STILL MAD

The World is Made of Poetry: The Art of
Ruth Stone (editor, with Wendy Barker)

Inventions of Farewell: A Book of Elegies (editor)

Eating Words (editor, with Roger Porter)

ALSO BY SUSAN GUBAR

Racechanges: White Skin, Black Face in American Culture

Critical Condition: Feminism at the Turn of the Century

Poetry After Auschwitz: Remembering What One Never Knew

Rooms of Our Own

Lo largo y lo corto del verso Holocausto

Judas: A Biography

Memoir of a Debulked Woman: Enduring Ovarian Cancer

Reading and Writing Cancer: How Words Heal

Late-Life Love: A Memoir

For Adult Users Only: The Dilemma of Violent Pornography
(editor, with Joan Hoff)

English Inside and Out: The Places of Literary Criticism
(editor, with Jonathan Kamholtz)

True Confessions: Feminist Professors Tell Stories
Out of School (editor)

STILL MAD

American Women Writers and
the Feminist Imagination, 1950–2020

SANDRA M. GILBERT
AND
SUSAN GUBAR

W. W. NORTON & COMPANY
Independent Publishers Since 1923

For information about permission to reproduce selections from this book, write to
Permissions, W. W. Norton & Company, Inc., 500 Fifth Avenue,
New York, NY 10110

For information about special discounts for bulk purchases, please contact
W. W. Norton Special Sales at specialsales@wwnorton.com or 800-233-4830

Manufacturing by LSC Communications, Harrisonburg
Book design by Ellen Cipriano
Production manager: Lauren Abbate

Library of Congress Cataloging-in-Publication Data

Names: Gilbert, Sandra M., author. | Gubar, Susan, 1944–, author.
Title: Still mad : American women writers and the feminist imagination, 1950–2020
/ Sandra M. Gilbert and Susan Gubar.
Description: First edition. | New York, N.Y. : W. W. Norton & Company, [2021] |
Includes bibliographical references and index.
Identifiers: LCCN 2021012937 | ISBN 9780393651713 (hardcover) |
ISBN 9780393651720 (epub)
Subjects: LCSH: American literature—Women authors—History and criticism. |
Feminism and literature—United States—History—20th century. |
Feminism and literature—United States—History—21st century. |
Women and literature—United States—History—20th century. | Women and
literature—United States—History—21st century. | American literature—
20th century—History and criticism. | American literature—21st century—
History and criticism.
Classification: LCC PS152 .G555 2022 | DDC 810.9/9287—dc23
LC record available at https://lccn.loc.gov/2021012937

W. W. Norton & Company, Inc., 500 Fifth Avenue, New York, N.Y. 10110
www.wwnorton.com

W. W. Norton & Company Ltd., 15 Carlisle Street, London W1D 3BS

1 2 3 4 5 6 7 8 9 0

For Dick Frieden and Donald Gray
and from each of us to each,
the irreplaceable other

Who knows? Somewhere out there in this audience [at the
Wellesley College commencement] may even be someone
who will one day follow in my footsteps and preside over the
White House as the President's spouse. I wish him well!

—BARBARA BUSH, ADDRESS TO THE
WELLESLEY COLLEGE CLASS OF 1990

Feminists are made, not born.

—BELL HOOKS, "CONSCIOUSNESS-RAISING:
A CONSTANT CHANGE OF HEART" (2000)

I was asked many times if I still believed in feminism! As if it
had been a fad like mood rings and pet rocks.

—HELEN REDDY, *THE WOMAN I AM: A MEMOIR* (2005)

I'm sometimes asked when will there be enough [women
on the Supreme Court]. And I say, "When there are nine."
People are shocked. But there'd been nine men, and nobody's
ever raised a question about that.

—RUTH BADER GINSBURG, LECTURE AT
GEORGETOWN (2015)

Our future will become
The past of other women.

—EAVAN BOLAND, "OUR FUTURE WILL BECOME
THE PAST OF OTHER WOMEN" (2018)

CONTENTS

SECTION V: RECESSIONS/REVIVALS IN
THE TWENTY-FIRST CENTURY

STILL MAD

INTRODUCTION

The Possible and the Impossible

THOSE WHO CAN'T MARCH, write. As many of our friends prepared to go on the January 21, 2017, Women's March, we knew that, with our various disabilities, we weren't physically able to join them. How could we stand in solidarity, we wondered? An answer to this question arrived a week before the massive protests in Washington, DC, and many cities around the globe, when we began collaborating on this book.

The passion then in the air recalled for us the intensity of the feminist movement in the seventies, a powerful social uprising that reflected a transformative political awakening for women and girls, and sometimes the men and boys around them. Looking back on that earlier time, the film critic Molly Haskell captured the sense of excitement: "We were rejecting the past, rejecting being circumscribed, rejecting the ways of our mothers. It was as if an entire landlocked race had climbed up a cliff and seen the vast wide sea for the first time. . . . Everything was possible."[1]

Of course, things were different in January 2017. What had seemed impossible—the defeat of a highly qualified woman candidate for the presidency by a boorish, utterly unqualified man—had not only become possible, it had *happened*. The countless worldwide protests were clearly fueled by feminism. If the women's liberation movement of the seventies hadn't had such far-reaching effects, the outcome of the election might not have seemed quite so scandalous, and the immediate need to protest might not have been so urgent. At the same time, though, even as the giant wave of protest mimicked the impassioned demonstrations of the seventies, it soon enough became obvious that this rebellion was inspired by despair. While the marchers of the seventies felt themselves to be advancing into a brave new world, the plaintiffs of 2017 were gazing at a fallen world, dominated by a corrupt figure both infantile and demonic.

To tell the story of what we consider the ongoing second wave of feminism, we have chosen representative women—poets, novelists, dramatists, singers, journalists, memoirists, theorists—who seemed especially charismatic to us. Taken together, they subvert the standard caricature of the women's movement as white, middle-class, and elitist. We've also chosen to concentrate on North American literary women, although all our other books examine the transnational relationships of women writing in English. But the shock of the election of a nativist president led us to narrow our focus to feminisms in our own country. And the permeable borders between Canada and America have made several Canadian women writers especially important to the American reading public.

Certainly, we could have picked other significant figures, but those we chose seemed to us to help keep things going while things were stirring, as the great nineteenth-century suffragist Sojourner Truth put it.[2] We were drawn not only to the publications of notable women but also to their lives, which dramatize the problems flesh-and-blood women face as they make the personal political. There has been much misrepresentation and some trashing of feminism's past, and maybe too much generalizing as well. We sought not to homogenize but to pay tribute to what the women's movement contributed not only to our present opportunities but also to an even more liberated future.

One of the debates in which women continue to engage swirls around the issue of how many "waves" of feminism there have been in American history: some say three, some say more. But the problems faced by women and the strategies devised by feminists evolved continuously throughout the late twentieth century and the first two decades of the twenty-first century. Just as we can trace the development of the first wave of the women's movement from the 1848 Seneca Falls Convention to the Nineteenth Amendment granting the right to vote in 1920, so we can conceptualize one second wave that grew from the nineteen fifties up to today: tremulous, tumultuous, tremendous, ongoing. With that perspective, we take to heart the fact that all of us are still in the midst of it, keeping things going while things are stirring.

To ensure future progress, we must all continue to contest, agitate, and advocate, for "if we wait till it is still," Sojourner Truth cautioned, "it will take a great while to get it going again." Sojourner Truth, who was "above eighty years old" when she spoke those words, believed that she was "kept here because something remains for me to do; I suppose I am yet to help to break the chain." We two, we too, feel similarly.

GLASS CEILINGS AND BROKEN GLASS

Mantras of bygone days still ring in our ears: *We've come a long way, professor! We're shattering glass ceilings! We can have it all! We're leaning in and the culture's changing!* But is the culture really changing? If it is, why are we and so many of our friends still mad? Mad as in the sense of enraged. Mad as in the sense of maddened, confused, or rebellious. Maybe if you come a long way, you encounter territorial backlash. Maybe if you shatter glass ceilings, you have to walk on broken glass. Maybe if you lean in, you topple over.

Four decades have gone by since we opened our first coauthored book, *The Madwoman in the Attic*, with the question "Is a pen a metaphorical penis?"[3] We were attempting to examine the centuries-long identification of authority with masculinity in order to excavate female literary traditions. Now we find ourselves mulling over a related question as we seek to understand the gender implications of American politics. In this presumably more liberated moment, when quite a few women have come forward as serious candidates for the presidency, we nevertheless find ourselves asking, Must the president have a penis?[4]

So far, all our presidential elections have suggested as much. In 2016, an unqualified, misogynistic television personality defeated a highly qualified, ambitious female politician in the Electoral College, although she won the popular vote by a margin of three million. But even more recently, a trio of vigorous, experienced women senators—Kamala Harris, Amy Klobuchar, Elizabeth Warren—dropped out of the Democratic primaries, leaving two elderly men standing, 78-year-old Bernie Sanders and 77-year-old Joe Biden; and finally, Joe Biden became the candidate. One factor that was put forward to explain these latest defeats? Electability. No "mere" woman, it was thought, could defeat the rabble-rousing, nearly psychotic Donald J. Trump, nor would a self-declared socialist like Sanders be able to trounce the monster. In a sense, however, Trump trounced himself with his bungled response to the pandemic that spread as the campaigns continued, so that the more empathic and rational Biden triumphed.

As Trump's bullying "lock her up" campaign against Clinton foretold, his term in office triggered an explosion of chaos, falsehood, and corruption that shattered all political norms, and its disorder peaked with his incompetent handling of COVID-19. At first denying the danger of the novel coronavirus, then promising that it was under his control, the president failed to organize the provision of testing, contact tracing, protective equipment, ventilators, national stay-at-home orders, and other medical necessities. While at some press conferences he boasted that only *he* could dictate the sheltering-in-place prescribed by epidemiologists and ordered by governors, at other briefings he claimed that the governors were in charge and he took no responsibility.

Toward the end of the second month of the viral rampage, Trump began, as Governor Jay Inslee put it, "fomenting domestic rebellion," tweeting out "LIBERATE MINNESOTA!" "LIBERATE MICHIGAN!" "LIBERATE VIRGINIA" in support of alt-right demonstrators protesting against the social distancing orders issued by his own government and adding ominously, "and save your great 2nd amendment [the right to bear arms]. It is under siege!"[5] Was he in fact fomenting *armed insurrection*? And did he seriously mean, a week or two later, to suggest that Americans should try to cure themselves of COVID-19 by injecting disinfectant into their bodies—for example, *Lysol*? Then he ordered the military to use flash-bang explosives, tear gas, rubber bullets, and helicopters against peaceful Black Lives Matter protesters in Washington, DC (so he could stage a photo-op while holding the Bible upside down).

When he was defeated by Joe Biden in the election of 2020, he refused to concede, firing advisers who tried to tell him he had lost and repeatedly posting such tweets as "NO WAY WE LOST THIS ELECTION" and "We won Michigan by a lot!" Finally, at a scandalous rally, he urged his enraged supporters to march down Pennsylvania Avenue to the Capitol, where on January 6, 2021, they invaded the seat of American government in a riot that left five people dead and many injured. Declared members of the House of Representatives in their impeachment brief, "He summoned a mob to Washington, exhorted them into a frenzy, and aimed them like a loaded cannon down Pennsylvania Avenue." Peter Baker of the *New York Times* compared him to a mad king at the end of a Shakespearean tragedy.[6]

Of course, in a traditional democracy, where each citizen has one vote and no Electoral College obstructs the will of the majority, Hillary Clinton, the first woman to run for president under the aegis of a major political party, would actually have won the 2016 election. An educated and experienced politician, she would surely not govern by tweet, not deny or evade the existence of a major medical threat, not foment rebellion among the citizens of her land or counsel people to ingest Lysol or enlist the military against civil rights protesters. In a counterhistory paralleling the anarchic narrative in which Americans became enmeshed, we can suppose that President Hillary Clinton would have run an orderly administration, no doubt with flaws and dissenters—but a stable government, much like, say, that of Angela Merkel.

Like us, this hypothetical president is the product of the seventies, and arguably it was seventies feminism that facilitated her unprecedented rise as the first female candidate for the presidency of the United States sponsored by a major party. She is also a paradigm of the seventies—a dramatic exemplar of the far-reaching possibilities of the women's liberation movement and at the same time a model victim of the backlash that the movement continually had to confront. During the seventies, Clinton earned a law degree, struggled to continue using the name Rodham, and determined that she didn't want to "stay home and bake cookies" because she wasn't "just some little woman standing by my man." As First Lady, she famously declared that "human rights are women's rights; and women's rights are human rights."[7] After her husband left office, she established a notable record as the first First Lady elected to public office—the first woman senator from New York—and then as a highly praised secretary of state.[8]

The historical transformations that rocketed Clinton into national politics were precisely those that propelled our generation into the professions. These upheavals would become the subject of intellectual inquiries that changed our lives as well as the lives and works of many of our contemporaries. As if in acknowledgment of this point and also to evoke the suffragists of the first wave of feminism, who wore white to proclaim allegiance to their cause, Clinton sported a white pantsuit when she accepted the Democratic nomination.

After the 2016 election, second-wave feminism had evidently both triumphed and failed. As the extraordinary Women's March on Washington of January 21, 2017, revealed, many were angry at the failure, but also puzzled by how it could have happened during a time of so many achievements. We were baffled too. The why of this book? Because we are still mad, we seek to understand feminism's past and present in order to strengthen its future. The 2016 election, which dramatized feminism's successes but also its failures, proves that women and men must learn over and over again what our generation started to learn and teach in the seventies and what we began learning during the semester we were teaching the material that would become *The Madwoman in the Attic*. Its aftermath also confirms that feminists today have begun channeling the rebellious rage of the madwoman we studied, a female figure incensed by patriarchal structures that have proven to be shockingly obdurate.

HOW THE SEVENTIES CHANGED OUR LIVES

Back in 1973, when we met in an elevator in the humanities building at Indiana University, we could not have foretold the transformations feminism would inspire throughout the nineteen seventies and afterward. Yet the year had begun with momentous alterations, as the subtitle of one book suggests—*January 1973: Watergate, Roe v. Wade, Vietnam and the Month That Changed America Forever.*[9]

In terms of the women's movement, think of the decade in its entirety. Remember the reproductive rights conferred by *Roe v. Wade*, and also the fight for ratification of the Equal Rights Amendment, Take Back the Night marches, the launching of *Ms.* magazine, the emergence of lesbian separatism and of battered women's shelters, and *The Hite Report.* Consider Title IX, which barred discrimination on the basis of sex in any education program or activity receiving federal aid, and the Equal Credit Opportunity Act, which for the first time ever enabled single, divorced, and widowed women to receive credit cards in their own names. Legislation finally assured women in all fifty states that they would serve on federal juries. At the start of the decade, *Our Bodies, Ourselves* appeared and the Statue of Liberty was draped with a huge banner: "Women of the World Unite." Toward the end, Congress passed an act prohibiting discrimination against pregnant women in all areas of employment.

Recall, if you are old enough, or Google, if you are younger, Judy Chicago and Miriam Shapiro's *Womanhouse* exhibition, Marlo Thomas's record *Free to Be . . . You and Me,* Billie Jean King's victory in the "Battle of the Sexes" tennis match, and Nancy Friday's best-selling book about women's erotic fantasies, *My Secret Garden.* Consider, too, that the lawyer later famous as the "Notorious RBG" began arguing against gender discrimination before an all-male Supreme Court; the first Black congresswoman, Shirley Chisholm, ran for president of the United States; and Barbara Jordan became the first African American and first woman to give a keynote speech at the Democratic National Convention.

Despite such advances, remember that until the twenty-first century, as the distinguished historian Ruth Rosen recently reminded
us, no one thought that a woman could actually run for the presidency (and gain a majority of the votes) with the sponsorship of a
major political party or that a woman could be elected Speaker of
the House of Representatives.[10] Chisholm's attempt at the former
accomplishment, fully backed by Gloria Steinem, proves that it was
imaginable; but since the odds of success were so low, it was a symbolic, theatrical, and deeply utopian undertaking, a harking forward to some better, future time when such a campaign would seem
perfectly realistic.[11] In the House, after all, the men's gym was not
open to women until 1985; the swimming pool remained exclusively
for the use of male members until 2009. As for the Senate, the first
woman without familial political connections was not elected to it
until 1980. And a bathroom facility was not provided for women senators until 1992; it wasn't up and running until 1993 (with only two
stalls, expanded to four in 2013).[12]

Nevertheless, women's hopes for equality continued to rise in the
seventies. Just as the National Women's Political Caucus emerged to
support female candidates, the National Women's Studies Association was formed to sponsor feminist academics. Professional publications flourished;[13] notably, many of these enterprises, along with the
activism that energized them, were situated on college and university
campuses, where they had been founded by feminist academics who
were as eager to investigate women's past as they were to redefine
women's future. For the supposedly insular ivory tower housed revolutionary ideas that would change all our lives.

Newly arrived at Indiana, we had never studied women's history
or women writers before. Nor had hardly anyone we knew, for such
categories were only beginning to be defined.[14] Neither one of us

had been taught by a female professor in undergraduate or in graduate courses. Yet our generation was on the brink of integrating a
feminist perspective into the humanities. We were also on the verge
of discoveries that not only established the fields of women's history
and women's literary history but also undertook equally important
investigations into the roles of women in anthropology, religion,
psychology, art, sociology, law, ethnic studies, business, and the sci-
ences, along with analyses of the concept of gender itself and long-
held views of sexual orientation. Together, all these rapidly emerging
inquiries profoundly reshaped the political, legal, and medical environments of twenty-first-century Americans.

We have come to believe that such major changes occurred
because our cohort lived with and through contradictions that produced the need to analyze our situation, paradoxes that women today
also face. Our own public exploration of gender began in 1974, when
we team-taught a class in literature by women. We knew nothing
about this field—indeed, it was not then "a field"—but we were drawn
to books we had always loved and put together a course that, after
much debate, we decided to call "The Madwoman in the Attic."

Teaching the class was transformative. Our syllabus included
women writers from Jane Austen to the Brontës, from Emily Dickinson to Virginia Woolf and Sylvia Plath—authors whose works we
read as girls and young women but whom we had never studied in college or graduate school. Reading and discussing them with twenty-
five responsive undergraduates, all of us were "changed utterly," as
William Butler Yeats (a man we *had* studied) would put it,[15] as were
the texts of the writers we analyzed.

This was a conversion experience, the scales of what seemed to
be a scaly masculinist past falling from our eyes, day in and day out.
An awakening was upon us, our own awakening to a history we had

never known, even though it had always been there. Kate Chopin had undergone a comparable experience while writing her novel *The Awakening* at the end of the nineteenth century, but the book had gone out of print; we did not know it. Zora Neale Hurston had too, in the nineteen twenties and thirties, but her work had also gone out of print; we did not know it. Ditto Charlotte Perkins Gilman: neither her celebrated story "The Yellow Wallpaper" nor her feminist tracts on women and economics were easily available. One memorable occasion, though, made us understand the obstacles that stood in our way.

We had invited the well-known poet Denise Levertov to visit our class. We met her at the Indianapolis airport and brought her to Ballantine Hall, where one of the students had made large-scale, abstract paintings to illustrate Levertov's verses. The chairs were arranged in a semicircle. Purple paintings lined the walls. Another student placed a tribute, a soft sculpture, at the poet's feet. We read some of her poems aloud, and the undergraduates discussed them as an expression of women's anger at confinement. "That's not what I meant at all," Denise Levertov said. The students nodded politely. We thought, *She does not know anything, but her poems know everything.* We thought, *It has always been there, as was its denial.* Later, quoting D. H. Lawrence, we told the students, "Never trust the artist, trust the tale."[16]

Denise Levertov did not want to be identified as a woman writer. She preferred to be recognized as an American writer, though she was born and raised in England. We encountered the same resistance when we sought to include Elizabeth Bishop in our co-edited *Norton Anthology of Literature by Women*. Indeed, her estate stipulated that we could include her verse only if we also reprinted a statement in which Bishop declared: "Undoubtedly gender does play an important part in the making of any art, but art is art and to separate writings, paintings, musical compositions, etc. into two sexes is to emphasize values in them that are *not* art."[17] Of course, Bishop, like Levertov, can be studied in multiple traditions: the history of twentieth-century poetry, American studies, lesbian history, travel literature, and trauma studies, among others. Still, why this resistance to the category of woman writer?

"Whoever is in power takes over the noun—and the norm—while the less powerful get an adjective," Gloria Steinem once observed.[18] To be a woman writer, from the point of view of Levertov and Bishop, was to be relegated to an inferior status as a less significant writer. Great authors, as literature syllabi had established for more than a century, were men. While we continued teaching and celebrating the genius of women artists, such moments led us to meditate on some women's resistance to gender identification and to feminism, as we will do in the pages to come.

Still, as we review our own history, we understand that our conversion experience in the seventies was hardly singular or unprecedented. It was one in a sequence of feminist lessons that women over the centuries have learned, and one in a sequence of feminist lessons that our generation had begun to learn in elementary school, maybe even earlier. Some of the problems that feminists confront today differ from the issues they or their mothers faced yesterday, but contradictions have always played a productive role in the second wave as women confront the paradoxes that shape their lives.

THE SCHOOLING OF HILLARY RODHAM AND HER GENERATION

Though she was often controversial, the woman who was called Hillary Clinton became a pivotal player on the public stage of feminist history and for us serves as a paradigmatic representative of her generation. How did a girl named Hillary Rodham, from a conservative midwestern family, come to embody the tensions of second-wave feminism in a twenty-first-century political campaign that became as much a battle of the sexes as a conflict of ideologies? At least one answer can be found in the crucial years between 1969 and 1979, when the women's movement was flourishing and Hillary Rodham was making life-altering decisions.

An honors major in government at Wellesley, the 21-year-old Rodham was the first student chosen to give the school's commencement address. And interestingly, she was one of four student speakers around the country whom *Life* magazine profiled in its June 20, 1969, issue. Though she had started college as a Barry Goldwater supporter, she had been radicalized in her undergraduate years. Now here she is in the pages of *Life*: long straight hair, no makeup, granny glasses, and an expression of frank determination. She could be one of countless revolutionary young American women in the heat and heart of campus protest.

And indeed, her confidently delivered commencement speech enacted an impromptu protest against the ideas of the Republican Senator Edward Brooke, the speaker who preceded her and whose remarks focused on what he considered frivolous student protests. As he spoke, a friend reported, she had scribbled a response in the margins of her text: "I find myself reacting just briefly to some of the things that Senator Brooke said," Hillary Rodham then announced, adding that "the challenge now is to practice politics as the art of making what appears to be impossible possible."[19]

Making the impossible possible: this is what young women of Clinton's generation—and ours—were brought up to believe we could do. "The question about possible and impossible was one that we brought with us to Wellesley four years ago," she declared, explaining that "we arrived not yet knowing what was not possible. Consequently, we expected a lot." Then she went on to expatiate on what she still, four years later, considered possible, or at least ideal: instead of "our prevailing, acquisitive, and competitive corporate life, . . . more immediate, ecstatic, and penetrating modes of living"—and, most important, "human liberation."

What mode of living would this idealistic young woman have to accept as she grew into her twenties? Hillary Rodham had already made close African American friends in her college years; with them, she mourned the death of Martin Luther King, Jr., dreamed of a better future, and transformed admissions protocols at her school.[20] In the seventies, she continued to meet with the kind of successes she had achieved at Wellesley. She decided to earn her J.D. from Yale Law School in 1973 partly because "there was a professor at Harvard Law School who looked at me—a bright and eager college senior, recently offered admission—and said, 'We don't need any more women at Harvard.'"[21] Then she went on to work in Washington (on the Nixon impeachment process). In 1975, with some ambivalence, she moved to Arkansas and married her law school boyfriend, Bill Clinton, soon to be that state's attorney general and, in 1979, its governor. In Arkansas, she continued working as an attorney, becoming the first female partner at the prestigious Rose Law Firm.

Fast-forward now, from 1969, with its seemingly unmitigated triumph, to that crucial year of 1979, when a 31-year-old Hillary Rodham—yes, still Hillary Rodham—is being interviewed about her new role as the First Lady of Arkansas.[22] Her self-presentation at this point seems quite different from that of the vaguely hippieish graduating senior. The governor's wife is dressed in a pink full-skirted suit, a frilly white blouse, and knee-high crimson boots: super feminine pink and white, and super serious boots, the kind that were "made for walking."[23] As she's grilled by a clearly hostile male interviewer, she maintains her calm, responding articulately to repeated questions that emphasize her radical difference from the Arkansas image of a governor's wife.

Does she even care about her duties as First Lady? the interviewer seems to want to know. What possesses her to keep not only her own name but her own professional career? She shifts a bit in her seat but is otherwise poised, as if she were humoring a fretful child. "I'm interested in social and civic events, but also in my professional life. *I don't see any reason to be an either/or person*," she patiently explains (italics ours). In a sweetly reasonable tone she notes, "I didn't want to mix my professional activities with [Bill's] political activities. . . . Keeping my name was part of that." In fact, she adds, "I came to Arkansas of my own free will," and she hopes that the state will accept someone who arrived "on her own terms."

A kind of splitting, one senses, is beginning here. The starry-eyed girl who dreamed of "human liberation" is being forced to confront the impossibility of the impossible. Does a part of her, steely with anger, stand apart from this demeaning encounter? She would seem to be someone who "has it all"—a handsome, successful husband and a gratifying career in the field for which she was trained. But she's jumping through hoops, performing, and on television, as if such public cross-examinations were merely what a person who "has it all" really ought to expect. Is the impossible really impossible? She doesn't seem to think so, at least not yet. She sits for this subtly hostile interview amiably, as if she is continuing to expect the great things that will come of her precocity as commencement speaker, as Washington insider, as practicing lawyer and law school professor, even as governor's wife. Why shouldn't all the parts of the puzzle come together?

Clearly Hillary Rodham, like so many other young women who were to dive into the second wave of feminism, had been raised to believe that she deserved a significant place in the world. Girls in the generation schooled in the fifties and sixties were the first to go to college en masse. As they—we—pored over our textbooks, we encountered the contradictions that were to shape Hillary Rodham's 1979 interview in Arkansas and the rest of her career—and many of our own careers too. Our books and teachers (especially at women's colleges but even on some coeducational campuses) urged us to excel, to win prizes, to graduate with honors, to become commencement speakers, to edit student newspapers, to go to law school, to publish poetry and fiction. Directly subverting all this encouragement, advice columnists, magazines for teenage girls, fashion stylists, and often enough our own parents admonished us to be decorative and demure, bosomy and domestic.

Even while we sat around seminar tables, eagerly interrogating the dialogues of Plato, many of us wore the long, full, ladylike skirts of the so-called New Look glamorized by Dior or the skimpy miniskirts that came later, along with bright red lipstick or dark black eyeliner, and (if necessary) padded bras, to assure others of our femininity. Yes, some of us did go to college not to win honors but to earn what used to be called "MRS degrees." But others—and Hillary Rodham was one of them—seem to have thought that one needn't be "an either/or person."

As the Arkansas years wore on and the subtle nagging about her name intensified, Hillary Rodham became Hillary Clinton. She had become convinced that one of the reasons her husband lost the 1980 governor's race "was because I still went by my maiden name."[24] Then she became Hillary Rodham Clinton, even as her hairstyles famously metamorphosed, no doubt in response to all too much public commentary. Meanwhile, Hillary herself—for now she began to be identified only by her first name, as if she were a pop musician or a princess—became increasingly secretive and, given the modesty of her husband's gubernatorial salary, increasingly anxious about money. She entered into confusing "deals" in and out of the Rose Law Firm that were to lead to much public trouble. And also, given her husband's sexual fecklessness, she was frequently forced to cover for him, to adopt a serene façade that did not come easily to her.

Once Bill Clinton became president, so deeply backed by her energy and intelligence that he and she became simply "the Clintons," what had been a constant low-level background of Arkansas nagging turned into an almost Wagnerian international chorus of disapproval, directed mostly at "Hillary." She grew more defensive than ever, yet her ambitions intensified. Eventually, she moved into an office in the West Wing rather than staying in the East Wing, where the First Lady and her staff are usually housed. And from then on, she was almost more a practicing politician than she was a First Lady, until, after her husband left the White House, she became first a senator and then a secretary of state.

As she morphed into a deeply guarded public figure, the former Hillary Rodham also became more compromised by the "prevailing, acquisitive, and competitive corporate life" she had once deplored. She bought into the Iraq war and was herself bought as a speaker, for stunning sums, by Goldman Sachs and other Wall Street sponsors. Beautifully groomed by an attentive staff and attired in Ralph Lauren pantsuits designed for her, she traveled the world to the point of utter exhaustion. Her message—"Women's rights are human rights"— must still have been a driving motivator, yet the distinctions on which she had once mused, between "authentic reality" and "inauthentic reality," began to blur. By the time of her first presidential campaign, when she was defeated in the primaries by a young Barack Obama, she downplayed her own feminism as a shaping force. "I didn't want people to see me as the 'woman candidate,'" she explained later, noting that our country would not have cheered but instead would have jeered at the narrative she badly wanted to tell: "My story is the story of a life shaped by and devoted to the movement for women's liberation."[25] In 2008, that tale was apparently untellable.

The ultimately calamitous campaign of 2016 returned her, willingly or not, to the arms of feminism. With the scandal-plagued Donald Trump bizarrely deriding her as "Crooked Hillary," she seemed determined to grin and bear it. She must still, in part of herself, have remained Hillary Rodham, the triumphant commencement speaker, a young woman who would make the impossible possible. After all, as one of her classmates had revealed to the *New Yorker* in June 2016, "we predicted Hillary would be the first female President of the United States."[26] And recently the best-selling novelist Curtis Sittenfeld has elaborated on that prophecy in the page-turning plot of *Rodham* (2020), a narrative that subverts a dismal reality with a fascinating fantasy in which Hillary finally becomes her "true" self.

In real life, the catastrophe of the election drove Hillary Clinton back, at least for a time, into the privacy she claimed to cherish. Yet as she emerged, once more, into the public eye, observers wondered what she thought, how she felt. In her 2017 book *What Happened* she did address the disgust and hatred of "sexism and misogyny" that she considered "endemic in America."[27]

We focus so intensely on the vexed fate of Hillary Rodham because the paradoxes of the young Wellesley graduate's brilliant career dramatized on an international stage the tensions and conflicts of seventies feminism. We were trained to succeed. We were scorned for succeeding. We were urged to marry. Marriage obstructed our aspirations. We were taught to fulfill ourselves. We were instructed to support our husbands' ambitions. We resolved to be authentic, to forget about makeup and making up to the world. We were constructed to be inauthentic, to dress up and dress well. When we experienced "sexism and misogyny," we bit our lips, clamped down on our rage—and then ran for office, for the editorial board, for CEO, for president of the United States.

THE CULTURAL CHAOS WE FACE

The years directly before and after the Trump triumph made it clear that we are entering an era when it will be more important than ever to examine women's lives, dreams, hopes, and despairs. Although at the turn of the century some thinkers declared the second wave over—there was much talk then about "post-feminism"—feminism and the need for feminism would no more fade away than did the state under communism.

Today, a deeply entrenched feminization of poverty means that a disproportionate number of women around the globe continue to struggle with economic hardship. Millions of women worldwide are trapped in the sex trade, receive no formal education, and are treated as property. Here at home, the glass ceiling remains mostly intact, despite Sheryl Sandberg's advice to "lean in."[28] For middle- and working-class mothers needing to earn a living, childcare is still an enormous challenge, and repeated legislative efforts, often fueled by Christian conservatives, have gradually eroded women's reproductive freedoms.

After the first Black president and his charismatic wife exited the White House, a cabinet dominated by conservative white billionaires was installed in office. Before and after his election, Obama's successor insouciantly admitted to groping women. And just before his inauguration, the *New York Times* reported on a survey on gender; of the women polled, 82 percent "said sexism was a problem in society today."[29]

Amid these conditions, feminism achieved a new cultural popularity. By August 2014, when Beyoncé performed at MTV's Video
Music Awards while the word "FEMINIST" glowed behind her,
celebrities had begun rebranding the movement. Emma Watson,
the actress who played Harry Potter's Hermione on-screen, spoke at
the United Nations about the need to understand gender as "a spectrum" rather than "two sets of opposing ideals," while Miss Piggy,
of Muppet fame, declared "*Moi* is a feminist pig." Contemplating the
#YesAllWomen movement, the feminist thinker Rebecca Solnit cele-
brated 2014 as "a year of feminist insurrection against male violence,"
in which women began speaking out in record numbers and "the
whole conversation changed."[30] To be sure, many of the problems
feminists addressed went unsolved, but at least our comediennes—
Tina Fey, Amy Schumer, and Samantha Bee—could help us laugh
when we watched them on YouTube or television.

In 2015, the TV critic of *HuffPost* welcomed "the feminist Golden
Age" of television as she considered such shows as *Orange Is the New
Black*, *The Mindy Project*, *Scandal*, *Grace and Frankie*, *Transparent*, and
Jane the Virgin.[31] The popularity of T-shirts with the logo "This Is What
a Feminist Looks Like" soared. And at the 2017 women's march Senator
Kirsten Gillibrand declared that all were participating in "the revival
of the woman's movement."[32] The Washington rally—and others—did
have the air of a revival meeting: a sense of dedication, of almost religious renewal and recommitment, as the marchers set out on a new
journey toward the centers of political power. What roads do they—do
we—see ahead for feminism? The growing realization that there would
have to be many roads became a certainty during the following months.

For as the misogynistic Trump administration took office, we
seemed on the brink of entering the nightmare world of Margaret
Atwood's 1985 novel *The Handmaid's Tale*, which started reappearing

on best-seller lists and which was serialized in the spring of 2017 in Hulu's television adaptation. Both the book's resurgence and the television series illustrate the growing relevance of second-wave feminism in the twenty-first century. An Orwellian fantasy, *The Handmaid's Tale* portrays the triumph of theocratic patriarchy in Gilead, a totalitarian state established in the ruins of a polluted America by Commanders who exploit rampant fears of foreign terrorism. Enslaved, women in Gilead cannot divorce or hold jobs, bank accounts, or political offices. Neither can they control their own bodies. Because of a poisoned planet, birth rates have plummeted. Abortion and birth control have been outlawed, and the Bible has been perverted by Commanders who manage to procreate despite the sterility of their wives by invoking Rachel and Leah, two barren wives in the Hebrew Bible who used their maids as surrogate mothers.

Atwood's Handmaid heroine Offred has been turned into a two-legged womb, wearing the red cloak and the white blinder bonnet of the fertile women who will bear the offspring of their Commander-owners. Her name signifies that she has become the chattel "of Fred." It also hints at a human being "offered," Atwood has explained, as "a religious offering or a victim offered for sacrifice."[33] During the monthly "ceremony" enacted when she is ovulating, Offred must lie between the spread legs of the Wife as the Commander inseminates her. Anatomy has become destiny for all the women of Gilead, who are assigned rigid roles.

The television series, like the novel, emphasizes societally enforced divisions between women: domestic servants and wives, Aunts and Jezebels, Econowives and Unwomen wear distinctive costumes and assume specialized roles.[34] Neither Atwood's novel nor the television series blames these rigid divisions between women entirely on men. The Wife in Offred's household named herself Serena Joy in the period before the Commanders took over, when she scrapped singing for making speeches "about the sanctity of the home, about how women should stay home. Serena Joy didn't do this herself, she made speeches instead, but she presented this failure of hers as a sacrifice she was making for the good of all."[35] Another collaborator with the patriarchy, Aunt Lydia—who uses clitoridectomy to punish rebellious handmaids into submission—spouts platitudes that once were feminist propositions: about pornography leading to rape and about women needing to preserve their maternal powers.

The Handmaid's Tale reminds us that ostensibly liberatory rhetoric can be lassoed by reactionary forces and that women have played significant roles in a succession of backlashes. We will see various feminist agendas hijacked by female opponents. We will also encounter real-life versions of Serena Joy appearing on the national stage from the fifties throughout the following decades, sometimes under the aegis of feminism itself. This deeply ironic and perplexing phenomenon is worth tracing; the problem of the anti-feminist woman remains a key conundrum for future activists and thinkers to tackle.

But the televised remaking of *The Handmaid's Tale* also speaks to another facet of feminism's long second wave: the recycling of earlier touchstone texts. The "feminist Golden Age" of television may have come into being in part because of the consciousness-raising of earlier feminists. In the early eighties, Alison Bechdel, the prizewinning author of the graphic novel *Fun Home*, started publishing a comic strip, *Dykes to Watch Out For*, recounting the everyday lives of a diverse cast of lesbians. In an installment from 1986 titled "The Rule," one character establishes three basic tests a movie must pass to get her approval: "One, it has to have at least two women in it, who, two, talk to each other about, three, something besides a man."[36] By 2010, the website bechdeltest.com was listing movies that passed the test.

While the Bechdel test cannot evaluate either the feminism or the excellence of a work of art, it certainly tracks the presence of women. For men and women today, Virginia Woolf's statement "we think back through our mothers if we are women" may sound somewhat retro;[37] however, the recycling of Atwood's novel as well as the appearance of protesters garbed as Handmaids at twenty-first-century demonstrations prove that we think back through our feminist predecessors when we aim to grapple with the persistence of gender trouble.

KEEPING THINGS GOING

In Gilead the Handmaids are not allowed to read and write. Like the slaves of the nineteenth century, they must be denied literacy because reading and writing always hold out the promise of liberation. It is no accident that the education of girls remains a crucial marker of a thriving democracy. University buildings in Gilead's Cambridge have been taken over by the Eyes of God (the secret police). Salvagings (public executions) occur in Harvard Yard.

That colleges and universities would have to be eliminated or colonized in a tyrannical regime based on Christian fundamentalism hints at another historic truth, at least in America during the second wave: campuses have served as incubators of feminism. Not all activists were academics, of course. But virtually all of them received degrees from institutions of higher education and contributed to or relied on the debates, languages, and approaches developed by the first generation of women to enter higher education not as tokens but as a sizable group capable of networking.

Many women of Hillary Clinton's generation went to college.[38] National defense scholarships and public institutions of learning boosted the numbers of young women receiving undergraduate and graduate degrees in a range of fields. Just as Hillary Clinton helped establish her reputation when in 1973 she published an essay in the *Harvard Educational Review* addressing the rights of children, so her cohort in the humanities produced works that would provide the methodologies to analyze discriminatory practices. At the same time, women who became creative writers sparked the ideas debated in critical conversations. Rarely, in fact, had the arts and the humanities played such a major role in a social movement. In the chapters to follow, we will discuss the cultural history underlying a contemporary feminism that is "still mad" today, a half century after the second wave of feminism named itself the women's liberation movement at the end of the sixties.

Our chapters proceed chronologically, from the stirrings of feminist revolt in the fifties and the eruptions of feminist protest in the sixties to the awakening of feminist thinkers and artists in the seventies, eighties, and nineties. But this is not a story of feminism progressing as it gets stronger and better. By the turn of the century, a number of the debates within feminism threatened to deteriorate into internecine squabbling. As in the far future of *The Handmaid's Tale's* conclusion—Atwood's novel ends with a satire of scholars dithering over Offred's taped testimony—by the nineties feminists sometimes seemed to be caught up in grandstanding or infighting. But this is also not a story of feminism's decline and fall or, for that matter, its death and resurrection, though we conclude with hope about the revival we witness today. Rather, *Still Mad* is an account of how generations of literary women tapped the enigmas of their own lives to shape visions of cultural transformation.

Why have we chosen to focus on literary women? For one thing, we've spent our lives celebrating their achievements. For another, the second wave was mightily influenced by women poets, novelists, dramatists, journalists, songwriters, essayists, memoirists, and theorists. For these thinkers, the capacity to imagine otherwise—to envision the possibility of alternative models and then what those alternative models might be—remains a prerequisite for generating more equitable social and political arrangements. Their contributions clarify the problems with which we will continue to contend.

What inspires Atwood's Offred to survive is a line of writing etched by her predecessor in the closet wall of the cell she inhabits in the Commander's house: "*Nolite te bastardes carborundorum.*" The faux Latin phrase means "Don't let the bastards grind you down." When the Commander hands Offred a forbidden writing instrument to copy the phrase, she thinks, "Pen Is Envy, Aunt Lydia would say . . . warning us away from such objects."[39] Many readers will get the Freudian joke—penis envy—understanding that the power of the pen, which women have effectively wielded for centuries, has historically and wrongfully stood for the mythical power of the phallus. Although the girl who had preceded Offred committed suicide, Atwood's heroine escapes, inspired and strengthened by her precursor's motto.

Ironically, these faux Latin words were framed and hung in the Washington, DC, office of Barry Goldwater—the 1964 Republican candidate for president who criticized the Supreme Court ruling mandating school integration in *Brown v. Board of Education*, supported the witch-hunter Joe McCarthy, and was in turn supported both by the Ku Klux Klan and by the rabidly anti-feminist Phyllis Schlafly. But Atwood proves that just as conservatives can co-opt liberatory rhetoric, so too feminists can sabotage reactionary rhetoric. The same sort of dynamic was at work after Senate Majority Leader Mitch McConnell protested against Senator Elizabeth Warren's reading of a letter from Coretta Scott King with a phrase that soon began appearing as a logo on all sorts of feminist regalia: "Nevertheless, she persisted."

We will complicate the idea that the second wave of feminism peaked in the seventies and eighties, receded at the turn of the century, and then resurged before and after the 2016 election, although there is some truth to that story. Yet as in individual lives so in the stages of social movements: periods that look quiescent or even retrograde may subtly produce tactics necessary to deal with future challenges. In the chapters that follow, feminism is a desire, a vision, a yearning, a fantasy, or a dream sometimes tragically at odds with reality but sometimes comically opening up the improbable possibilities of an alternative reality. Throughout its evolution over the past seven decades, we will argue, feminism sustains itself as a profoundly imaginative endeavor that includes a range of imaginings.

Without completely telegraphing our narrative about how seventies feminism came into being and what happened to it, we can disclose our claim that during every decade from the nineteen fifties onward, the contradictions in women's lives spurred the need for learning and relearning sophisticated ways of formulating the strategies needed to keep things going while things are stirring. Like their successors, our predecessors and contemporaries rarely agreed. They quarreled with and qualified each other, but they nevertheless persisted. By exploring how they managed to keep things going, we can devise ways to counter the shocking legitimization of misogyny in our time. Together we can now read the writing on the wall: *Nolite te bastardes carborundorum.*

SECTION I

STIRRINGS IN THE FIFTIES

1

Midcentury Separate Spheres

THE PARADOXES THAT SHAPED the second wave of feminism were rooted in the neo-Victorian sexual culture of the era that the poet Robert Lowell famously called "the tranquillized Fifties," a decade that espoused iron-clad gender conformity for women: girdles, stockings, bullet bras, and crinolines.[1] Like Hillary Rodham, most seventies feminists went to school in the fifties, and we experienced the dizzying contradictions that marked the early lives of such literary women as Sylvia Plath, Diane di Prima, Lorraine Hansberry, and Audre Lorde.

Dizzying contradictions, and sometimes sickening ones. For even the fiercest among us seem at some point to have been complicit in the mores of the era, especially young women raised in the white middle class. Adrienne Rich, who was to become *the* poet laureate of seventies feminism, recalled the delight with which—in rebellion against her father, who wanted to be "Papa Brontë" with geniuses for children—she "spent hours writing imitations of cosmetic advertising" and "mercifully . . . discovered *Modern Screen, Photoplay*, Jack

Benny, 'Your Hit Parade,' Frank Sinatra."[2] Sylvia Plath, raised from the age of 9 by a widowed mother who encouraged both academic excellence and gender conformity, was even more passionate about the popular culture of her day. Presenting herself as a perfect all-American girl, she began her career impersonating a sort of intellectual pinup and ended, after her death, becoming (in the words of one critic) "the Marilyn Monroe of the literati."[3]

Monroe was of course the iconic sweetheart of the decade—voluptuous, whispery, and "blonde all over"—though she'd started her adult life as a busty brunette working in an airplane factory.[4] If she was the antithesis of the "good" girl that middle-class fifties girls were pressured to be, she was the incarnation of the desirable woman whom they knew their boyfriends wanted and whom they themselves secretly longed to impersonate.

Sylvia Plath *vs.* Marilyn Monroe? Sylvia Plath *as* Marilyn Monroe? Plath herself once recorded a dream in which

Marilyn Monroe appeared to me . . . as a kind of fairy godmother. . . . I spoke, almost in tears, of how much she and Arthur Miller meant to us, although they could, of course, not know us at all. She gave me an expert manicure. I had not washed my hair, and asked her about hairdressers, saying no matter where I went, they always imposed a horrid cut on me. She invited me to visit during the Christmas holidays, promising a new, flowering life.[5]

Strikingly, Plath had this fan-girl dream when she was an accomplished resident of the artists' colony Yaddo, in 1959. Yet like a teenager, she was still hoping to be helped along by Marilyn Monroe. Her other fairy godmothers were more suitable to her literary aspirations: among living poets, "Edith Sitwell & Marianne Moore, the aging giantesses

& poetic godmothers ... May Swenson, Isabella Gardner & more close, Adrienne Cecile Rich," although "Phyllis McGinley is out— light verse; she's sold herself," and Plath planned to "eclipse" Rich.[6]

The juxtaposition of godmothers—luscious Marilyn Monroe, quirky Marianne Moore—dramatizes the extraordinary confusions of the fifties for young women whose lives reflected but also rebelled against the conformity of the decade. Women in rapidly expanding suburbs claimed to be in love with their new fridges and pledged allegiance to the *Joy of Cooking* author whom Plath called her "blessed Rombauer." Speaking for the new society of Westchester, Phyllis McGinley preached "suburban rapture" for young women.[7] Yet in urban centers and small towns, psychoanalysts and sexologists disputed the nature of female sexuality, as the Beats promoted deviance, African Americans organized to protest racism, interracial couples joined civil rights activists in defying segregation, and lesbians established their own places and publications.

Amid these jostling imperatives, the evolution of the good, bad, and mad literary women who would become celebrities in seventies feminism shatters normative notions of this notoriously normative decade. Within the cauldron of the fifties' contradictions, seventies feminism incubated.

SYLVIA PLATH'S PAPER DOLLS

For Sylvia Plath, a middle-class girl from an upwardly mobile immigrant family—and, during the Second World War, a vexingly German American one at that—the cultural pressures were intense. A voracious consumer of "girls'" magazines (*Seventeen, Mademoiselle*) and periodicals that targeted housewives (*Ladies' Home Journal, Good Housekeeping*), Plath began creating her own paper dolls and their stylish outfits when she was 12. Her idealized figures were babes, not babies—dolls that had movie star figures and seductive costumes, some of which she named as if she were writing copy for *Vogue*: "Heartaches," "Fireside reveries," "Evening in Paris."[8]

A decade later, when she was studying at Cambridge on a Fulbright, she presented herself as a living doll in an article for the university newspaper titled "Sylvia Plath Tours the Stores and Forecasts May Week Fashions."[9] Here she appears in a ball gown, a cocktail dress, and most strikingly in two cheesecake poses (one on the front page of the paper) in which she is wearing a "white one-piece" bathing suit "with black polka dots, bow tied over each hip." With or without irony—her intention is unclear—she sent clippings to her mother, autographing one "with love, from Betty Grable."[10] When she wrote this piece for *Varsity*, for which she was a reporter, Plath was already deeply involved with the scruffily handsome Ted Hughes, who owned only "one pair of dungarees" and a dirty black corduroy jacket.[11]

On the one hand, she adored him: he was the only man "huge enough for me," a genius, etc.[12] On the other hand, she wanted him to wash his hair more often, to clean his fingernails, to buy newer, nicer clothes. Together, she believed, they would conquer the literary world. And within months they romantically married on Bloomsday, 1956, then honeymooned like Hemingway characters, in the south of Spain, living on potatoes, eggs, tomatoes, and fish for next to nothing; writing ferociously; swimming and getting marvelously tanned. At the same time, forbidding her mother to disclose her secret marriage, Plath yearned for a real American wedding: "a shell pink dress . . . delectable drinks . . . and much much food both meats and sweets," plus "all stainless steel kitchenware, brown-and-aqua baking dishes; and if possible, a white and forest-green bathroom towel set."[13]

Even in Benidorm, Spain, living like a beatnik, Plath lamented the absence of ingredients stipulated by Rombauer's *Joy of Cooking*. Yet she soldiered on, happily preparing three meals a day ("caffe latte" for her and "brandy milk" for Ted in the morning, picnics of deviled eggs on the beach, fish and potatoes on a single burner for dinner).[14] Why, then, did her widower write one of his strongest poems in *Birthday Letters* about their honeymoon, disclosing that, as its title declared, "You Hated Spain"? Though she couldn't speak Spanish and was merely "a bobby-sox American," she "saw right down to the Goya funeral grin" as her "panic / Clutched back towards college America."[15]

Hughes's insight was acute. Despite his wife's exuberant descriptions of Spain in letters home, she was glad to leave early, yearning for refrigeration. "College America," with its dating games and Bermuda shorts, writing contests and junior proms, had made her into a living oxymoron, an intensely ambitious writer who was also a boy-crazy Betty Grable. Here is the teenage Plath, musing in a 1950 journal entry on her own image, as she strolled through Boston on a date: "I walked along, loving, narcissus-like, my reflection in store windows." Here, in another journal entry from about the same time, she records that "I sit here, smiling, as I think in my fragmentary way: 'Woman is but an engine of ecstasy, a mimic of the earth from the ends of her curled hair to her red-lacquered nails.'" And here she is, a few years later, proclaiming a moment of social triumph: "Miraculous, and quite unbelievably . . . I am going to that magnificent event, the Yale Junior Prom with him: the one boy in the whole college I give a damn about."[16]

But then in entry after entry she railed against her sexual position, the social admonitions to preserve chastity, the imperative to marry and become a dutiful wife and mother. "I dislike being a girl, because as such I must come to realize that I cannot be a man," she wrote with a certain hesitancy. Elaborating on her feelings, she explicitly described her discontent with having been born a woman:

> Being born a woman is my awful tragedy. From the moment I was conceived I was doomed to sprout breasts and ovaries rather than a penis and scrotum; to have my whole circle of action, thought and feeling rigidly circumscribed by my inescapable femininity. Yes, my consuming desire to mingle with road crews, sailors and soldiers, bar room regulars— . . . all is spoiled by the fact that I am a girl, a female always in danger of assault and battery. My consuming interest in men and their lives is often misconstrued as a desire to seduce them, or as an invitation to intimacy. Yet, God, I want to talk to everybody I can as deeply as I can. I want to be able to sleep in an open field, to travel west, to walk freely at night . . .[17]

By the time she wrote *The Bell Jar*, Plath put the situation even more dramatically. Her narrator/protagonist, Esther Greenwood, confides that after a boyfriend told her she wouldn't want to write poems once she had children, "I began to think maybe it was true that when you were married and had children it was like being brainwashed, and afterwards you went about numb as a slave in some private, totalitarian state."[18] In its examination of fifties culture as manifested in the hothouse world of a fashion magazine, Plath's only extant novel explores all the ills that American girls were heir to in a society that enjoined them to compete for prizes while presenting themselves as dolls.

The experience that inspired the novel was as bitterly confusing as the supposedly fictive narrative. In June 1953, Plath herself was a "guest editor" of *Mademoiselle*, then *the* magazine for the gung ho college girls whom Ted Hughes called "bobby-sox Americans." In the journal's stylish Madison Avenue offices, undergraduate women who won this prestigious position confronted the conflicts that haunted fifties femininity in especially dramatic ways. Sitting around long tables in conference rooms that resembled the seminar rooms they were used to on campus, they were asked to analyze not Plato or Shakespeare but the incoming season's set of pleated plaid skirts and frilly blouses, in which all were then costumed to pose for the special issue they were ostensibly "editing." On excursions that seemed like strange field trips, they were gifted with trousseau linens, perfumes, and even new hairstyles. In writing assignments curiously evocative of prompts for college papers, they were encouraged to discourse on fashion, not fiction, or to summarize cosmetic options rather than critical opinions.[19]

The 20-year-old Plath lived with the other guest editors in the women-only Barbizon Hotel, where she struggled to keep up both physical and social appearances, felt oppressed by the alienating New York dating scene, was depressed by Eisenhower-era politics, and was especially horrified by the globally controversial electrocution of Julius and Ethel Rosenberg on June 19. By the time she left town to return to her mother's house for the rest of the summer, she was sickened by what was supposed to have been a glamorous month in the big city. Like Esther Greenwood, she flung all her fancy New York clothes off the roof of her hotel, then went home to insomnia, shock therapy, a failed suicide attempt, and a stay at a mental hospital.

Over the following years, Plath brooded on the intersection between sexual and American politics that she felt she had encountered that troubled summer. Long an accomplished graphic artist, in 1960 she put together a sardonic collage summarizing her view of the era whose avatar she herself was to become. At the center of the piece is Eisenhower, a deck of cards in his hands and Tums on his desk, along with a camera pointed at a model in a swimsuit with the slogan "Every Man Wants His Woman on a Pedestal." But a bomber is pointing at the female belly, and there's another caption: "It's HIS AND HER time all over America."[20]

HIS AND HER TIME

What made the apparently "tranquillized" fifties such a bewildering turning point? For one thing, a new ideology of marriage shaped the middle-class white America in which both Plath and Rich grew up. In the society depicted in Plath's collage, dominated by Eisenhower Republicans, "HIS AND HER time" epitomized the separate spheres of the sexes: the breadwinner and the housewife. When "the man in the gray flannel suit" returned home from his daily labors, his suburban helpmate, clad in the "New Look" of the fifties, with its long, full skirts and decorous sweater sets, was waiting for him in a tidy, clean, Betty Crocker/Betty Furness kitchen.[21]

Middle-class women had long since put aside the padded shoulders of the forties, as well as Rosie the Riveter's bandana and trousers, and they had ostensibly, too, relinquished ambitions to work outside the home—though they could expertly drive station wagons to schools and commuter platforms. In the forties, Phyllis McGinley's celebratory sonnet "The 5:32" had already set the scene for the romantic fantasy of suburbia, when the breadwinner returns in sentimental sunlight to the housekeeper poet who is his dutiful wife. "She said, If tomorrow my world were torn in two, . . . I think I would remember . . . This hour best of all the hours I knew: // When cars came backing into the little station, . . . the women driving . . . and the trains arriving, / And the men getting off with tired but practiced motion."[22]

Oddly, given the dichotomized roles of breadwinner and house-wife, an ideology of "togetherness" was dominant, as was an ethic of "adjustment" and "maturity." McGinley's own life was apparently as idyllic as the world of her sonnet. Not long ago, one of her daughters remembered that her family was "a sanguine, benign, adorable version of 'Mad Men' "—which would seem almost as much of a contradiction in terms as Plath's intellectual Betty Grable pose.[23] But television itself was new and cheerful in those days. Families gathered on weekends to marvel at the *Ed Sullivan Show* or Sid Caesar's *Show of Shows*, and slick serial comedies—*I Love Lucy, Ozzie and Harriet*—chronicled the charmingly nutty antics of middle-class wives and children (though in the end everyone professed to agree that, as the title of another series put it, "father knows best").

Marriage rates rose rapidly: "almost everyone was married by his or her mid-twenties"—Plath married at 23; Rich married at 24—and "most couples had two to four children, born sooner after marriage and spaced closer together than in previous years."[24] Girls started "going steady" early and then hoped to be "pinned." Plath continually insisted that she and Hughes wanted five children; Rich had three before she was 30. During the baby boom, the historian Elaine Tyler May has explained, "childlessness was considered deviant, selfish, and pitiable."[25] In one poem Plath herself excoriated the "Barren Woman" as a "museum without statues." In another, she brooded that "Perfection is terrible, it cannot have children. / Cold as snow breath, it tamps the womb."[26] Yet looking back on her child-rearing years in the fifties, Adrienne Rich was to remember that "every mother has known overwhelming, unacceptable anger at her children."[27]

A glossy surface, darker stirrings below. Both Sylvia Plath and Anne Sexton attended Robert Lowell's verse-writing workshop in Cambridge, Massachusetts, where they would have had to confront the implications of "the tranquillized Fifties."[28] And tellingly the word "tranquillized" reminds us that the ideology of separate sexual spheres arose in what W. H. Auden in 1947 called "an age of anxiety"—personal and public.[29] The smiling suburbanites of the "silent generation" silently suffered from heartburn and headaches. The personal anxieties troubling the lonely crowd were often soothed by Miltown, a newly formulated tranquilizer that became widely popular. Public anxieties, no doubt doubling private ones, were focused on the mushroom cloud that ended the Second World War.

Fear of the atomic bomb intensified a need for security that was increasingly associated with home and hearth. While children "took cover" under classroom desks during air-raid drills, their parents built backyard bomb shelters and stockpiled them with canned goods. The McCarthy hearings and the investigations led by the House Un-American Activities Committee fanned the red scare by blacklisting the supposedly subversive doings of liberal intellectuals and artists. Loyalty oaths, the Korean War, and the execution of the Rosenbergs escalated the sense of dread, as did purges from the government of "sexual misfits," prosecuted and persecuted as "security threats."[30]

Even the poetry that dominated the literary scene for much of the decade was tightly formal and aesthetically conservative. Plath trained herself in her craft by churning out sonnets and villanelles and, in the manner of that "aging giantess" Marianne Moore, carefully counted syllabic verse. At this point, Moore incarnated the American ideal of a woman poet: spinsterish and eccentric, wearing a cape and tricornered hat à la George Washington, and in 1955 gamely trying to think up names for the shark-finned car that Henry Ford was eventually to call the "Edsel," after his brother. (Among other monikers, Moore proposed "The Resilient Bullet," "The Intelligent Whale," and "Utopian Turtletop.")[31]

Not only did Plath start out as an admirer of Moore, Moore herself was for a while an admirer of Plath, awarding her a prize in a 1955 Mount Holyoke verse-writing contest and posing amiably for a joint photograph. But the relationship soured, in part because the chasm between married and single women deepened during "HIS AND HER time all over America." Moore was one of three judges (along with W. H. Auden and Stephen Spender) who awarded a major first-book poetry prize to Hughes's *Hawk in the Rain,* and it soon became clear that she preferred the husband's work to the wife's. After Plath sent Moore poems for critical appraisal, she admonished the younger woman not to be "so grisly" and not to be "too unrelenting."[32]

When Plath wrote her asking if she'd be a referee for a Guggenheim Fellowship, and, according to one scholar, "unwisely asserted the value of her experience as a mother,"[33] the spinsterish Moore took offense. By 1961, when she was queried about Plath's candidacy for the Guggenheim, Moore was bizarrely hostile:

Sylvia Plath Hughes won a Glascock Award at Mt. Holyoke when I was a judge: work was attractive as well as talented. I thought and think her very gifted but feel cold toward this "project." And way of presenting it. You are not subsidized for having a baby especially in view of world population explosion. You should look before you leap and examine your world-potentialities of responsibility as contributory parent. Sylvia Plath has been specialing [*sic*] lately in gruesome detail, worms and germs and spiritual flatness. Her husband Ted Hughes has moral force and twice the talent that she has, won the YMHA verse-book contest with W. H. Auden, Stephen Spender, and me, as judges and I'd rather give the money to him to continue his work than give it to Sylvia.[34]

As Vivian Pollak remarks in a discussion of this letter, "Hughes is not faulted for fathering children."[35] Nor had he, in fact, applied for a Guggenheim (he'd already had one).

Of course, Moore's comments reveal much more about her than they do about Plath: in particular, they suggest the extraordinary complexity of the period's attitudes toward marriage and maternity. What Moore had avoided in pursuing a career as a single woman had rewarded her with power and prestige. What Plath celebrated—her determination to be a "triple threat woman, wife, mother and writer"—went beyond the bounds and bonds of womanhood.[36] A young lady should be one or the other, should not aspire to "have it all," as Plath did. Thus, the domesticity in which Plath might seem so dutifully to have reveled was paradoxically seen by Moore (and no doubt by others) as a rebellious gesture rather than a decorous one.

And, as we have seen, Plath herself had wanted to rebel against the "awful tragedy" of sprouting "breasts and ovaries rather than a penis and scrotum." Yet once she had encountered Hughes she enthusiastically (and defiantly) celebrated the joys of a creative partnership in childbearing, child-rearing, householding, *and* art. Nonetheless, she refused to be a "housewife poet" like McGinley ("she's sold out"). She yearned to be "The Poetess of America"—not suburbia—and for Ted to be "The Poet of England."[37] Her ambitions would have seemed, in different ways, problematic to Moore and McGinley—and each of them seemed problematic to Plath.

ANATOMY AND DESTINY

What biological and psychological assumptions about femininity shaped the clashing views of marriage, maternity, and creativity espoused by such divergent figures as Moore, McGinley, and Plath? Before feminists took on the subject of sexuality, it was monopolized by male as well as female psychologists and psychiatrists who made their names by advancing conventional strictures about women's proper place in the nuclear family. To be happy and healthy, they preached, a young woman had to subordinate herself to a man and to children. Freudian theories of psychosexuality dominated the thinking of the fifties, even while the sexology research of Alfred Kinsey started to contest them.

Neither the wifely and maternal Plath nor the spinster Moore would have fit the bill of Freudian "normalcy." Moore's avoidance of marriage, her George Washington getup, and her decision to hang out with the Big Boys of modernism (Pound, Williams, Eliot, et al.) made her classically neurotic from a psychoanalytic perspective. And Plath's passion to become "a triple threat woman, wife, mother and writer" put her, too, at odds with established fifties ideals. After her death, in fact, she was to be accused by the psychoanalytic critic David Holbrook of "false male doing."[38]

In the fifties, psychoanalysis seemed "modern," while as a discipline sexology evoked such fin de siècle figures as Havelock Ellis and Richard von Kraft-Ebbing. Yet many of Freud's disciples reinforced Victorian notions of femininity, whereas Alfred Kinsey and his colleagues subverted some traditional ideas of female sexuality. Ironically, too, a number of the leading experts translating Freudian psychoanalysis to Americans were women playing the penalizing role of Serena Joy in Margaret Atwood's *The Handmaid's Tale*, disciplining other women to submit to their (grim) anatomical destiny. Both sides focused for the most part on white women and both fixed on organs rarely discussed before in American letters: penises, vaginas, and the clitoris.

Once experienced as liberating, Freudian ideas became strangely punitive by this decade, with Freud's descriptions of female psychosexual development used to diagnose as mentally disturbed anyone who deviated from his definition of femininity. The psychiatrist Marynia Farnham can be viewed today on YouTube in a clip from a 1950s newsreel in which the narrator intones with archaic phrasing, "Strongly against careers for women is Dr. Marynia Farnham."[39] Coauthor with the journalist Ferdinand Lundberg of the best-selling *Modern Woman: The Lost Sex* (1947), she sternly argues that abandoning traditional roles has made women, their husbands, and their children unhappy. (We see footage of an unattended kid almost hit by a car, kindergartners playing with fire.) Eschewing the conventional roles that she promotes, Farnham is costumed as a specialist—white coat, stethoscope, short-cropped hair, in a hospital office, with a seated secretary dutifully taking shorthand. During a period when women were a tiny scattering of tokens in the medical establishment, she attributes all the ills of society to women working outside the home as professionals or laborers.

Modern Woman: The Lost Sex, widely read in the fifties, claims that women who have deserted homemaking for the labor force have made themselves and their society sick. For they themselves have been sickened by "the feminist complex," a pathology of epic proportions. Specifically, they are "afflicted with a severe case of 'penis-envy.'"[40] Angry feminists, "hostile to women," encourage women to "commit suicide as women and attempt to live as men." According to Lundberg and Farnham, the rampant penis envy induced by the reign of feminism dooms women to sexual dysfunction. The "apparently new" phenomenon of "frigidity" arose and became complicated because "mere orgasm can never be the entire sexual goal for a satisfactorily functioning woman." Not orgasm but babies must be her aim: "for the sexual act to be fully satisfactory to a woman she must, in the depth of her mind, desire, deeply and utterly, to be a mother." A woman who does not desire to become a mother or who seeks pleasure in "the sex act" itself is doomed: "Women cannot make its immediate pleasure an end in itself without inducing a decline in the pleasure."[41]

Those who cling to the "infantile sexual activity" centered on "clitoral stimulation" are guilty of "a denial of femininity" that accounts for most "marital sexual difficulties." Schooling intensifies the problem: "The more educated the woman is, the greater chance there is of sexual disorder" that will impair her offspring. Needless to say, the "unmarried mother . . . is a complete failure as a woman," as is the spinster. The neurotic married mother produces delinquents and criminals when she is "rejecting" or "dominating"; she produces castrated "sissies" when she is "over-affectionate." Most of these disorders are attributed to women's "morbidly intense ego-strivings."[42]

As one historian of American sexual thought has noted, *Modern Woman: The Lost Sex* simplified the theories of Helene Deutsch "for a popular audience."[43] In *The Psychology of Women* (1944), Deutsch laid the foundation for Lundberg and Farnham's screed against feminism by establishing the three defining traits at the "core" of "the feminine personality," a temperament that finds its contentment at home with hubby and babies: "narcissism, passivity, and masochism."[44] This core feminine personality arose from Deutsch's alarming revision of Freud's view that girls become envious when they see the clitoris as an inferior penis.

Some girls may find the clitoris an "inadequate outlet," Deutsch concedes, but others find it "so rudimentary that it can barely be considered an organ": "the little girl is frequently 'organless'"; "it is simply not there!" This "genital trauma" persists because "the vagina—a completely passive, receptive organ—awaits an active agent to become a functioning excitable organ." The adolescent girl must navigate between "the Scylla of having no penis and the Charybdis of lacking the responsiveness of the vagina."[45]

According to Deutsch, pain is inseparable from pleasure in "coitus," which is "closely associated with the act of defloration, and defloration with rape and a painful penetration of the body." She defends herself against her peer Karen Horney, who criticized Deutsch for believing that "what woman ultimately wants in intercourse is to be raped and violated; what she wants in mental life is to be humiliated."[46] But Horney is right: Deutsch does claim that "the 'undiscovered' vagina is—in normal, favorable instances—eroticized by an act of rape." Inevitably for Deutsch, "the intellectual woman is masculinized; in her, warm intuitive knowledge has yielded to cold unproductive thinking." Caught within a "masculinity complex," the ambitious woman, like "the sadistic witch," displays a "surplus of active-aggressive forces" that should be attributed to "the girl's genital trauma."[47] Regardless of the personal sources of Deutsch's views,[48] as in the case of Marynia Farnham a female professional was instructing other women to eschew professional aspirations. For women, curtailing other women's rights—in this case, their economic, educational, and erotic rights—turned out to be a gainful business.

While the psychoanalysts viewed the clitoris as a puny penis or as nonexistent, the sexologist Alfred Kinsey defined it as the usual source of female orgasmic pleasure. Less theoretical than empirical, Kinsey's 1953 *Sexual Behavior in the Human Female* judges the frequency of orgasm—resulting from a range of activities—to be the best measure of sexual activity. In direct opposition to Freudian thinkers, Kinsey questioned the existence of " 'vaginal orgasm,' " which, he argued, "is a physical and physiologic impossibility for nearly all females."[49]

Kinsey's table of contents lists his massive investigations into women's sexual behaviors, although over the years critics have questioned the representativeness of his sample. Were all the people he interrogated "average," or were they subject to what skeptics dismissively called "volunteer bias"?[50] How many midcentury women would be willing to talk honestly about erotic intimacies? Still, the very number of interviews he recorded subverts the Freudian idea that there is a single model for female sexuality. And the book, dedicated "To the nearly 8000 females who contributed the data," does stress that "many males do not understand that [the clitoris] may be as important a center of stimulation for females as the penis is for males." It also emphasizes that "it is difficult for most males to comprehend that females are not aroused by seeing male genitalia," a reminder that retains its relevance.[51]

The outcry following the publication of Kinsey's best-selling *Sexual Behavior in the Human Female* expressed shock about his findings that eventually resulted in his losing funding from the Rockefeller Foundation.[52] Especially scandalous was his report on the numbers of women engaged in sex before marriage and in adulterous affairs during marriage. Yet Kinsey's findings illuminate what we know about most of the literary women of the fifties whose lives and letters we investigate here. Neither Plath nor Rich, neither di Prima nor Lorde, were "virgins" when they married. And many letters mailed to Kinsey expressed gratitude. His documentation of women's responsiveness to masturbation, fantasy, and interpersonal contacts before, during, and outside marriage clearly appealed to a culture fascinated by the steamy eroticism of *A Streetcar Named Desire* and *Peyton Place*, the crooning of Frank Sinatra, the sexual gyrations of Elvis Presley, the voluptuous performances of Marilyn Monroe and Jayne Mansfield.

Did this fetishization of the erotic have consequences as troublesome as Freudian psychosexual theory—equating sexual success with appropriate climaxing? It was no coincidence that Hugh Hefner and his Playboy clubs were longtime supporters of Kinsey's research.[53] "Pussies" and penises, not heads and hearts, seemed to matter most both to the Freudians and the Kinseyites. Yet in a society that increasingly celebrated women who were sexy "playmates," by the end of the fifties 25 percent of women with children were working outside the home.[54] But even for the most diligent young working women, the culture of the period posed knotty problems.

Want ads in newspapers were gender-specific, with most of the employment available to women clustered in low-status, low-paying, or service-oriented jobs: "pink-collar" jobs as secretaries, receptionists, telephone operators, or sales clerks, with luckier women working as teachers or nurses. On the financial front, single, divorced, or widowed women could not get financial credit. What we now call "reproductive freedom" was barely existent. The so-called rhythm method of birth control produced quite a few babies, and illegal backstreet abortions killed quite a few women.[55]

In fact, the classic picture of the tranquilized fifties belies the furious though sometimes furtive resistance of women who never bought into the fantasy of docile femininity or women whose surface conformity masked deep dissent. The decade that shaped the gender roles dramatized in the twenty-first-century television series

Mad Men produced a number of singularly determined and eccentric mad women who would make their mark on history. Although the bourgeois, white society in which Plath, Rich, Moore, Farnham, and Deutsch were each embedded may have been the hegemonic culture of the fifties, it was hardly the only one. Neither the Freudians nor the Kinseyites seem quite to have grasped the social, intellectual, and racial complexity of the world in which they promoted their ideas.

2

Race, Rebellion, and Reaction

W HILE P LATH AND R ICH were dutifully studying at Smith and Radcliffe, then bearing children, and, for quite some time, stifling their rebellion or simply confiding it to secret journals, bohemians, Beats, and Blacks were protesting the pieties of midcentury America. In 1955, their dissatisfaction rose to a howl in Allen Ginsberg's poem of that name. Gay, Jewish, left-wing, and disaffected, Ginsberg made himself heard from coast to coast when he protested what he considered the horrific state of things:

> Moloch! Solitude! Filth! Ugliness! Ashcans and unobtainable
> dollars! Children screaming under the stairways! Boys sobbing
> in armies! Old men weeping in the parks!
> . . . .
> Moloch! Moloch! Robot apartments! invisible suburbs! skeleton
> treasuries! blind capitals! demonic industries! spectral nations!
> invincible madhouses! granite cocks! monstrous bombs![1]

But even before Ginsberg's rant enthralled an increasingly wide circle of dissidents, there were young women who struggled to escape
the clutches of a culture that they defined as soulless.

DIANE DI PRIMA AS A FEMINIST BEATNIK

Like Plath, Diane di Prima was born to immigrant parents (di Prima's were Italian) in 1934 and performed brilliantly in high school—
in her case, Hunter College High School, a highly selective public
school for girls in New York City. And like Plath, di Prima was
encouraged to go on to an equally elite college, Swarthmore. But
there the resemblance ends. Though di Prima might as well have
been Plath's double—same age, same kind of background—she was
defiantly, stubbornly *opposite.*

Where Plath wrote, for the most part, exuberantly about her
time at Smith, di Prima hated Swarthmore, "the pretentious, awkward intellectual life, clipped speech, stiff bodies, unimaginative
clothes, poor food, frequent alcohol, and deathly mores by which
I found myself surrounded." Nor did she find solace in most other
options open to her. "Nine-to-five was a prison; family was prison.
Cold intellect of campus, another prison." Seeking, like her early
idol John Keats, the life of art and "the holiness of the heart's affec-
tions," she chose "the life of the renunciant . . . outside the confines
and laws of that particular and peculiar culture" of the fifties.[2]

Dropping out of college, she left home and settled into an
impoverished but freethinking bohemian life on New York's Lower
East Side. In her fictionalized autobiography *Memoirs of a Beatnik,*
di Prima recalled "a strange, nondescript kind of orgy" with Allen
Ginsberg, who slid "from body to body in a great wallow of flesh":

"It was warm and friendly and very unsexy—like being in a bathtub with four other people."[3]

Di Prima had no feminist vocabulary to draw upon. However, she knew perfectly well that the poetry scene she had entered was male-defined, sometimes "pompous, self-righteous," but she has claimed that "we walked together on the roads of Art. . . . And seeing it thus made it possible for me to walk among these men mostly un-hit-on, generally unscathed." While Plath—like so many of her contemporaries—was seeking boyfriends, lovers, or potential husbands, di Prima defined the men around her as "friends and companions of the holy art."[4]

According to *Recollections of My Life as a Woman*, her 2001 memoir of New York in the fifties, she had many lovers. The first person with whom she fell in love was a woman named Bonnie, and the second was the African American poet LeRoi Jones. Even before these passionate affairs, though, she had decided at the age of 22 to have a baby: "I do remember . . . the words in my mind. That if I didn't have a baby I was going to get sick," she recalled in her memoir, adding, strikingly, "Not that I for one minute thought of including a man in my life, in my home. That was out of the question. . . . As far as I could see, all they were was trouble."[5]

After giving birth to her first daughter, di Prima raised her while co-editing a literary magazine, *The Floating Bear*, with LeRoi Jones. Working in a Village bookstore, founding the Poet's Theater with a group of friends, entering into a "marriage of convenience" with Alan Marlowe (it lasted six and a half years), she published her own poetry and eventually mothered four more children. Her relationship with LeRoi Jones was intense and vexed. When it began, she has written, "She defined herself as a duo: herself and the child. She defined herself as her work. . . . Stepped into the 'love affair' not knowing where it would lead."[6]

Where it led might, from Plath's perspective, seem disastrous, for Plath's pride in her love match with Hughes was inextricably entangled with possessiveness, and she was enraged if her husband even walked down the street with an attractive "other woman." But from di Prima's point of view, it was essential to remain "self-defined in the midst of it all," even infidelity. "Roi slept around, he lied. . . . He didn't show up when he was going to, showed up unexpectedly, treated me like a peer, a queen, a servant. . . . All that went without saying I took it as it came."[7] And then, despite his protests—for he was already married, with two children—she bore his child, her second daughter, on her own.

He would "often call me Lady Day," di Prima writes of her time with Jones, when they would make love to the music of Billie Holiday, "especially the fiercer, sadder pieces"; but she confesses, "At that time I was only half aware that the songs carried the bitterness, the dilemma of our 'interracial' love," though she knew "there was no world where it was simply okay for us. Not for our black and whiteness. Not for me, a single woman with a child."[8] Her memory of her time with Jones, who would later change his name to Amiri Baraka and in the sixties become part of the Black Arts movement, dramatizes the significance of African American culture in the fifties. For although popular narratives represent the world as having been lily-white, such a view is as deceptive as the mostly white offices of Madison Avenue.

GWENDOLYN BROOKS'S BRONZEVILLE

If Black people appeared at all in most fifties' films and sitcoms, they were stereotyped as mammies or Uncle Toms. Yet it was in this decade that Gwendolyn Brooks, who was eventually to become the first Black woman appointed poet laureate of the United States, composed meticulously detailed portraits of a culture very different from the one chronicled in the poems of Phyllis McGinley or indeed in *The Bell Jar*. Her short poem "The Bean-Eaters," published in 1959, captures a partnership in poverty and resilience: a couple who "eat beans mostly" with "tin flatware" on "a plain and creaking wood."[9] Brooks focuses not on the raptures of suburbia but on the problems—and pleasures—of her South Side neighborhood, Bronzeville, the Black ghetto in her hometown of Chicago to which many African Americans journeyed during the second Great Migration from the oppressions of the South to the possibilities of the North.

Brooks's Bronzeville is more complex than McGinley's placid suburbia. Her only novel, *Maud Martha* (1953), traces the coming-of-age of a girl who is distressed by being darker—"blacker"—than her older sister and darker, too, than the more "yellow" man who becomes her husband; in this way it prefigures Toni Morrison's debut novel, *The Bluest Eye*, which tells a similar though more calamitous story.[10] At the same time, however, in "Bronzeville Woman in a Red Hat," Brooks wrote scathingly of the kitchen confrontation between two cultures—the world of the white bourgeoisie and the world of "bean-eaters" and Maud Marthas who have to become their domestic workers.

Subtitled *"hires out to Mrs. Miles,"* the story of "Bronzeville Woman in a Red Hat" is told from the perspective of the haughty white employer, who instantly reifies the "woman in a red hat":

They had never had one in the house before.
The strangeness of it all. Like unleashing
A lion really. . . . A black
Bear.

There it stood in the door,

Under a red hat that was rash, but refreshing—

In a tasteless way, of course[.][11]

The woman whom Mrs. Miles sees as an "it" or a "Bear" has been sent by an agency to substitute for a missing "Irishwoman . . . Who was a perfect jewel, a red-faced trump."[12] Clearly Mrs. Miles is unkind to any servant, but her shock at her child's innocent affection for the Bronzeville woman dramatizes the often-unacknowledged tensions in the supposedly shiny fifties kitchen. When her child "Kiss[es] back the colored maid," Mrs. Miles experiences disgust and rage:

Heat at the hairline, heat between the bowels,

Examining seeming coarse unnatural scene,

She saw all things except herself serene:

Child, big black woman, pretty kitchen towels.[13]

Of course, the kinds of pink-collar jobs that young white women could apply for—jobs as file clerks and secretaries—were rarely available at that time to young Black women, or to Black women of any age. None of Sylvia Plath's fellow guest editors at *Mademoiselle* were Black (or, for that matter, Asian or Hispanic). Brooks's Maud Martha, like her Bronzeville woman, is offered a job as a domestic.

Despite such racial stratification, however, the fifties was in many ways a decade shaped and complicated by the successes of African American culture. The music scene was as rich as it ever has been, with the new genres of bebop and jazz dominated by such figures as Charlie Parker, Thelonious Monk, Miles Davis, and John Coltrane. Louis Armstrong was still around, blasting his horn, and Harry Belafonte sang "Man smart, woman smarter" in Caribbean accents.[14]

Nor did women lag behind. Billie Holiday was still an idol, Ella Fitz-gerald had just begun to record her classic songbooks, and in 1958 Nina Simone, born a year before Sylvia Plath, had inaugurated her brilliant and defiant career with the album *Little Girl Blue*.

Like a steady drumbeat under this pattern of syncopation, the civil rights movement was gaining strength. After Gwendolyn Brooks produced *Annie Allen*, which won the Pulitzer Prize in 1950, Ralph Ellison won the National Book Award for *Invisible Man* and James Baldwin published *Notes of a Native Son*. Martin Luther King, Jr., led the Montgomery bus boycott in 1955, after Rosa Parks refused to move to the back seat of a public bus. It was in this context that the Black playwright Lorraine Hansberry wrote her powerful *A Raisin in the Sun*, which opened on Broadway in 1959 and became a smash hit.

THE STAGES OF LORRAINE
HANSBERRY'S MILITANCY

Memorialized in Nina Simone's popular R&B song "To Be Young, Gifted and Black," the short but activist life of Lorraine Hans-berry evolved with the civil rights movement. Her first publication, the poem "Flag from a Kitchenette Window"—Hansberry's father amassed his wealth by renting kitchenette apartments to his Black neighbors in segregated Chicago—paid homage to Gwendolyn Brooks's "Kitchenette Building."[15] Yet in contrast with Brooks, Hans-berry has received relatively little attention until quite recently—a startling omission, since she was the first Black playwright to receive the New York Drama Critics Circle Award (for *A Raisin in the Sun*). On opening night, when Sidney Poitier brought her up to the stage for a standing ovation, she was 28 years old.

Paradoxes abound in the facts we do know. Born in 1930 into

a well-to-do and college-educated family, Hansberry became an insurgent after her mother sent her to school in a white fur coat and the other kids beat her up: "from that moment I became—a rebel" by choosing friends from among the assailants.[16] Since one of her youthful heroes was the Haitian revolutionary Toussaint L'Ouverture, this identification with the dissident and disenfranchised was not altogether surprising. She could have gone to historically Black Howard University, where her uncle was a professor of African studies, but she chose to spend two years at the University of Wisconsin, which, like many institutions of higher learning, did not then provide on-campus housing for Black students.[17] In a story set on the campus, Hansberry's surrogate finds college "a bust," proposes the toast "Long live—the Kinsey Report!," and dedicates herself to the proposition that the distinction between " 'nice girls' and 'bad girls' belonged in the Middle Ages."[18] Progressive activism more than art engaged her before she dropped out.

Hansberry attributed the skepticism qualifying her faith that humanity can "command its own destiny" to the atomic bombing of Nagasaki and Hiroshima when she was a teenager and the inauguration of the Cold War when she was entering her twenties.[19] Hobnobbing with intellectuals in New York's bohemian Greenwich Village, she studied with the influential philosopher W. E. B. Du Bois, and soon questioned the idea that words like "modern" or "progress" should be used as if synonymous with the West: "it is the women of Ghana who vote and the women of Switzerland who do not."[20]

In the early fifties, Hansberry rose from staff writer to associate editor of the singer-actor Paul Robeson's *Freedom* magazine, contributing articles on Egyptian protests against British rule and substandard Harlem schools. She earned $31.70 a week, which accounted, she joked, for her slimness. The essays were produced while she was

increasingly "sick of poverty, lynching, stupid wars, and the universal maltreatment of my people."[21] When she attended the Inter-
American Peace Conference in Uruguay in place of the grounded
Paul Robeson—he had been deprived of his passport because of his
affiliations with the Communist Party—she knew that upon her
return the FBI would start surveilling her.[22]

During this same period, she signed a photograph of herself with
the name "young Ida B.," a reference to Ida B. Wells, the journalist famous for crusading against lynching.[23] This self-identification
explains the nature of some of Hansberry's activism: she coordinated
an artistic program in honor of Ida B. Wells, eulogized the career of
the Black musical theater actress Florence Mills, and covered a conference of a group called Sojourners for Truth and Justice—Black
women protesting the Korean War as well as racial discrimination.
Increasingly militant about civil rights, Hansberry married the Jewish critic, producer, and song writer Robert Nemiroff, a rebellious
act since interracial marriage was illegal at the time in most states.
The night before the wedding, they protested the death sentence
of the Rosenbergs. The couple attained economic security when
Nemiroff earned a hefty sum from his 1956 coauthored song "Cindy,
Oh Cindy," which was recorded by Eddie Fisher.[24]

The next year, with Hansberry free to focus on her writing, she
celebrated Simone de Beauvoir's *The Second Sex* as "the most important book in America." According to Hansberry, gossip about the
author's relationship to Jean-Paul Sartre or "her alleged 'lesbianism' "
testifies to the truth of the book's assertion that men compel women
"to assume the status of the Other." Since Beauvoir refuses "to accept
the traditional view" of marriage's "sacred place in the scheme of
human development," accusing her "of not respecting marriage is
quite like accusing a communist of not 'respecting' free enterprise."

Unlike those who disparaged Beauvoir, Hansberry portrays her own reverential response: she is "the twenty-three-year-old woman writer closing the book thoughtfully after months of study and placing it in the most available spot on her 'reference' shelf, her fingers sensitive with awe . . . ; her mind afire at last with ideas from France once again in history, *egalité, fraternité, liberté—pour tout le monde!*"[25]

Woman, Hansberry declares, is "chained to an ailing social ideology which seeks always to deny her autonomy and more—to delude her into the belief that that which in fact imprisons her the more is somehow her fulfillment." And she concludes by tackling the detrimental effects of the celebration of domesticity: "The ancient effort to glorify the care of the home into something which it is not and cannot be is one of the greatest assaults against womanhood." As if directly opposing Farnham and Deutsch, she proclaims that women who devote themselves entirely to their husbands and children become "one of the most neurotic sections, no doubt, of our entire population."[26]

Yet the central character of *A Raisin in the Sun*, completed while Hansberry wrote so fervently about Simone de Beauvoir, is the widowed Mama whose heroic act consists in abdicating her power to her son. At the end of the play, Mama decides to make her son Walter Lee the "head" of the family "like you supposed to be."[27] And her quest—to move the family from the South Side of Chicago to a suburban home—would seem to replicate precisely the domestic ideology that Hansberry herself critiqued. Indeed, the genius of the play consists in Hansberry's testing the American dream of the fifties against the experiences of working-class Black people and finding it sadly wanting.

In doing so, she not only gained the wide audience needed to get a play produced on Broadway (then made into a movie and later revived repeatedly on stage); she also addressed the gender and racial biases of her time.[28] *A Raisin in the Sun* recasts the experience of Hansberry's parents when they moved from a Black neighborhood in Chicago to an affluent white neighborhood, where the 8-year-old was threatened by brick-wielding whites—one brick crashed through the front window, almost hitting her—and her mother patrolled the house with a loaded Luger. The little girl was "spat at, cursed and pummeled in the daily trek" to and from a Jim Crow school whose mission was "*not* to give education but to withhold as much as possible."[29] After the family was evicted by an Illinois court, her father worked with the NAACP to win a favorable decision from the Supreme Court, although it would not address the larger issue of racially restrictive real estate covenants until another case, eight years later.

More impoverished than Nannie and Carl A. Hansberry, most of the Younger adults in *A Raisin in the Sun* undertake domestic work outside as well as inside the house. When the widowed Lena Younger, "Mama" in the play, receives $10,000 of insurance money, she uses it to put a down payment on a house in a white neighborhood, although her son Walter Lee wants to invest in a liquor store. In the final act, Mama willingly renounces her financial power over Walter Lee, just as he, defrauded by his partner in the liquor scheme, refuses to sell out to white racists and decides instead to lead the family into the new house. No one knew better than Hansberry what the Younger family had waiting for them there.

Regardless of the racism Mama will continue to have to face, her triumph at the end of the play consists in her realization that her son has "finally come into his manhood today." Their generational struggle has not converted Walter Lee to his mother's religious piety, but it has convinced him not to grovel or capitulate to those who think his family would "dirty up" the white folks' neighborhood.[30]

A Raisin in the Sun addresses feminist themes in its portrayal of the generational conflict that strengthens Mama's daughter-in-law and daughter, each of whom manages to confront what Langston Hughes called "dreams deferred" without drying up "like a raisin in the sun."[31] Walter Lee's wife, Ruth, determines whether to abort a pregnancy when there is barely room in their cramped apartment for their little boy. And Walter Lee's sister, Beneatha, struggles with her desire to become a doctor, given the scarcity of money and the pressure to marry.

Especially through the overtures of her two quite different suitors, Beneatha—who in the course of the play decides to close-crop her "unstraightened" hair—realizes that her rejection of the "assimilationist" suitor who is "willing to give up his own culture and submerge himself completely in the dominant, and in this case *oppressive* culture" does not necessarily mean that she should marry her Nigerian suitor and make Africa her homeland.[32] The acolyte of Beauvoir created in Beneatha a female character who seeks autonomy and professional satisfaction.

But through the resonant figure of Mama, Hansberry predicted that feminists of color would adopt agendas differently inflected from those espoused by white feminists. Hansberry's Mama wants not independence from the home but a home of her own. She seeks not to challenge male domination but rather to reaffirm the damaged manhood of her son; and, as bell hooks has explained in a different context, Mama realizes that "masculinity need not be equated with sexist notions of manhood."[33] Mama does not need the right to work—she has worked her whole life outside and also inside her home—but instead she hopes to secure the future of her family. According to the prescient Hansberry, both gender and race must be addressed by activists committed to liberation.

A few weeks before the opening of *A Raisin in the Sun*, Hansberry delivered a passionate plea to Black writers who, in her view, needed to produce socially engaged art in order to refute the prevailing platitudes of the day: "women are idiots"; "people are white"; "European culture is the culture of the world."[34] Taking issue with the Beats, whose appropriation of Black language seemed patronizing to her, and with Norman Mailer's "The White Negro" (1957), which seemed prompted by misbegotten primitivism, Hansberry urges African American authors to tackle the "hideous malignancy" of "color prejudice" that continues to result in Blacks murdered "with and *without* rope and faggot, in all the old ways and many new ones."[35] Though she has witnessed terrible injustice, she bases her hope for the future on the thousands who marched in Montgomery and the nine children who determined to attend school in Little Rock. It must have been a source of satisfaction to her that one of the nine students sent her a fan letter after seeing a performance of *A Raisin in the Sun*.

Before Hansberry died of pancreatic cancer at 34, she analyzed the forces that had led her to mistitle this landmark 1959 speech—which was not published until 1981—"The Negro Writer and *His* Roots" (italics ours). The 1961 essay "In Defense of the Equality of Men," which went unprinted until we included it in the first edition of *The Norton Anthology of Literature by Women* (1985), castigates a social order that effectively keeps women in a "second-class situation, but which is less often criticized for imposing *upon males* the most unreasonable and unnecessary burdens of 'superiority' and 'authority,' which, in fact, work only to insult their humanness and *deny the reality of their civilized state.*" Citing Mary Wollstonecraft, Susan B. Anthony, Elizabeth Cady Stanton, and Harriet Tubman, Hansberry repeatedly demythologizes the homemaker: "*The Feminists did not create the housewife's dissatisfaction with her lot—the Femi-*

nists came from out of the only place they could have come—the housewives of the world!" (italics hers).[36] Before Betty Friedan, there was Lorraine Hansberry.

Alternately empowered and plagued by the celebrity that came with a Broadway hit, and separated from her husband, Hansberry pursued projects arising from her commitment to combat racism at home and colonialism overseas. "Jimmy" Baldwin, who called her "Sweet Lorraine," partied with her and accompanied her to meetings and protests. To Nina Simone, whose performances she enjoyed at the Village Gate, she could confide her melancholy and her shame at being alone: "I have closed the shutters so that no one can see. Me. Alone. Sitting at the typewriter on Easter eve; drinking; brooding; alone."[37]

Readers today can gain a sense of some of Hansberry's writings about her erotic relations with women in Imani Perry's *Looking for Lorraine*, which captures the dazzling beauty and wit of a woman who lived before her time. Yet Adrienne Rich was right in noting the damages wrought by external and internal censorship.[38] Hansberry's proposed project "The Sign in Jenny Reed's Window" had morphed into *The Sign in Sidney Brustein's Window*, a show that closed the night she died. In its last version, her next play, *Les Blancs*, which originally featured female characters, highlighted male protagonists. She never got the time to write her projected full-length drama on Mary Wollstonecraft, a strong spokeswoman "destroyed many times over."[39] And Hansberry's pseudonymous contributions to the lesbian publication *The Ladder*—founded in 1955 by the Daughters of Bilitis—address the pressures on lesbians to marry, homosexual persecution, and anti-feminist dogma.[40]

In 1964, Hansberry obtained a Mexican divorce, although she kept Robert Nemiroff as her literary executor. In the same year, in a letter to the *New York Times*, she referenced civil rights militancy by dwelling on the italicized last words of Langston Hughes's poem about what happens to a dream deferred: if it does not dry up like a raisin in the sun, *"does it explode?"*[41]

AUDRE LORDE'S LESBIAN BIOMYTHOGRAPHY

During the red scares of the fifties, when homosexuals were routinely outed as security risks and then flushed out of their jobs, many lesbians were necessarily closeted. However, in this repressive decade, the poet Audre Lorde joined a dynamic, mostly underground lesbian community centered in Greenwich Village. As she reported in *Zami: A New Spelling of My Name*, which she labeled a "biomythography," she once attended a party where guests raved over a platter of slices of rare meat "lovingly laid out and individually folded up into a vulval pattern, with a tiny dab of mayonnaise at the crucial apex."[42]

But she had always been a defiant sort. Diane di Prima, who was her longtime friend and classmate at Hunter High, captured the intensity of her presence: "there was always Audre Lorde—who was later to become a poet of note—Black and fierce, and in those days often unreadable. She kept us guessing with her eyes and her silence. A kind of knowing and a kind of contempt."[43] Still, she chose the title *Zami* for her memoir, a word in "Carriacou, meaning *women who work and live together*," because her mother used it to mean "just friends": "it probably came from Patois, which is a combination of French and Spanish, probably from 'les amies,' the friends."[44]

Lorde arrived at the gay bars after a difficult youth marked by the discrimination her Caribbean-born parents faced during the Depression. Throughout a Harlem childhood, her fiercely protective mother—impotent against the racism of the white nuns at her daughter's Catholic school—regularly thrashed Audrey, the youngest of three sisters. Chubby, spirited, and legally blind, Audrey needed to be taught not to expect fair treatment, her mother believed, since it would never be forthcoming. A precocious little girl, she learned to read and write early, savored her mother's Caribbean cooking and storytelling, and enjoyed dropping the "y" from her first name because she relished the resulting "evenness" of her two names.[45]

Growing up lonely, with the conviction that she was an outsider inside her family, Lorde had one resource: whenever anyone asked her "How do you feel?" she would "recite a poem, and somewhere in that poem would be the feeling, the vital piece of information." At the children's room of the public library, she memorized poems. They became "the first reason for my own writing, my need to say things I couldn't say otherwise when I couldn't find other poems to serve." Saying her first poems aloud helped her "find a secret way to express my feelings."[46]

No one in the family spoke about "race as a reality." At age 6, Lorde asked her two older sisters, "What does *Colored* mean?" Since her mother looked white enough to pass, the child decided to identify herself as "white same as Mommy," only to be plunged into confusion by her siblings' horrified reaction.[47] At Hunter High, there were only a scattering of Black students, and according to *Zami*, the one Lorde befriended committed suicide after possibly being abused by her father.[48]

Despite the trauma of that event—recalled in "Memorial II," the opening poem of her *Collected Poems*—Lorde gained a strengthened commitment to verse through a group of literary white girls whom she calls "The Branded": "the Lunatic Fringe, proud of our outrageousness and our madness, our bizarre-colored inks and quill pens."[49] Aspiring poets and the daughters of immigrants, among them Diana di Prima, these feisty girls skipped classes and held séances, calling up the spirits of the dead poets they revered.[50] Always active in *Argus*, the school literary magazine, Lorde also at 17 published a poem in, yes, *Seventeen*.

During a stint of factory work in Stamford, Connecticut, Lorde had an affair with her first significant lover, another worker, who entranced her but also instructed her on prevailing attitudes toward lesbian sex. "*Snappy little dark eyes, skin the color of well-buttered caramel, and a body like the Venus of Willendorf. Ginger was gorgeously fat, with an open knowledge about her body's movement that was delicate and precise*" (italics hers). Although Ginger perceived Lorde "as a citified little baby butch," she learned from Ginger how much she had not learned in high school: about Black history and about lovemaking, which brought her "home to a joy I was meant for, and I only wondered, silently, how I had not known that it would be so." However, Ginger would not acknowledge "a relationship between two women as anything other than a lark," and Ginger's mother casually informed Lorde, "Friends are nice, but marriage is marriage."[51]

Meanwhile, Lorde's grueling work at Keystone Electronics—running a commercial X-ray machine and then processing quartz crystals used in radio and radar machinery—would take its toll: "Nobody mentioned that carbon tet [tetrachloride] destroys the liver and causes cancer of the kidneys. Nobody mentioned that the X-ray machines, when used unshielded, delivered doses of constant low radiation far in excess of what was considered safe even in those days."[52] This retrospective passage in *Zami* was written after Lorde's first diagnosis of cancer.

Later, in New York, Lorde became aware of her vulnerability as a Black in the lesbian world, a lesbian in the Black world, and anathema to progressives who were fearful of government surveillance. A (closeted) English major at midtown Hunter College, downtown she frequented Village bars: Swing Rendezvous, the Pony Stable Inn, and the Bagatelle. Experimenting with communal sex, earning money at a library job, making ends meet by shoplifting, Lorde enrolled in night courses. Before and then after the breakup of a committed partnership—which filled her with the "red fury" that "used to burst into nosebleeds instead of tears" in her mother's house—she found solace in the bars.[53]

Yet the lesbian bars were predominantly white. "To be Black, female, gay, and out of the closet in a white environment, even to the extent of dancing at the Bagatelle, was considered by many Black lesbians to be simply suicidal." Social interaction was also rigidly structured. Lorde felt anomalous when categorized as one of "the 'freaky' bunch of lesbians who weren't into role-play, and who the butches and femmes, Black and white, disparaged with the term Ky-Ky, or AC/DC. Ky-Ky was the same name that was used for gay-girls who slept with johns for money. Prostitutes." In Lorde's self-assessment, "I wasn't cute or passive enough to be 'femme,' and I wasn't mean or tough enough to be 'butch.'" Then there was the added danger of plainclothes policewomen "looking for gay-girls with fewer than three pieces of female attire. That was enough to get you arrested for transvestism."[54]

Depressed despite ongoing therapy, Lorde struggled with Black women who dubbed her crazy, Black men who sexually assaulted her, a white partner who thought that "gay-girls were just as oppressed as any Black person," and white strangers who viewed her as an intruder, if they didn't mistake her for the folksinger Odetta just because they both had natural hair.[55] The conundrums of her life in the fifties are made clear in *Zami*: after an unsatisfactory relationship with a boyfriend, her terror at undergoing an illegal abortion; her delight in discovering a community of lesbians in Mexico, where she could not afford to settle down.

These problems help explain why in the sixties the woman whose name would become synonymous with Black lesbian activism found herself "raising two children and a husband in a three-room flat on 149th Street in Harlem."[56] Sometimes conflicted, Lorde nevertheless shared with Plath, di Prima, and Hansberry a determination to find or forge words to break the shackles that bound her.

JOAN DIDION'S *VOGUE* VERSUS BETTY FRIEDAN'S PROBLEM THAT HAS NO NAME

Even while rebels like di Prima, Hansberry, and Lorde stalked the cafés of the Village, *Mademoiselle* persisted in flattering, fluttery efforts to indoctrinate college girls in campus glamour. Nor was Sylvia Plath the only would-be literary star to grace its pages. In 1955, a mousey-looking white girl from an old Sacramento family stepped into the tepid summer air of what used to be called Idlewild Airport, already worried that her dress wasn't fashionable enough.

A 20-year-old UC Berkeley undergraduate, Joan Didion understood right away that New York was where she needed to be. After a month in the perfumed corridors of *Mademoiselle*, she went back to school, fulfilled her Milton requirement, and returned to the Big Apple as the winner of *Vogue*'s *prix de Paris*, an even more prestigious award than her earlier gig. Now she was becoming a real pro, learning to "write to count."[57] In one of her first assignments, she profiled another winner of the *prix de Paris*, Jacqueline Bouvier, who had claimed in her prize-winning essay that she dreamed of becoming a "sort of 'Overall Art Director of the Twentieth Century,' watching everything from a chair hanging in space."[58]

Didion never liked JFK—she was a dyed-in-the-wool Republican—but she recognized that his wife would become an icon of the new era, "leading a rebellion in beauty" so significant that, she observed, after Jackie's appearance on the scene the "insistence on a certain nose, a special profile, is dead."[59] At the same time, Didion loathed the Beats, especially Ginsberg; disliked Lorraine Hansberry; and understood Sylvia Plath to be a rival at *Mademoiselle*. Yet despite her conservative politics, Didion was workaholically ambitious. Though she was never to be a feminist, she was never to become a conformist wife and mother either, and she was always to pursue her goals with a kind of cynical energy. Her New York boyfriend, Noel Parmentel, described her working twelve hours a day at the office and then twelve hours at home writing her first novel.[60]

As 1959 slid into 1960, with Hansberry on Broadway, Lorde and di Prima at Swing Rendezvous, and Plath at Yaddo, Didion was climbing the ladder at *Vogue* and, soon, at *Life*, the *Saturday Evening Post*, and the *National Review*, as well as (eventually, in the early sixties) in Hollywood. While Mattel manufactured the Barbie doll created by Ruth Handler, and Hugh Hefner hosted a variety/talk show on TV, Didion elaborated on her feelings for Jackie, noting: "She came along, and suddenly we forgot about the American girl—that improbably golden never-never child who roved through the world's imagination with a tennis racket . . . —and fell in love instead with the American woman, a creature possessed of thoughtful responsibility, a healthy predilection for the good and the beautiful and the expensive."[61] Given her astute journalistic instincts, Didion would seem to have predicted the next national romance.

But even while Didion was celebrating the glamour of the "good and the beautiful and the expensive," a left-wing Jewish labor journalist and mother of three was researching the quotidian lives of American women, including not just supposedly happy housewives but many who felt themselves to be captives of suburbia and, in a larger sense, of the American dream. A summa cum laude graduate of Smith College, Bettye Goldstein Friedan began circulating a questionnaire among her classmates in 1957, asking them to comment on their home and work situations.

With a commission from *McCall's*, Friedan had set out to use the Smith alumnae questionnaire "to write a major magazine article refuting *Modern Woman: The Lost Sex* and proving education didn't make American women frustrated in their role as women."[62] Surely Farnham and Lundberg were wrong. "Surely, education made us *better* wives and mothers," she thought.[63] But what she learned was startling. One respondent after another testified to boredom, even despair, complaining of an entrapment in domesticity. Drawing on such evidence of widespread discontent, Friedan—who had been a psychology major in college—attacked not just Farnham and Lundberg and Deutsch but also the Freudian theories in which their ideas were rooted, declaring that Freud was a "prisoner of his own culture" about gender issues and cataloguing a range of dissatisfactions while prescribing a kind of GI Bill for American mothers and housewives.[64]

Though she herself was a left-wing outsider, Friedan targeted white middle-class readers, hoping to publish in just the same women's "slicks" where Plath sought to place stories. Anxious about the tail end of McCarthyism, she kept her politics under wraps. But she did, in a confessional era, explain her personal connection to her subject matter: "I suffered for a time, the reactions of terror—no future—feelings I had no personality that I have heard described by so many other women."[65] And her writing was infused with the anger that would later make her famously difficult to get along with in the feminist activist circles where she would become a founder of key women's organizations.

Perhaps because her writing was so passionate, *McCall's* rejected it, as did the *Ladies' Home Journal*, *Mademoiselle*, and *Redbook*. Then, refusing to be silenced, she reworked an article into a book proposal and sold it to W. W. Norton. When *The Feminine Mystique* was published in 1963, with an initial print run of 3,000 copies, it touched a chord and flew, amazingly, off the shelves of bookstores. However, Betty Friedan didn't invent the discontent she chronicled, nor was she the first to explore it. As she herself observed, "the trapped American housewife" had become a recurring theme in magazines and newspapers from *Life* to *Newsweek* and the *New York Times*. Declared one commentator, "The road from Freud to Frigidaire, from Sophocles to Spock, has turned out to be a bumpy one."[66]

Indeed it had. As Friedan proclaimed, "In 1960, the problem that has no name burst like a boil through the image of the happy American housewife."[67]

ERUPTIONS IN THE SIXTIES

3

Three Angry Voices

THE FIFTIES KEPT ON being "the fifties" well into the sixties, though there was one dramatic public change. The youthful John F. Kennedy and his elegant wife replaced the fatherly Eisenhower and his rather frumpy wife, Mamie, in the White House. But as representatives of the new decade, JFK and Jackie would seem to have been icons of all that the fifties had desired: a wealthy, intelligent husband and a glamorous "society" wife. The Eisenhowers, after all, were holdovers from the forties.

At state dinners Mamie presided over meals featuring American standards straight out of *Good Housekeeping*. A feast for the king and queen of Greece included "Shrimp Cocktail, Saltine Crackers, Celery Hearts, White Fish in Cheese Sauce, Coleslaw, Boston Brown Bread Sandwiches, White Wine, Crown Roast of Lamb Stuffed with Spanish Rice" and "Lemon Iced Diamond Shaped Cookies," among other down-home specialties. By contrast, Jackie hosted a luncheon for Princess Grace and Prince Rainer that was as chic as a Chanel sheath: "Soft-Shell Crab Amandine, Puligny-Montrachet 1958," followed by "Spring Lamb à la Broche aux Primeurs, Château Croton Grancey 1955, Salade Mimosa, Dom Pérignon 1952," and topped off by "Strawberries Romanoff, Petits Fours Secs, Demi-tasses." (Note, too, that in Jackie's menu, plain old "white wine" has been replaced by Puligny-Montrachet 1958.)[1]

For all her glamour, though, Jackie was dutifully domestic and, with her two children, photogenically maternal, enacting the feminine mystique for a national audience and declaring in her breathy voice that the job of the president's wife is "to take care of the president."[2] That this president was a ferocious Lothario—and that his discreet wife knew as much—was not then grasped by most of the couple's fans. The mission she assigned herself in her first years as First Lady was also properly domestic, though more ambitious than the job ordinary housewives would face: no less than the redecoration of the entire First Interior.

With the TV personality Charles Collingwood, Jackie toured the rooms to show off the result. Explaining that the White House had fallen into such neglect that it almost looked "like a hotel decorated by a wholesale furniture store," she noted that she had even had to replace the glassware in the State Dining Room. The elaborately produced program—pitched primarily to women—drew 46 million viewers.[3] When Marilyn Monroe, in a clinging gown, went onstage at Madison Square Garden to sing "Happy Birthday Mr. President" in a breathy voice not unlike Jackie's, it seemed only right that the era's sex idol should pay such a tribute. John F. Kennedy was, all things considered, one half of the perfect couple. Jackie herself would call the brief three years that they occupied the White House the era of Camelot.

Nonetheless, as in the fifties, transgressive forces still simmered under an apparently calm surface. In 1960, the first birth control pill,

Enovid, went on the market. It would make possible an unprecedented sexual revolution. Then, in August 1962, three months after Marilyn Monroe crooned "Happy Birthday" to JFK, she died of an overdose of barbiturates. Almost immediately Andy Warhol, as emblematic of sixties pop art as Monroe was of midcentury eroticism, turned her into the objet d'art she had always really been.[4]

On February 11, 1963, Sylvia Plath—in the midst of a rancorous separation from her husband—set mugs of milk and slices of bread next to her children's cribs, opened their windows and sealed their door against fumes, then went downstairs to her kitchen and turned on the gas. On the desk in her bedroom, she left a manuscript that was like a bomb. Before her suicide, in an angry letter to her mother, she burst out, "Don't talk to me about the world needing cheerful stuff! . . . It is much more help for me . . . to know that people are divorced and go through hell, than to hear about happy marriages. Let the *Ladies' Home Journal* blither about those."[5]

Eight days later, on February 19, 1963, W. W. Norton published Friedan's *The Feminine Mystique*. Though initial reviews were mixed, the book would sell three million copies by the year 2000. In 1963, too, Norton published Adrienne Rich's third book, *Snapshots of a Daughter-in-Law*, which the poet Marilyn Hacker was later to call "The Young Insurgent's Commonplace Book"—and so it was.[6]

On August 28, 1963, 250,000 people from all over the country marched on Washington, DC, where, standing in front of the Lincoln Memorial, Martin Luther King, Jr., delivered his resounding "I Have a Dream" speech. A few months earlier, Lorraine Hansberry had stormed out of a meeting with Robert Kennedy after exclaiming, "I am very worried . . . about the state of the civilization which produced that photograph of the white cop standing on that Negro woman's neck in Birmingham."[7] Two months later, the President's

Commission on the Status of Women, which had been established by JFK and chaired by Eleanor Roosevelt until her death in 1962, issued its report titled *American Women*, noting the many inequalities faced by women in a supposedly liberated society.

On November 22, 1963, John F. Kennedy was assassinated as his motorcade passed through downtown Dallas. Almost immediately, as he had with Marilyn Monroe, Andy Warhol turned Jackie into an objet d'art. In *Twenty Jackies* (1964), he captured her downcast face as she stood in front of a uniformed guard at her husband's funeral.[8]

The fifties, with their decorous dreams of romance, were over, as dead as Monroe, JFK—and Sylvia Plath Hughes. Embedded in her personal history, the proto-feminist poems Plath left as her legacy prefigure the complaints against patriarchy expressed by her contemporary Adrienne Rich and the protests sung by Nina Simone, who channeled the energies of the civil rights movement into women's issues.

PLATH DESPAIRS WHILE *ARIEL* TAKES WING

If Sylvia Plath Hughes was dead, Sylvia Plath was certainly still alive. *Ariel* saw to that, as Ted Hughes may have sensed it would, once he saw the manuscript lying on his dead wife's desk.

The marriage had unraveled in one domestic calamity after another, despite all of Plath's efforts at the sort of "nesting" the fifties had taught her to want. After the birth of their daughter Frieda, the couple had searched for a larger space and finally found an idyllic country place: Court Green, a thirteenth-century thatched-roof house in Devon. Hughes, a country man raised in Yorkshire, was drawn to the land, the orchard, the history. Plath was less certain, yet her urge for domestic and poetic accomplishments convinced her that here she could raise the five children she wanted, and spend

mornings in a study facing an ancient graveyard. Cooking, garden-
ing, and writing, she would inherit the English history of which her
husband was already an heir. In the summer of 1961, the two poets
and their baby daughter moved to Court Green, where they would
live together for a brief fourteen months.

In the mornings, Hughes took care of Frieda so that Plath could
write. In the afternoons, he wrote while she made excursions into
town with the baby or sewed curtains for the house. Then, on January
17, 1962, she gave birth to their son Nicholas, at first "blue and glistening" in an alarming way, then with a "handsome male head." After
a difficult labor that she recounted in detail in her journal, she noted
that now, "It felt like Christmas Eve, full of rightness & promise."[9]

And indeed, the births of both her babies had been not just personal but poetic gifts for Plath. In a break with modernist tradition,
she began writing intense maternal poems to her children. Historically, this was unprecedented. Fathers since the Renaissance had
written to sons, and in the nineteenth-century sentimental "poet-
esses" had penned obsequies for dead babies. But Plath was composing sophisticated works in a new genre. *Ariel* deliberately opened with
"Morning Song," a beautiful aubade for Frieda. Beginning "Love set
you going like a fat gold watch," the piece celebrates not the sexual
love that set the baby going but maternal love, as Plath describes the
age-old scene of a mother nursing her infant at dawn.

> One cry, and I stumble from bed, cow-heavy and floral
> In my Victorian nightgown.
> Your mouth opens clean as a cat's.[10]

Later, in "Nick and the Candlestick," another nursing poem, she
records waking at night to feed her child, but contextualizes the scene

of love with a world of suffering, in which the possibility of nuclear annihilation hovers over the baby in whom "the blood blooms clean," noting that "The pain / You wake to is not yours."[11]

Within a few months of Nicholas's birth, the "rightness & promise" of the "Christmas Eve" scene the night he was born had disintegrated. Though there were wonderful moments—for instance, when the Court Green garden bloomed with masses of daffodils, about which both poets wrote—the loneliness of country life, together with the arduousness of caring for two little children while keeping house in an old manor without central heating or a modern kitchen, exhausted the pair. "We can hardly see each other over the mountains of diapers and demands of babies," she told her mother.[12] Even before the melodrama that overtook them in the summer of 1962, the marriage had begun to fray.

The story of what happened next is well known to historians of twentieth-century poetry: how Assia and David Wevill, to whom the Hugheses had sublet their London apartment, came for a weekend, with the glamorous Assia having already confided to a colleague that she planned to "seduce Ted." (Sylvia's kitchen calendar shows she served corn chowder, beef stew, and gingerbread for dinner that night.) How Ted fell for Assia right away. How Sylvia, with what her husband called her "death ray quality," intuited that something was wrong. How Ted sent Assia a love note, how Assia responded affirmatively with a symbolic blade of grass in an envelope. How the lovers met and steamily copulated in various hotel rooms. How Assia called Ted, speaking in a pseudo-masculine voice, and Sylvia, picking up the phone before he could get to it, tore the black machine out of the wall "by its roots"—so that it would be impossible for months to reconnect the phone service. How her mother, who was visiting for a month, saw so much marital discord that Sylvia was horrified. How she forced Ted out but sought for his return. How Frieda, witnessing her parents in tears, exclaimed, "Mummy sad, daddy sad!"[13]

In August 1962, Ted left for London, where he would scrounge for living spaces from friends before permanently exiting Court Green in October. Sylvia stayed in Devon, alone with two little children, a large house, a garden, and an orchard of "seventy trees / Holding their gold-ruddy balls / In a thick gray death-soup."[14] Abandoned and insomniac, she depended on barbiturates for sleep, then woke at five in the morning, when the medication wore off, and went straight to her desk—the elmwood plank that Ted and her brother Warren had polished for her—and began writing the poems of *Ariel*. "Have managed a poem a day before breakfast," she wrote her mother. "All book poems. Terrific stuff, as if domesticity had choked me."[15]

She was and was not the person she had been. Her scrupulous kitchen calendar still recorded meals; she was still keeping bees, cooking, mothering. But now she began to take riding lessons and to cast about for other options—Ireland? Spain? London? She searched frantically for nannies and confided to her mother and her brother how anxious she was. And yet, despite her panic—or perhaps, more accurately, because of it—the amazing poems continued to arrive at "that still, blue, almost eternal hour before cockcrow, before the baby's cry, before the glassy music of the milkman, settling his bottles."[16]

And now they were poems boasting of an achieved new self, a self, to be sure, that was being constructed on the page. Significantly, that re-created paper-self was a feminist, even if its author had not read Simone de Beauvoir. Finally she cast off old stereotypes in poem after poem—from "Fever 103°" to "Ariel," "Lady Lazarus," and "Stings." Especially in the last of these works, written on October 6, 1962, when Hughes was at Court Green to pack his things, she insisted, as she bent to her beekeeping, that "I am no drudge / Though for years I have eaten dust / And dried plates with my dense hair."[17]

This was the domesticity that had almost "choked" her, not only in the literal dust of Court Green but in the figurative dust of its long past and in both the literal and figurative dust she had inhaled as she kept house for her husband, typing his poems, cooking his meals, washing his dishes. No, she decided at last, "I / have a self to recover, a queen":

> Now she is flying
> More terrible than she ever was, red
> Scar in the sky, red comet
> Over the engine that killed her–
> The mausoleum, the wax house.[18]

The mausoleum: the tomb of history in which women are imprisoned? The mausoleum of her imagination in which her dead father, a professor of entomology (author of *Bumblebees and Their Ways*), was still somehow alive, though he had died decades before? And the wax house: not just the literal wax house of the bees, but the false house of fifties domesticity, forever beckoning in the pages of the *Ladies' Home Journal*? Or Court Green itself, that fantasy of English history, in which she was buried alive with her two children, while her husband cavorted in London with his mistress and his literary friends?

A week later, on October 12, 1962, Plath wrote "Daddy," perhaps the most famous of her poems. Apparently straightforward and bouncy as a nursery rhyme, the piece was initially seen by its author as bleakly *funny*. Shortly after writing it, Plath read it to a friend, and the two burst into gales of laughter.[19] And indeed "Daddy" is revisionary comic verse, just as it is a revisionary nursery rhyme of the sort Plath was regularly reading to Frieda. At the same time, though, in a remarkable literary sleight of hand, it is a work of feminist theory, the major one that Plath would produce in her short lifetime—and as such it looked forward to writings by Plath's contemporary Adrienne Rich and by Kate Millett, whose *Sexual Politics* was to appear in 1970.

To be sure, when the poem was first published in the States, it was read by some as a personal attack on the poet's dead father, Otto Plath, the professor who had died of gangrene when she was only 8, and to a lesser extent as an attack on her husband, Ted Hughes. Casting the German-born "daddy" as a Nazi and his frightened daughter as "a bit of a Jew," Plath threaded imagery of Hitler's Germany through the piece: "Dachau, Auschwitz, Belsen. . . . your Luftwaffe . . . Panzer-man. . . . Not God but a swastika / So black no sky could squeak through."[20] To the BBC, she explained before reading the poem on the air that it was "a poem spoken by a girl with an Electra complex."[21] But her first American audience, in particular, was having none of this. When "Daddy" appeared in *Ariel*, the poem was singled out for violent rebukes from critics who imagined that Plath was actually accusing her father of being a Nazi.

In fact, throughout the poem Plath brilliantly conflated her biological father with a patriarchal Father, with God the Father, with Germany's "Führer," and, eventually, with her black-jacketed husband, Ted Hughes. Analyzing the (sometimes self-willed) abjection of women in patriarchal culture ("Every woman adores a Fascist, / The boot in the face, the brute / Brute heart of a brute like you"), she outlined her rebellion against "daddy's" diabolical system, a rebellion that simultaneously looks back on childhood and animates childhood.

To begin with, she remembers being merely a foot, "poor and white, / Barely daring to breathe or Achoo"—a daddy's girl experiencing herself as no more than a humble body part inertly enclosed in the black shoe of the Father. Worse still, she recalls her inability to speak even the most primordial words of his language: "It stuck in a barb wire snare. / Ich, ich, ich, ich"—even the simplest word for self, for "I" in German, became an unpronounceable "Ich" that was also icky.[22] And the repeated, pounding rhythm of "Ich, ich, ich, ich" goose-steps across the page like a Nazi soldier.

But this poem is powered by ambivalence, for the angry speaker confesses that, abandoned by the real father when he died, and implicitly too by the deific Father, she tried to die "And get back, back, back to you," as Plath herself did in her suicide attempt at the age of 20. When she was rescued ("they pulled me out of the sack, / And they stuck me together with glue"), her only recourse was to "[make] a model of you": a husband whose fascistic charisma replicated the allure of the patriarchal Father, reviving the daughter's thralldom to his "Marble-heavy" command.[23]

In the end, then, Plath—or, shall we say, "Daddy's girl"?—reimagines both the daunting "daddy" and the husband who is his clone as a vampire whom she must murder in just the way that the Transylvanian villagers killed Dracula in Bram Stoker's novel—and in numerous popular films:

There's a stake in your fat black heart
And the villagers never liked you,
They are dancing and stamping on you.
They always knew it was you.
Daddy, daddy, you bastard, I'm through.[24]

At one point this poem was so significant for Plath that she thought she would title her new manuscript *Daddy*.

Eventually, though, after Hughes left for London, Plath's riding skills improved and she began to spend early mornings cantering across the moors on a horse named Ariel, whose liberatory speed she celebrated in a dazzling poem. As the piece, also named "Ariel," begins, she and her horse are standing on the edge of a field in the darkness just before dawn. But their "Stasis in darkness" is quickly disrupted by a gallop toward the sunrise, as she and her horse seem to meld into one speeding creature. Finally, in an orgasmic climax, the journey lets her free herself from her past, "unpeel— / Dead hands, dead stringencies," like a "White / Godiva" as she plunges swift as an arrow toward the rising sun, which is both the "red / Eye"—like the burning eye of a god? or like a regenerated I?—and "the cauldron of morning": a kind of celestial kettle in which the fierce light of a new day coils and boils.[25]

Is she, then, galloping toward rebirth at the break of day? But what about the sound of that last phrase? Can it be mistaken for "cauldron of *mourning*"? Previously in the poem, after all, she has noted that the dew "flies / Suicidal" toward the sun. Is she a drop of dew, doomed to evaporate in the heat she approaches, or is she, as she declares, "an arrow" seeking a target?[26] Given the intense alternation between braggadocio and despair in these late works, it is hard to decide.

In any case, the name Ariel was crucial to her: she had always been obsessed with Shakespeare's exploration of father–daughter love in *The Tempest*, whose governing spirit is a sprite called Ariel. And she knew that in Hebrew *Ariel* signifies "God's lioness." Facsimiles of the manuscript she left on her desk that bleak February morning show how she wavered between two titles: one, "Daddy," that looked back—perhaps with anger, perhaps with laughter—to the dependency of girlhood, and the other that flew into the future as Ariel, not only a raging lioness but a spirit freed by the patriarchal Prospero into autonomous selfhood or, perhaps, autonomous self-immolation.[27]

Finally, as we know, Ariel defeated Daddy, at least on the page, where Plath the poet struck out "Daddy" and replaced it with "Ariel." But for Plath the woman, torn between the ideology of the fifties that had shaped her and the feminism of the sixties that she was inventing for herself, the choice was not so easy. In December, she moved to London, where she could have all the literary company she wanted, live in a stylish flat ("in Yeats's house!"), and buy new clothes with a check from her Smith College patroness, Olive Higgins Prouty. "I . . . feel and look like a million," she wrote her mother in one of her feverish late letters. "Got a Florence-Italy blue and white velvet overblouse, a deep brown velvet Italian shirt, black fake-fur toreador pants, a straight black velvet skirt and metallic blue-and-black French top."[28]

And, too, in the days before she took her life, Plath saw her estranged husband repeatedly. One snowy evening they walked around Soho Square, as she begged, according to one of his poems, "Tell me / We shall sit together this summer / Under the laburnum," the ornamental tree (sometimes called the "golden chain tree") that sheltered part of the garden at Court Green.[29] He reassured her and took her to his flat, where she wept and screamed all night—screamed so loud that the upstairs neighbors knocked through the ceiling for quiet. In some part of herself, she realized the golden chain of the marriage was broken.

Then the next day she told him to leave the country, that she wanted to be on her own.

On February 4, she wrote to her American psychiatrist: "I am suddenly in agony, desperate, thinking Yes, let him take over the house, the children, let me just die & be done with it."[30] And then, a week later, as if joining the world of "Daddy"—of "Dachau, Auschwitz, Belsen"—she put her head in the oven and turned on the gas, entering the history she had struggled so hard to resist.

ADRIENNE RICH AS A CULTURAL DAUGHTER-IN-LAW

More than a decade after her daughter's death, Aurelia Schober Plath put together a carefully pruned collection of Sylvia's "intimate correspondence with her family from the time she entered Smith College," in an effort to prove that the author of "Daddy" had a happier childhood than her posthumously published poems would suggest. When it appeared in print as *Letters Home by Sylvia Plath*, the volume carried a glowing blurb on its back cover: three sentences from Adrienne Rich, Plath's near contemporary: "Finally now, young women writers can cease to identify with the apparent self-destroyer in Sylvia Plath and begin to understand the forces she had to reckon with. What comes across in the letters is a survivor, who knew that to be a writer means discipline, indefatigable commitment, and passion for hard work. By no means all is told here, but the features emerge of a real, not a mythic, woman artist."

Always an astute reader, Rich discerned in the letters not just what was there but what had been cut: not only the forces Plath had to "reckon with" but the force in her that deeply wanted to survive the wreckage of her dream of marriage. Rich grasped these personal and cultural dynamics because they were forces that had animated her own career from childhood onward.

Born in 1929, a few years before Plath, Rich also grew up in an academic household, though one that was far more affluent than Plath's home and that, besides, featured two parents instead of a struggling widow. Her father, Arnold Rich, was a secular Jew and a distinguished professor of medicine; her Gentile mother had been trained as a concert pianist. A dutiful child, Rich was homeschooled for some years by her mother, who taught her to play Bach and Mozart, and, more overwhelmingly, by her father, who set daily literary tasks for her and her younger sister. But beneath an obedient veneer, the poet had begun to rebel. From her father's perspective, she was "satisfyingly precocious," but like Plath she was "groping for . . . something larger" by the time she began her studies at Radcliffe.[31] The forces she had to reckon with? As in Plath's case, they were the dynamics of the fifties that preached not only feminine but writerly decorum.

And in fact, Rich's early work, like much of Plath's, is expertly crafted but often evasive and glitteringly impersonal in a way that was popular at the time. When she was just 21, her first collection of poems, *A Change of World*, won the Yale Younger Poets Prize, an award for which Plath had fruitlessly yearned. The introduction to her book, written by the masterful W. H. Auden, was strikingly appropriate to an era marked by the "feminine mystique." Rich's poems, declared Auden, were "neatly and modestly dressed, speak quietly but do not mumble, respect their elders but are not cowed by them."[32] A few years later, in patronizing words on her next volume, *The Diamond Cutters*, Randall Jarrell sounded the same trivializing note, observing that the author of the book seems "to us a sort of princess in a fairy tale."[33] But yes, Rich herself, writing what she was to call her "praised and sedulous lines" to please her professorial father, did indeed produce some poems that were "neatly and modestly dressed."[34]

The princess-poet's first act of overt rebellion was to marry "a divorced graduate student" from an observant Jewish family.[35] (Her parents were so disapproving that they refused to come to the wedding, held at Hillel House on the Harvard campus.) Then she began to write "'modern,' 'obscure,' 'pessimistic' poetry," and eventually she had "the final temerity to get pregnant."[36] Visiting Cambridge in 1958, Sylvia Plath discerned what Auden, Jarrell, and perhaps even Rich's father had failed to grasp. In her journal she described Rich, with some respect, as "all vibrant short black hair, great sparkling black eyes and a tulip-red umbrella: honest, frank *forthright* & even *opinionated*" (italics ours).[37] At the same time, Plath was fiercely competitive toward this contemporary whom she rightly understood to be the only woman of her generation who shared her drive and talent. "Who rivals?" she asked herself once in her journal. "Most close, Adrienne Cecile Rich," she responded.[38]

The "final temerity to get pregnant": married in 1953 to Alfred Conrad, a graduate student in economics who went on to teach at Harvard, Rich quickly had three sons but was later to declare that "motherhood radicalized me."[39] In her ambitious treatise *Of Woman Born: Motherhood as Experience and Institution* (1976), she confessed that the domestic life that Plath had glamorized depleted and depressed her. After evading analysis of it for a while, she began to write her first, breakthrough feminist poem, "Snapshots of a Daughter-in-Law," which took her two years to compose, between 1958 and 1960. The poem, she remembered, was "jotted in fragments. . . . I despaired of doing any continuous work at this time. Yet I began to feel that my fragments and scraps had a common consciousness and a common theme, one which I would have been unwilling to put on paper at an earlier time because I had been taught that poetry should be 'universal,' which meant of course nonfemale."[40]

But though the poem appears fragmented—it is, after all, a *sequence*—it is no more fragmentary than the verse sequences of, say, T. S. Eliot or Wallace Stevens, both of whom Rich had studied intensely as an undergraduate. In particular, like Eliot's *The Waste*

Land, it is both elliptical and allusive, deploying a scholarly range of quotations in support of its central argument. And like Eliot's "Love Song of J. Alfred Prufrock," it is a portrait of a distinctive individual, in this case a young woman who chafes against the bonds imposed upon her by her status as a daughter-in-*law*—not just, that is, somebody's wife and therefore the daughter-in-law of his parents but also a daughter of the *law* of patriarchal culture. Like Plath in "Daddy," then, Rich was struggling to define the role into which her society had cast her and to envision a way of transcending that role.

As she begins the poem, she focuses on a woman of an earlier generation, perhaps her own Southern mother, as she addresses a "You" who was "once a belle in Shreveport" but who has never grown out of her early triumph as a seductive young woman. For now, though this beauty is in the "prime" of life, her mind is "moldering like wedding-cake, / heavy with useless experience." Quite literally, slices of wedding cake, heavy with candied fruits and nuts, are designed to be saved, though there is always the danger that they'll be saved so long that they "molder."[41]

In a larger sense, the very idea of wedding cake announces the theme of the poem: marital domesticity and its discontents, or, to put it another way, the fate of women as daughters-in-law. For even while the older woman's mind crumbles "to pieces under the knife-edge / of mere fact," her rebellious daughter "grows another way," and the next section of the ten-section sequence focuses on her rage as, trapped in her kitchen, she hears "angels," messengers of difference, "chiding": "*Have no patience. . . . Be insatiable. . . . Save yourself; others you cannot save*" (italics hers).[42] These are commands that must have haunted Rich herself, who was struggling to nurture three small boys while also fostering her own talent. Might she too, she must have wondered, become a victim of the moldering wedding cake, the sickening meal fed to brides when they become daughters-in-law?[43]

The next eight sections of "Snapshots" are essayistic, reportorial, as if, like Betty Friedan or Simone de Beauvoir, Rich was surveying the female condition—what it means to be the second sex and therefore obliged to acquiesce in the feminine mystique under the foundational law of patriarchal culture. "A thinking woman sleeps with monsters," she asserts in the opening sentence of section 3. "The beak that grips her, she becomes." *Are* women monsters, especially those who presume to think? And if you fear becoming a thinking (female) monster, if you are gripped by the harpy beak of terror, will you become a comparable freak of nature? In a society that instills such anxieties, women are estranged from each other and become each other's enemies, stabbing each other in the back: "The argument *ad feminam*, all the old knives / that have rusted in my back, / I drive in yours, / *ma semblable, ma soeur!*" My likeness, my sister.[44] Whatever applies to the sisterhood of thinking women, some of whom may be her readers, applies also to her, or so Rich suggests here.

Like "Daddy," "Snapshots" is a poem that is trapped until the very end in its own bitterness. As a cultural document, then, it seems for the most part to be a camera lens of the early sixties looking back in anger at the fifties and taking snapshots of that era. To be sure, in section 4 Rich broods on Emily Dickinson "writing, *My Life had stood—a Loaded Gun—* / in that Amherst pantry," broods with such intensity that for a moment she might herself be sighting her subjects not with a camera but with a loaded gun.[45] Mostly, though, she assembles a range of quotations from literary history to illuminate the rules and roles of the feminine mystique.

Dulce ridens, dulce loquens,
she shaves her legs until they gleam
like petrified mammoth-tusk.[46]

"Sweetly laughing, sweetly speaking"—the quote from Horace in section 5, and the next line too, might describe a fifties coed getting ready for a Big Date, until the last line of this three-line stanza drops the hypocrite reader into the abyss of prehistory. What would a New York beauty editor say to this: *Honey, do you really want your legs to look like petrified mammoth-tusk?* And do they look that way because such feminine cosmetic primping is also prehistoric?

"When to her lute Corinna sings / neither words nor music are her own": here is an outraged observation coming from a poet and literary scholar who of course knows the line about Corinna from the work of the Elizabethan poet Thomas Campion. But why should Corinna author anything? After all, as Rich acerbically notes, she lives only for romance: "Pinned down / by love." And what does love teach? "Has Nature shown / her household books to you, daughter-in-law, / that her sons never saw?"[47] Is a woman, whose existence is shaped by her sexuality, closer to "Mother" Nature than are her husband and sons—and therefore closer to understanding the "household books" of the natural world?

Considering Corinna's passivity, that seems unlikely. And what if Corinna were to rebel, like Mary Wollstonecraft, whom Rich quotes in the next section? Because that foundational feminist "fought with [against] what she partly understood," "she was labelled harpy, shrew and whore." And then there is the ultimate insult to women writers: "*Not that it is done well, but / that it is done at all.*" This means, to Rich, that "our mediocrities" are "over-praised." If Corinna makes up a little verse of her own, her male interlocutors will gallantly praise her. But if she dares "to cast too bold a shadow / or smash the mold straight off"? The reward is "solitary confinement, / tear gas, attrition shelling."[48]

The dangers of authorship and authority match the dangers of domesticity. What can a daughter-in-law choose? If she seeks to smash the mold, she will be assaulted; if she acquiesces in the mold, she will molder. There seems to be no hope for women until the very last section of "Snapshots," when the stasis of the camera is replaced by a visionary image. Here drawing on a passage from Beauvoir's *The Second Sex*, the poet fantasizes the "coming" of a utopian redeemer, and although she concedes that this unprecedented figure has been "long about" her arrival, she is somehow imminent:

> I see her plunge
> breasted and glancing through the currents,
> taking the light upon her
> at least as beautiful as any boy
> or helicopter,
> poised, still coming,
> her fine blades making the air wince[.][49]

Note that although she is "breasted," the visionary woman here is likened to a boy or a helicopter: she is alien, androgynous, almost out of science fiction.

Years later, Rich was to claim that "Snapshots" was faulty because "too literary, too dependent on allusion. I hadn't found the courage yet to do without authorities, or even to use the pronoun 'I'—the woman in the poem is always 'she.'"[50] For their part, early reviewers, shocked by her repudiation of her youthful "modesty," found the work grating.[51] But with its camera eye on the targets of patriarchal culture, "Snapshots" focused on centuries in which daughters-in-law were fed on moldering cake and responded with fury: *"Be insatiable. . . . Save yourself; others you cannot save."* One wishes that Sylvia Plath could have said those words to herself, that icy night in February when she turned on the gas.

But within a few years, Rich herself would be trying to save others. In the mid-sixties she moved with her family to New York, and by 1968 she was working in the SEEK (Search for Education, Elevation, and Knowledge) program at City College, where she taught Black literature to African American students. She had sought the job, she explained, "after King was shot, as a political act of involvement."[52] And among her new colleagues were Black writers and participants in the civil rights movement who would become some of her closest friends: Toni Cade Bambara, June Jordan, and especially Audre Lorde. By now, too, Rich had become a fervent admirer of Diane di Prima's onetime lover, LeRoi Jones. In one of the "Blue Ghazals," dated September 29, 1968, and dedicated to Jones, she declared that "Terribly far away I saw your mouth in the wild light: / it seemed to me you were shouting instructions to us all."[53]

NINA SIMONE, DIVA

One of the major voices adding women's issues to the protests mounted by the male-dominated civil rights movement issued from the mouth of a singer who had been denied the higher education she had sought. By 1963, Nina Simone was at the apex of a career in music that defied categorization. An accomplished classical pianist, she sang jazz, blues, pop, R&B, gospel, soul, calypso, and country as well as Broadway show tunes, French cabaret numbers, and Israeli folk music. According to Angela Davis, "She helped to introduce gender into our ways of imagining radical change." Toni Morrison saw her as "indestructible, incorruptible. She even scared me a little." When Morrison confessed to Nina Simone that she "wasn't ready to take up arms [against racism] and that I'd rather take up my pen," the singer would "get mad." But "I guess she wasn't ready to take up arms either because she channeled it all into her music": "Nina Simone saved our lives," Morrison believed. And Amiri Baraka, a longtime friend, defined her work as "American classical music."[54]

As in a Grimm brothers' fairy tale, the transformation of Eunice Kathleen Waymon into Nina Simone involved three rebuffs, each followed by a telling response.[55] An 11-year-old prodigy, she was about to perform her first piano recital in her segregated hometown when she saw her parents being removed from front-row seats to make room for a white family. The little girl promptly refused to play until her parents were reseated "and to hell with poise and elegance" (she characteristically added in her autobiography).[56]

The second snub came after high school and a stint of lessons at Juilliard preparing for a scholarship examination at the Curtis Institute of Music in Philadelphia. Shocked at being rejected by the Curtis Institute, only later did she understand that "if blacks were going to be admitted then they were not going to accept an unknown black, that if they were to accept an unknown black then it was not going to be an unknown black girl, and if they were going to admit an unknown black girl it was not going to be a very poor unknown black girl."[57] Her reaction to this rejection explains the birth of her name. She started making money by playing the piano in an Atlantic City bar and, because it was a job requirement, singing along. Nina (the nickname bestowed by a boyfriend) Simone (an homage to the French actress Simone Signoret)[58] came into being to shield her preacher-mother from knowledge of her daughter's dabbling in the devil's music.

A classical musician improvising jazz, Nina Simone began infusing Bach fugues into her songs and demanding from audiences the sort of attention more common in concert halls than in drinking dives. From this point on, she would gain a reputation for being imperious and temperamental. When she played at the Village Gate, she arrived with bodyguards "to protect the public from her, not to protect her from the public," some believed, since at times she lashed out at noisy fans. She would go on to insist throughout her career, "If they're going to compare me to somebody, they should compare me to Maria Callas. She was a diva, I'm a diva."[59]

However, Nina Simone's response to the third insult of her life illuminates the vulnerability of a woman who bore herself with regality on stage. After a dinner party to celebrate her engagement to Andy Stroud, a New York City policeman, his jealousy led to a brutal beating: "He hit me in the cab, on the pavement outside my apartment building, in the lobby of the building, in the elevator up to the twelfth floor and along the passageway to my apartment."[60] Tied up and battered, she recounted later, she was then raped. Yet she decided to marry Andy Stroud and let him take over the management of her career and her money.

Why is not altogether clear, though Simone sensed that "loneliness and insecurity made my mind up for me": "Andy was a strong man and I loved him. I forced myself to believe he wouldn't hit me any more."[61] She knew that she had talent, but she was also "a girl" with "desires like other girls": "I wanted it all. I wanted everything."[62] She embarked on "a traditional marriage," in which the husband would decide "This is how it will be."[63]

With Andy Stroud as her manager, a new baby named Lisa, and a triumphant solo show at Carnegie Hall, the 30-year-old Nina

Simone looked to be getting it all by the time she was ensconced in Mount Vernon, only 10 miles away from Lorraine Hansberry's place in Croton-on-Hudson. On April 12, 1963, the night of Simone's debut at Carnegie Hall, Hansberry phoned to discuss what could be done about "Martin Luther King Jr.'s arrest in Birmingham."[64] A godmother to Lisa, Hansberry sparked Nina Simone's "thinking about myself as a black person in a country run by white people and a woman in a world run by men." They talked about "Marx, Lenin, and revolution—real girls' talk." Although Andy Stroud tried to focus her on career goals, she was galvanized by the imprisonment of King, by the murders of Medgar Evers and of four little girls in a bombed Birmingham church. "It was more than I could take, and I sat struck dumb in my den like St. Paul on the road to Damascus: all the truths that I had denied to myself for so long rose up and slapped my face."[65]

The sequence of traumas made her think of killing someone, so she tried to make a zip gun. When her husband intervened—"I knew nothing about killing and I did know about music"[66]—she wrote her first civil rights song, the brilliant and haunting "Mississippi Goddam." Protesting the instructions of whites to "Go slow," with a chorus emphasizing that "Do it slow" is precisely the problem, she signals the passion that would catapult civil rights rhetoric into Black power demands. Its lyrics resound like gunshots:

You told me to wash and clean my ears
And talk real fine just like a lady
And you'd stop calling me Sister Sadie

Oh but this whole country is full of lies
You're all gonna die and die like flies.[67]

According to her daughter, Nina Simone dated the break between her "pre-getting mad" and her "post-getting mad" voice to this 1963 hit: "it was as if her voice just dropped, and it never returned to its former octave," Lisa recalled.[68] Quite a few members of her audiences at civil rights rallies would get mad along with her, while in more conventional venues others, not unlike the usually intrepid Toni Morrison, would be unnerved by the militancy of her performances.

During the mid-sixties, Nina Simone raged against the situation of Black women. The new songs she sang—some adopted and reinterpreted, others of her own creation—grew out of a tormented identity: "*I can't be white* and I'm the kind of colored girl who looks like everything white people despise or have been taught to despise," she wrote in an undated note in her diary. "If I were a boy, it wouldn't matter so much, but I'm a girl and in front of the public all the time wide open for them to jeer and approve or disapprove."[69] Simone's presentations of "Pirate Jenny," "Go Limp," and "Four Women"— works very different in tone and structure—manifest her insights into the sexual politics of race.

Transporting Jenny, one of the resentful whores in Bertolt Brecht and Kurt Weill's *Threepenny Opera*, to a flophouse in South Carolina, Simone introduced "Pirate Jenny" by explaining that Jenny is going to kill everyone in the town and go home. Jenny's taunting lyrics—as she scrubs the floors, makes the beds, but defiantly grins—are juxtaposed with a menacing refrain about a black freighter in the harbor, with a skull on its masthead and guns on its bow. "You gentlemen can wipe that smile off your face," Jenny the domestic, maid, and prostitute declares while considering her destiny as Jenny the pirate. It begins with her "stepping out in the morning / Looking nice with a ribbon in my hair." The men swarming on the black freighter bring her a succession of chained people. "Kill them NOW, or LATER?" they ask. Pirate Jenny whispers urgently, "Right now!" As the bodies pile up, she adds, "That'll learn ya!" With slow, descending notes, Jenny describes the freighter disappearing out to sea: "And on it is me."[70]

Piratical Jenny's dreams of killing all the gentlemen who have been ordering her around come true on the black freighter. According to Angela Davis, Simone redefined "the content of this song to depict the collective rage of black women domestic workers." By evoking *The Threepenny Opera*, another commentator noted, "Simone associated her own anti-racism with Brecht's antifascism."[71] An apocalyptic revenge fantasy against what she would later call the United Snakes of America, "Pirate Jenny" puts on display Simone's acting skills even as it envisions an escape to a Black homeland.[72]

A more whimsical Nina Simone crooned the parodic folksong "Go Limp," a mother–daughter dialogue warning against the sexual exploitation of young women in the civil rights movement, but performed with teasing innuendos and encouragements of audience participation. In an adaptation of lyrics by Alex Comfort, the mother cautions her daughter against marching with the NAACP, "For they'll rock you and roll you / and shove you into bed." But the daughter will defend her virginity by arming herself with a "brick in [her] handbag / And barbed wire in [her] underwear." To the tune of "Sweet Betsy from Pike" and interspersed with the audience singing "Too roo la, too roo li ay," the stanzas recount the daughter meeting a young man at a march. "And before she had time / To remember her brick . . ."—Simone pauses here long enough for the expected rhyme to elicit laughs before she delivers, "They were holding a sit-down / On a nearby hay rick."[73]

In some of the recordings of "Go Limp," Simone inserts a stanza that speaks to her ongoing alienation from the repertoire of pop music she was marketing. "If I have a great concert," she warbles, "Maybe I won't have to sing those folk songs again." However, this folk parody then goes on to deliver a tongue-in-cheek analysis of the injunction "go perfectly limp and be carried away" that was used to encourage nonviolence upon arrest at protests. When the young man suggests a kiss, the daughter "remembered her brief / And did not resist." Her carried-away character concludes the song with reassurances to the mother: "No need for distress / For the young man has left me / His name and address." If they win their struggle for equality, her baby will not have to march "Like his da-da and me."

While in "Mississippi Goddam" Nina Simone questioned nonviolence in the face of mounting Black anger against racial injustice, in "Go Limp" she queries the usefulness of passive resistance in the relationship between the sexes. For all of its joviality, "Go Limp" targets the masculinist bias of the Black power movement that Angela Davis called the "unfortunate syndrome among some Black male activists . . . to confuse their political activity with an assertion of their maleness."[74] Though Simone counted Stokely Carmichael a friend, "Go Limp" anticipates and critiques his infamous comment that "the position of women in SNCC is prone."[75]

One of the most haunting songs that Simone herself composed broaches the difficult subject of color prejudice within the African American community. In it, she examines the fetishizing of light, nearly "white" skin. First recorded in 1965, "Four Women" offers the monologues of four very different women: each character describes her skin tone, hair texture, and body (in that order), all of which have overdetermined their collective fates.[76] Although it was banned from some radio stations for being disrespectful, "Four Women" captures a self-alienation that Simone also addressed in the song "Images": "She does not know her beauty . . . She thinks her brown body has no glory."[77]

With black skin, woolly hair, and a back strong enough to take repeated pain, the first persona of "Four Women" declares, "My name is Aunt Sarah." In an interview, Nina Simone pictured Aunt Sarah as elderly and exhausted from overwork, living in Harlem, but talking in a Southern dialect. Her name derives from " 'Auntie,' like the whites used to call the mammies to suckle their babies."[78] With yellow skin and long hair, the second character belongs to two worlds, since her rich, white father raped her mother, and she concludes, "My name is Saffronia." Simone described Saffronia as one of those "yellow bitches who think they're better," but then added, "It's bad enough to be born black in America, but to be burdened down with the problems within it is too much." With tan skin, fine hair, inviting hips, and a mouth like wine, the third speaker declares herself a "little girl" whom anyone "who got enough money" can buy, announcing, "My name is Sweet Thang." Simone's comments gloss over the situation of the prostitute, only commenting that she's "fine" with herself; "she don't give a damn."

At this point there is a pause in "Four Women" and what Simone calls "a big rumble" of magnificent arpeggios before the emergence of the fiercest figure. With brown skin and a tough manner, the last woman, who would "kill the first mother I see," has led a rough life and feels "bitter these days because my parents were slaves": "My name is"—and she pauses—"Peaches." The name, belted only once, enacts what Simone calls one of her "razor cuts": "at the end, I cut you, I make you think and it's immediate." Peaches reminded Nina Simone of "Stokely Carmichael"; she is a fierce woman who has "gone to Africa, she's got her ass together," and "she probably was the sweetest of all."

"When any black woman hears that song," Simone remarked, "she either starts crying or she wants to go out and kill somebody."

Simone's longtime guitarist, Al Schackman, considered Peaches "part of the persona that Nina became. You did not want to mess with her—she pulled out a knife in a second, she didn't take any of the shit that the other three did or play the white folks' games that the others did."[79] But, of course, it is possible to view Simone as a composite, an actress capable of identifying with four stereotypes foisted on women not born into white privilege: the mammy or domestic, the tragic mulatto, the Jezebel or whore, the tough bitch. The sadness underlying the piece resides in part in the formal soliloquies: there is no possibility of a conversation between these women.

Nina Simone does not comment on the single line that is repeated in every stanza without any variation, right before the declaration of each name: "What do they call me?" The issue of what "they call me" goes back to "Mississippi Goddam": "You'd stop calling me Sister Sadie." It suggests that the language inflicted on Black women comes from alien forces. Are the names of Simone's women all wrong? What sorts of names are Aunt Sarah and Sweet Thang? Do the names of these women really define their true selves?

"Four Women" appeared four years after the publication of her friend James Baldwin's best-selling collection of essays, *Nobody Knows My Name* (1961). The characters in Simone's song struggle to establish an identity: "Black women didn't know what the hell they wanted because they were defined by things they didn't control, and until they had the confidence to define themselves they'd be stuck in the same mess forever—that was the point the song made," Simone wrote in *I Put a Spell on You*.[80] Before the term *black feminism* was bandied about, Nina Simone was expressing its insights.

Yet despite her creative success, Nina Simone's sense of being coerced mounted. In 1967 she recorded Billy Taylor and Dick Dallas's "I Wish I Knew How It Would Feel to Be Free": "I wish I could break all the chains holding me."[81] By the end of the sixties, she saw two faces in the mirror, "knowing that on the one hand I loved being black and being a woman, and that on the other it was my colour and sex which had fucked me up in the first place."[82] On stage, the diva would emphasize her roots by means of flamboyant jewelry, African fabrics, her hair sculpted into a coned crown or baroquely braided; but feverish recording schedules and hectic tours exhausted her, and she worried about her responsibility for a throng of musicians and dependents.

Her husband's working her "like a carthorse" made her feel that he "loved me like a serpent": "He wrapped himself around me and he ate and breathed me, and without me he would die."[83] Their mutually abusive relationship, as well as her undiagnosed mood swings and the unrelenting traveling, took a toll. About her self-division, she said, "Eunice is a woman who doesn't get enough time off," while Nina Simone is "the machine who must perform every night."[84] Experimenting with drugs, disillusioned about the efficacy of antiracist activism, in 1969 Simone deposited her wedding ring in her bedroom and left for Barbados, where a relationship with another woman left her distressed that she was "*stuck between desire for both sexes.*"[85]

It was the beginning of a peripatetic unraveling, struggles with mental illness, and a search for a homeland that would extend until her death . . . but not before she composed the tribute to Lorraine Hansberry, "To Be Young Gifted and Black," that she performed on *Sesame Street* and that the Black organization the Congress of Racial Equality (CORE) deemed the "Black National Anthem."[86] With its title quoting Hansberry's inspirational words to black youth,[87] the song would continue to uplift students on college campuses, protesters at rallies, and concertgoers around the world.

4

The Sexual Revolution and the Vietnam War

NINA SIMONE'S RIBALD JOKES and daring garb reflect a shift in both racial and sexual attitudes. As powerful as the civil rights movement and coexisting alongside it, the sexual revolution began with the invention of the birth control pill but soon shaped changes in behavior that defied long-held prescriptions about virginity. Sexual intercourse originated "In nineteen sixty-three," the poet Philip Larkin famously pronounced, adding plaintively "(Which was rather late for me—)."[1]

Larkin might have been thinking about a publishing revolution after legal battles, both in the States and England, overturned obscenity laws banning sales of D. H. Lawrence's *Lady Chatterley's Lover* and Henry Miller's *Tropic of Capricorn*.[2] Or he may have had in mind the popularity of the Pill—a medical breakthrough funded in part through the efforts of the birth control activist Margaret Sanger. Approved in 1960 for contraceptive use, by 1963 it had freed millions of women from fear of unwanted pregnancy.[3] Two years later, the

U.S. Supreme Court case *Griswold v. Connecticut* legalized the use of contraception by married couples.

While William Masters and Virginia Johnson began reporting their data on the physiology of human sexuality, journalists and essayists—Gloria Steinem and Helen Gurley Brown, Susan Sontag and Joan Didion—were responding first to the sexual revolution and then to the emergence of the counterculture. All their quite different perspectives were amplified by a maelstrom of protests against the Vietnam War that erupted, during the momentous year 1968, into the women's liberation movement.

SEX IN NEW YORK CITY: GLORIA STEINEM VERSUS HELEN GURLEY BROWN

Gloria Steinem and Helen Gurley Brown were particularly notable as avatars of the sexual revolution, and though they followed different paths to success, the two had a lot in common. Both were raised by single mothers in Depression-era poverty. Both would later attribute their ambition to regret at the difficulties their mothers faced. Although Gurley could not afford college, she worked her way up as a secretary and then an advertising copywriter until, like Steinem, she entered the world of journalism. Both stayed unmarried—Gurley until 37, Steinem until 66—and both chose to remain childless. In the early sixties, Steinem and Brown focused on the situation of the urban single woman. Both rejected the double standard of monogamy for women and promiscuity for men, though again in different ways.

Amid the glitterati of the sixties, the photogenic Gloria Steinem—with her miniskirts and long hair (the aviator glasses would come later)—embodied the sexual revolution. Before she defined herself as a feminist, she lived an unusually independent life. Though she was involved in a series of what she called "little marriages" with men she admired, she had no wish to marry.[4] She had landed in Manhattan after an education at Smith—overlapping Plath's time there and, like Plath, attending with a scholarship—followed by a stint in India. Steinem shared an apartment with a girlfriend and dated a series of eminent men, some of whom aided her breakthrough into the world of magazine journalism. When a New York City Playboy Club opened, the editors of *Show* encouraged her to go undercover. She used her grandmother's name (Marie Ochs) and Social Security card to apply for a job as a Bunny and then to expose what she later called "the phony glamor and exploitative employment policies" of Hugh Hefner's enterprise.[5]

Steinem's 1963 essay "I Was a Playboy Bunny" takes the form of a diary in which the 28-year-old Steinem records shaving four years off her persona's record because she was "beyond the Bunny age limit." Knowing how dumb bunnies should be, she purposely answered several questions wrong on the entrance test. She also had to submit to a gynecological examination before donning a bright blue satin Bunny costume, which was tight enough to make her fear bending over: "The bottom was cut up so high that it left my hip bones exposed as well as a good five inches of untanned derrière. The boning in the waist would have made Scarlett O'Hara blanch, and the entire construction tended to push all available flesh up to the bosom."[6] (She was encouraged to stuff plastic dry-cleaning bags into the bodice to inflate her breasts.) Bunnies were expected to pay for their own cosmetics, costume cleaning, black nylons, and shoes dyed to match. Half of Steinem-Ochs's tips went to the club. The glowing ads to attract applicants camouflaged the grueling and not especially lucrative labors of the Door Bunnies, Camera Bunnies, and Table Bunnies, all sporting fluffy tails and floppy ears.

Why did Hefner fix on the Bunny for the centerfolds in his magazine and the waitstaff in his clubs? The bunny is "a fresh animal, shy, vivacious, jumping—sexy," he explained.[7] (That they are hyper-reproductive did not seem to enter his thinking, though the phrase "fuck like a bunny" probably did.) Mainstreaming porn, Hefner marketed *Playboy* so successfully that the magazine appeared in many middle-class homes. The soft porn centerfolds made one young girl—who grew up to become the cultural critic Carina Chocano—think of "the taxidermied animals at the national-history museums."[8]

Working at the club, Steinem-Ochs froze at the front door or served at the bar while her legs numbed from the knee up, her feet swelled, her hands—bearing heavy trays—ached, and her skin was rubbed raw from the costume stays. During her two-week stint, distress at propositions from patrons paled in comparison to exhaustion and starvation: she lost 10 pounds because the only food available was snatched on the run. At one point, Steinem considered her essay on this experience an "early mistake" because of the notoriety it spawned.[9] But in a 1983 postscript, she declares that "all women are Bunnies."[10] The piece itself testifies with more nuance to the disconnect between the glamour surrounding the Playboy Bunny and the unpleasant realities that confronted the naive young women who signed on to the role.

At the time, Steinem believed, the "sex jokes" provoked by the Bunny exposé "swallowed up" her first major article: a 1962 *Esquire* report on the contraceptive revolution.[11] "The Moral Disarmament of Betty Coed" described interviews with college administrators and students on campus sexual mores. Although some college presidents still considered premarital sexual relations "offensive and vulgar," among undergrads "the belief that pleasure in sex was created only to ensure the production of children seems to have disappeared." Steinem describes coeds taking responsibility for affairs by obtaining diaphragms and lying to physicians about their marital status to do so. But it was the "first completely safe and foolproof contraceptive pill" that, "accepted so quietly," quickly transformed women's lives.[12]

"More aesthetic than mechanical devices," the Pill did not need to be taken at the time of sexual intercourse and it was proven to be "one hundred percent effective." What happens to young women when pregnancy fears are removed? Steinem wonders. She suspects that fearless girls gain libido while deciding "that their sex practices are none of society's business." Encountering young women who expect to find their identities "neither totally without men nor totally through them," she claims: "The development of the 'autonomous' girl is important, and in large numbers, quite new."[13] Such a girl has been freed by the Pill to postpone marriage while pursuing a career without renouncing sexuality.

Steinem understands the downside of the trend she celebrates. "Society has begun to make it as rough for virgins and women content to be housewives" as it once did for independent women. With this insight, she foresees that the tension between single and married women in the fifties would morph into the friction in the seventies between so-called liberated women and those who are "only housewives." Yet she praises educators who have begun questioning the pronouncements of Sigmund Freud and Helene Deutsch by suggesting that "women's role is more learned than physically determined."[14]

With these words, Steinem addresses the debate between what in the eighties would come to be called "essentialism"—the idea that the sexes are biologically hardwired—and what would come to be called "social constructionism": the insistence that, as Simone de Beauvoir put it, men and women are made by culture, not shaped by nature. Similarly prescient, the conclusion of "The Moral Disarmament of Betty Coed" considers the "real danger of the contraceptive revolution": "the acceleration of woman's role-change without any corresponding change of man's attitude toward her role."[15] Maybe, Steinem suggests, there won't be enough sexually liberated men to go around.

That view about the predominance of unliberated men helps explain the assumptions of *Sex and the Single Girl*, a breezy best seller published by Helen Gurley Brown in 1962. At the start, Brown emphatically agrees with Steinem that women should have a longer interval before marriage as a stage for pleasure and career: "I think marriage is insurance for the *worst* years of your life," she tells her readers. "During your best years you don't need a husband. You do need a man of course every step of the way, and they are often cheaper emotionally and a lot more fun by the dozens."[16] Both the in-your-face flaunting of promiscuity ("cheaper . . . by the dozens") and the opening proviso ("You do need a man . . . every step of the way") distinguish her stance from Steinem's, for Helen Gurley Brown was marketing a "fun" form of sexual libertarianism that encouraged women to enjoy plentiful sex before marriage while tapping their sex appeal to get their material needs met. "Good girls go to heaven," she quipped, "but bad girls go everywhere."[17]

Sex and the Single Girl functions as a self-help guide for the career gal who needs to know how and where to meet men. On which men are eligible, Brown advises her readers "not to rule out married men but to keep them as pets": "While they are 'using' you to varnish their egos, you 'use' *them* to add spice to your life. I say 'them' advisedly. One married man is dangerous. A potpourri can be fun." The key to attracting guys is to be "a sexy woman"—that is, "a woman who enjoys sex." Accessories help: "the sheer stocking, the twenty-four-inch waist, the smoldering look." Whereas "Clean hair is sexy," evident "hair under your arms, on your legs and around your nipples, isn't."[18] And so forth. If men are not liberated, women nevertheless have the means at their disposal to milk them for what they are worth.

To be sure, Helen Gurley Brown believed that employment remains crucial before or even instead of marriage. She therefore pitches her own impoverished origins to set out the ways in which girls in lean times can live in style while saving for and investing in the future. Needless to say, these instructions include never going out "Dutch treat." An instant success, *Sex and the Single Girl* critiqued a culture that defined sexually active young women as shameful. Amid advice on how to furnish an apartment as a "sure man-magnet," how to entertain and diet, and how to exercise and use makeup (even "plastic surgery is very, very 'natural'"), Brown emphasizes the importance of speaking honestly about women's desires. She wants to blow to smithereens publications that portray "the problems of single women in the same vein as their articles on [nuclear] fall-out." Marriage is "no longer the big question for women," and therefore, "You, my friend, if you work at it, can be envied the rich, full life possible for the single woman today."[19]

As her biographer Jennifer Scanlon demonstrates, Helen Gurley Brown was attacked from the right (for promoting immorality) and from the left (for encouraging women to use sex in exchange for benefits from wealthier men).[20] Yet, as Scanlon also shows, Brown appealed to those young career women who wanted to exploit a system biased against them. Embarking on diets that kept her 5'2" frame pencil-thin at 100 pounds, Brown devoted herself to selling the programs required by a deliberate performance of femininity. Her single girls are not prudes, sluts, bimbos, or old maids; they are ambitious to

rise from rags to riches while savoring their work and their affairs—
as Brown did until she settled down to the editorship of *Cosmopolitan*,
which soon included articles on the ways in which the Pill improved
women's sex lives.

In 1966, the year the National Organization for Women (NOW)
was founded to end sex discrimination, William H. Masters and
Virginia E. Johnson's *Human Sexual Response*—also an instant best
seller—echoed Helen Gurley Brown's view that women are as sexually desirous as men and then upped the ante. In order to measure
sexual response, the two researchers created "artificial coital equipment": transparent plastic penises. Equipped with a camera, the dildo
could be "controlled completely by the responding individual." Nick-
named Ulysses, this plastic penis led the scientists to declare that
"clitoral and vaginal orgasms are not separate biological entities." In
their view and in opposition to the Freudians, the clitoris is "unique,"
the only organ "totally limited in physiologic function to initiating
or elevating levels of sexual tension. No such organ exists within the
anatomic structure of the human male."[21] One psychiatrist, Mary
Ann Sherfey, immediately concluded: "There is no such thing as a
vaginal orgasm distinct from a clitoral orgasm."[22]

Ulysses led Masters and Johnson to the realization that "many
well-adjusted women enjoy a minimum of three or four orgasmic
experiences before they reach satiation." Unlike men, women are
"capable of rapid return to orgasm immediately following an orgasmic experience," and they can maintain "an orgasmic experience for a
relatively long period of time." Masters and Johnson want to "emphasize the physiologic similarities in male and female responses rather
than the differences"; however, their data prove that "female orgasmic
experience usually is developed more easily and is physiologically more
intense . . . when induced by automanipulation as opposed to coition."[23]

Masturbation, not intercourse, evidently generated the most intense orgasmic experiences. At home, Penelope no longer had to wait passively for Ulysses, weaving and unweaving her tapestry. By the end of the sixties, feminists would tease out the significance of the view promulgated by *Human Sexual Response*: men, liberated or unliberated, were instrumental for reproduction, but were no longer needed to bring about female sexual satisfaction.

SUSAN SONTAG, JOAN DIDION, AND SAN FRANCISCO

Long before Ulysses the plastic penis was a glitter in the eyes of Masters and Johnson, the 26-year-old Susan Sontag meditated on the orgasm. "Good orgasm vs. bad. Orgasms come in all sizes," she mused in her journal in 1959, adding, "Woman's orgasm is deeper than the man's. 'Everybody knows that.' Some men never have an orgasm; they ejaculate numb." A few months later, she was still brooding on the same subject. "The coming of the orgasm has changed my life," she noted, and went on to declare: "The orgasm focuses. I lust to write. The coming of the orgasm is not the salvation but, more, the birth of my ego."[24] Sontag would continue to welcome the new forms of eroticism ushered in by the sexual revolution, while another public intellectual, Joan Didion, would deplore them.

Famous for her brilliance as a critic, Sontag was both intellectually and sexually precocious. At an early age she had decided that she was either bisexual or homosexual, and as a 15-year-old freshman at the University of California, Berkeley, she had an affair with a classmate, Harriet Sohmers, who would become an on-and-off fixture in her life. With Harriet, she cruised the gay bars in San Francisco, got drunk, and made wild love while also applying to the University of

Chicago, drawn by its Great Books program. Then, at 16, she left Berkeley for Chicago.

During her second year of college, Sontag listed the lovers she had from "1947 (age 14) to 8/28/50 (age 17)": they added up to thirty-six. According to her biographer Benjamin Moser, the list, titled "The Bi's Progress," shows that she "was trying to train herself into heterosexuality by increasing the proportion of heterosexual encounters."[25] After a brief courtship, she married her sociology instructor, the 28-year-old Philip Rieff, when she was just 17. Shortly before the wedding, she wrote a single, solemn entry in her journal: "1/3/51: I marry Philip with full consciousness + fear of my will toward self-destructiveness."[26] Retrospectively, alluding to the pedantic antihero of George Eliot's *Middlemarch*, she often said, "I married Mr. Casaubon."[27]

Despite anxiety about her marriage, she thrived on Chicago's Great Books, graduating as a member of Phi Beta Kappa when she was 18 and giving birth to her only child, David Rieff, when she was 19. During these years, she also collaborated with Philip Rieff on his well-received *Freud: The Mind of a Moralist* (1959), for which he claimed sole authorship but which she later insisted she had co-written. From Chicago, Rieff went on to teach at Brandeis, and Sontag pursued further studies at Harvard while teaching freshman English at the University of Connecticut and—at the same time—caring for young David.

By the time she was awarded an American Association of University Women Fellowship to Oxford, though, the marriage was crumbling. Sontag went to Europe on her own in 1957, leaving David with his grandparents and essentially abandoning Rieff, though he did all he could to keep her. Disliking Oxford's formality, she left for Paris after one term, ostensibly to study at the Sorbonne but really to immerse herself in the culture of the Rive Gauche. There she

fell again into the arms of Harriet Sohmers and, almost simultaneously, longed to make love to the Cuban playwright Irene Fornes,
Sohmers's current inamorata, who would later become her own partner in New York. There she heard Simone de Beauvoir "talk on the
novel" and concluded that she is "lean and tense and black-haired and
very good-looking for her age, but her voice is unpleasant."[28] And
there she learned to be the cosmopolite—the "intellectual-diva,"[29] as
one observer called her—who would become a youthful star among
the New York intellectuals of *Commentary* and *Partisan Review.*

She was striking, with a mane of dark hair that would, as she
aged, be marked with a signature streak of white. Commentators
even compared her to "Marilyn" and "Judy"—glamour girls with
whom enthralled admirers like to think themselves on a first-name
basis. "Jackie" too would fit into this category, and "Gloria." But
none of them had an intellectual glamour as dazzling as their celebrated looks: only "Susan" had that. As if to emphasize this point, her
first book, a sort of "antinovel" titled *The Benefactor* (in which, said
the *New York Times* reviewer, "the characters do not lead lives, they
assume postures"),[30] featured no blurbs on the back jacket but only a
sumptuous portrait of the author, looking pensive and French, in a
black turtleneck.

Though *The Benefactor* (1963) wasn't much of a success, by the
time the feminist critic Carolyn Heilbrun interviewed her in 1967
Sontag was such a celebrity that, said Heilbrun, "Everyone knows
who she is. . . . One need not have read her books, nor even have
heard of Partisan Review. . . . [She is] smart enough to tell America
off, and glamorous enough to make America like it."[31] What cata-
pulted her into the pages of the popular press was her essay "Notes
on Camp," which appeared in 1964 and drew so much attention that
Time magazine did a story about it.

In setting down a collection of cultural decrees, Sontag assumes a kind of Wildean role, transforming herself into a philosopher of pop culture. "Camp," she declared, "sees everything in quotation marks. It's not a lamp, but a 'lamp'; not a woman, but a 'woman.'" And then, "Camp is the triumph of the epicene style. (The convertibility of 'man' and 'woman,' 'person' and 'thing.')"[32] With these two "notes" (numbered 10 and 11), Sontag, "out" neither as a feminist nor as a lesbian, might as well have been inventing some of the theoretical notions of the nineties feminists who claimed that there is no ontological *woman*, only a socially constructed "woman." (But then, remember that Sontag had been listening attentively to Simone de Beauvoir in Paris, and perhaps inhaling Beauvoir's view that "one is not born, but rather becomes, a woman.")[33]

"Notes on Camp" was also, to be sure, a celebration of what had long been an underground gay aesthetic, so in elaborating these ideas Sontag was allying herself (a supposedly closeted lesbian) with a long tradition of transgressive transvestism. No wonder that the essay particularly enraged both the right-wing critic John Simon and the Old Left thinker Irving Howe.[34] From the perspective of both men, Sontag's blurring of genre distinctions was close to barbaric.

By the time she had published *Against Interpretation*, Sontag had indeed come to be an acolyte of what the historian Theodore Roszak shrewdly called the counter culture,[35] and as a partisan of that subversive movement she had become not only a defender of the new revolution represented by, say, hippie flower children in San Francisco but also an antiwar activist, horrified by the role that the American military had come to play in the Vietnam War. If "Notes on Camp" had been shocking in its espousal of a gender-bending gay aesthetic, "What's Happening in America," published in 1966, was perhaps even more scandalous in its attack on "the arch-imperium" of "today's

America, with Ronald Reagan the new daddy of California and John Wayne chawing spareribs in the White House." Cataloging America's flaws—"the most brutal system of slavery in modern times," "a country where the indigenous culture was simply the enemy . . . and where nature, too, was the enemy"—she notoriously concluded that America is the apotheosis of the civilization of "the white race" and that "the white race *is* the cancer of human history . . . which eradicates autonomous civilizations wherever it spreads [and] which has upset the ecological balance of the planet."[36]

Against this backdrop of what she considered the "Yahooland" of America, Sontag argued that the rebellious youth of the sixties heralded a brave new world. Responding to an attack on hippies by the critic Leslie Fiedler (who feared that long-haired pot-smoking young men were "the new mutants" bringing about a "radical metamorphosis of the Western male"), she celebrated what she called the "depolarizing of the sexes" as "the natural, and desirable, next stage of the sexual revolution." "From my own experience and observation," she confided, "I can testify that there is a profound concordance between the sexual revolution, redefined, and the political revolution, redefined." For what "some of the kids understand is that it's the whole character structure of modern American man . . . that needs rehauling."[37]

If one were to postulate an anti-Sontag, Joan Didion would be an almost inevitable choice. Yet like Helen Gurley Brown and Gloria Steinem, the two had a lot in common. They were nearly the same age, and both so photogenic that their portraits often appeared instead of copy on their book jackets. Both were California-bred, both studied at UC Berkeley, and both were successful journalists. But where Sontag started her career in intellectual quarterlies, Didion wrote for *Vogue*, *Life*, and the *Saturday Evening Post*. Both were drawn to film, but where Sontag studied the avant-garde and eventually directed a few innovative movies, Didion worked in Hollywood. Where Sontag promoted revolution in cultural, aesthetic, and sexual mores, Didion was having none of it. Where Sontag (born Susan Rosenblatt) came from an immigrant Jewish family and never knew her father, who died when she was 5, Didion was born into a WASP ranching family that had long been established in Sacramento.

Even more important, where Sontag aligned herself with the Old (and then the New) Left, Didion cleaved to Republican conservatism. Where Sontag drew a parodic picture of "John Wayne chawing spareribs in the White House," Didion limned a misty-eyed portrait of "Duke's" true grit in "John Wayne: A Love Song."[38] And where Sontag was drawn to the political and sexual changes that were immanent in the experimental lives of "the kids" in the sixties, Didion traveled from Los Angeles to San Francisco to research their ways because she wanted to study "the evidence of atomization, the proof that things fall apart."[39] The result of her entirely sober trip into the center of drug-induced tripping was her most famous essay, "Slouching Towards Bethlehem."

The piece—whose title was drawn from W. B. Yeats's apocalyptic "The Second Coming"—begins with a passage of unmitigated gloom, which is worth quoting at some length:

The center was not holding. It was a country of bankruptcy notices and public-auction announcements and commonplace reports of casual killings and misplaced children and abandoned homes. . . . It was a country in which families routinely disappeared . . . and adolescents drifted from city to torn city, sloughing off both the past and future as snakes shed their skins. . . . It was the United States of America in the cold late spring of 1967, and the market was steady . . . and a great many articulate people seemed to have a sense of high social purpose and it might have been a spring of brave hopes[,] . . . but it was not, and more and more people had the uneasy apprehension that it was not.[40]

From this set of bleak assumptions about the mid-sixties as an American landscape that is, on the one hand, a sort of post-apocalyptic waste land and, on the other hand, a weirdly Orwellian society in which "a great many articulate people" profess duplicitous optimism, Didion begins her investigation of San Francisco, "where the social hemorrhaging was showing up," and "where the missing children were gathering and calling themselves 'hippies.'"[41]

She locates herself in Haight-Ashbury, during the famous 1967 "summer of love," where a conglomeration of "beatniks," "hippies," and "flower children" are smoking dope, listening to the Doors or the Grateful Dead, dropping acid, and celebrating "be-ins" in Golden Gate Park. Here she befriends a crew of mostly inarticulate teenage drifters—Don, Max, Sharon, and so forth, along with an equally inarticulate Officer Gerrans, who is shrewdly introduced by Max as "our Officer Krupke" and who explains that "the major problems [in the Haight] are narcotics and juveniles. Juveniles and narcotics, those are your major problems."[42] Didion's stance toward this cast of characters is, as one might expect from the opening paragraphs of her essay, both icily objective and bitterly ironic. A sophisticated documentarian, she lets many of her subjects speak for themselves:

"I've had this old lady for a couple of months now, maybe she makes something special for my dinner and I come in three days late and tell her I've been balling some other chick, well, maybe she shouts a little but then I say, 'That's me, baby,' and she laughs and says, 'That's you, Max.' "

"I remember I wanted to be a veterinarian once. . . . But now I'm more or less working in the vein of being an artist or a model or a cosmetologist. Or something."

"I found love on acid. But I lost it. And now I'm finding it again. With nothing but grass."[43]

Gradually the tone darkens as Didion enters less laughable scenes. Searching for the mysterious Chester Anderson, a 30-something "legacy of the Beat Generation" who posts "communiques" all over the district, she records one of them verbatim:

Pretty little 16-year-old middle-class chick comes to the Haight to see what it's all about & gets picked up by a 17-year-old street dealer who spends all day shooting her full of speed[,] . . . then feeds her 3,000 mikes & raffles off her temporarily unemployed body for the biggest Haight Street gangbang since the night before last. . . . Rape is as common as bullshit on Haight Street. Kids are starving on the Street. Minds and bodies are being maimed as we watch, a scale model of Vietnam.[44]

When the summer of love began, the hippie part of San Francisco, mellowed by the comparative innocence of marijuana and energized by, yes, the legacy of the Beats, seemed as hopeful as Sontag had thought it was. Participants in all the revolutionary "movements" of the decade—the free speech movement, the civil rights movement, the antiwar movement—mingled with paisley-clad, long-haired, runaway teenagers. But dealers moved in and earnest students went back to school, leaving quite a lot of debris behind them.

Runaway girls had children, for instance, whose plight Didion represented in riveting detail: Michael, a "very blond and pale and dirty" 3-year-old who doesn't talk but loves to play with lighted joss sticks; and Susan, a 5-year-old who is on acid and explains that her mother sends her to "High Kindergarten."[45] (Years later, in a documentary, Didion was to confide that her discovery of Susan was a journalistic treasure: "gold, pure gold.")[46]

"Minds and bodies are being maimed . . . a scale model of Vietnam." In fact, as the historian Michael J. Kramer has pointed out, the connections between the increasingly horrific war in Southeast Asia and the insurgent hippie movement were intricate. "Girls say yes to boys who say no" appeared on antidraft posters blowing in the wind. And "just as the war became a central theme in the counterculture, the counterculture became central to the GI experience in Vietnam," where marijuana use among soldiers "increased 260 percent" between 1967 and 1968, while the military brass tried to soothe the troops by adding "additional 'acid rock' programming" on Armed Forces Radio Vietnam. Wrote one observer in a letter to the *Berkeley Barb*, "There probably would be no Haight Ashbury without the war."[47]

As the summer of love turned into a rainy winter in San Francisco, the faraway war became disconcertingly present. Writers and rebels wanted to go to Vietnam to understand for themselves what was happening. Didion yearned to report on the war, only to realize that she had just adopted a baby and couldn't possibly bring little Quintana to the front with her, as she had insouciantly planned to do. But Sontag was distraught—and eventually would journey to Hanoi. The Vietnam War, she wrote, "blew up in my face. That and its aftermath derailed me for about 10 years."[48]

WOMEN STRIKE FOR PEACE

On March 16, 1965, the first antiwar protester to immolate herself on American soil (in imitation of Buddhist monks who were similarly protesting in Vietnam) was Alice Herz, a member of Detroit's Women Strike for Peace. An 82-year-old German Jew who had fled Hitler's regime in the early thirties with her young daughter, she had spent years demonstrating, but growing rage at President Lyndon Johnson's approval of a massive bombing campaign in North Vietnam led her to declare that "I have chosen the flaming death."[49] Later that year, a delegation of ten American women, organized by Women Strike for Peace, met in Indonesia with high-ranking North Vietnamese officials and women from the National Liberation Front of South Vietnam.

The Americans' reports of damaged or destroyed hospitals, churches, and schools moved the New Left activist Todd Gitlin to the realization that the Vietnam War was real now: "There were witnesses, individuals with names and faces at stake, asking for help."[50] Soon more female witnesses would amass in the United States to testify to their outrage at the aggression they experienced daily as women. No one single literary woman can represent the multiplicity of voices raised in 1968, feminism's annus mirabilis, when the connection between masculine aggression abroad and feminine servitude at home sparked major protests by what would become the women's liberation movement.

At first, though, women's demonstrations against the war were based on the conventional idea that women's life-creating capacity conferred on them the authority to protest the death-dealing apparatus of warfare. Although by the mid-sixties Women Strike for Peace was focused on the Vietnam War, the organization began back in 1961 when 50,000 women marched against the testing of nuclear weapons. "For the first time since the 1920s," the historian Ruth Rosen has explained, "women emerged not as part of a mass movement, but *as* that movement, ready to take up the political activism that McCarthyism had interrupted."[51] They pursued lawsuits, engaged in sit-ins and boycotts, and published a cookbook, titled *Peace de Resistance*, often stressing their traditional roles as housewives, mothers, and widows. Strontium-90 from nuclear fallout, they contended, contaminated mothers' milk as well as the milk of cows. "End the Arms Race—Not the Human Race" was one of their rallying cries.

Women Strike for Peace supported the growing number of antiwar protesters in the Free Speech, civil rights, New Left, and student movements who were united in efforts to end what was increasingly viewed as unjust aggression and to derail the draft system that facilitated it. At countless teach-ins and draft-card burnings, celebrated poets—Robert Lowell, Robert Bly, Adrienne Rich, Nikki Giovanni, Denise Levertov, Robert Duncan—read antiwar poems to large audiences.[52] Denise Levertov in particular captured the horror experienced by civilians who were watching the first televised war in history. Although in the seventies she distanced herself from the women's movement, during the sixties Levertov declared that protest poetry made the antiwar campaign "a more revolutionary movement" in which ending the war could no longer be seen as "a single issue . . . divorced from racism, imperialism, capitalism, male supremacy."[53]

Levertov marched and spoke at rallies, as she began writing poems like "Life at War," which focuses on what it means to see pictures of warfare on a TV screen or a magazine page. "The disasters numb within us," she declares, and then she explores the anesthetizing effect of media coverage on viewers whose minds become "filmed over with the gray filth of it." We turn "with mere regret / to the scheduled breaking open of breasts whose milk / runs out over the entrails of still-alive babies." The poet struggles to grasp the reality of such atrocities: "these acts are done / to our own flesh; burned human flesh / is smelling in Viet Nam as I write."[54]

The grotesque burning of babies takes center stage in "Advent 1966," which also emphasizes the perspective of civilians horrified by what they watch. "Because in Vietnam the vision of a Burning Babe / is multiplied," Levertov contrasts it with the singularity of "the flesh on fire" in Thomas Southwell's sixteenth-century poem "The Burning Babe," where the burning baby Jesus prefigures the purification and rebirth that Christ will bring to Christians. The flesh burning in Vietnam is neither visionary nor unique, neither purifying nor redemptive. Human, it is "repeated, repeated, / infant after infant, their names forgotten, / their sex unknown in the ashes."[55] Also writing as a numbed onlooker, Muriel Rukeyser placed the war in the context of twentieth-century carnage and similarly stressed the horror of war at a distance: "The news would pour out of various devices / Interrupted by attempts to sell products to the unseen."[56]

The literary women who traveled to Vietnam insisted, as Mary McCarthy did, that "the worst thing that could happen to our country would be to win this war"; they emphasized its corroding effect on their own country, its language, and sometimes, paradoxically, on themselves.[57] Upon her arrival in 1967 Saigon and then especially in 1968 during her visit to the North, McCarthy lost her own "assurance of superiority" as a "confident American."[58] When Sontag's "Trip to Hanoi" appeared in 1968, McCarthy noted that she and Sontag were both "driven to an examination of conscience."[59] Like a number of their male contemporaries, McCarthy and Sontag moved from denouncing the American warmongers to cheering the North Vietnamese communists.

But they also found themselves struggling with the propaganda of their hosts. Even McCarthy's objectivity feels "uncomfortable, like a trademark or shingle advertising a genuine Mary McCarthy product."[60] And Sontag—finding the Vietnamese sexless, bland— exposes her own imperial gaze: "I still feel like someone from a 'big' culture visiting a 'little' culture." She ended up deciding that "the Vietnamese are 'whole' human beings, not 'split' as we are."[61] Grace Paley also suffered the shame of American aggression when she traveled to North Vietnam to bring home prisoners of war.

She tried to understand her countrymen in a quintessential Paley moment: "It's true, they are overkilling the Vietnamese countryside and the little brooks, but that's America for you, they have overkilled flies, bugs, beetles, trees, fish, rivers, the flowers of their own American fields. They're like overgrown kids who lean on a buddy in kindergarten and kill him." Yet the analogy does not hold, for Paley comes to believe that the American program is not accidental but genocidal. "Some people do not like the word 'genocide' and we will leave the words alone; still, in this kind of war, every person takes part, and the next thing a logical military brain hooks into is the fact that every person is a military target, or the mother of a military target, and they live in the same house; since all military targets must be destroyed, it follows that the whole people must be destroyed."[62]

Most of the writers publishing tracts against the war found their witnessing discounted after Martin Luther King and Robert Kennedy were assassinated in 1968, Hubert Humphrey obtained the Democratic nomination at a riot-torn Chicago convention, and President Nixon expanded the war to Laos and Cambodia. Levertov suffered the end of a crucial relationship when her friend the poet Robert Duncan equated her political zeal with the sacrifice of her individuality to a "demotic persona." In his poem "Santa Cruz Propositions," Duncan characterizes her as the Hindu goddess of destruction, Kali, "whirling her necklace of skulls, . . . Revolution or Death." She responded defensively in one section of a long poem: "No, / I am no Kali, I can't sustain for a day / that anger."[63] In a later letter, Duncan attributed her antiwar verse "to the deep underlying consciousness of the woman as a victim in a war with the Man," to which she replied, "That is unmitigated bullshit, Robert."[64]

But had Duncan glimpsed a powerful dynamic at work? To what extent did the anger of antiwar women arise from a "deep underlying consciousness of the woman as a victim in a war with the Man"? Surely the Americans who traveled to Vietnam were aware that the North Vietnamese insisted that women be included in delegations to their country. Female delegates from the States were often invited to meet separately with Vietnamese women. According to the historian Sara Evans, "the Vietnamese elevated the status of women delegates further by always requesting that they speak first, stressing their importance in view of the fact that there were many barriers to women becoming active, and pointing out the accomplishments of the Vietnamese women in surmounting them."[65] One American delegate felt her trip to Vietnam "was my most clearly women's liberation experience."[66]

When young activists participated in the Jeannette Rankin Brigade on January 15, 1968, they seized on the connection between violence in Vietnam and violence in the States, and the women's liberation movement dramatically surfaced. Claiming the name of the congresswoman who had voted against both world wars, the Brigade's organizers determined to hold a rally in Washington, DC, calling for the immediate withdrawal of American troops from Vietnam. The younger radicals—objecting to the idea of protesting as housewives, mothers, or widows—targeted male aggression and women's historic complicity in it. They arrived to bury traditional womanhood, not to praise it.

Within the ferment of the Jeannette Rankin Brigade rally, older reformers in Women Strike for Peace watched with ambivalence as youthful radicals paraded in a "funeral procession with a larger-than-life dummy . . . complete with feminine getup, blank face, blonde curls, and candle." "Traditional Womanhood" had died "after 3,000 years of bolstering the egos of Warmakers and aiding the cause of war," explained the feminist theorist Shulamith Firestone, who was one of the marchers. The Radical Women's Group rejected any reliance on "women's traditional role which encourages men to develop aggression and militarism to prove their masculinity." Their leaflets asked the Brigade's older members to refrain from serving as "supportive girl friends and tearful widows": "We must not come as passive suppliants begging for favors, for power cooperates only with power."[67]

Despite the schism between younger and older participants, Firestone insisted that the protest "confirmed our belief that a real women's movement in this country will come." A phrase coined by the protester Kathie Amatniek—"Sisterhood Is Powerful!"— resounded for the first time.[68] The young activist changed her name to Kathie Sarachild, in honor of her mother, as she dedicated herself to organizing for women's liberation and created the term and the process of "consciousness-raising."[69] When the Jeannette Rankin demonstration was mocked by the left-wing *Ramparts* magazine as a "miniskirt caucus," the alienation of sexual liberationists from their movement compatriots deepened.[70] The transformation of radical women—their separation from left-wing men—began to accelerate as consciousness-raising groups sprouted across the country.

VALERIE SOLANAS AND THE RISE
OF THE SECOND WAVE

Against the backdrop of Vietnam, the violence of the sixties acceler-
ated: peace protesters jailed, students beaten by the police for trying
to register voters, university strikes, political assassinations, inner-
city riots, mayhem at rock concerts. One eccentric act of violence
on June 3, 1968, quickly became associated with the birth of feminism, although its perpetrator repeatedly denounced feminists: the
provocateur Valerie Solanas arrived at Andy Warhol's famed Factory, waited till he appeared, rode with him in the elevator to his
loft, pulled out a gun, and fired three shots, one of which hit him in
the stomach.

At her arrest, Solanas enjoined journalists to read the mimeographed manifesto she was trying to get into print. Both the vicious
act and the vitriolic *SCUM Manifesto* reflected a life of childhood
sexual abuse, two babies delivered (and given away) before she was 16,
and grifting that somehow led to undergraduate study at the University of Maryland and a year of graduate work at Minnesota before she
landed in New York City.[71] Despite its incoherence, the pamphlet she
had peddled on the streets signaled a crest of anger that was fueling
emerging female liberation groups.

Surreal in the intensity of its author's rage, the *SCUM Manifesto* calls for the destruction of the male sex, arguing, "The male is
a biological accident: the Y (male gene) is an incomplete X (female
gene). . . . In other words, the male is an incomplete female, a walking abortion, aborted at the gene stage." Studded with barbs, the dia-
tribe turns common assumptions topsy-turvy: women "don't have
penis envy; men have pussy envy"; "A 'male-artist' is a contradiction
in terms." In the new regime she wants to usher in, Turd Sessions will

be conducted, "at which every male present will give a speech beginning with the sentence, 'I am a turd, a lowly, abject turd,' then proceed to list all the ways in which he is." On behalf of "thrill-seeking, freewheeling, arrogant females," Solanas also directs her animus against "Daddy's Girls," who are "dependent, scared, mindless."[72] Women should abstain from intercourse so that men will disappear.

Although the acronym SCUM stands for the Society for Cutting Up Men, the pamphlet called for a revolt of those its author identified as the wasted, the trashed, the scum of the earth. A deviant fantasy, it addressed Solanas's own paranoia as she panhandled, turned tricks, shoplifted, acted in one of Warhol's movies, hung out with dykes and drag queens in the Village, signed a literary contract that tormented her with the delusion that she no longer owned her own words, and ended up homeless. She had become obsessed with the idea that Warhol had reneged on promises to produce her play, *Up Your Ass*, and had stolen a copy of *SCUM*. He never fully recovered from the wounds she inflicted.

Before and after her incarceration in a mental institution, Solanas and her *SCUM Manifesto* served as a catalyst, sparking radical feminists' split from liberal feminists. At her pretrial hearing, the activist-lawyer Florynce Kennedy represented Solanas. Her case was also taken up by Ti-Grace Atkinson, who left NOW because it was distancing itself from Solanas's man-hating.[73] WITCH (Women's International Terrorist Conspiracy from Hell) picketed at Solanas's trial. The group's founder, the child-actress-turned-poet Robin Morgan, raised funds for her.[74] Kate Millett, who likened the manifesto to Swift's *Modest Proposal*, saw in the shooting "a female artist driven to terrible lengths by the response—or lack of response—from the art world around her, and then finally lashing out in this way against the superhero or leader of the avant-garde."[75]

Solanas exploited or libeled most of these radicals—she identified herself as a lone maverick and later threatened to throw acid in Robin Morgan's face[76]—but *SCUM* was published because of publicity about the shooting and inaugurated the late-sixties era of scandalized headlines about feminist militancy. Fed up with playing an auxiliary role in the sixties' protest movements, women began forming groups of their own. Participants in such collectives as the Seattle Radical Women, the Women's Radical Action Project in Chicago, D.C. Liberation, and New York Radical Feminists debated strategies. At consciousness-raising get-togethers, small groups of women "discussed everything from faked orgasms and concerns about the size of their breasts to long-repressed rapes or black-market abortions," as Gail Collins put it. Kathie Sarachild expressed exhilaration about a grassroots movement in which each woman felt as if she was "standing up and saying, 'I was shot into this movement and they're going to have to shoot me to get me out of it.'"[77]

Three months after the arrest of Solanas, a *New York Post* banner, "Bra Burners & Miss America," launched the myth that Robin Morgan and her cohort burned bras to protest the Miss America pageant in Atlantic City. What the protesters did do was crown a live sheep Miss America and hurl girdles, spike heels, falsies, cosmetics, and copies of *Playboy*, *Cosmopolitan*, and the *Ladies' Home Journal* into a Freedom Trash Can.[78] On Halloween in 1968, representatives of WITCH began demonstrating on Wall Street. Wearing witchy outfits, a coven would later invade the Bridal Fair at Madison Square Garden, chanting "Here comes the bribe" and "Always a bride, never a person" while releasing white mice.[79] Soon, too, one hundred protesters would occupy the headquarters of the *Ladies' Home Journal*—famous for its column "Can This Marriage Be Saved?"—demanding that its editors alter their portrayal of women.

"In 1968," the poet-novelist Erica Jong recalls, "there was a great feeling of hope that things might change, that women might . . . find . . . economic parity with their brothers and fathers. Not to mention their husbands." By 1968, the members of a Chicago underground dedicated to assisting women in need of illegal abortions had fixed on the plain name "Jane" to protect their identities, though Jane did not acquire a last name, "Howe," until the next year. "It seemed appropriate: Jane could tell you how." In the fall of 1968, Shirley Chisholm celebrated a historic election to the House of Representatives, but thirty-five years later she recalled facing "far more discrimination being a woman than being black" in the political arena. By Christmas, Audre Lorde—arriving at the home of Diane di Prima to serve as the midwife of another baby—knew that she would be leaving her husband and taking her daughter and son with her to start an openly lesbian existence.[80]

The WITCHy guerrilla theater, like *SCUM*'s rhetoric, can be read as a retort to the violent side of the sexual revolution: drug trips gone wrong and accounts of widespread sexual predation at be-ins and rock concerts, on the streets of neighborhoods where long-haired boys and girls in unisex costumes found rape "as common as bullshit." After the countercultural Jerry Rubin visited the acidhead murderer Charles Manson—in jail with his harem for the horrific killings of the pregnant actress Sharon Tate and six others—the self-proclaimed Yippie wrote that he had fallen in love with the killer when he first saw him on national TV.[81]

But the feminist protests can also be viewed as a reaction to the misogyny of some of the leaders of the Black power movement. Back in the mid-sixties, Mary King and Casey Hayden had circulated a protest against the secondary roles assigned women in the civil rights struggle: "Assumptions of male superiority are as widespread and deep rooted and as crippling to the woman as the assumptions of white supremacy are to the Negro."[82] The word *sexism*, which had surfaced in the thirties to describe prejudice against women, began to circulate as an analogue to the word *racism*. Soon resolutions on "the liberation of women" were being discussed at resistance conventions, albeit amid hoots and catcalls, for women continued to confront the sexism of the men with whom they were aligned in fighting racism.

In *Soul on Ice* (1968), for example, Eldridge Cleaver described how he "started out practicing" rape on "black girls in the ghetto" until he considered himself "smooth enough" to cross over the tracks and prey on white women: "Rape was an insurrectionary act. It delighted me that I was defying and trampling on the white man's law, upon his system of values, and that I was defiling his women."[83] Cleaver claimed to be acting on behalf of Black women raped by white men, but his period of "practicing" belies that claim. The same misogynistic rage fueled a poem by LeRoi Jones, now renamed Amiri Baraka. In "Babylon Revisited" (1969), Diane di Prima's ex-lover curses a white woman "and her sisters, all of them," who should receive his words

> in all their orifices like lye mixed with
> cocola and alaga syrup
> feel this shit, bitches, feel it, now laugh your
> hysteric laughs
> while your flesh burns and your eyes peel to red mud.[84]

According to one director of a freedom school program, "every black SNCC worker . . . counted it a notch on his gun to have slept with a white woman—as many as possible." It must have been "traumatic for the women," who "hadn't thought that was what going south was about."[85] Kathleen Cleaver admitted that she had to "genuflect" to the men in the Black Panther Party; and about the everyday sexism in SNCC, Frances Beale, one of its few prominent Black women, pointed out that "when it comes to women," "the black militant male" who sets out to upend white values "seems to take his guidelines from the pages of *Ladies Home Journal.*"[86]

Sexism in the Free Speech, New Left, and antiwar movements also raised the consciousness of female activists. Left-wing women were beginning to realize that they were "typing the speeches the men delivered, making the coffee but not policy, being accessories to the men whose politics would supposedly replace the Old Order."[87] While both the men of Columbia and the women of Barnard braved police brutality at the 1968 Columbia University uprising, only the women cooked "in a kitchen the size of a telephone booth"; and later that summer the dissidents' spokesman, Mark Rudd, "advised his girlfriend that she could go to 'chicklib' class while he was busy with other things."[88]

As New Left organizations splintered, Chicago's feminist group started issuing the newsletter *Voice of the Women's Liberation Movement*; on the East Coast, female liberationists mimeographed the first feminist journal, *Notes from the First Year*, in 1968. Anne Koedt, an associate editor, had heard Valerie Solanas speak about SCUM at the Free University and wondered at the performance: "What do you *do* with that rage? Some of it must have been founded in truth, but where do you direct it?"[89] Koedt directed it into her widely read essay "The Myth of the Vaginal Orgasm." Teasing out the implications of Masters and Johnson's findings, Koedt judged men's fear that "they will become sexually expendable" to be perfectly valid, since "lesbian sexuality could make an excellent case, based upon anatomical data, for the extinction of the male organ": the clitoral orgasm threatens "the intersexual *institution*."[90]

The editor of *Notes from the Second Year*, Shulamith Firestone, included a boxed notice of the "Aunt Tom of the Month" in its back pages; within it was the name of Helen Gurley Brown. On the concluding page, readers were informed that additional copies of *Notes* could be ordered from Redstockings: 50 cents for women, $1 for men. The group's name came from the eighteenth-century "bluestockings": the female intellectuals of the past had been turned red by revolutionary fervor. At a Redstockings speak-out on abortion in 1969, Gloria Steinem experienced a moment of illumination—what would soon become famous as a "click."[91] "Suddenly, I was no longer learning intellectually what was wrong. I knew": "If one in three or four adult women shares this experience, why should each of us be made to feel criminal and alone?"[92] She sat down to write "After Black Power, Women's Liberation" (which contained no mention of her abortion).

As Stonewall erupted, as the first pamphlet version of "Our Bodies, Ourselves" surfaced, as Chicana student activists in Long Beach, California, formed their first organization and (male) students at Boston College challenged the firing of Mary Daly, whose *The Church and the Second Sex* had alienated Jesuit administrators, Marge Piercy's "The Grand Coolie Damn" lambasted the leaders of the New Left: "Fucking a staff into existence is only the extreme form of what passes for common practice" in left-wing circles: men have "created in the Movement a microcosm of . . . oppression and are proud of it."[93]

In "Goodbye to All That," circulated in the first month of 1970, Robin Morgan—who had played the tomboy Dagmar in the popular TV series *Mama* and been named "The Ideal American Girl"—said goodbye to "the male-dominated Left" with its "Stanley Kowalski image and theory of free sexuality but practice of sex on demand for males" and to "Hip culture and the so-called Sexual Revolution, which has functioned toward women's freedom as did the Reconstruction toward former slaves." Casting aside the Robin Morgan doll that had been manufactured as a collector's item and the Dagmar doll named for the TV character she played, Morgan adopted a new image: "We are rising, powerful in our unclean bodies; bright glowing mad in our inferior brains; wild hair flying, wild eyes staring, wild voices keening. . . . We are rising with a fury older and potentially greater than any force in history, and this time we will be free or no one will survive."[94]

Unlike the sixties, the seventies arrived right on time with an explosion of incendiary feminist publications.

SECTION III

AWAKENINGS IN THE SEVENTIES

5

Protesting Patriarchy

IN THE SUMMER OF 1970, to celebrate the fiftieth anniversary of women's suffrage, some 20,000 women marched down Fifth Avenue in the largest demonstration yet of the Women's Strike for Equality. As if to reflect the intellectual intensity of the movement, the cover of *Time* magazine featured a portrait of the feminist thinker Kate Millett produced by the painter Alice Neel.[1] The core demands of the marchers: equal opportunity in education and employment, the right to abortion, and child care. The core argument of Kate Millett's best-selling *Sexual Politics* (1970): relationships between men and women are shaped by a patriarchal ideology that subordinates the female of the species.

By October 1971, activists and theorists alike were elated that the House of Representatives had passed the Equal Rights Amendment after only a short debate. Surely, most believed, the ERA would quickly become the law of the land, for it was a simple affirmation: "Equality of rights under the law shall not be denied or abridged by the United States or by any State on account of sex."[2] It would extend

Title VII of the 1964 Civil Rights Act, which barred employment discrimination based on race, religion, national origin, and sex. In 1972 and 1973, such optimism found confirmation first in Title IX of the Education Amendment Act, outlawing discrimination on the basis of sex in any educational program or activity receiving federal financial assistance, and then in the 7–2 decision of the Supreme Court in *Roe v. Wade*, which based the nationwide legalization of abortion on the privacy rights guaranteed by the Fourteenth Amendment.

The article accompanying the 1970 *Time* cover described Millett as "the Mao Tse-tung of Women's Liberation" while explaining that she had struggled in childhood with a truculent father who beat her and her sisters before abandoning them, and with a mother whose college degree initially earned her a job demonstrating a potato peeler in a department store.[3] Like Millett, some of the women marching in New York had first seen the painful effects of female subordination in the frustration of their own mothers, though others may have been inspired because their mothers went to work during or after the Second World War. The generation that would trigger a revolution in sexual politics determined to break from the claustrophobic domesticity that hindered the lives of many female relatives, while carrying out what might have been their mothers' thwarted projects.

Both the origin and the personal consequences of Millett's landmark book speak to the nature of seventies feminism. That *Sexual Politics* started as a protest speech at Cornell University and evolved into a doctoral thesis at Columbia University reflects the synergy of activism and the academic humanities at a moment when women for the first time began studying—and teaching—their own histories, as we did at Indiana University. After the publication of *Sexual Politics* caused a firestorm of publicity and Millett was singled out as a leader, she and many of her compatriots were angered by the notion that any one person could represent a movement dedicated to the communitarian ideal that, as Robin Morgan's 1970 book title put it, *Sisterhood Is Powerful.*

Since the publicity resulted in Millett's being outed first as bisexual, then as lesbian, she grappled not only with a media circus but also with hostility from her feminist compatriots and her family. At the height of seventies feminism, the differences between women—ostensible leaders and supposed followers, radicals and liberals, lesbians and heterosexuals, and women of color and white women—would produce passionate, sometimes wounding conversations addressing multiple forms of subjugation. The sexual liberationists' struggle on behalf of *woman* in the sixties became the feminists' fights for *women* by the end of the seventies and thereafter.

At the start of this tumultuous decade, amid distress at the carnage of the Vietnam War, the bombings of Cambodia, and the killings of student protesters at Kent State, many women shared painful stories in consciousness-raising groups. The phrase *male chauvinist* clung to the noun *pig.* The personal was becoming political. A number of lesbian organizations emerged, one of the most famous being the Combahee River Collective, a Boston-based coalition of Black lesbians named after the river on whose banks Harriet Tubman led a Union raid that freed hundreds of slaves.[4] Women were learning "that politics was not something 'out there' but something 'in here' and of the essence of my condition." These words—appearing in Adrienne Rich's landmark essay "When We Dead Awaken"—capture the heady insights of the seventies: "It's exhilarating to be alive in a time of awakening consciousness; it can also be confusing, disorienting, and painful."[5]

The metaphors of feminism—of awakening, enlightenment, illumination, epiphany, conversion, revival—sound spiritual, and the movement did exert a force not unlike that of religion. In addition, the language of first and second "waves" expresses the oceanic urges associated with diving into darkness and surfacing toward light. "The women's liberation movement," recalled Rich, "embodied for a while the kind of creative space a liberatory political movement can make possible: 'a visionary relation to reality.' Why this happens has something to do with the sheer power of a collective imagining of change and a sense of collective hope."[6]

Rachel Blau DuPlessis, a poet and feminist critic who was a graduate student at Columbia in the late sixties and early seventies, is one of many who glowingly describes her experience of what Elaine Showalter called "a Great Awakening": "The experience was powerful, energizing, defining, the birth of commitment and conviction."[7] Thinking back on the years between 1969 and 1979, the activist Ann Snitow also recalled a common feeling in feminist groups—"a mixture of outrage and hope hard to recapture now. . . . [W]e expected everything was going to change."[8] On a more material plane, during the seventies "a visionary relation to reality" produced women's health initiatives, political caucuses, childcare centers, battered women's shelters, rape crisis centers, affirmative action policies, feminist art collectives, bookstores and presses, women's studies programs, and countless journals.[9] Affecting the lives of millions of women, this great awakening generated all the feminisms that continue to shape our lives.

Especially energized were the literary women who gave the movement words. While such polemicists as Kate Millett and Susan Sontag deconstructed the family romance, novelists from Toni Morrison and Erica Jong to Rita Mae Brown and Marilyn French analyzed debilitating feminine roles—as Sylvia Plath had in the legacy she bequeathed to her readers. All of us asked, To what were we awakening? Quite a few woke in shock at the oppression that had led to a state of female paralysis or nullification.

KATE MILLETT'S TOUCHSTONE BOOK

Many readers were surprised that Kate Millett began *Sexual Politics* by discussing pornographic passages penned by Henry Miller and Norman Mailer. Millett wrote the book with its "'to hell with it' first chapter" because her participation in the 1968 Columbia University strike led to her getting fired from her Barnard teaching job.[10] A $4,000 advance from Doubleday supported her while she produced one of the first works of feminist literary criticism. In it, she pioneered many of the approaches later scholars would use: the critique of masculinist texts, the recovery of female-authored and proto-feminist works, and theoretical speculations on the evolution of patriarchal institutions.

In the opening chapter of *Sexual Politics*, Millett investigates misogynist representations of "intercourse in the service of power":[11] Henry Miller's and Norman Mailer's raunchy depictions of phallic dominance over outlandishly appreciative or flaccid female bodies. The exalted potency of Miller's and Mailer's male surrogates reduces female characters to helpless carnality. Millett counters her discussions of Miller's and Mailer's triumphal fantasies with readings of works by Jean Genet, who "writes about gay men's mimicry of heterosexuality": "the only model they have is the dominant heterosexual paradigm and by parodying it they reveal it as the farce that it is."[12] By drawing on Genet, she implicitly demonstrates that all bodies can be masculinized or feminized. Taken together, the male-authored texts persuade Millett of the need to eliminate "the most pernicious of our systems of oppression": the "delirium of power and violence" inherent in sexual politics.[13]

At the heart of her book, Millett emphasizes the universality of a system that subjects women to men's monopolies of the military, industry, technology, higher education, science, politics, and finance. According to Millett, the family is the institution that creates the (aggressive or sadistic) masculine and the (passive or masochistic) feminine traits needed for the maintenance of this structure. In effect, the family manufactures psychological *gender roles* distinct from *anatomical sex*. Women, dependent for their survival on those who support them, are set against each other. Patriarchy, with God the paradigmatic Father on its side, exploits foundational myths—of Pandora or Eve bringing evil into the world—to blame the ills of the human condition on unruly women who must be made to submit to male control. Submission is achieved through "the interiorization of patriarchal ideology" that leads women to acquiesce in their own subordination.[14]

The rest of *Sexual Politics* outlines the history of ideas about sexuality from 1830 to 1960 and analyzes literary texts by returning to Millett's earlier trio of Miller, Mailer, and Genet but this time prefaced by D. H. Lawrence. Despite the long history of misogyny, her conclusion seems more optimistic than Shulamith Firestone's in *The Dialectic of Sex*, another feminist classic published the same year. Agreeing with Millett that the family generates the masochistically feminine and sadistically masculine roles necessary for the continuity of patriarchy, Firestone can envision liberation only in a future era when technology frees women from pregnancy. Millett, however, welcomes the social changes promised by the women's movement: "it may be that a second wave of the sexual revolution might at last accomplish its aim of freeing half the race from its immemorial subordination."[15]

Yet Millett's hopeful conclusion contrasts strikingly with the difficulties she encountered immediately after the book's publication, many of which are described in her stream-of-consciousness memoir

Flying (1974). An anti-elitist herself, Millett lamented the "media's diabolic need to reduce ideas to personalities," yet nonetheless her fame provoked quite a few feminists not chosen for the spotlight to attack her. She remembers commiserating with Simone de Beauvoir after Beauvoir suffered from French leftists who "insulted her for her efforts, she was an elitist, a star." When consulted by *Time* about its cover, Millett had asked for an image of many women, so she felt betrayed by the Neel portrait that sparked so much antagonism. At a meeting of "the core of the movement, the Feminists, the Radical Feminists, the Redstockings, members of consciousness-raising cells," she joked about coming out . . . this time as a pacifist, noting about the topic under discussion—"violence *in* the movement"—that she was an expert on the subject of "our trashing each other."[16]

Everyone laughed at her joke, because this inner circle of organizers knew Millett had been forced to come out as a lesbian right after *Time* described her as a bisexual living with the Japanese sculptor Fumio Yoshimura and also erotically engaged with women. Pictures were printed of her "kissing Fumio"; she was misquoted as saying, "Lesbianism was 'not my bag.'" At a feminist panel on the gay and women's liberation movements, one audience member demanded she use the L-word. "Five hundred people looking at me. Are you a Lesbian? . . . 'Say it! Say you are a Lesbian.' Yes I said. Yes. Because I know what she means. The line goes, inflexible as a fascist edict, that bisexuality is a cop-out. Yes I said yes I am a Lesbian. It was the last strength I had."[17]

In fact, although there are many sensual descriptions of Millett engaged in joyous lesbian sex in *Flying*, there are also quite a few sensual descriptions of her engaged in joyous heterosexual sex. And *Sexual Politics* had been dedicated to her husband. Why did she lie? Before the Women's Strike for Equality march, at the Second

Congress to Unite Women, the Lavender Menace Zap had galvanized the women's movement. A group of radicals cut off the microphones and put out the lights to protest Betty Friedan's use of the phrase "lavender menace" to distance NOW from lesbian groups like the Daughters of Bilitis. With the lights switched on, the radicals wore Lavender Menace T-shirts as they handed out copies of "The Woman-Identified-Woman," which begins by asserting: "A lesbian is the rage of all women condensed to the point of explosion."[18]

Millett, wanting to certify herself as a radical, said "yes I am a Lesbian," although during this period she was leading a bisexual life. The lie was also spoken by the browbeaten Millett because friends like the *Village Voice* columnist Jill Johnston denounced bisexuality as a cop-out: "Bisexuality is staying safe by claiming allegiance to heterosexuality."[19] As Ti-Grace Atkinson put it, "Feminism is the theory, lesbianism the practice." Johnston herself believed that "feminism at heart is a massive complaint. Lesbianism is the solution."[20]

Negotiating these rifts, Millett realizes that she has pained her mother. *Flying* returns frequently to Millett's sadness at her mother's revulsion. Fame turned Millett into "a hate object while you wept in St. Paul because the neighbors heard *Time* say I was queer, my life's shame home at last." After Millett tells her mother that she is writing an autobiographical book, her mother's response—"You're not going to put that awful stuff about Lesbianism in it?"—makes her feel "guilty as in childhood. I am a freak." While her mother wails, Millett asks for acceptance of the memoir she is composing, to which her mother responds that "I'm killing her": "I tell her Doris Lessing said mothers don't die as easily as they claim. Now she's just crying. So am I."[21]

Yet the reference to Doris Lessing alludes to the mentoring that sustained Millett. After the publication of *Sexual Politics*, she had visited the author of *The Golden Notebook* (1962), a novel that touched "the thousands of women who read it," and discussed the trashing Lessing received at a New York event: "Movement heavies coming to cheer Lessing as their heroine, but she infuriates them by saying she doesn't hate men at all and finds other world conditions—peace, poverty, class—all far more pressing than the problems of women."[22]

The scene that meant the most to Millett in *The Golden Notebook*, she explained to Lessing, is the moment the heroine "finds herself in a toilet at the outset of her period. . . . Happens every month of adult life to half the population of the globe and no one had ever mentioned it in a book." In return, Lessing encouraged Millett to continue writing by confessing that her own mother announced her intention to die with every book she wrote, and "I went on hoping eventually I might manage to please her . . . only to produce another funeral." When Millett lamented the fact that seven years of protesting had not stopped the Vietnam War, Lessing assured her, "But you have begun something else more remarkable if less efficacious. A great pendulum of social force, a change, a movement among millions of Americans spreading now abroad too."[23]

Brooding on the fallout from publicity, armed with the wisdom of Beauvoir and Lessing, Kate Millett turned down an invitation to attend a debate with Norman Mailer that would be filmed as *Town Bloody Hall*.[24] She devoted the rest of her life to her own art, the artist colony she established for women in upstate New York, her relationship with and eventual marriage to the Canadian journalist Sophie Keir, and a fight against the obscenity of violence—trained against children, sex workers, the sick, the aged, and the victims of Islamic fundamentalism—despite her own struggles with mental illness.

Mailer had to make do on April 30, 1971, with braying and snorting at Jacqueline Caballos, the president of the New York chapter of NOW; Germaine Greer, the author of *The Female Eunuch* (1970), who said that Sylvia Plath, trying to be a poet as well as a housewife, "was such a perfectionist and ultimately such a fool"; Jill Johnston, who stated that "all women are lesbians except those who don't know it"; and the literary critic Diana Trilling, who judiciously asserted that Mailer had failed to imagine "the full humanity of women" and yet she "would gladly take even Mailer's poeticized biology in preference to the no biology at all of my spirited sisters."[25]

In *The Prisoner of Sex* (1971), Mailer's rants against contraception, masturbation, clitoral orgasm, and homosexuality repeatedly excoriate Kate Millett while defending Henry Miller, D. H. Lawrence, and most especially Mailer himself. Irving Howe, who also attacked Millett, argued that *Sexual Politics* was a "vulgarized form" of *The Second Sex* that sounds as if it were "written by a female impersonator."[26] But in his own fashion Gore Vidal came to Millett's defense, in a review of Eva Figes's *Patriarchal Attitudes* (1970). Mailer's tirades, Vidal declared, "read like three days of menstrual flow." In fact, he argued that "the Miller-Mailer-Manson man (M3 for short)" is on the defensive about "girls" like Figes and Millett who threaten M3's "tribal past."[27]

At the free-for-all in the town hall meeting, the boos of the audience failed to inhibit Mailer's braggadocio. Audience members Betty Friedan, Elizabeth Hardwick, Susan Sontag, and Cynthia Ozick rose to defend the feminists on the panel and to question his cocky performance. When Sontag got the mike, she wanted to pose "a very quiet question to Norman" and then queried his use of the word "lady," which she found patronizing. "I don't like being called a lady writer," she said quietly. Ozick prefaced her question by explaining that she had a fantasy of putting it to Mailer ever since she read his *Advertisements for Myself*, where he stated that "a good novelist can do without everything but the remnant of his balls": "For years and years," Ozick mused, "I have been wondering, Mr. Mailer, when you dip your balls in ink, what color is it?"[28]

By the end of the seventies, Kate Millett had come to see the situation of the "second sex" as almost inevitably deadly. In her 1979 book *The Basement*, she agonized about "a human sacrifice": 16-year-old Sylvia Likens, whose torture and murder she had been brooding on since 1965, when the crime took place.[29] A lively teenager, Sylvia had been left, along with a crippled younger sister, in the Indianapolis home of the ultimate sadistic babysitter, one Gertrude Baniszewski, by her father, a traveling circus roustabout. Baniszewski had seven children of her own, most of whom were pressed into service torturing Sylvia, who was ultimately bound, gagged, and left to die in the family basement, with more than 150 wounds on her naked body. Though she screamed, neighbors didn't respond. In the end, malnourished and deprived of water, she chewed through her own lips.

Reviewing Millett's painful meditation in the *New York Times*, Joyce Carol Oates coolly commented that

> Miss Millett's identification with the murdered girl is extraordinary, and one can only respect, if not fully comprehend, the depth of its power: "I was Sylvia Likens. She was me." Elsewhere, as part of a long, reasoned, admirably sustained meditation on the historical fate of women in general (which includes a discussion of clitoridectomy and other genital mutilations still practiced today), [Millett] comes to the conclusion: "To be feminine, then, is to die."[30]

One wonders, Is this what the arguments of *Sexual Politics* had to come to? To be female is to die? Despite the measured tones of Joyce

Carol Oates's review, in 1970 she had published the brilliant story "Where Are You Going, Where Have You Been?" about a young girl who implicitly accepts the decree that to be feminine is to die.

SUSAN SONTAG AS FEMINIST PHILOSOPHER

Ten years before Millett produced *The Basement*, Susan Sontag included "The Pornographic Imagination," in *Styles of Radical Will*, one of her books. Here, meditating on "Pauline Réage's" sadomasochistic *The Story of O*—in which a chained and naked young woman whose name is merely O, a null or a hole, willingly acquiesces to a variety of tortures—Sontag appeared to celebrate exactly the female sexual degradation that horrified Millett. Rather than a hapless victim, she argues, "O is an adept . . . grateful to be initiated into a mystery [that] is the loss of self."[31] Moreover, though she seems passive, she is active; her entrance into mystery is also an entrance into mastery:

> O learns, she suffers, she changes. . . . The plot's movement is not horizontal, but a kind of ascent through degradation. . . . O's quest is neatly summed up in the expressive letter which serves her for a name. "O" suggests a cartoon of her sex, not her individual sex but simply woman; it also stands for a nothing. But what *Story of O* unfolds is a spiritual paradox, that of the full void and of the vacuity that is also a plenum.[32]

Sontag's language verges on the mystical. But most feminists would have none of it—especially Susan Griffin, who declared that although Sontag "defends *The Story of O* not only as art but as an extension of consciousness," consciousness in this novel "extends ultimately only into its own annihilation."[33]And of course, unlike *The Basement*, "Réage's" story is not grounded in reality but is embedded in a fever dream of eroticism: it first took shape when the real "Réage"—a young French intellectual named Anne Desclos—wrote a series of sexual letters to titillate the imagination of her lover Jean Paulhan. It is hard to believe that Sontag would have been so enthusiastic about *The Story of O* if she thought the work had its origin in living flesh rather than fantastic imagery.

In fact, a crucial sentence in Sontag's meditation on the book hints at a turn her thinking would take in the early seventies: " 'O' suggests a cartoon of her sex, not her individual sex but simply woman; it also stands for a nothing." As if Sontag were haunted by this notion, in feminist essays published in 1972, 1973, and 1975 she sought to dismantle the notion of woman as null, submissive, and irrational.

The first of these pieces, "The Double Standard of Aging," focuses on the terrible truth that aging female bodies are considered "obscene," whereas older men are viewed as powerful, even virile. Old women are witches, older men are tribal leaders. The "rules of this society are cruel to women. Brought up to be never fully adult, women are deemed obsolete earlier than men." Moreover, Sontag goes on to observe, femininity is performative: to "be a woman is to be an actress. Being feminine is a kind of theater, with its appropriate costumes, *décor*, lighting, and stylized gestures." Thus, "from early childhood on, girls are trained to care in a pathologically exaggerated way about their appearance."[34] Trained, in other words, to be the null O, who is merely a decorated body.

But women's thralldom to the body is even more problematic than the performativity in which girls are trained. For, notes Sontag in "A Woman's Beauty: Put-Down or Power Source?," "Women

are taught to see their bodies in *parts*, and to evaluate each part separately. Breasts, feet, hips, waistline, neck, eyes, nose, complexion,
hair, and so on—each in turn is submitted to an anxious, fretful, often
despairing scrutiny." Her vision here suggests that women are taught
to subject themselves to an almost Picasso-esque fragmentation, by
which body parts are moved around according to the ways that their
beauties are prioritized. No wonder, then, that Sontag dryly comments, "To preen, for a woman, can never be just a pleasure. It is also
a duty. It is her work." Indeed, she concludes, "One could hardly ask
for more important evidence of the dangers of considering persons as
split between what is 'inside' and what is 'outside' than that intermi-
nable, half-comic half-tragic tale, the oppression of women."[35]

In "The Third World of Women," Sontag's major feminist
essay of this period, the oppression of women is no longer dismissed
as "half-comic half-tragic." Responding to a questionnaire from
the editors of *Libre*, a Spanish-language, loosely Marxist journal,
Sontag—who was often identified as an *anti*-feminist—outlined radically subversive, feminist views of what, like Millett, she defined as
a patriarchal culture. Her central thesis: the "oppression of women
constitutes the most fundamental type of repression in organized
societies. That is, it is the most *ancient* form of oppression, pre-dating
all oppression based on class, caste, and race. It is the most primitive
form of hierarchy."[36]

The substance of the piece then elaborates on the consequences
of this primordial oppression, as Sontag ranges from cultural practices to the "grammar of family life" to grammar itself. "The 'femininity' of women and the 'masculinity' of men are morally defective
and historically obsolete conceptions," she argues, adding that the
"liberation of women seems to me as much a historical necessity as
the abolition of slavery"—indeed, "even more momentous than abo-

lition in its psychic and historical consequences." As for the linguistic fate of women, she points out that "grammar, the ultimate arena of sexist brainwashing, conceals the very existence of women. . . . Thus we *must* say 'he' when we mean a person who might be of either sex. 'Man' is the accepted way to refer to all human beings; 'men' is the literary way of saying people."[37]

On the fundamental organization of society, she notes that the "modern 'nuclear' family is a psychological and moral disaster. It is a prison of sexual repression, a playing-field of inconsistent moral laxity, a museum of possessiveness, a guilt-producing factory, and a school of selfishness." On the basis of these premises, she formulates a series of radical prescriptions for social change, significantly akin to those ideas put forward by equally radical thinkers more usually associated with the women's movement. First, "the only sexual ethic liberating for women is one which challenges the primacy of genital heterosexuality."[38] Second, the

women's movement must lead to a critical assault on the very nature of the state—the millennial tyranny of patriarchal rule being the low-keyed model of the peculiarly modern tyranny of the fascist state. . . . Fascism, in other words, is the natural development of the values of the patriarchal state applied to the conditions (and contradictions) of twentieth-century "mass" societies. Virginia Woolf was altogether correct when she declared in the late 1930s, in a remarkable tract called *Three Guineas*, that the fight to liberate women is a fight against fascism.[39]

Finally, in a dazzling and sometimes sardonic riff on what women should do, and how, Sontag stipulated a series of large and small actions that women should take in the battle against oppression.

Only groups composed entirely of women will be diversified enough in their tactics, and sufficiently "extreme." Women should lobby, demonstrate, march. They should take karate lessons. They should whistle at men in the streets, raid beauty parlors, picket toy manufacturers who produce sexist toys, convert in sizable numbers to militant lesbianism, operate their own free psychiatric and abortion clinics, provide feminist divorce counselling, establish make-up withdrawal centers, adopt their mothers' family names as their last names, deface billboard advertising that insults women, disrupt public events by singing in honor of the docile wives of male celebrities and politicians, collect pledges to renounce alimony and giggling, bring lawsuits for defamation against the mass-circulation "women's magazines," conduct telephone harassment campaigns against male psychiatrists who have sexual relations with their women patients, organize beauty contests for men, put up feminist candidates for all public offices.[40]

"You . . . are precisely a liberated woman," the editors of *Libre* remarked in the questionnaire that they addressed to Sontag, to which she rather ironically replied, "I would never describe myself as a liberated woman. Of course, things are never as simple as *that*. But I have always been a feminist."[41]

But had she? Decades of commentary on her work defined her as either indifferent to feminism or as anti-feminist. And interestingly, the feminist essays we've been discussing never appeared in any of her collections. Instead, they are relegated to "Uncollected Essays," a section at the back of the Library of America's 2013 volume of her essays of the 1960s and 1970s, edited by her son, David Rieff.[42]

One major feminist who found Sontag's commitment to the

movement disappointing was Adrienne Rich, who in 1975 addressed a critical letter to the *New York Review of Books* about Sontag's sophisticated, nuanced (and hostile) discussion of Leni Riefenstahl in "Fascinating Fascism." How, Rich wondered, did the "same mind" produce "this brilliant essay" and the "equally brilliant essay" on "The Third World of Women"? Responded Sontag, "Easy. By addressing itself to a different problem, with the intention of making a different point."[43] But why didn't Sontag note the profound misogyny animating Nazism? (That she had done so in "The Third World" doesn't seem to have mattered.)

"The feminist movement," wrote Rich, "has always been passionately anti-hierarchical and anti-authoritarian." Feminists have also been "justly alert to and critical of women who have 'made it' in the patriarchy"—a definition that paradoxically could have described not only Riefenstahl and Sontag but Rich herself. In a magisterial tone, Sontag observed that "I would assume that Riefenstahl offends some feminists (though I wish it were for a better reason than her being on that ominous-sounding enemies list, 'male-identified "successful" women')." Furthermore, she added, if Rich "is going to start baiting that heavy bear, the intellect, then I feel obliged to announce that anyone with a taste for 'intellectual exercise' will always find in me an ardent defender."

Point, set, and match. But perhaps not. According to Rich's biographer Hilary Holladay, the two women decided to meet and talk in person following this in-print debate. At Sontag's apartment they "started out talking and ended up making love."[44] At the same time, Sontag's biographer Benjamin Moser notes that "Sontag's attack on Rich alienated many feminists, who would never consider her one of their own: a breach that may explain why Sontag's own feminist writings were mothballed." Moser attributes her public disavowals of feminism and lesbianism to her ambition to serve "as a universal arbiter" of culture: "To be known as a feminist, much less as a lesbian, would have pushed her to the margins."[45] But perhaps Sontag's evasiveness about feminism and lesbianism, her intellectual arrogance, her grandiosity both on and off the page, arose from wounds that she could never acknowledge.

In a sardonic elegy for her, the literary critic Terry Castle proclaimed in the *London Review of Books* that she was "sibylline and hokey and often a great bore," though she was "a troubled and brilliant American."[46] More poignantly, in Sigrid Nunez's memoir *Sempre Susan*, we see the author of *Against Interpretation* in the flesh, living in a cockroach-haunted apartment on the Upper West Side, unable to stop smoking, fearful of being alone, acting as a kind of theatrical mother-in-law to Nunez, who was also living in the apartment and dating David Rieff.[47] Life, even the life of the intellect and of underground feminism, can be strange.

Very few feminists in the seventies knew about Sontag's radically feminist essays. Certainly, we did not. We discovered them only in the process of composing this book, some four decades after they appeared. And of course, Sontag defined herself primarily as a creative writer rather than an essayist, as the author of novels, plays, and screenplays, few of which appealed to the elite audiences that adored her as "the Dark Lady" of American letters.

BEST SELLERS IN THE WOMANHOUSE: FROM TONI MORRISON TO MARILYN FRENCH

While Sontag's creative works rarely received the acclaim she thought they deserved, a number of her contemporaries were quite successful in producing feminist fiction that captivated readers. In novels pub-

lished throughout the seventies, writers of Sontag's generation countered Miller's and Mailer's suppositions about compliant bimbos by
illuminating Kate Millett's concept of "the interiorization of patriarchal ideology" and Sontag's thesis about "sexist brainwashing," both
of which explain young women's submission to dysfunctional societal institutions. They take as their subject a process of socialization
detrimental to their characters' well-being: their induction into femininity. Toni Morrison, Alix Kates Shulman, Erica Jong, Rita Mae
Brown, Margaret Atwood, and Marilyn French portrayed female
lives deformed by mind-sets destructive to women's full humanity.[48]

Dense with details about the indignities of growing up female,
feminist fiction in the seventies describes the secrecy around the
onset of menstruation, the furtive discovery of clitoral masturbation, the first (generally unsatisfactory) experience of heterosexual
intercourse, the shame inculcated by a sexual double standard, the
overvaluation of love and of male protection, and an all-pervasive
fetishization of the female body as well sexual harassment, illegal
abortion, domestic abuse, and rape. Heterosexuality, the institution
of marriage, and the nuclear family are presented as blighting the
lives of girls and women.

There can be no more poignant rape victim than 11-year-old
Pecola Breedlove in Toni Morrison's eloquent first novel, *The Bluest Eye* (1970), who—even before an incestuous act of violence—is
undone by her internalization of white standards of beauty. Convinced that she is unlovable, enthralled by pictures of blue-eyed Shirley Temple, Pecola grows up trying "to discover the secret of [her]
ugliness" and praying for *"pretty blue eyes."*[49] Her mother, Mrs. Breedlove, had also been corrupted by one of "the most destructive ideas in
the history of human thought": the assumption that (white-defined)
physical beauty is a virtue.[50] Pregnant at a movie theater, she had

curled her hair *"almost just like"* Jean Harlow's when a bite of candy pulled a tooth out of her mouth. At that moment, she *"settled down to just being ugly"* and eventually gave birth to a daughter with a *"Head full of pretty hair, but Lord she was ugly."*[51]

Toni Morrison composed her first novel while she was working for Random House and raising her two sons. She had been brought up in Lorrain, Ohio, by parents who "assumed that black people were the humans of the globe; but had serious doubts about the quality and existence of white humanity": "So I grew up in a basically racist household," she explained, "with more than a child's share of contempt for white people."[52] Such a view must have been strengthened when a landlord once set the family's house on fire to force them to leave, although her hardworking father put out the flames and refused to leave.

Only at Howard University, where she began to study literature, did she change her name from Chloe Anthony Wofford to Toni Wofford. After writing a master's thesis at Cornell on the works of William Faulkner and Virginia Woolf, she married and divorced the Jamaican architect Harold Morrison, hinting that she objected to his conventional notions of marriage. She wrote *The Bluest Eye* in part to examine the motto of the civil rights and Black power movements: "Black is beautiful."

Sweetly sickening and addictive, white-defined ideals of feminine beauty explain why the Breedlove family in *The Bluest Eye* sport the maiden name of the millionaire Madam C. J. Walker, who produced hair-straightening and skin-lightening products, and why Pecola's first name recalls Peola, the daughter torn between her lauded white appearance and her scorned Black identity in Fanny Hurst's novel *Imitation of Life*.[53] Morrison pointedly depicts other female characters who haven't been tainted by an overvaluation of white standards of attractiveness, but gullible Pecola plummets into madness in part because "adults, older girls, shops, magazines, newspapers, window signs—all the world had agreed that a blue-eyed, yellow-haired, pink-skinned doll was what every girl child treasured."[54]

What pushes Pecola into schizophrenia, however, is the evil act of a man himself victimized by racism. Pecola's father, Cholly, had been violated as a boy by white men who surprised him in an earnest first attempt at lovemaking by "shining a flashlight right on his behind" and goading him, "nigger," to "make it good": Cholly was not old enough to hate the white men so instead "he hated, despised the girl" who "bore witness to his failure, his impotence." Yet even in the act of raping his daughter, her misery kindles his need to protect her and this "confused mixture" leads him "to fuck her—tenderly." Despite the horror of the rape, one of the narrators of *The Bluest Eye* believes that Cholly "was the one who loved [Pecola] enough to touch her," though "his touch was fatal."[55]

Such a cursory summary of the central plot of *The Bluest Eye* does not do justice to its aesthetic power, but it does illuminate its analysis of a beauty myth that affects Blacks and whites differently. Morrison's insight into that disparity surfaced in an essay on women's liberation published a year after *The Bluest Eye*. As she considered the segregation signs common in the South, Morrison found one type oddly reassuring. To her mind, "White Ladies" and "Colored Women" properly labeled white females as soft, helpless, and dependent, in comparison to their Black counterparts who "were tough, capable, independent."[56]

The novels of Alix Kates Shulman and Erica Jong tackle a feminine dependence on men, shaped by the training of "White Ladies," that has no place in *The Bluest Eye*. In *Memoirs of an Ex-Prom Queen* (1972), Shulman links an overemphasis on good looks with her heroine's single-minded determination to attract men. To Sasha Davis, "being beautiful mattered so much that I always suspected I was just passing my prime." Schoolyard bullies—she accepts "the boy's hatred of us as 'normal'"—cause her to focus her attention on an appearance that will attract male protection, though she fears being labeled a slut. Sasha absorbs the shock of "bleeding *down there*"; the shame of discovering a "joy button" that no one else apparently has or has named; the attacks of boys who abduct her into the woods and, like her boyfriends, *"always go as far as they can"*; the frustrating contrast between the pleasure of petting and the nonevent of penetration; and the putdowns of envious sorority sisters who confirm her belief that *"Surely I must be beautiful."*[57]

The insecurity generated by these events convinces Shulman's heroine that she remains "worthless without a man." In college, predictably, Sasha's love of philosophy gets channeled into her seduction of a 43-year-old married-with-children philosophy professor. When he jerks out of her to come in her mouth, she considers it "an honor," though his wife soon intervenes with the information that he has had a succession of youthful playmates.[58] Instead of Prince Charmings, real-life husbands arrive to prove to Sasha that marriage is no happily-ever-after.[59]

Shulman's self-destructively licentious heroine resembles the ribald central character in Erica Jong's *Fear of Flying* (1973). Isadora Wing's frankness about orgasm, oral sex, threesomes, and the messiness of dealing with menstrual blood without a tampon earned the accolades of Henry Miller and John Updike, while other reviewers castigated the novel's vulgarity.[60] Yet Jong agreed with Morrison that "Black women were at least a century ahead of white women in banishing the slave in the self,"[61] and also with Shulman that the crucial problem of white women hinges on their dependence upon men. (In the first wave, the turn-of-the-century South African feminist Olive Schreiner called this problem "sexual parasitism.")[62]

Lusty Isadora Wing finds herself tormented by a need for sta-
bility, on the one hand, and a desire for adventure, on the other;
however, she associates both options with men: security with her
staid Freudian psychoanalyst-husband Bennett and freedom with her
hippy Laingian psychoanalyst-lover Adrian Goodlove. No wonder,
since she has been "brainwashed," as are all girls who grew up with
"cosmetic ads, love songs, advice columns, whoreoscopes, Hollywood gossip": "you longed to be annihilated by love, to be swept off
your feet, to be filled up by a giant prick spouting sperm, soapsuds,
silks and satins, and of course, money." Isadora nevertheless defines
herself as a feminist because she wants to be a poet, not a typist: "the
big problem was how to make your feminism jibe with your unap-
peasable hunger for male bodies."[63]

Resisting taboos against bawdy women, Isadora Wing realizes
that all her ideas about orgasm are suspect, coming as they do from
Freud and D. H. Lawrence. She looks in vain for a woman writer
"who had juice and joy and love and talent," finding only Colette
and the shadowy Sappho. Through her heroine's fantasies, Jong made
her name as a juicy writer extolling "the Zipless Fuck." Impersonal,
fleeting, no strings attached, the satisfactions of the zipless fuck seem
related to the independence Isadora seeks in her sensual poetry and
in her adultery with Adrian. But when Isadora goes on a hot road trip
with him—"for the first time in my life, I live out my fantasy"—he
"goes limp as a water-logged noodle and refuses me." Although men
"wanted their women wild," when "women were finally learning to
be wanton and wild," the "men wilted."[64]

The discrepancy between fantasy and reality is pointedly emphasized at the end of *Fear of Flying*. After Isadora resists the Freudian
psychobabble of her husband and the existentialist sermons of her
lover, a stranger does try to push his hand between her legs in an

empty train compartment, only to elicit her outrage. Isadora ends up submerged in her absent husband's hotel bathtub, not knowing whether her story will end in love, as it would in the nineteenth century, or in divorce, as it would in the twentieth. The indeterminate ending of *Fear of Flying* involved lots of outtakes, Jong has explained. "In one, Isadora writes long letters, à la Herzog, to Freud, to Colette, to Simone de Beauvoir, to Doris Lessing, to Emily Dickinson. In another, she dies of a botched abortion. In another, she blows off Bennett and goes to Walden Pond to live alone in the woods. In another, she promises eternal slavery, and he takes her back."[65] Instead, Jong leaves Isadora Wing—unable yet to fly away—submerged in the waters of a potential rebirth.

Shulman and Jong clearly ridicule the victimization of their heroines. In this respect, they put the lie to Joan Didion's condemnation of "the coarsening of [the] moral imagination" in feminist thinking. In a 1975 essay, "The Women's Movement," Didion sneered at the "Everywoman" of feminists who is "everyone's victim but her own: She was persecuted even by her gynecologist, . . . raped by her husband, and raped finally on the abortionist's table."[66] With a heroine who refuses victimhood, Rita Mae Brown deplored not female dependence upon men but the heterosexual script upon which that dependence was built. Molly Bolt's good looks, insatiable desire for lots of sex, and indomitable spirit empower her to defy her mother's prejudice—the mother is generally a regressive agent of socialization in these novels—in *Rubyfruit Jungle* (1973).

Rita Mae Brown's landmark novel, which was turned down by all the agents and publishers she approached, found its way into print through the small feminist publishing house Daughters, Inc. When they "couldn't keep up with the demand," the novel was sold to Bantam Books, and to Brown's shock she received a check for $125,000.

She also got "notoriety, a ton of hate mail, numerous threats on my life including two bomb threats, increased outrage from the conservative wing of the feminist movement and scorn from the radical dykes": "Straight people were mad because I was gay. The dykes were mad because I wasn't gay enough."[67]

While the inquisitive, racially ambiguous, and illegitimate Molly Bolt experiments throughout *Rubyfruit Jungle* with all sorts of polymorphous couplings, Brown explodes the idea—inherited from Radclyffe Hall's resonantly titled *The Well of Loneliness* (1928)—that lesbians are freaks doomed to a miserable fate. She does so by satirizing the Freudian idea that buttresses such a plot. Never a male wannabe, Molly reacts to the sight of a childhood friend's penis not with envy but with an entrepreneurial scheme to make money by charging neighborhood kids for a good look.[68] From a young age, Molly—disdaining Shirley Temple dolls and experimenting by kissing girls as well as boys—determines to do exactly as she pleases: "Why does everyone have to put you in a box and nail the lid on it?"[69]

The straight people Molly goes on to encounter in college and later in New York City assume that lesbians are sick or that they must relinquish an immature form of eroticism. Yet their own heterosexuality—like that of the man who "gets his kicks out of being blasted with grapefruits"—is portrayed as downright kinky.[70] The gay scene offers its own problematic boxes for people divided into butches and femmes: Molly scoffs, "What's the point of being a lesbian if a woman is going to look and act like an imitation man?" At the end of the novel, she manages to complete a degree in film and make peace with her mother. Nonetheless, she notes the prosperity of male peers—who specialize in pornography—while she herself is offered a job as a secretary.[71]

Margaret Atwood extends her contemporaries' attacks on fairy tales, romantic movies, Hollywood idols, and pornography in *Lady Oracle* (1976). Atwood's humorous metafiction takes aim at thin heroines and stories that ultimately fail to starve her escape artist into anorexic submission. Resisting a skinny, tyrannical mother (who ices a cake for her daughter with Ex-Lax), Joan Foster finds herself in the grip of what has come to be called *matrophobia*, a fear and hatred of the mother that leads her to consume huge amounts of food. At first Joan's "jiggly thighs" and "bulges of fat" debar her from performing the role of butterfly in a dance recital: "who would think of marrying a mothball?" she frets. By 15, however, she feels a "morose pleasure" when everyone looks away from her 245-pound figure.[72] Girth lends her invisibility and protection from male harassment. She starts to fantasize about an exhibitionist Fat Lady walking skillfully on a high wire—wearing pink tights, a sparkling tiara, and satin slippers, and carrying a diminutive pink umbrella.

We are what we eat, but also what we read and write. After Joan loses weight to gain an inheritance, she embarks on a series of relationships with men, all of whom seem seductively Byronic to her, but all of whom turn out to lead dreary pedestrian lives. Joan hardly notices, because she is juggling the impostures that fund her life with them: her secret identities as the mystic poet of a successful book of verse, *Lady Oracle*, and as the romance writer of lucrative costume gothics. In sharp contrast to the Fat Lady, both these thin avatars of Joan are tangled in stories of feminine victimization.

Joan, the photographed poetess, is haunted by the tragic fate of female artists in legends: the Lady of Shalott, who leaves her weaving to die in the real world, and the dancer in *The Red Shoes*, who is "torn between her career and her husband" and whose shoes end up dancing her into an oncoming train. "All my life I'd been hooked on plots," Joan realizes, in which "you could sing and dance or you could be happy, but not both."[73] The author of costume gothics fares no better than the poet, for her commercially successful stories reward persecuted heroines with happy endings. Her fearful central characters trespass into grim ancestral mansions while competing with ravenous wives and confronting heroes who might just be nefarious villains. In the interpolated passages from *Stalked by Love* upon which Joan works throughout the novel, the wife Felicia is supposed to die so her successor Charlotte can rest her throbbing breast against the chest of the equivocal master of the mansion.

As Joan fragments under the stress of her multiple identities—wife, mistress, celebrity poetess, Harlequin author—even her daydreams about the Fat Lady turn sinister. But after a fake suicide lands her safely out of Canada, Joan returns to the Fat Lady and also to the standard gothic plot: "I was getting tired of Charlotte, with her intact virtue and tidy ways. Wearing her was like wearing a hair shirt, she made me itchy. Even her terrors were too pure, her faceless murderers, her corridors, her mazes and forbidden doors."[74] Joan needs to change the plot so that she can escape the pernicious influence of Charlotte Brontë.

When the main character appears in the last installment of *Stalked by Love*, it is the wife Felicia, not the virginal Charlotte, who walks deep into the maze to arrive "in the central plot" where four women sit on a bench. All identify themselves as Lady Redmond, including the Fat Lady. Her various avatars, Joan realizes, have been trapped in an identical story, as the master appears either to whirl Felicia into the marriage plot or to kill her into the death plot, while Joan's act of revision suggests that the two stories might be identical, as they are in the Bluebeard tale that fascinated Atwood. If, as Oscar Wilde claimed, life tends to imitate art, then the only way to get a life liberated from the tyranny of romantic clichés is to engage in revisionary imaginative acts, a point brilliantly made by the British storyteller Angela Carter with her reworked fairy tales in *The Bloody Chamber* (1979).

Four years before *Lady Oracle*, Atwood had explored not only psychological but also national colonization in a novel about an unhinged character traumatized by the endings of her relationships with her parents and a partner. In *Surfacing* (1972), the nameless heroine travels north into the Canadian wilderness with a new boyfriend as well as a couple who dramatize the sadomasochistic heterosexuality that Atwood anatomized in her verse: "you fit into me / like a hook into an eye // a fish hook / an open eye."[75] The suicidal heroine searches her parents' lakeside cottage and her own memories to confront the injuries that have devastated her.

Repelled by the pollution of the wilderness, she swims toward the lake bottom, looking for the Native cliff drawings that her father had been photographing before he disappeared. Coming upon not a painting or a rock but "a dead thing," she associates the body (probably that of her father) with something "in a bottle curled up, staring out at me like a cat pickled. . . . Whatever it is, part of myself or a separate creature, I killed it. It wasn't a child, but it could have been one." Previous tales about a lost marriage had been a smokescreen for this other loss of an aborted fetus, which alienated her from her parents and from the unborn baby's father. Feeling contaminated by the destructiveness of the colonizers she calls "Americans," the narrator determines to divorce herself from the human world, the realm of "men and women both."[76]

Before Atwood's heroine sets out to get in touch with the sacred gods and animals of nature, she uses her boyfriend to inseminate herself: she can feel her lost child "surfacing within me, forgiving me, rising from the lake where it has been prisoned for so long." In and around the cottage, she goes about destroying vestiges of culture: rolls of film, her own illustrations of fairy tales, her parents' maps, albums, plates; she makes a lair, and lives on remnants from the garden. The attempt to shed false selves and regain a primeval animal self is of course doomed to failure; however, she experiences a succession of visions that lead her to conclude that she has one overarching responsibility: "This above all, to refuse to be a victim"—which in part involves recanting "the old belief that I am powerless."[77] Spare as a fable about an anonymous everywoman, *Surfacing* speaks for all the seventies heroines who struggle to shatter the stale conventions of the past and seek rebirth into wilder forms of being.

The starkness of *Surfacing* contrasts with the broad historical sweep of *The Women's Room*, which made a splash when it hit the best-seller list in 1977. Yet Marilyn French also presented a pessimistic view of "men and women both." The first half of her novel reads like a depressing confirmation of Betty Friedan's insights into fifties domesticity.[78] All the wives suffer the misery of dependence on men who might work, or not; who might drink, or not; but "you're no one without them." Married to (the properly named) Norm, French's heroine Mira—who sardonically thinks of herself as Mrs. Perfect Norm—finds herself "sick unto death of four thousand years of males telling me how rotten my sex is. Especially it makes me sick when I look round and see such rotten men and such magnificent women, all of whom have a sneaking suspicion that the four thousand years of remarks are correct."[79]

But in the second part of the novel, about the sixties, feminism fails to save most of French's characters. Its most important advocate, the divorce survivor Val, has given over hating her husband or "any of them. They can't help it: they're trained to be bastards." After her teenage daughter is raped, though, Val slips into vitriol as she argues that "in their relations with women, all men are rapists, and that's all they are. They rape us with their eyes, their laws, and their codes."[80] *The Woman's Room* quickly became a symbol of feminism, though it was greeted with ambivalence by many feminists.[81]

Still, its desolation reflects the uncertainty of the other seventies heroines who find themselves at the end of their stories wandering between two worlds, one dead and the other struggling to be born. The landscapes they inhabit resemble the rooms in *The Womanhouse* installation that Judy Chicago and Miriam Shapiro created in 1972 in an old mansion in Hollywood: the Menstruation Bathroom with its trash can overflowing with used tampons, the Dollhouse with its miniature interiors filled with hidden monsters, the Nurturing Kitchen with its eggs and breasts covering the walls and ceilings, and especially the Bridal Staircase with a life-size doll fixed on a landing in full regalia.[82]

Reading many of these novels while we were working on *The Madwoman in the Attic*, we were astonished how they highlighted the more submerged protests voiced by Jane Austen, Charlotte Brontë, and Elizabeth Barrett Browning. But unlike many of the central characters of Austen, Brontë, and Barrett Browning, the heroines of feminist fiction do not end up living happily ever after in committed heterosexual relationships. Maddened, unhappily married, divorced, or single, they offered their authors the opportunity to evaluate the institution of marriage during a period when divorce rates surged at least in part because the traditional relationship between the sexes was being so defiantly attacked by feminists.[83]

PLATH'S ELECTRIC TAKE ON THE FIFTIES

One of the most widely read novels of this decade was a critique of traditional American femininity, whose contradictions drive its depressed protagonist/narrator to madness—and a suicide attempt. Sylvia Plath's *The Bell Jar* was first published in London in 1963, under the pseudonym Victoria Lucas, less than a month before its author's suicide. After her death, both her husband and her mother hesitated to let it appear under her own name in England, and were even more anxious about letting it appear in the United States. Finally, in 1971, the novel came out in America, to mixed reviews but also to eager readers, many of whom were aware that the plot of the work followed the grievous arc of Plath's own history while also foreshadowing her grim future.

For a long time, Plath had hoped to write a novel in a "fresh brazen colloquial voice," like Joyce Cary or, as it ultimately turned out, J. D. Salinger.[84] And certainly her narrator, Esther Greenwood, has just the sardonic perspective on the world that Holden Caulfield has. But even darker: without Holden's contempt for "phonies," Esther is bizarrely alienated from the culture that has shaped her as she drifts toward self-immolation. The first paragraph of the book sets its tone: "It was a queer, sultry summer, the summer they electrocuted the Rosenbergs, and I didn't know what I was doing in New York." (Esther was in New York, of course, because, like Plath herself, she had won a guest editorship at a young women's magazine.) But even before she begins to explain what she's doing in New York, Esther continues to obsess about the Rosenbergs: "The idea of being electrocuted makes me sick, and that's all there was to read about in the papers. . . . I kept hearing about the Rosenbergs over the radio. . . . I knew something was wrong with me that summer because all I could think about was the Rosenbergs and how stupid I'd been to buy all those uncomfortable expensive clothes, hanging limp as fish in my closet."[85]

Esther's obsession with the Rosenbergs isn't surprising. She is beginning a sort of novel/memoir about the fifties, with all that decade's McCarthyism and anti-Semitism—an anti-Semitism promoted even by the Jewish lawyer Roy Cohn, the prosecutor who sought the death sentence for the Rosenbergs and who was later to become Donald Trump's personal fixer. Ethel Rosenberg's electrocution was especially scandalous since there was little evidence that she had participated in the espionage engineered by her brother and her husband, so she is even more important to Plath. Her electrocution introduces a theme that is central to the *Bell Jar*: the dangerous misuse of electric shock therapy, from Plath's point of view an analog of electrocution, from which she herself was to suffer in 1953.

Esther's adventures during what ought to have been a triumphant month in New York are all misadventures. She admires the managing editor for whom she is interning, deeming that Jay Cee "had brains"—but is put off by the editor's "plug-ugly" looks. Among her sister guest editors, she is drawn to two opposites: the rebel Doreen and the all-American Betsy, whom Doreen labels "Pollyanna Cowgirl."[86] Together with her widowed mother—a teacher of shorthand and typing, who urges Esther to learn the same skills—these figures might seem to represent different facets of herself or different roles she vaguely aspires to. But at the same time, none is adequate to her secretly stirring ambitions. In fact, together they are imprisoned in a world that is literally poisonous. All the guest editors—except, tellingly, for Doreen—are felled by food poisoning at a luncheon hosted by the magazine *Lady's Day*. How did Doreen survive? By skipping what was meant to be a treat. But she too had earlier vomited and passed out from too much alcohol, supplied her by a freewheeling DJ she picked up in a taxi.

Nor are the men Esther encounters adequate to her desires. Her high school boyfriend, Buddy Willard, is as bourgeois as her mother, and his mother is even more culture-bound. Mrs. Willard strives to marry Buddy to Esther while also urging Esther to become a cookie-cutter cookie-baking fifties housewife. "What a man is is an arrow into the future," Mrs. W. opines, "and what a woman is is the place the arrow shoots off from." But what Esther wants is to be herself an arrow into the future. In any case, Buddy doesn't present her with anything sexually attractive. When she finally gets a look at his genitalia, the first set of male reproductive organs she's ever seen, she likens them to "turkey neck and turkey gizzards."[87] As for the other men she gets involved with—a Peruvian who tries to rape her, a passive simultaneous translator, a math professor who deflowers her (and triggers a massive hemorrhage)—all have nothing to offer while embodying everything to fear.

Esther's anomie arguably signals the oncoming mental breakdown that will require shock treatments and hospitalization in the second half of the novel. But it's also clearly a consequence of just the "normlessness" described by the sociologist Émile Durkheim in his famous study *Suicide* (1897). Such normlessness—a breakdown of previously agreed-on standards and values—increasingly characterized the smug culture of the fifties. Consider, after all, Esther's colleagues in New York, at home, and later in the mental hospital. Each represents an entirely different way of being. In a world that idealizes the Betsy types—and Betsy was eventually to become a cover girl—rebellious Doreen continues to flourish, and Esther's helicopter mother supports herself by teaching stenography at university, Mrs. Willard propounds the platitudes of *Good Housekeeping*, and Jay Cee is powerful but unattractive. All different, yet each in her way as compelling a cultural image as any of the others. No wonder Esther finds herself riveted by what she calls "the vision of the fig tree," in which she imagines herself sitting under a fig tree, whose fruits traditionally represent female vulvas and here symbolize the range of roles represented by the women around her; as she is unable to decide which fig to choose, each withers and falls to the ground.[88]

After she has sleepwalked through her month in New York, Esther throws away all her new fancy clothes—the costumes of fifties womanhood—and goes home to spend her days trying to kill herself, finally almost succeeding by swallowing a bottle of sleeping pills and entombing (or enwombing?) herself in her mother's basement. Not only has her "normless" month of anomie in New York driven her to this Grand Guignol gesture; her first encounter with electric shock therapy, badly misapplied, is a calamity prefigured by the horrifying fate of the Rosenbergs. In "Hanging Man," one of her *Ariel* poems, Plath was also to write about this experience: "By the roots of my hair some god got hold of me. / I sizzled in his blue volts like a desert prophet."[89]

When Plath wrote all this bleak stuff in the early sixties, she didn't name herself a feminist. Nonetheless, she and her work, both in prose and poetry, embodied what was to become seventies feminism: an alienation from the rigid female roles of the fifties, a nauseated response to sexuality—both virginity and its loss—and even a secret sense that, as in Millett's *The Basement*, "to be female is to die." By one of those quirks of fate out of which futures rise, Betty Friedan's *The Feminine Mystique* was published a month after *The Bell Jar* appeared in England in 1963, and a little more than a week after Plath killed herself. Both books can be said to struggle with what Friedan labeled "the problem that has no name,"[90] and together, along with Millett's *Sexual Politics*, they birthed seventies feminism, as did the compellingly tragic life story of Sylvia Plath.

When *The Bell Jar* appeared in the States, it was rightly seen as an analysis of just the fifties culture against which seventies feminists were rebelling. As in some story of time travel, Esther Greenwood herself might be seen as a seventies feminist, complete with ambition, anger, and an awakening consciousness, transplanted to the fifties. Together with such poems as "Daddy," which takes on the "marble-heavy" image of a patriarch, and "Lady Lazarus," which announces the rebirth of a fire-breathing woman, the novel names on every page the problem that has no name.

No wonder its publication, added to the mystery that continued to surround Plath's suicide, triggered a kind of literary riot. Robin Morgan's poem "Arraignment," appearing in 1972 in her first book, *Monster*, set the stage for feminist assaults on Ted Hughes, who was held accountable for his wife's death.

> How can
> I accuse
> Ted Hughes
> of what the entire British and American
> literary and critical establishment
> has been at great lengths to deny
> without ever saying it in so many words, of course:
> the murder of Sylvia Plath?[91]

Hughes declared that Morgan's poem was libelous and threatened to take her to court; his lawyers banned publication of the poem in the United Kingdom and elsewhere in the Commonwealth. But feminists in England, Canada, and Australia produced pirated editions of the book while others set to work "desecrating" (or, from their perspective, revising) the name on Plath's headstone: Sylvia Plath Hughes was repeatedly truncated to Sylvia Plath. Stones and shells from Devon that Ted Hughes had placed on the grave were regularly removed. Heated letters were exchanged in the pages of the *Guardian* and other papers.

Privately, Hughes said to a friend, "It doesn't fall to many men to murder a genius," adding, "I hear the wolves howling in the park"— Regents Park Zoo was near Plath's apartment, where he was living with their two children—"and it's very apt."[92] But in *Birthday Letters* (1998), the elegiac sequence of poems written to the ghost of Sylvia Plath, he chafed against the assaults of feminists who held him accountable for what had happened. One piece, in particular, dedicated to his children, expresses the sense of grievance he felt. Titled "The Dogs Are Eating Your Mother," the poem warns that it's "Too late / To salvage what she was," then describes how he and his children lovingly decorated her grave, before "a kind / of hyena" appeared to desecrate the spot, to "batten" on her body and "Bite the face off her gravestone."[93]

Lawyers and libel suits, riots and fierce retorts. When Hughes traveled to Australia for a poetry festival in 1976, he was met by women carrying a forest of signs that read "Murderer!" His response was to have a two-year-long affair with Jill Barber, his Australian hostess, while also bedding a number of other women. But he survived to become the Poet Laureate of England, to go fishing with the Queen Mother, and to have Prince Charles put up a sort of shrine to him in his royal household. In the meantime, Plath survived not only in her best-selling writings but in her material leavings: a hank of hair preserved in the Lilly Library at Indiana University, skirts and dresses recently auctioned off for large sums in London, and paper dolls also at Indiana.

In the 2015 poem "Self-Portrait with Sylvia Plath's Braid," Diane Seuss declares that Plath wielded her beauty like a weapon until her husband left her and when she took it up again it became "a word-weapon, / a poem-sword."[94] Seuss was working in a strain of verse about Plath established by writers from Erica Jong and Anne Sexton to Catherine Bowman. Jong's "Alcestis on the Poetry Circuit," which focuses on a female slave who beats herself "with the fine whip / of her own tongue," describes the fate awaiting such a creature:

If she's an artist
& comes close to genius,
the very fact of her gift
should cause her such pain
that she will take her own life
rather than best us.

& after she dies, we will cry
& make her a saint.[95]

Anne Sexton's "Sylvia's Death" mourns the loss of her friend but envies Plath's decision "to lie down . . . into the death I wanted so badly and for so long."[96] In the verse collection *The Plath Cabinet*, Catherine Bowman links the preserved lock of hair and the paper dolls to the airless cabinet in which women poets have been canonized. Plath's posthumous life has extended much longer than her lived life.[97]

For quite some time, Ted's sister Olwyn, a literary agent, acted as lioness at the gate of the Plath estate. Now Plath's daughter Frieda Hughes—the sole survivor of the little family, because Nicholas hanged himself in Alaska in 2009, at the age of 47—guards a treasure trove that has remained controversial.

Yet for some readers the fantasy that Plath has somehow survived is still hard to relinquish. Not that long ago, the *London Review of Books* published a review of the complete Plath letters, teased on its cover as "Sylvia Plath at 86." Its author, Joanna Biggs, concluded by imagining that

Sylvia Plath didn't die at all: she survived the winter of 1963 and she still lives in Fitzroy Road, having bought the whole building on the profits of *The Bell Jar* and *Doubletake*, her 1964 novel about "a wife whose husband turns out to be a deserter & philanderer although she had thought he was wonderful and perfect." She wears a lot of Eileen Fisher and sits in an armchair at the edge of Faber parties. . . . She is baffled by but interested in MeToo. . . . She stopped writing novels years ago, and writes her poems slowly now she has the Pulitzer, and the Booker, and the Nobel. She is too grand to approach, but while she's combing her white hair and you're putting on your lipstick in the loos, you smile at her shyly in the mirror[.][98]

6

Speculative Poetry, Speculative Fiction

A DECADE OF FERVENT ACTION, the seventies was also an era of intense speculation: speculation in the etymological sense of looking *at* things from a distanced, theoretical perspective and speculation in the fantasizing sense of *what if*—what if things were different, better, or (even) worse. In these years, while Adrienne Rich and other activists were writing a poetry of speculation, many of their colleagues began producing feminist science fiction that was more speculative than the hard-core work their male counterparts were publishing. Both in poetry and in fiction, aspirational women began examining and deploying the ancient genres of dystopia and utopia.

Though we wouldn't have said so at the time, it's no exaggeration to say that we suddenly understood ourselves to be living in a dystopia—that is, in the literal sense of the Greek term, in "a bad place." In a moment, in the blinking of an eye, everything that had once seemed "normal" and "normative" appeared fantastic. For women who came to feminism in the seventies, the history that we had been taught in school and that had seemed, though bloody, inevitable, was the history of a patriarchal system that—if you thought about it as had Kate Millett and Susan Sontag—was a nightmare from which we were trying to awake.

The cold hillside of the Cold War on which we awoke seemed to us as dystopian as the history we were trying to escape. While the Vietnam War raged on, while the conspiracies of Watergate unfolded in a country where most of the promising (male) leaders—JFK, MLK, RFK—had been assassinated, there were virtually no female leaders, certainly not at the national level. In 1970 there was one woman in the Senate (Margaret Chase Smith); there were a mere eleven women in the House of Representative (2.1 percent of the membership); and no women were on the Supreme Court. And in private life, women's bodies were sexualized as never before: micro-miniskirts left us unable to bend over at drinking fountains without exposing our underwear. Complemented by tights or knee-high boots, our daily dress made us look like the sexy aliens that male sci-fi writers had long fantasized as inhabitants of extraterrestrial worlds in which creatures gendered female existed only to serve and service men.

How had this happened? Most of us had never studied women's history. "History" was the chronicle of male heroes and villains, of wars and colonizations. When women were part of it, they existed as prizes, like Helen of Troy or Eva in Wagner's *Die Meistersinger*. "History," said Jane Austen's Catherine Morland in *Northanger Abbey*, a book we now read with revisionary fervor, "tells me nothing that does not either vex nor weary me. The quarrels of popes and kings, the men all so good for nothing, and hardly any women at all. It is very tiresome."[1]

We knew that there had been a suffrage movement, and that women got the vote only after the First World War. Most of us, though, didn't know that for centuries women couldn't own property, that their children "belonged" to their husbands, and that a husband could beat his wife with impunity using a "whip or rattan no bigger than [his] thumb in order to enforce . . . domestic discipline."[2] And on and on. What we hadn't known could, and eventually did, fill volumes of the women's history feminists were beginning to research.

But then, there was what we yearned for and longed to bring into being. A utopia, an ideal world of liberation and equality. A world in which the old imaginings of gender were understood to be what they really were—fictions. A world no longer shaped by "the quarrels of popes and kings" or of masculinist presidents and misogynistic dictators. A good world but, given the etymology of *utopia* (derived from the Greek *eu-topia*, "good place," and the Greek *ou-topia*, "no place"), a seemingly impossible world.

THE METAMORPHOSES OF ADRIENNE RICH

When Adrienne Rich thought back to the period that had transformed her life, love, and art, she wondered, "What is the connection between Vietnam and the lovers' bed? If this insane violence is being waged against a very small country by this large and powerful country in which I live, what does that have to do with sexuality and with what's going on between men and women, which I felt also as a struggle even then?"[3] For this always self-reflective poet, the turmoil of one revolutionary decade—the sixties—had engendered the transfigurations of what she experienced as an even more revolutionary decade: the seventies.

Metamorphosis would be at the root of her experience in these years. Like the feminist science fiction writers whose works we explore later in this chapter, she would find herself yearning to imagine a world "changed, changed utterly" (as Yeats wrote about an earlier rebellion) by insurrection.[4] For her, the awakenings that marked the cresting of feminism's second wave were simultaneously political, poetical, and personal. And they inspired a newly engaged speculative poetry that struggled against dystopias while imagining utopian revisions of culture.

Political: Rich's increasing commitment to public issues in this period has been widely documented. In 1966, she and Alfred Conrad moved to New York with their three young sons. Conrad had come to chair the economics department at City College; Rich taught for a while at Columbia and then joined the radical SEEK program, also at City, where she taught language arts mostly to underprivileged African American and Puerto Rican students. Both were involved in the civil rights and antiwar movements. Conrad, the coauthor of the groundbreaking article "The Economics of Slavery in the Antebellum South" (1958), was at least as outspoken in his rage against the "militarism, callousness, and the racism of this society" as Rich was in her increasingly polemical poems.[5]

Together the couple hosted gatherings of activists in their Central Park West apartment, and together, too, they participated in protests against the war in Vietnam. Conrad supported his wife's work in SEEK; he was "deeply impressed" with the "maturity and realism" of her students, Rich wrote to the poet Hayden Carruth, one of her principal confidants.[6] And Conrad's fierce support of the fight to achieve an open admissions policy at City led to his resignation, in May 1969, from his position as chair of the economics department. While he had always been sympathetic to his wife's ambitions, however, he was taken aback by the intensity of the feminist commitment whose outlines she had first sketched in "Snapshots of a Daughter-in-Law."

Poetical: As Rich rejected the domesticity of the fifties, she began writing the associative, testimonial verse that was to make her name.

To an interviewer in the nineties she explained that as her public and private worlds began to fall apart and re-form, she had to "find an equivalent for the kinds of fragmentation I was feeling, and confusion." She was drawn to the ghazals of the Urdu poet Ghalib, where she "found a structure which allowed for a highly associative field of images"; she was also "going to the movies more than I ever have in my life" and was powerfully influenced by, for instance, "Godard's use of language and image in films."[7] In fact, according to Hilary Holladay, in 1971 she ghostwrote a book on horror movies and "said that if she'd had to choose a different career path, she might have written film criticism."[8]

Personal: both Rich's commitment to public politics and to poetic revision accompanied what she herself called a "re-vision" of her private life. Her marriage to Conrad had never been perfect; there were, as one commentator puts it, "infidelities on both sides,"[9] but the compact had been definitive. Now, as her professional and political life widened, Rich's personal life began to change and, from Conrad's point of view, fall apart. Depressed for much of the sixties—she had long suffered from rheumatoid arthritis and now developed a fear of stairs—she went into psychotherapy with the existential psychoanalyst Leslie Farber (author of a noted volume, *Ways of the Will*), who became, for a while, the most important person in her life.

By the end of the sixties, she decided to move out of the Central Park West apartment, leaving her sons with Conrad, so that she could live on her own in a small studio nearby. In October 1970, Michelle Dean tells us, she wrote to Hayden Carruth that "Alf & I [are] talking a lot, in the car on leaf-strewn roads, or by the stove evenings"; yet soon she noted that "I feel Alf is in bad trouble—I can't help him anymore & I am trying at best not to provide damaging occasions for him." Then, Dean adds, the "same day she wrote the letter, Conrad wrote a check for the gun" with which he would soon shoot himself not far from the couple's Vermont vacation home.[10]

Conrad's suicide was "shattering for me and my children," Rich always remembered. "It was a tremendous waste. He was a man of enormous talents and love of life."[11] At the same time, this act of personal violence symbolized for the poet not just the rift between one individual couple but what Rich herself had begun to consider an almost unbridgeable gulf between the sexes. As Hayden Carruth remembered, "she was becoming a very pronounced, very militant feminist," so much so that "Alf came to me and complained bitterly that Adrienne had lost her mind." Later, after Conrad shot himself, Carruth added that he thought "Alf was a very disappointed person, who, as Adrienne became more celebrated, became more depressed."[12]

As for Rich herself, after her husband's death she reportedly cut off almost all contact with male friends and for many years sought only the company of women, increasingly taking on the role of a prophet for feminism and eventually coming out as a lesbian.[13] "She got swept too far," complained her sometime friend Elizabeth Hardwick. "She deliberately made herself ugly and wrote those extreme and ridiculous poems."[14] But the "extreme and ridiculous poems" spoke to a generation of young women and swept them too to new, far-out places. For arguably, after Conrad's suicide, the political, poetical, and personal fused in Rich's literary career, re-creating her as a public intellectual who channeled the anger of her generation.

Rich claimed to dislike the confessional strain in American poetry, preferring the pronouns "we" and "you" to "I." Yet it was the personal crisis of "shattering" grief that left an indelible mark on both her poetry and her politics. Rarely openly autobiographical, she mostly "told all the truth but told it slant," in a Dickinsonian manner.[15] Or to put the matter another way, as she implied in a late verse, she wrote her story into her poetry in invisible ink, which can be read only when held over a deciphering flame.[16]

Diving into the Wreck, her landmark 1973 collection of poems, was certainly a record of her feminist awakening; but the book's power also arises from its sorrowful yet angry gaze at the *wreck* of her husband's life, her marriage, and, in her view, the institution of patriarchal heterosexuality that forged the connection between "Vietnam and the lovers' bed." Indeed, if Sylvia Plath's *Ariel* was a kind of self-elegy, mourning the death of the fifties while dreaming of renewal in the sixties, *Diving into the Wreck* was an elegy for the fifties marriage of Adrienne Rich and Alfred Conrad that sought to describe what the title poem calls "the ribs of the disaster"[17] the couple confronted in the sixties and seventies.

Wrote Margaret Atwood in the *New York Times Book Review*, "When I first heard the author read from it, I felt as though the top of my head was being attacked, sometimes with an ice pick, sometimes with a blunter instrument," and she concluded that it was "one of those rare books that forces you to decide not just what you think about it, but what you think about yourself."[18] Tellingly, Rich's imagery of diving and discovering in her title poem parallel Atwood's similar imagery in *Surfacing*, as though both writers intuited the theme of deep exploration into a patriarchal past that marked so much feminist thinking in this decade.

In a 1972 issue of *Commentary*, Rich's psychotherapist Leslie Farber published an essay titled "He Said, She Said," in which he marveled at the ways in which "the new feminism has thrown into question all those institutions under whose auspices men and women through the centuries have sought to combine their lots or join their fates."[19] An interventional analyst who actively engaged with his patients, he might have gained this grasp of seventies feminism from discussions with one of his patients—Adrienne Rich. For as she awakened from the dreams of heterosexual "true romance" that had shaped the marriage plans of her generation, Rich bore witness to *seeing* with increasing clarity the oppressiveness of the "institutions under whose auspices" she had been living all her life. Even while obliquely exploring loss and grief, *Diving into the Wreck* analyzes the changes she and her generation had undergone and also reiterates—to use the title of the book she published just before this one—her own "will to change."

"The tragedy of sex / lies around us, a woodlot / the axes are sharpened for," Rich wrote in "Waking in the Dark," as she recorded her sense that she was dwelling in what had been "A man's world. But finished."[20] What exactly constituted her vision of "the tragedy of sex"? Few of the poems in *Diving* are as specific about this matter as a passage in a slightly later poem, "From an Old House in America," in which Rich broods on the history of the family vacation house in Vermont near which Conrad shot himself in 1970. Here is a traumatic "he said, she said" dialogue more dramatic than those Leslie Farber examined in his 1972 essay.

But can't you see me as a human being
he said

What is a human being
she said

I try to understand
he said

what will you undertake
she said

will you punish me for history
he said[21]

By the time Conrad shot himself, Rich was enraged at history, which she had come to see as a dystopian narrative of the culture that had always defined woman as secondary. In "Trying to Talk with a Man," she came to see all men as beings whose "dry heat feels like power," whose "eyes are stars of a different magnitude."[22] Vision and re-vision became obsessive themes in her work, as did fury at what she saw when, in Blakeian terms, the "doors of perception were cleansed."[23] "Underneath my lids another eye has opened / it looks nakedly / at the light," she wrote in "From the Prison House." And in "The Stranger" she imagined herself as an androgyne, with "visionary anger cleansing my sight / and the detailed perceptions of mercy / flowering from that anger."[24]

Rich's "Diving into the Wreck," at the center of the volume with that name, allegorizes with dreamlike intensity the quest for truth and rebirth at the heart of her feminist project. She begins this speculative account of a voyage that Jung would define as a night sea journey with three crucial acts of preparation: she reads *"the book of myths"* that shape her world, she loads *"the camera"* so she can record what she sees, and she checks "the edge of the *knife-blade*" that may either protect her or enable her to dissect what she discovers (italics ours). Then, imagining herself as a lone diver, she steps away from the reality of twentieth-century New York, attires herself in diving gear—"the body-armor of black rubber / the absurd flippers / the grave and awkward mask"—and descends into what is symbolically the dark ocean of the collective cultural unconscious to examine "the wreck" in which she discovers the drowned body of a man and a woman.[25]

As she enacts her journey downward and inward, Rich suggests that the poem itself is identical with her descent into the underworld. "The words are purposes. / The words are maps." Magically, her writing of the poem becomes a way of plunging deeper into the tragedy of sex that turned her own marriage into a shipwreck. "I came to see the damage that was done / and the treasures that prevail," she declares, as she notes that she is seeking to understand "the wreck and not the story of the wreck / the thing itself and not the myth." Arriving at the reality of the wreck and circling its debris, she ultimately discovers that she is not just the mermaid and merman swimming "into the hold," she is also a victim of the calamity, as is her male counterpart.[26] It is not just the traditional married couple but the tradition of heterosexual coupledom that has drowned:

I am she: I am he

whose drowned face sleeps with open eyes
. . . .
we are the half-destroyed instruments
that once held to a course
the water-eaten log
the fouled compass[27]

The "instruments / that once held to a course": in some of Rich's poems from earlier volumes, notably "A Marriage in the 'Sixties" and "Like This Together," she had celebrated her husband as a "Dear fellow-particle" with whom she was twinned.[28] Now what had been has been hopelessly lost, not only the self that "he" was but the self that "she" had. Thus, in the last stanza of "Diving into the Wreck" the explorer who ventured into the oceanic depths of the past must be not only spiritually and sexually but even grammatically revised and reborn, as s/he confronts the endless factuality of the wreck. Strikingly, a confusion of pronouns at the poem's conclusion suggests an infusion of the barely speakable new into the old, as the reader, too, is drawn into the action: "We are, I am, you are . . . the *one* who find our way / back to this scene / carrying . . . a book of myths / in which / our names do not appear" (italics ours).[29] Standard English grammar does not suffice for the articulation of this thought: Rich drowns it as she struggles to find new ways of saying and new ways of being so original that "the book of myths" has never before recorded the existence of such a utopian being.

"We are the one." We are one. Only one. What is left of the couple is the one who survives, carrying within her not just the story of ruin but a hope of rebirth. *Diving into the Wreck* does not conclude with Rich's turn toward a new kind of love. Her relocation of herself on what she was to call "the lesbian continuum" happened slowly, once she had begun to define heterosexuality as not just a pervasive but a "compulsory" institution. But the book closes with a few poems that celebrate her progress into the personal, poetical, and political change for which she had longed. Most notably, the wistful poetic epistle to her dead husband, "From a Survivor," offers a clear-eyed look at the broken marriage ("The pact that we made was the ordinary pact / of men & women in those days"), mourns his willful suicide ("you are wastefully dead"), and describes the arc of change that was to define the decade whose spokeswoman she became. The "leap / we talked / too late of making"—divorce? personal reinvention?—is what "I live now / not as a leap / but a succession of brief, amazing movements // each one making possible the next."[30]

Those amazing movements included the composition of a number of groundbreaking essays, a book-length research project into the "experience and institution" of motherhood, and the intensely erotic "Twenty-One Love Poems," which reimagine the traditional sonnet sequence as a female-authored paean to lesbian love. Rich's prose works in this period included incisive analyses of *Jane Eyre* and of the poetry of Emily Dickinson, but the most influential of them were "When We Dead Awaken: Writing as Re-Vision" and "Compulsory Heterosexuality and Lesbian Existence."

In "When We Dead Awaken," she extolled the consciousness-raising that marked the decade ("The sleepwalkers are coming awake, and for the first time this awakening has a collective reality"), then affirmed that "Re-vision—the act of looking back, of seeing with fresh eyes, of entering an old text from a new critical direction—is for women more than a chapter in cultural history: it is an act of survival."[31] These sentences summarized the feminist rethinking of literary culture that was to become a vital mode of critical thinking; "When We Dead Awaken" is a founding text of women's studies as well as of feminist criticism. Equally central, the essay "Compulsory Heterosexuality" critiqued the cultural "ideology which *demands* heterosexuality" (italics hers) as she sought to excavate the reality of a "lesbian continuum" in which "women's choice of women as passionate comrades, life partners, co-workers, lovers, community" would be a social and erotic possibility.[32]

In her own poetic oeuvre, the arguments of these prose works inform "Twenty-One Love Poems," the sequence at the heart of *The Dream of a Common Language* (1978). These thirteen- to twenty-line poems aren't really sonnets, but on the page they look very much like sonnets, and like traditional, male-authored sequences they trace the arc of a love affair—in this case, between two women: as Holladay tells us, Rich and her psychiatrist Lilly Engler (who had also been Susan Sontag's lover). According to Rich's friend Robin Morgan,

Engler was hardly a wild erotic goddess. On the contrary, she was "a classic sort of middle-European, slightly older than middle-aged, zaftig, sweet-looking, dumpy woman."[33] But in Rich's bold sequence, she becomes an idealized female other with the aura of a Venus.

Like many of Rich's poems in this period, these quasi-sonnets are set in New York City, with its tenements, playgrounds, and elevators, where, as the speaker says,

No one has imagined us. We want to live like trees,
sycamores blazing through the sulfuric air,
dappled with scars, still exuberantly budding,
our animal passion rooted in the city.[34]

And, like most of Rich's work in this era, the poems are as politically committed as they are emotionally energized. Loving each other, the two women still have to "stare into the absence / of men who would not, women who could not, speak / to our life." Yet despite the sense that she and her lover have to confront a cultural "absence," Rich's testimonial sonnets are infused with an almost exalted desire: "I want to travel with you to every sacred mountain. . . . I want to reach for your hand as we scale the path, / to feel your arteries glowing in my clasp," she declares in poem XI; and in the next poem she affirms that "in any chronicle of the world we share / it could be written with new meaning / we were two lovers of one gender / we were two women of one generation."[35]

One generation. Placed as it is at the end of a central poem, the word "generation" takes on special force, implying not just a station in time but a renewal, rebirth, regeneration. And the explicitly erotic unnumbered poem titled "The Floating Poem," meant to be read at any point in the sequence, dramatizes the generative sexual awakening that drives the poet toward metamorphosis. "Whatever happens with us, your body / will haunt mine," she promises as she praises her beloved in a series of blazons—using the technique that (male) Renaissance writers deployed to list the beauties of a woman's body: "your traveled, generous thighs," "the live, insatiate dance of your nipples," "your strong tongue and slender fingers." Now she includes a reversal that equally celebrates the body of the speaker/lover, "reaching where *I* had been waiting years for you / in *my* rose-wet cave"[36] (italics ours)—not only the moist vagina of the desirous speaker but also the originary female home where the poet had been waiting through decades of "compulsory heterosexuality" for a moment when the lesbian within her could "[begin] to stretch her limbs."[37]

"Twenty-One Love Poems" concludes with an affirmation of choice in which, again, the poet transports herself back into the past, where she models for her readers the *will* to change. Imagining herself among the "blue and foreign stones / of the great round rippled by stone implements" that is and is not the archaic site of Stonehenge, she argues that this isn't just Stonehenge:

> . . . but the mind
> casting back to where her solitude,
> shared, could be chosen without loneliness,
> not easily nor without pains to stake out
> the circle, the heavy shadows, the great light.
> I choose to be a figure in that light,
> half-blotted by darkness, something moving
> across that space, the color of stone
> greeting the moon, yet more than stone:
> a woman. I choose to walk here. And to draw this circle.[38]

Whereas "Diving into the Wreck" concluded with a confusion of pronouns, "Twenty-One Love Poems" ends with a powerful gesture of self-definition: the speaker names herself as a woman by choice, and a woman who has chosen to walk in a certain place, and to situate herself in the center of a circle at the beginning of time. By now she has moved far away from the streets of Manhattan where she trysted with her lover. Now, in the solitude of a self-made self she has become a strange new creature—a woman almost as hard to imagine as a figure from science fiction or fantasy.

DYSTOPIAS AND UTOPIAS

Like Rich's speculative poetry, much of the female-authored science fiction of the decade similarly set dystopias against utopias. The writers of these texts were working in a tradition that had significant antecedents in feminist thought. For, as we studied our own literary history, we discovered lost texts that brood on these twin themes of dystopia and utopia. Some of us in the seventies began exploring the works of the turn-of-the-century feminist Charlotte Perkins Gilman. We began to teach her story "The Yellow Wallpaper" (1892), a first-person narrative that delineated a dystopian world in which a young mother is separated from her child and imprisoned in an attic room where she can neither read nor write and goes mad attempting to decipher menacing figures in the yellow (ancient? musty?) wallpaper. The text's utopian twin, which we also now began to study, was Gilman's novel *Herland* (1915), an account of an egalitarian, all-female society into which three male explorers have stumbled.[39]

Both these works prefigured the speculative fiction to which many feminists turned in the sixties and increasingly in the seventies. If the great awakening of the decade could be understood as a heightened consciousness that the system of gender in which we had all been living was not the way things *had* to be but was a kind of dystopia, by contrast the revised and revisionary system for which feminism labored was a utopia. And in the writings of Rich's contemporaries who turned to fantasy and science fiction, a revulsion against patriarchal dystopia is as crucial as an aspiration for a feminist—perhaps matriarchal—utopia. Unlike "realist" novelists, feminist sci-fi writers dramatize both the oppressions and the aspirations of women by setting them on fantastic planets or in grimly dystopic geographies.

Three major authors of works in these genres—Alice Bradley Sheldon, Joanna Russ, and Ursula K. Le Guin—became textual and political companions. Though all three were compelling writers, Alice Sheldon was the most fascinating of these figures. Throughout the seventies, she wrote as James Tiptree, Jr., and was thought for nearly a decade to be a male author and was critiqued as such. Le Guin, Russ, and everyone else in the lively, disputatious science fiction community knew Tiptree's work, but most feminist readers didn't, probably because of the cover of "Tiptree's" male pseudonym. Yet Sheldon/Tiptree set dystopias against utopias in a series of short stories with significant feminist implications. And perhaps because of her (literary) male impersonation, her feminist writing was received with special applause.

ALICE SHELDON/JAMES TIPTREE, JR.

The "real" Alice B. Sheldon was the beautiful wife of a CIA official. Born in Chicago in 1915, she had been a wealthy debutante with lesbian longings, but later became a successful graphic artist, married and divorced a wealthy playboy, joined the Women's Army Auxiliary Corps during the war, married her second husband in Paris, and then joined the CIA when he did. She earned a Ph.D. in psychology in 1967, around the time she began writing science fiction. Seeking a pseudonym, she turned toward a jar of British marmalade in her local supermarket and exclaimed "James Tiptree," to which her husband jokingly appended "Junior."[40] But—no joke—Tiptree was to become her other self, and "he" was to bring her extraordinary success. As a "man," did she seem to some to be a "better" feminist—a *male* feminist?

Certainly, the cleverly constructed "masculine" voice in which she told her tales liberated her from the constraints of a conventional "femininity" even while it enabled her to dissect the conventions of "masculinity" from the position of someone who might belong to a sort of third sex. For when she was just establishing herself as Tiptree, Sheldon proposed to her literary agent that she should write a book titled "The Human Male." As her biographer, Julie Phillips, notes, "by talking about men from a woman's point of view, [the book] would illustrate women's way of looking at the world" while remedying the problem that "everything we know about the human male comes from his own mouth and is suspect."[41] Arguably, though Sheldon managed to outline only a few chapters ("Getting It There: The Central Drama of the Male," "Beyond Sex: Dominance, Territory, Bonding and All That," "Things That Go Wrong with Men"), much of Tiptree's fiction is an investigation of the questions she had planned to address in "The Human Male."

Whether you read her shrewd "The Women Men Don't See" as male- or female-authored, it is delightfully subversive. Set in the Yucatán, the Hemingwayesque story begins with the crash of a small plane onto a tropical sandbar. The plane's occupants seem ordinary enough: Don Seldon, the narrator, a "gray used-up Yank dressed for serious fishing"; the Mayan Captain Estéban; and two unprepossessing women, a mother and daughter, who claim to be headed for someplace in Guatemala. At daybreak, Don and the older woman, whose first name is Ruth, go off into the swamp in search of drinking water, leaving Ruth's daughter, Althea, to mind the wreck with the wounded Estéban. Like their luggage, the Parsons pair are "small, plain and neutral-colored," an easy-to-overlook "double female blur."[42] As Don and Ruth trudge through watery wilderness, Don learns that the two work for the government in Washington, DC. Just as he had supposed, he decides, both are merely cogs in the wheels of bureaucracy.

Yet after a day or so, Ruth spots a Mayan ruin and seems to be waiting for something—which turns out to be an alien spacecraft, sweeping flashes of light across the swamp. And when Don tries, "heroically," to protect her, she makes it clear that she doesn't at all want his protection but instead plans to escape with the aliens, together with her daughter, who may have been impregnated by the handsome Mayan Estéban.

The speech in which Ruth explains herself to Don is a classic feminist polemic, as well as a cynical prediction that the ERA would be doomed to failure.

Women have no rights, Don, except what men allow us. Men are more aggressive and powerful, and they run the world. When the next real crisis upsets them, our so-called rights will vanish like . . . smoke. . . . And whatever has gone wrong will be blamed on our freedom, like the fall of Rome was. You'll see. . . . What women do is survive. We live by ones and twos in the chinks of your world-machine. . . . Think of us as opossums, Don. Did you know there are opossums living all over? Even in New York City.[43]

The final scene, in which Ruth persuades the aliens to take her and her daughter away with them ("Please take us. We don't mind what your planet is like; we'll learn—we'll do anything!") is a kind of comic cosmic imbroglio. The cartoon aliens, all white tentacles and blank faces, define themselves as "Ss-stu-dens . . . S-stu-ding . . . not—huh-arming," while Don tries to persuade Estéban to help him keep the women from going. But in the end, he has to confront the extraordinary facts: "Two human women, one of them possibly pregnant, have departed for, I guess, the stars; and the fabric of society will never show a ripple."[44] For all its charm, "The Women Men Don't See" is a dark parable: from the perspective of women who live like opossums in the chinks of a patriarchal "world-machine," anywhere in the interstellar reaches would be preferable to this dystopian human planet.

With the exception of tentacled aliens, the world-machine from which the Parsons women escape is very much a realm of *now*. But two of Tiptree's most disturbing dystopias, "The Girl Who Was Plugged In" and "The Screwfly Solution," are set in terrestrial futures, where they illuminate strikingly different gender disorders.

The first, "The Girl Who Was Plugged In," recounts the pathetic tale of one Philadelphia Burke (mostly referred to as P. Burke), a girl of 17 who suffers from the deformations of pituitary disease in a society that worships beautiful "gods" and "godlings."[45] After P. Burke tries to kill herself, she is arrested and turned into a "waldo"—in sci-fi terms, a remote manipulator of, in her case, an adorable godling named "Delphi," who becomes the glamorous other self for which miserable Phila*delphia* has always yearned. Elfin, brainless Delphi becomes famous, but trouble comes when the privileged son of one of the masters of this particularly cynical world-machine falls in love with her, assuming that she too is real. The awful misunderstanding climaxes when Delphi's lover tracks down P. Burke and tries to disen-tangle his girlfriend from her waldo. Inevitably, the horrid hulk flops down dead at his feet, and little Delphi expires too.

Here Tiptree took on the imperatives of what feminists used to call "looks-ism," delineating the nightmare of P. Burke's life by con-trasting it with Delphi's career. At the same time, the *thinking* por-tion of Delphi is ugly P. Burke, in her electronic/neurological cabinet, while the seductive aspect of P. Burke is Delphi, made-to-measure by computer geniuses into a futuristic Galatea.

It's impossible to read this story—for which Tiptree won a Hugo Award—without feeling for the pathos of P. Burke and, too, for the mindless passivity of her "other" self. The text illuminates the power of the beauty myth even while deconstructing the experience of the supposedly "beautiful" heroine. In a sense, then, it meditates eerily on the mind-body problem from a feminist perspective. If the ugly but electronically potent P. Burke is lovely Delphi's "mind" so that only together do they constitute one perfect "woman," does this imply that a woman's mind is necessarily ugly though desirous? And does it also suggest that, like Delphi, a beautiful girl is nothing more than "a warm little bundle of vegetative functions"?[46]

To be sure, P. Burke/Delphi has to be taught to be adorable, that is, to manage the performance of femininity "DELICIOUSLY." Her "training" is "exactly what you'd call a charm course." Yet, as Tiptree writes in her toughest tough-guy lingo, P. Burke is excep-tionally "apt" because somewhere "in that horrible body is a gazelle, a houri, who would have been buried forever without this crazy chance. See the ugly duckling go!"[47] Forty years ago, we'd have considered it a tale of the madwoman in the computer, though its author would have seemed to be a Raymond Chandler type, writ-ing noir sci-fi. For, deploying a macho style, Tiptree writes this story slangily without any indication of sympathy for the two-in-one heroines.

Indeed, whereas P. Burke and Delphi are (together) performing femininity, their author is deftly performing masculinity, even though Allie Sheldon/James Tiptree, Jr., are (together) interrogating the Delphic oracle of the Feminine. Miss America? Barbie? Are they no more than dummies—and if you aren't a dummy, are you just an ugly duckling? As for the reader, the rough tough narrator addresses "us" on and off as "dummy," "zombie," etc. We too, "he" implies, would be taken in by Delphi's fake seductiveness. But while we are complicit with the narrator in our attraction to Delphi, the tough-guy narrator is "himself" complicit in a dynamic that reduces women to dummies or ugly ducklings, a society shaped by more of the many "things that go wrong with men."

Using a different, later pseudonym—Raccoona Sheldon—Alice Sheldon dissected more of the major ways in which men go wrong. "The Screwfly Solution" tracks the dilemma of a scientist setting up "a biological pest-control program"[48] in Colombia through a series of letters and other documents sent to him by his wife in Michigan. Relatively cheerful to begin with, she writes him about a new misogynistic cult calling themselves "the Sons of Adam." Somehow, they are associated with a series of "femicides" recounted in a stack of newspaper clippings that a colleague has asked her to send him.

The situation darkens as the husband understands that the brutal femicides of the Sons of Adam are multiplying like, well, a plague. Racing home to protect his wife and his young daughter, he realizes en route that he, too, has been infected by the pandemic of misogynistic blood lust. Dreaming of erotic fulfillment with his wife, he sees that the "sex was . . . driving some engine of death." A new missive from his colleague includes a note from another professor: "A poten-

tial difficulty for our species has always been implicit in the close
linkage between the behavioral expression of aggression/predation
and sexual reproduction in the male," suggesting that the "present
crisis" might be "viral or enzymatic in origin."[49]

Returning home infected, the scientist murders his cherished
daughter and then kills himself. In the end, his wife takes refuge in
the northern woods, maybe the last human female left. What is the
"screwfly solution"? It's a method of insect control based on the introduction of sterile males into a target population, thereby preventing
reproduction. In Raccoona Sheldon's story, a thought experiment
reversing this technique, human male sexuality is exaggerated into
blood lust, killing off the females of the species so that no humans
can reproduce. Why? Visitors from outer space are scoping out our
real estate.

The slick sci-fi ending, blaming the catastrophic pandemic on
extraterrestrial intervention, helps divert attention from the philosophical center of the tale: its analysis of "the close linkage between
the behavioral expression of aggression/predation and sexual reproduction in the male." While "The Girl Who Was Plugged In" suggests that femininity is no more than a performance, "The Screwfly
Solution" implies that masculinity might be biologically vulnerable
to violent tendencies, sexual lust always in danger of metastasizing
into blood lust.

Compared to such dystopic fantasies, Tiptree's exuberant representation of a utopia appears in her Hugo Award–winning "Houston, Houston, Do You Read?," a novella that might be a revision of
Charlotte Perkins Gilman's *Herland*.[50] A classic space opera, this tale
traces the misadventure of three lost astronauts—the Bible-quoting
Major Norman Davis, his bawdy second-in-command Captain Bud
Geirr, and their sensitive onboard scientist, Dr. Orren Lorimer—as

they find themselves and their ship, the *Sunbird*, spun forward three centuries in time and rescued from death in the sky by the all-woman crew of the *Gloria*, a big "low-thrust" spaceship from the future that looks, says Bud, "like a flying trailer park." Even before they board the *Gloria*, Lorimer and his companions are told that they and their world, in particular their sex, are part of history. Over their radio, one woman explains that "the first *Sunbird* mission was lost in space." But in fact, the three astronauts now enter a society in which men, with their "rigid authority code" and its "dominance-submission structure," no longer exist.[51]

The women's utopian world, it turns out, is not only egalitarian but also sophisticated and low-tech. As Lorimer enters the women's space, he notes that the "future is a vast bright cylinder, its whole inner surface festooned with unidentifiable objects, fronds of green"— which turn out to be greenhouse plants, chickens, somebody's leather work, somebody else's beading rack, a loom, and a "damned kudzu vine." In a spoof of twentieth-century American domesticity, this futuristic Herland is stuffed with what, from Lorimer's irascible masculine point of view, is hatefully "cozy."[52]

Yet, as Tiptree points out, this world *works*, in every sense of the word. Not only do its inhabitants explore space, but on their home planet—Earth—they farm, fish, and manufacture necessities. More strikingly, because all the males perished in an apocalyptic epidemic, these women clone themselves and educate their daughters. They need no government, but collaboratively organize their industries. And when Bud openly masturbates after his attempt to rape one of them, the intended "victim" efficiently catches his semen in a plastic bag—presumably for use in introducing another genotype into their culture.

The dystopian behavior of the men in "Houston, Houston" is

even more central to the story than is the utopian equilibrium of the women. For this novella is not only another analysis of "the human male" but an elegy for him. The three astronauts are, to be sure, stereotypes. From the intellectual Lorimer's perspective, the Major and the Captain are "alpha males"—but two different versions. Major Davis, the Bible-quoting commander, dramatizes the "dominance-submission" structure of the space crew he rules, not just because of his technical expertise but because of his patriarchal theology. His underling, "Bud" Geirr, is a bad buddy, a foulmouthed would-be rapist.

Yet Lorimer can't help admiring just those Alpha-male qualities that endanger the serene community of the *Gloria*. When Bud sexually assaults one of the women, provoking a melee in the spaceship's greenhouse, Major Davis pulls out a gun, declaring, "Let the women learn in silence and all subjection." But by the end of the tale, the men, alpha or not, have been overwhelmed by the greater efficiency of the women, who are, after all, ingenious survivors. As the women tow the supine Major and his fallen Captain out of the greenhouse, Lorimer declares, "elegiacally," that "they were good men," and knows he is "speaking for it all, for Dave's Father, for Bud's manhood, for Cro-Magnon, for the dinosaurs too, maybe," noting rebelliously that he and his fellow men "built your precious civilization." One of the women responds that though "we enjoy your inventions and we do appreciate your evolutionary role[,] . . . what you protected people from was largely other males, wasn't it? We've just had an extraordinary demonstration in that. You've brought history to life for us."[53]

There is no Houston at the end of this story to "read" the tale and its moral, Tiptree implies, nor should there be. The women of the *Gloria* aren't "Amazonia" or "Liberation." They are quite simply the human race, as if bringing to life the recent T-shirt slogan

THE FUTURE IS FEMALE. The human male with his obsessive "dominance-submission" is gone like the dinosaurs. Even while impersonating masculinity, Tiptree/Sheldon seems to wonder: what redemption can there be for the dystopian "masculinity" we have known?

JOANNA RUSS'S MISANDRY

Joanna Russ's *The Female Man*—published in the middle of the seventies but written at the very beginning of the decade—turned away from masculinity, except in its most melodramatic forms, to examine the spectrum of possibilities that constitute the feminine. In this experimental novel, Russ dramatized four possible iterations of the world in which one woman, the author/narrator Joanna, might live. Joanna, Jeannine, Janet, Jael: together this quartet of women constitutes the split-up consciousness of the "female man"—that is, the Woman Human Being. Elegantly constructed as it is, however, *The Female Man* is not dispassionate. While Tiptree examines masculinity by impersonating the masculine, Russ dreams of murdering cartoon men.

Tiptree, an admirer of Russ's, instantly recognized the all-consuming anger that flames through *The Female Man* and other works. "Holy peanut butter, dear writer," she told Russ in one letter, "do you imagine that anyone with half a functional neuron can read your work and not have his fingers smoked by the bitter, multi-layered anger in it? It smells and smolders like a volcano buried so long and deadly it is just beginning to wonder whether it can explode."[54] Explode it did, throughout the seventies and into the eighties. "Gee, isn't it awful for women to hate men?" Russ asked sardonically in *The Village Voice* in a piece titled "The New Misandry," adding bitterly, "What male reviewer found Hitchcock's 'Frenzy' one-20th as revolting as Solanas's

'Scum Manifesto'? Of course Solanas went out and did it, but then so do many men"[55]—including the serial rapist-killer at the center of *Frenzy*.

The plot of *The Female Man* is triggered by the appearance on earth of Janet, an emissary from the utopian all-female planet of Whileaway—a place that is in the future "but not *our* future."[56] Janet appears in what is simultaneously the impoverished society of Jeannine—an America where the Depression has never ended and the Second World War has never happened—and the more "realistic" (though equally depressing) society of Joanna, who inhabits the real American seventies. Jeannine, a dreamy librarian, longs for marriage yet is ambivalent about the sexual practices of her impotent boyfriend. Joanna takes Janet to a party where a panoply of goofy men make passes at her, while Swiftian cartoon women—Lamentissa, Aphrodissa, etc.—mouth stereotypically "feminine" anti-feminist platitudes. Clearly Jeannine and Joanna are products of dystopian culture, whereas Janet's utopian Whileaway, where she lives with her wife, Vittoria, enacts a fantasy of lesbian separatism, not unlike that of the community on Tiptree's *Gloria*.

The true incarnation of feminist/female rage comes onstage toward the end: Jael, the murderess, appears with subtly concealed steel claws and teeth. She is from a future of endless sexual warfare where Manland and Womanland are in mortal opposition. When she whisks the other three off to Manland, she demonstrates her skill as an assassin, violently eviscerating a smug bossy type. After this, she returns to her home, where she makes love to a beautiful robot named "Davy"—a sex toy not unlike Delphi in Tiptree's "The Girl Who Was Plugged In."

As Pat Wheeler put it, "Russ's seminal novel . . . keyed into the zeitgeist of radical feminist politics of the day"—the disgust with stale sex roles, the yearning for a utopia of one's own, and the rage at pompous patriarchs.[57] Indeed, like Rich, Russ was demanding to replace not just the deadly dystopia that created Jael but also the humdrum dystopias inhabited by Jeannine and Joanna with Janet's utopia right away. At the same time, recognizing the impossibility of such a project, she was mourning its impossibility. The sardonic yet lyrical passage with which she concludes the novel comically summarizes her ambition for change.

> Go, little book, trot through Texas and Vermont and Alaska and Maryland and Washington and Florida and Canada and England and France; bob a curtsey at the shrines of Friedan, Millet [sic], Greer, Firestone, and all the rest. . . . Wash your face and take your place without a fuss in the Library of Congress. . . . Do not get glum when you are no longer understood, little book. Do not curse your fate. . . .
> Rejoice, little book!
> For on that day, we will be free.[58]

URSULA LE GUIN'S ANDROGYNY

Whereas Tiptree was a widely traveled woman posing as a widely traveled man, and Russ was an impassioned lesbian academic, Ursula K. Le Guin usually defined herself as "a Portland housewife."[59] Yet she was no ordinary homemaker, of the kind Friedan had profiled. The daughter of the distinguished anthropologist Alfred Kroeber and the writer Theodora Kroeber, she married Charles Le Guin in her early 20s and settled down to mothering three children in the fifties and sixties. While her husband worked as a history professor, Le Guin started writing speculative fiction. Her householding partnership

with her husband seems neither to have obstructed her productiv-
ity nor quelled her ambition. Her gender-bending chef d'oeuvre, *The
Left Hand of Darkness*, appeared in 1969 and inspired plaudits from
both Russ and Tiptree, who became frequent correspondents.

A detailed ethnography of the planet Gethen (or Winter, in
English), *The Left Hand of Darkness* examines the sociocultural implications of an androgynous world and might well have influenced
Carolyn Heilbrun's 1973 meditation on gender, *Toward a Recognition
of Androgyny*. Le Guin's Gethenians are sexually neutral for twenty-
six days of the month, and then they go into "kemmer," or what we
would consider estrus in certain animals. When in kemmer, any
Gethenian can become male *or* female; if female and impregnated,
"she" remains female throughout pregnancy and lactation. (Even the
king can be pregnant, one of Le Guin's favorite adages.) Then "she"
reverts to androgynous neutrality. Many Gethenians, as Le Guin's
terrestrial narrator explains, have both birthed and sired children,
though descent is traced through the maternal line.

And "consider," Le Guin declares, the meaning of such ambisexuality. For one thing, "anyone can turn his hand to anything
[since] everybody has the same [sexual] risk to run or choice to make.
Therefore nobody here is quite so free as a free male anywhere else."
And "consider," too, that a "child has no psycho-sexual relationship
to his mother and father," so there "is no myth of Oedipus on Winter." Moreover, "there is no unconsenting sex, no rape," nor is there
any "division of humanity into strong and weak halves. In fact the
whole tendency to dualism that pervades human thinking may be
found to be lessened or changed, on Winter."[60] Nor is there war on
Winter, because the testosterone-fueled aggressiveness that animates
Terran masculinity is absent in ambisexual beings. The Gethenians
are capable of treachery, but they have no armies, no battles.

Le Guin's experimental analysis of ambisexuality was the most striking achievement of feminist science fiction in the twentieth century. But Le Guin's planet Winter was hardly a utopia: the novel's plot features intrigue, betrayal, a desperate flight across the icy crest of the world, and the death of the Gethenian whom the narrator has come to love. Moreover, as Le Guin herself conceded, her representation of ambisexuality was marred by her use of the pronoun "he" throughout the book.[61] Though we know that her Gethenians are both women and men, the pronoun leaves us imagining them as men—who might just become pregnant.

Within a few years, Le Guin addressed this problem: when republishing another Gethenian tale, "Winter's King" (1969), in *The Wind's Twelve Quarters* (1975), she changed the problematic "he" of the original version to "she," explaining that "in revising the story for this edition, . . . I use the feminine pronoun for all Gethenians— while preserving certain masculine titles such as King and Lord, just to remind one of the ambiguity."[62] And several decades later, another story similarly uses "she" for everyone who is not in kemmer.[63]

A decade later, Le Guin produced a more utopian vision of our own planet in the short story "Sur," an exhilarating account of an all-woman expedition to the South Pole. In 1908, her narrator tells us, a group of nine South American women—from Peru, Argentina, and Chile—ventured through the Antarctic to the South Pole with the help of a kindly ship's captain, who deposited the party on the otherwise unreachable ice shelf. Le Guin provides her story with a map of the area explored by the dauntless women, not unlike the maps usually appended to accounts of the expeditions led by such male polar explorers as Scott, Shackleton, and Amundson.

However, her female explorers are very different from their male contemporaries. For one thing, the women are less hierarchical: from the start, they decide that they'll be "all crew." Then, arriving at "Hut Point," the polar station made famous in Scott's *Voyage of the Discovery* (1905), they are repelled by the "mean disorder" left behind by the male explorers: "Empty meat tins lay about; biscuits were spilled on the floor." But then, they remind themselves, "housekeeping, the art of the infinite, is no game for amateurs."[64]

That these women are no amateurs is revealed by the base camp they make for themselves. Digging into the ice, they carve out an elegant dwelling with comfortable burrows for sleeping, a stove that draws well, skylights, and even sculptures—whose maker "cannot bring them north. That is the penalty of carving in water." Then, for a while, as they explore the frozen landscape, they note that there "was nothing to see at all," yet because they had "come to that white place on the map, that void, . . . we flew and sang like sparrows."[65]

As they explore the region further, they begin to bestow revisionary names on notable features of the terrain. What Shackleton called "the Beardmore" glacier, they rename the "Florence Nightingale" glacier; various peaks are called "Bolivar's Big Nose," "Whose Toe?," and "Throne of Our Lady of the Southern Cross." Finally, reports the narrator, on "the twenty-second of December, 1909," they reach the South Pole, a "dreary place," and decide to leave "no sign there, for some man longing to be first might come some day, and find it, and know then what a fool he had been, and break his heart."[66]

A postscript to the polar journey: when the narrator returns to the base camp, she discovers that one of the explorers is pregnant and on the verge of giving birth. Innocent Teresa hardly knows the facts of life and merely thought she was getting fat! When her daughter arrives, she calls the child "Rosa del Sur." Thus the story of "Sur" is not just a narrative of polar exploration, it is the tale of the birth of a girl child.

Is "Sur" a utopia? For a few minutes, as the women cavort like sparrows while crossing the ice, their delight seems utopian. Yet their utopia is soon subsumed into the master narrative of patriarchal history. The women bury their tale in attics and bureau drawers, just as they had buried their dwelling place beneath the ice of the glacier. Back in so-called civilization, little Rosa del Sur dies of scarlet fever at the age of 5. The narrator has written her story only for her descendants: "Even if they are rather ashamed of having such a crazy grandmother, they may enjoy sharing in the secret." But there is no need to tell Mr. Amundsen! The hero must have his day and way. "We left no footprints, even."[67]

A poem Adrienne Rich wrote in 1974 serves as a kind of precursor narrative to "Sur," although it is based on a real-life incident. "Phantasia for Elvira Shatayev," spoken in the voice of a Russian explorer who along with the seven other women of her climbing team died in a blizzard while attempting to ascend Lenin Peak in Kyrgyzstan, elegizes and eulogizes the dead climbers.

> *A cable of blue fire ropes our bodies*
> *burning together in the snow   We will not live*
> *to settle for less   We have dreamed of this*
> *all of our lives*[68]

Utopia? Dystopia? The dream of the climbers was utopian: their community was linked by the sisterly love that Rich characterizes as a "cable of blue fire." Yet their immolation in the ice suggests that the price of their ambition was death. While the explorers of "Sur" left no footprint, returning to decorous lives as wives and mothers, Rich's climbers leave their frozen bodies as marks on the landscape of *Lenin* Peak, a mountain named for a male hero. Must feminist defiance be either secret or suicidal?

7

Bonded and Bruised Sisters

A S THE SEVENTIES UNFOLDED and feminist networks expanded, creative women working in different media were inspired by a utopian ideal of sisterhood. Revisiting the decade, Vivian Gornick celebrated "the joy of revolutionary politics," quoting from Wordsworth: "bliss was it in that dawn to be alive. Not an I-love-you in the world could touch it. . . . We lived then, all of us, inside the loose embrace of feminism."[1] Many women more isolated than the well-connected Gornick discovered that by working together they could challenge male-dominated organizations and traditions.

Yet quite a few confronted the ways in which the women's movement could degenerate into dystopic misunderstanding, infighting, and trashing. Even those enraptured by a dream of sisterhood mourned ruptures in relationships with their "sisters." While Gloria Steinem, Alice Walker, and Audre Lorde weighed the political fallout of bonding and bruising on America's second wave, Maxine Hong Kingston's memoir and Judy Chicago's *Dinner Party* installation more graphically investigated issues of sisterhood—and daughterhood.

Unfortunately, efforts at coalition building between straight and gay, radical and liberal, white and Black, native-born and foreign-born women were undermined by the onset of a national backlash that was organized—at the apex of seventies feminism—by one woman, Phyllis Schlafly. At the end of the seventies, while feminists were beginning to address their disagreements, express their differences, and commemorate their achievements, it was not yet apparent that the high hopes generated by Title IX and *Roe v. Wade* would be dashed when ratification of the Equal Rights Amendment stalled. Only during the next decade, after the ERA was scuttled, would it become clear that equality of rights would continue to be abridged by the United States on account of sex.

GLORIA STEINEM AND ALICE WALKER AT *MS.*

Gloria Steinem's alliances with women reflect the supportive and divisive relationships that characterized the seventies women's movement, although she proved herself to be an unusually generous survivor of many upheavals. While the loyal (more than the rivalrous) dealings of women became a central topic of feminist discussion, Steinem traversed the country giving lectures and testifying for the adoption of the ERA, generally partnered with an African American activist: the child-welfare advocate Dorothy Pitman (Hughes) or the flamboyant lawyer Flo Kennedy or the civil rights activist Margaret Sloan. If her partner was the feisty Kennedy, "I always had to speak first because if I went after Flo, it was such an anticlimax." These affiliations preceded her sponsorship of Alice Walker, a life-long friend whom she revered: "We can change for the better if we know her," Steinem attested.[2]

Pairing up on the lecture circuit helped cure Steinem's jitters on public platforms, but it also demonstrated that feminism was not merely a white movement. Steinem refused to pose for a *Newsweek* cover in 1971 because, like Millett, she wanted to divert attention from herself to the women's movement, but a photographer shot her secretly with a telephoto lens. Through her journalism and public speaking, she became a representative feminist who could also counter homophobic stereotypes. When asked on the road if she were a lesbian, she genially responded, "Not yet."[3] Her appearances dispelled assumptions about all feminists being lesbians and all lesbians being battle-axes.

Working with Betty Friedan, Shirley Chisholm, and Bella Abzug, Steinem helped establish the National Women's Political Caucus. But it was the appearance of the glossy, popular *Ms.* magazine in 1972 that solidified Steinem's standing. The first, preview issue included Jane O'Reilly's "The Housewife's Moment of Truth," Letty Pogrebin's "Raising Kids without Sex Roles," Vivian Gornick's "Why Women Fear Success," Judy Syfer's "I Want a Wife," and what was billed as "Sylvia Plath's Last Major Work," her "Three Women: A Play for Three Voices."

The essays Steinem wrote for *Ms.* and other outlets—from "Why We Need a Woman President in 1976" to "If Men Could Menstruate"— were witty, as were her speeches. But backlash arrived fast. In 1973, when only five more states were needed to ratify the ERA, *Screw* magazine published an image of a nude in aviator glasses, oversized labia on display, with the headline "Pin the Cock on the Feminist." There were penises on the border to choose from. That same year Hugh Hefner wrote a memo, leaked by a staff member: "These chicks are our natural enemies. It is time to do battle with them."[4]

Less predictably, Betty Friedan began claiming that Steinem was in league with a destructive form of anti-male "female chauvinism." Friedan smeared Steinem as a latecomer ripping off the movement.[5] In *Esquire*, Nora Ephron mocked Friedan as brooding about her ownership of feminism: "It's her baby, damn it. Her movement. Is she supposed to sit still and let a beautiful thin lady run off with it?" While Nora Ephron was thinking of Betty Friedan as the "Wicked Witch of the West" and of Gloria Steinem as "[Princess] Ozma, Glinda, Dorothy—take your pick," she found herself walking down the street with her weeping friend after the Democratic National Convention. "I'm just tired of being screwed, and being screwed by my friends," Steinem said.[6]

She was thinking of powerful men in the Democratic Party and the media, but leaders in the women's movement were also harassing her. In 1974, the feminist constituents Friedan had reprimanded as a "lavender menace" joined forces against Steinem. *Lesbian Nation* brought an "indykement" against *Ms.* in a mock lawsuit, charging the magazine with "gross neglect and Psychic genocide against Lesbian women,"[7] despite evidence to the contrary. Distressed, Steinem began cutting down her public appearances, although she continued to mentor younger women.

One of those women celebrated the attachments and experienced the acrimony that would affect Steinem. Alice Walker, the youngest child of Georgia sharecroppers, had left the historically Black Spelman College for Sarah Lawrence. On a white-dominated campus, the mentoring of the poet Muriel Rukeyser—an early feminist beloved by younger poets—helped Walker decide to become a writer and led to her first publication. Subsequent works described the voter registration and welfare rights movements in Mississippi, where she lived under threatening circumstances with her white husband, the civil rights activist-lawyer Mel Leventhal. The stress of being part of an interracial couple—and then bringing up their daughter, Rebecca— as well as the cultural aridity of Jackson led the pair to move north but also led to the unraveling of their marriage.

At the invitation of Steinem, who had fallen "in love with Alice on the page," Alice Walker joined the *Ms.* staff in 1974.[8] Her essays took as their central theme the collaboration between women that was facilitating her own career. The same year that she started working at *Ms.*, she joined Adrienne Rich and Audre Lorde in "refusing the terms of patriarchal competition" for the National Book Award and "declaring that we will share this prize among us, to be used as best we can for women."[9] Ironically, but rarely mentioned when this tale is told, there was another woman finalist, the 22-year-old impoverished Eleanor Lerman, who needed the money and refused to join the pact: if she had won the prize, she stated, "I would have taken it and cashed the check." Decades later, she was still angry, remembering the pressure that had been put on her by "these elitist, educated, fancy-schmancy women."[10]

In 1974, too, Walker's "In Search of Our Mothers' Gardens" appeared in the pages of *Ms.* and quickly became a landmark text. Walker begins by meditating on the thwarted creativity of Black women that turned them into "crazy Saints" staring "wildly, like lunatics—or quietly, like suicides." As she wonders how a Black woman could become an artist under inhumane circumstances, she finds it necessary to revise Virginia Woolf's discussion in *A Room of One's Own* of the impediments to female creativity, noting that unlike the middle-class white women on whom Woolf focuses, enslaved women faced the horrors of "chains, guns, the lash, the ownership of one's body by someone else, submission to an alien religion." Walker quotes Woolf's meditation on the "contrary instincts" that would have doomed Shakespeare's sister and then considers the "contrary instincts" evident in the slave-poet Phillis Wheatley's encomium to a golden-haired goddess of liberty, lines that later earned derision from critics.[11]

"No more snickering" at Wheatley, Walker proclaims: "We know now that you were not an idiot or a traitor; only a sickly little black girl, snatched from your home and country and made a slave," struggling to speak with a "bewildered tongue." As for those who did not manage to sing the song that was their gift, Walker asserts that they, too, found ways to express their creativity. Turning to her own origins, she describes the quilts, stories, and gardens that her mother produced. Our conception of artistry must be widened, she argues, to include the creativity of generations of women like her mother. When she concludes by considering Phillis Wheatley's mother, Walker speculates that perhaps she "was also an artist. Perhaps in more than Phillis Wheatley's biological life is her mother's signature made clear."[12] Lyrically, Walker establishes a Black aesthetic matrilineage to affirm cross-generational, transnational links between women.

One year later, Walker recounted her effort to pay homage to her most significant literary precursor in that matrilineage. "In Search of Zora Neale Hurston," which also appeared in the pages of *Ms.*, resurrects a forgotten author who would soon become quite influential. Walker had fallen in love with Zora Neale Hurston on the page and decided to impersonate the author's niece to find out what she could about the Harlem Renaissance genius whose work was no longer in print and who may have died of "malnutrition."[13] Wading through weeds in a south Florida cemetery, terrified of snakes, Walker finds what she believes to be Hurston's grave, chooses a cheaper marker than the one she wants, and hands over the inscription to the engraver:

ZORA NEALE HURSTON
"A GENIUS OF THE SOUTH"
NOVELIST   FOLKLORIST
ANTHROPOLOGIST
1901   1960

Later, an acquaintance of Hurston's insists she *"didn't* die of malnutrition."[14] Facts remain obscure even among the few people who
remember Hurston (as it turns out, for instance, Hurston was born
in 1891, not 1901), but they would be clarified by Walker's support of
later Hurston scholars.

Both essays display the passion with which Walker encouraged
women writers as an editor at *Ms.*, where she promoted the publication of Mary Gordon, Ama Ata Aidoo, and Ntozake Shange, the
author of the 1976 Broadway hit *For Colored Girls Who Have Considered Suicide When the Rainbow Is Enuf.* Attacks by male critics had distressed Shange, who found refuge in a social group, the Sisterhood,
that the poet June Jordan organized and Walker joined, along with
Toni Morrison. When Morrison's *Sula* was criticized in the *New York
Times*—its author was informed that she needed to "transcend" the
"classification 'black woman writer'"—Walker came to the defense
with a letter that Morrison deemed "splendid."[15]

The 31-year-old Walker must have been disheartened, then,
when her college mentor Muriel Rukeyser objected to her portrait
of Hurston, who, Rukeyser claimed in a letter, was helped by "white
women," just as Walker had been aided by Rukeyser herself at Sarah
Lawrence and "in comparable ways." Rukeyser asked Alice Walker
to "correct" her accounts of Hurston's life and of Rukeyser's positive
role in Walker's own career.[16] In response, Walker tried to explain
both her indebtedness and her need to distance herself: "Have you
ever considered how like a beggar I felt those days when all of you

were 'helping' me?"[17] She admitted to overlooking Rukeyser's assistance publicly, but also wondered why Rukeyser, whose letter hints that she had known Hurston, had not taught Hurston's works in her courses on Southern writers.[18] Undoubtedly painful for both of them, the damage done to their relationship reflects the tensions that troubled allies in the women's movement.

In 1975, Gloria Steinem was wounded by attacks that came from feminists she had supported. The anger of two sixties radicals, Kathie Sarachild and Carol Hanisch, had been brewing for some time. According to Susan Brownmiller—who published her groundbreaking book *Against Our Will: Men, Women and Rape* that year and later documented the period—Sarachild and Hanisch "did not understand how it had come about that the mainstreamers at *Ms.* were speaking for the entire movement while they, the founders, were shut out of the public discourse."[19]

Sarachild and Hanisch released document packets at a media event that began by denouncing Steinem's "ten-year association with the CIA . . . which she has misrepresented and covered up"; they then stated that "*Ms.* magazine . . . is hurting the women's liberation movement."[20] While the radicals insinuated that Steinem had lied about her impoverished childhood, Ellen Willis, another Redstockings founder, left *Ms.*, charging it with "a mushy, sentimental idea of sisterhood." But Susan Brownmiller informed Betty Friedan that she would not help air the CIA charge against Steinem: it was "not only laughable, it was loony."[21]

In 1959, Steinem had worked at a nonprofit educational foundation encouraging young Americans to attend International Communist Youth Festivals to represent free-world values. Responding to the attacks by retreating behind her usual nonconfrontational style, Steinem agonized and lost weight. In a belated statement to the press, she explained, "I naively believed then that the ultimate money source didn't matter, since . . . no control or orders came with it." Decrying her attackers, she concluded: "Every page of this meandering 'release' contains other distortions. To answer each one would be like [shaking] hands with an octopus."[22] Internecine quarrels about the validity of the charges against Steinem effectively destroyed the Sagaris Collective, a visionary summer retreat in Vermont that had presented itself as a utopia for feminist educators.[23]

The accusations inspired the republication in *Ms.* of the essay "Trashing"; written by "Joreen" (Jo Freeman), it begins with her dismay while she watches "as the Movement consciously destroys anyone within it who stands out in any way."[24] The article provoked numerous letters, many from those who had been trashed. In interviews, Friedan recycled reports that Steinem was a government informant, decried a "cannibalization of leadership" in the women's movement because ratification of the ERA had begun to stall, and claimed that "followers of Total Womanhood or the Pussycat League or the League of Housewives" have started "moving in backlash against us."[25]

Ironically, they were all probably being spied upon throughout this period on the orders of the head of the FBI, J. Edgar Hoover, who used surveillance strategies against what he called WLM, the Women's Liberation Movement.[26] When it became clear that the FBI had sent informants to infiltrate feminist groups all across the country, Letty Cottin Pogrebin wondered in a 1977 issue of *Ms.* at all the smears in the extensive FBI files: " 'They' kept tabs on 'us' with the aid of special agents, informers, observers, infiltrators, other law enforcement agencies, and Red alert signals from conscientious citizens." Sadly, she concludes that the FBI "compiled a catalog of the Women's Movement's self-destructiveness and our lost opportunities—a

requiem for once thriving coalitions killed by the death wish of ideological purists and a nostalgic reminder of extinct organizations and
names since burned out and retired from activism."[27]

Steinem was hardly the only one trashed, as her biographer Carolyn Heilbrun has explained, but she was "the most famous and the
most publicized, therefore the most ardently hated."[28] Drawing on
her own experience of being trashed, Erica Jong identified seventies feminists as a "whiplash generation" and wondered, "Why are
women so ungenerous to other women?" Then Jong diagnosed the
problem: "Unable to turn our assertiveness against men, we turn it
against each other."[29] She was implicitly agreeing with the psychologist Phyllis Chesler: "My feminist generation ate our leaders. Some
feminists who were really good at this became our leaders." Chesler,
too, had an analysis of the dynamic: "Like other powerless groups,
my generation of feminists found it easier to *verbally* confront and
humiliate another feminist than to *physically* confront patriarchal
power in male form."[30]

By the time Steinem arrived at the eagerly anticipated 1977
National Women's Conference in Houston, reactionary opponents
of feminism had begun exploiting not the divisions among feminists
but, ironically, their unanimity. A "high point of liberal feminism,"
the convention was inaugurated by a relay of female athletes who carried a torch lit in Seneca Falls and a new Declaration of Sentiments
written by Maya Angelou.[31] Some "20,000 women participated, 35
percent of the delegates were nonwhite and nearly one in five was
low income."[32] Along with Kate Millett, Andrea Dworkin, Billy Jean
King, Margaret Mead, and Coretta King, First Ladies Rosalynn
Carter, Betty Ford, and Lady Bird Johnson appeared at a bipartisan
event that the anti-feminist Phyllis Schlafly was to identify as the

moment when she knew that she would defeat the ERA: specifically, when the "libbers" voted to extend the feminist platform to include lesbian rights. In later years, Schlafly used films of the vote to damage feminism, even showing the footage on television in advertisements against the ERA. "In her view," the educator Sheila Tobias has noted, "the display of feminist solidarity with lesbians that day in Houston clinched her victory."[33]

In Houston in 1977, Schlafly also staged a counter-conference that brought together thousands of men and women opposed to the ERA and abortion with those antagonistic to gay rights. "God Made Adam and Eve, Not Adam and Steve" waving placards declaimed.[34] What Schlafly represented as an unholy trinity—feminism, women's control of reproduction, and homosexuality—would soon consolidate the New Right.[35] To the various religious denominations assembled, she emphasized "their common belief in the primacy of divinely created gender roles and familial structure."[36] The STOP in STOP ERA meant Stop Taking Our Privileges.

Other prominent women prefigured the preachings of Atwood's Serena Joy. The former beauty pageant winner Anita Bryant started her "Save Our Children" campaign against gay men who, she weirdly argued, set out to molest "our children" because they cannot produce children of their own.[37] And a character based on the teachings of Marabel Morgan—the best-selling author of the anti-feminist seduction manual titled *The Total Woman* (1973)—appeared on the TV show *Maude*, greeting her homecoming husband attired in nothing but plastic wrap.[38] But Phyllis Schlafly outdid them all, which may explain why Donald Trump eulogized her at her funeral. A lawyer, political candidate, author, and orator, she castigated feminism as an assault on the privileges enjoyed under the law by stay-at-home wives and moms.

AUDRE LORDE DISMANTLES
THE MASTER'S HOUSE

Despite right-wing backlash, hopes for the passage of the ERA remained high throughout the seventies. And if anyone could confront head-on the divisions within feminism, that person was Audre Lorde. *Sister Outsider* (1984), the title of Lorde's collected essays—most of which were delivered as lectures in the late seventies—captures the role she played in addressing fractures in the second wave, as do the talks themselves. An oxymoron, it reflects her commitment to the sisterhood of the women's movement as well as her insistence on positioning herself as an outsider questioning its boundaries.

After a marriage during the sixties to a closeted homosexual and the births of two children, Lorde found her vocation when in 1968 she went to Tougaloo College in Mississippi as poet-in-residence: "I began to learn about courage, I began to learn to talk." Suspecting that the marriage was going nowhere and that her next partnership would be with the academic Frances Clayton, Lorde realized that "teaching was the work I needed to be doing."[39] Back in New York, she embarked on a career in the SEEK program at City College and at Lehmann and John Jay Colleges.

Throughout the subsequent years, Lorde grappled as a lesbian with homophobia in the Black community. As an African American, she denounced white feminists' eurocentrism. As the mother of a son as well as a daughter, she scolded gay separatists. As a Black woman who had married a white man and was parenting with a white woman, she chided racial separatists. A poet, she excoriated economic injustices too often ignored by privileged academics. When she became a cancer patient, she reprimanded medical authorities. By tapping the anger of an outsider, Lorde became a quarrelsome sister. Not an easy person to get along with, she courageously mined "the crucibles of difference" that shaped the prose writing she crafted to gain a larger audience than the readership garnered by verse.[40] Her talks and essays, drawing on her earlier experiences, encouraged twentieth-century feminists to guard themselves against the racism of nineteenth-century suffragists and learn from their painful disagreements.

Living with her daughter Beth, her son Jonathan, and Clayton on Staten Island, Lorde could publish her third collection of verse, *From a Land Where Other People Live*, only by acquiescing to the editor's insistence that she delete "Love Poem": "And I knew when I entered her I was / high wind in her forests hollow / fingers whispering sound / honey flowed / from the split cup."[41] The male editor of a prestigious Black book series couldn't imagine the poem being spoken by a woman.[42] Yet "speaking up was a protective mechanism" for her—a way of fending off antagonists—so she published "Love Poem" in *Ms.* magazine in 1974 and tacked it up on the wall in John Jay's English department.[43]

Lorde's essay "Scratching the Surface" tackles the "lesbian-baiting" in Black communities that undermines the bonding of Black women with each other and with non-Black women. She accuses Black men of creating environments that discourage Black women's sense of solidarity and program them instead to compete for male approval. The energy wasted in the Black community on "antilesbian hysteria" scapegoated people like her and her colleagues in the Combahee River Collective.[44] In poetry and in other essays, Lorde argues that "Black male consciousness must be raised to the realization that sexism and woman-hating are critically dysfunctional" because "they arise out of the same constellation that engenders racism and homophobia."[45]

While the homophobia and sexism of the Black community hor-rified her, the racism of white feminists did too. "An Open Letter to Mary Daly" urges the post-Christian feminist theologian to deal with the "history of white women who are unable to hear Black wom-en's words." When reading Daly's account of the goddess in *Gyn/Ecology* (1978), Lorde was baffled at the "white, western european, judeo-christian" images: "Where was Afrekete, Yemanje, Oyo, and Mawulisa? Where were the warrior goddesses of the Vodun, the Dahomeian Amazons and the warrior-women of Dan?"[46] These are the muses invoked in the poems she was producing.

Lorde had long worn a dashiki and head wrap, but now she regularly donned them for readings and signed her letters "In the hands of Afrekete."[47] According to Lorde, Daly's book presents non-European women "only as victims," specifically by focusing on geni-tal mutilation and ignoring positive aspects of African culture. Even Lorde's own words seem misused by Daly: "Did you ever read my words, or did you merely finger through them for quotations which you thought might valuably support an already conceived idea con-cerning some old and distorted connection between us?"[48]

That the letter to Daly degenerates into threats—"I would like not to destroy you in my consciousness"[49]—seems especially odd in view of a fact supplied by Lorde's biographer, Alexis De Veaux. Although the letter opens with a note that Lorde published it after receiving no reply, De Veaux quotes Mary Daly's polite response, which Lorde did receive, and goes on to speculate that the obfus-cation arose from "Lorde's love-hate-competitive relationships with white women": "There was an element of 'sibling rivalry' in her view of the sisterhood between Rich and Daly that Lorde found herself outside—insecure and intensely jealous."[50] De Veaux asso-ciates Lorde's possessiveness with her "sexual aggressiveness"—in affairs she kept secret from Clayton and in sexual overtures rebuffed by friends like Barbara Smith, Adrienne Rich, and Rich's partner, Michelle Cliff.

Collaboration or competition: Lorde veered back and forth. When in 1974 she was nominated for the National Book Award for poetry, as we have seen, Lorde joined Rich and Walker "in refusing the terms of patriarchal competition." And Adrienne Rich facilitated Lorde's connection to the editor John Benedict at W. W. Norton, the publishing house that issued *Coal* in 1976. But a list of Rich's books advertised at the back infuriated Lorde. Their dialogues about gender and race could not alleviate her edginess about a better-known rival. Yet Lorde knew that Rich was herself deeply committed to antiracist work as a teacher and thinker, so their disputes functioned for her as symbolic debates "in a space of Black woman/white woman where it's beyond Adrienne and Audre, almost as if we're two voices."[51]

Lorde's anger informed her most gnomic maxims. In "Power," a poem excoriating a white policeman who was freed after shooting a 10-year-old in Queens, Lorde unleashed her fury at racial injustice: "The difference between poetry and rhetoric / is being ready to kill / yourself / instead of your children."[52] Her most famous saying, "the master's tools will never dismantle the master's house," appears as the title of an essay provoked by her appearance at a conference otherwise devoid of Black women and lesbians. According to Lorde, white feminists were using "the tools of a racist patriarchy . . . to examine the fruits of that same patriarchy." They ignore different forms of oppression at their own peril. By not dealing "with the fact that the women who clean your houses and tend your children while you attend conferences of feminist theory are, for the most part, poor women and women of Color," they produce "racist feminism." She ends by asking each member of her audience to *"reach down into that*

deep place of knowledge inside herself and touch that terror and loathing of
any difference that lives there. See whose face it wears."[53]

In 1977, at Rich's suggestion, Lorde reached down to touch
her own terror and produced a talk called "The Transformation of
Silence into Language and Action." Fear of cancer had overwhelmed
her during a scare that proved to be unfounded: the biopsied tumor
turned out to be benign. During her three-week confrontation
with "the final silence" of death, what Lorde regretted most were
her silences. Her personal discovery—"My silences had not protected me"—morphed into a more general message: "Your silence
will not protect you." Fear "of visibility, of the harsh light of scrutiny and perhaps judgment, of pain, of death" makes us vulnerable,
but free speech also furnishes "the source of our greatest strength,"
for words "bridge the differences between us": "it is not difference
which immobilizes us, but silence. And there are so many silences to
be broken."[54] Like Tillie Olsen, whose essay "Silences" appeared in
1962 and whose book *Silences* appeared in 1978, Lorde spoke for the
empowerment of the dispossessed through language.

Extrapolating from her childhood experience with verse writing,
Lorde's essay "Poetry Is Not a Luxury" sees poetry as "the way to help
give name to the nameless so it can be thought" and especially as a way
to give name to emotions. If the "white fathers told us: I think, therefore I am," the "Black mother within each of us—the poet—whispers
in our dreams: I feel, therefore I can be free." In "Uses of the Erotic:
The Erotic as Power," eroticism is defined as "an assertion of the life-
force of women; of that creative energy empowered, the knowledge
and uses of which we are now reclaiming in our language."[55]

On the tenth anniversary of the Stonewall Riots, Audre Lorde
gave a speech at the huge National March on Washington for Lesbian and Gay Rights that her longtime friend and sometime lover

the historian Blanche Cook called "galvanizing."[56] By 1979 she had become a charismatic spokeswoman, even though the year before, at the age of 44, she had undergone a mastectomy. In the words of her son Jonathan, "her life took on a kind of immediacy that most people's lives never develop."[57]

Quickly determined to break the conspiracy of silence surrounding breast cancer, Lorde refused to wear a prosthesis and began writing essays about cancer. Her 1979 account of her mastectomy in *Sinister Wisdom* is a draft for what would become *The Cancer Journals* (1980). Lorde describes the pain she endured, the community of women who healed her, and her determination to confront "the whole terrible meaning of mortality as both a weapon and power," for she wanted "not to turn away from the fear, but to use it as fuel" to find herself "furiously empowered."[58]

She would go on in the next decade to become a pioneer in patients' rights as she questioned the procedures of breast reconstruction and addressed the environmental causes of cancer while setting the standard for a genre of patient memoirs that continues to challenge medical assumptions and practices. Facing schisms within the women's movement, Lorde believed that "anger expressed and translated into action in the service of our vision and our future is a liberating and strengthening act of clarification."[59] Because she is perceived to have "own[ed] anger the way that Monet owns water lilies," her vigorous spirit continues to inspire contemporary feminists.[60]

MAXINE HONG KINGSTON'S GHOSTS AND WARRIORS

Far from the seething center of feminist politics on the East Coast, West Coast feminists too were struggling to convert silence into language and action. Tillie Olsen was a grande dame, but she was joined by Ursula K. Le Guin, Joanna Russ, Dorothy Bryant (*The Kin of Ata Are Waiting for You*, which Alice Walker pronounced "one of my favorite books in all the world"),[61] Susan Griffin (*Woman and Nature: The Roaring Inside Her*), Ruth Rosen (*The Maimie Papers*), Angela Davis, and many others, eventually including such fugitives from the East Coast as Alice Walker and Adrienne Rich.

In 1976, just as the concept of "identity politics" was starting to surface, a new kind of feminist text was published by a West Coast writer. Maxine Hong Kingston's *The Woman Warrior: Memoirs of a Girlhood among Ghosts* added to seventies conversations about the differences between women and men and the differences among women an appreciation of a host of other differences—geographical, linguistic, culinary—that mark what it means to grow up female.[62] Although at the time the book was published Kimberlé Crenshaw had not yet developed her theory of "intersectionality," the experiences of Kingston's protagonist, simultaneously resisting misogynistic Chinese traditions and long-standing American prejudice against Chinese immigrants, dramatize the dynamics that Crenshaw was to delineate in the eighties.[63]

The Woman Warrior is compulsively readable: it won a National Book Award, became a best seller, and was one of the most frequently taught contemporary works throughout the eighties and nineties. But despite its riveting style, this memoir—or rather these memoirs—are fragmentary, constituting a tale told in theatrical flashes rather than a straightforward narrative. Yet when read carefully, *The Woman Warrior* is a *Künstlerroman*, recounting the girlhood and education of a literary artist who just might be Maxine Ting Ting Hong Kingston. Certainly there are many parallels between the narrator of this book and its author: both grow up in a close-knit Chinese immigrant community in Stockton, California; both come from large families whose parents never learn English;[64] both have mothers who "talk-story"; both experience the ambivalence toward the "home" country that is characteristic of first-generation Americans; and both are talented in all their studies.

Perhaps because of these parallels, even Kingston's title is ambiguous. Much of the book is a kind of collaboration between the narrator's mother, who "talks-story" *to* her daughter, and the narrator herself, who "talks-story" *about* her mother.[65] Who, then is the Woman Warrior after whom the book is named? The figure is a blur, both mother (whose name is "*Brave* Orchid"—italics ours) and daughter (who reimagines herself/her mother as a version of the famous Chinese woman warrior Fa Mu Lan). Both women are warrior women; however, some of their most significant battles are against each other, suggesting that "Maxine," or Little Dog (as she is sometimes called in the book), is suffering from an ambiguous case of matrophobia.

And what about the subtitle—*Memoirs of a Girlhood among Ghosts?* Again, the book is not a single cohesive memoir, but rather memoirs of both mother and daughter. *Among Ghosts?* This crucial word may be the most resonant. For Chinese immigrants, Americans/white people seem to be "ghosts"—not really, as the narrator's mother hints, "human beings": "America has been full of machines and ghosts—Taxi Ghosts, Bus Ghosts, Police Ghosts, Fire Ghosts, Meter Reader Ghosts. . . . Once upon a time the world was so thick with ghosts, I could hardly breathe."[66]

The White Ghosts are terrifying not just because they appear to be inhuman creatures but also because they are oppressive, openly or subtly showing contempt for the immigrant Chinese. But those American ghosts aren't the only phantoms haunting this book. Back in China, Brave Orchid encounters monstrous ghosts, both in her own experience and in stories through which she learns the nature of her culture. Are they ghosts of real people, as in traditional Western lore? Mostly not: more like diabolical spirits continually transforming themselves.

The most significant ghost, though, appears in "No Name Woman," the monitory opening tale in the book. "You must not tell anyone," Brave Orchid tells her daughter (who betrays her mother and tells us), "what I am about to tell you": the horrifying story of a young sister-in-law who became illegitimately pregnant as the consequence of a coupling whose origins are shadowy. The woman's husband had left for America; was she raped? or did she drift into an affair? She became pregnant; then the family was assaulted by enraged "villagers" just as she was about to give birth; then she bore her child in the pig pen and drowned herself and the baby in the well. "My aunt haunts me," the speaker confesses. "I am telling on her, and she was a spite suicide. . . . The Chinese are always very frightened of the drowned one, whose weeping ghost . . . waits silently by the water, to pull down a substitute."[67]

"No Name Woman" begins the *Woman Warrior* with dread. Brave Orchid tells her daughter the tale as a warning of the dangers of female sexuality. Girls must be chaste and plain. Yet even if they are appropriately docile, their fate may be as awful as the nameless aunt's. In one of her meditations on the hypothetical possibilities of the inexplicable story, the narrator muses that the unknown lover had "commanded" No Name Woman "to lie with him," and she submitted because "she always did as she was told," even though, as the narrator also muses, "he organized the raid against her."[68]

As if to emphasize the hopelessness of this aunt's destiny, Kingston inserts a chilling reference to the ancient Chinese practice of foot-binding into the tale. As her mother told her, sisters "used to sit on their beds and cry together . . . as their mothers or their slaves removed the bandages for a few minutes each night and let the blood gush back into their veins."[69] The bound feet of the women, some-times considered symbolic of elegance and delicacy, actually ensured that girls from the age of 7 on would sit still to do their weaving. At the same time, the cultural practice signified the same hopelessness into which No Name Woman was born: a space of female oppression from which there could be no escape.

But while *The Woman Warrior* begins with a bleak morality tale, Kingston's memoirs flow onward into a fantasy of escape. In the epi-sode titled "White Tigers," "Maxine" imagines herself ascending a magic mountain where she will be trained to become another Fa Mu Lan, a legendary Chinese sword fighter who takes her father's place at the head of an army determined to overthrow corrupt regimes. Thus if "No Name Woman" introduces us to a retrograde dystopian China, "White Tigers" replaces that country with a utopian realm in which women wield swords, leap over houses, command armies, and revenge themselves on a world they never made.

Everything is almost Disney magical in "White Tigers": a semidi-vine older couple who take the little girl in and train her to be brave and strong, a rabbit who benevolently immolates himself in a campfire when the child is starving on a cold mountainside, an enchanted water bowl in which she can see her parents far away in the valley below.[70] As she grows stronger, she becomes a savior of the China that would otherwise have annihilated her. Her parents tattoo a text of revenge onto her bare back. She leads an army and is truly Fa Mu Lan, the warrior who takes her own father's place as a commander in a patriarchal world.

But then—but then—she's back in Stockton, where she breaks the dishes she's been told to wash, delights in being called a "bad girl," and declares that she'd like to grow up to become "a lumber-jack in Oregon." In her real Chinese life people say, "When fishing for treasures in the flood, be careful not to pull in girls," and she has to "get out of hating range." In fact, she concludes, the "swordswoman and I are not so dissimilar. . . . What we have in common are the words at our backs. . . . The reporting is the vengeance— . . . the words. And I have so many words—'chink' words and 'gook' words too—that they do not fit on my skin."[71]

In "Shaman," the narrative traces Brave Orchid's acquisition of a medical degree in China and her return to her native village, where she practices medicine and encounters more weird apparitions. Of all the sections, this one is most firmly situated in what can only be described as a haunting landscape of China, populated by odd birthings, grateful patients, a village madwoman, Japanese bombers, and the memories of two children who died early. Here Brave Orchid becomes a professional woman who makes her own way in the world.

By contrast, when she emigrates to the ghost world of America, she is consigned to endless days in the stereotypical Chinese laundry that the family operates, and to cooking meals that her "American" children find revolting.

> My mother has cooked for us: raccoons, skunks, hawks, city pigeons, wild ducks, wild geese, black-skinned bantams, snakes, garden snails, turtles that crawled about the pantry floor and sometimes escaped under refrigerator or stove, catfish that swam in the bathtub. . . . She had one rule to keep us safe from toadstools and such: "If it tastes good, it's bad for you. . . . If it tastes bad, it's good for you." We'd have to face four- and five-day-old leftovers until we ate it all.[72]

Brave Orchid cooks boldly for her children; her children find China impossible to swallow: indigestible.

Yet if China poses a conundrum for the children, America is a riddle that the parents are incapable of solving. When Brave Orchid's younger sister Moon Orchid arrives in America thirty years after Brave Orchid has left China, the older sister assumes that the younger one will want to reunite with the husband who had much earlier emigrated and now lives in Los Angeles. But as "At the Western Palace" reveals, for all her canniness in talking-story and sautéing skunk, "Maxine's" mother utterly misunderstands the situation, insisting on Chinese traditions in an American context while even forgetting some key Chinese realities.

Although Moon Orchid and her daughter point out that the husband has remarried and himself has three "American" children, Brave Orchid insists on driving the mother and daughter to L.A. so they can "claim" their rights. The trip is a disaster. Frail and shy, Moon Orchid refuses to confront the errant husband; and as for the husband, he smells "like an American" and has "black hair and no wrinkles," reminding Brave Orchid that "in China families married young boys to older girls."[73] Accomplished and authoritative, he has become an Americanized brain surgeon, and this trauma ultimately drives Moon Orchid mad. Thus if "Shaman" showed Brave Orchid at her best in the heart of China, "In the Western Empire" reveals her vulnerability in America, the puzzle she cannot solve.

All this is learning material for "Maxine," who progresses from terror at the constraints of Chinese femininity to a more nuanced understanding of her mother's weaknesses. Because Brave Orchid never steps outside the narrow community of Chinese "villagers," she sets herself up for defeat. In "Song for a Barbarian Reedpipe," however, "Maxine" finally struggles with her own place in America. Here, as she is whipsawed between Chinese school (where everyone is noisy and free) and American school (where she covers blank pages with black ink and cannot speak), she finally expresses her rage at the American silencing of the Chinese girl, as she bullies a mute Chinese double. Her behavior is wicked, so she is punished by a long illness. Yet at the same time, she has won through to her own song—the song for a "barbarian reedpipe" that was sung centuries ago by a captive Chinese poetess, who probably told her how she could herself become another Chinese poetess, telling her own story among the barbarians of America. Or would she become an American poet, telling her own story against the alien backdrop of China? Reconciling the tensions between the fantastic homeland of the past and the confusing home of the present, she emerges triumphantly as both Chinese and American in a talk-story of the dialogue between two cultures.

THE DINNER PARTY

While Kingston was teaching high school in Hawaii and beginning to draft *The Woman Warrior*, we were team-teaching in Blooming-ton, Indiana, and then beginning to write *The Madwoman in the Attic*. At that time, the idea of gathering a constellation of women writers who had never been assembled before felt like putting on a celebra-tory dinner party.

But perhaps it was also a kind of wake, a space of mourning. For we celebrated the genius of nineteenth-century literary women, but at the same time saw the painful circumstances of their lives—Jane Austen hiding her manuscript under a blotter when guests came to call; Charlotte Brontë responding to Robert Southey's dictum that "Literature cannot be the business of a woman's life, and it ought not to be" by noting, "I have endeavored not only to observe all the duties

a woman ought to fulfil, but to feel deeply interested in them"; Emily
Dickinson taking a young friend up to her room and locking the door
with the comment "Matty: here's freedom."[74]

The contradictions between the achievements of these literary
women and the constraints that bound them were compelling. We
knew we had to write a book and as soon as we parted in the fall of
1974, we began to write—and to write like mad. Through the intervention of a friend, we got a contract with Yale University Press, but
we were somewhat alarmed by the size of the manuscript we'd produced: nearly a thousand pages, which would turn the book into a fat
700-page volume.

At a Modern Language Association meeting, we plunked half the
pages into one typewriter paper box, half into another, hoping that
our wonderful editor, Ellen Graham, would think we were giving
her two copies of the work. But she was too shrewd: "That's the first
half of the book and that's the second, isn't it?" she said in her lovely
Southern accent. It was the shoebox of cards for the massive index
that almost did us in; but then *The Madwoman* was quickly reviewed,
and one of its first reviewers, the eminent scholar and mystery writer
Carolyn Heilbrun, would become a beloved mentor. In 1979, the year
the book came out, every day felt like a surprise party.

And then there was a celebratory artwork, called *The Dinner
Party*, to top things off. The feminist artist Judy Chicago, who chose
as her last name the name of the city where she grew up so she could
discard the patriarchal names of father and husband, planned a massive installation to honor both the female domestic arts of needle-
work, pottery, and weaving and the female heroes of history. Festive
banners honoring the goddess lined the entrance to the exhibit.
Their solemn message was utopian:

And She Gathered All before Her
And She made for them A Sign to See
And lo They saw a Vision
From this day forth Like to like in All things
And then all that divided them merged
And then Everywhere was Eden Once again[75]

In the huge, dimly lit room of the installation, a large trian-
gular table evoking the delta of Venus was loaded with hand-sewn
runners, goblets, and beautifully painted plates representing thirty-
nine female heroes whom Chicago had chosen to celebrate. These
ranged from Boadicea to Virginia Woolf, from Hrosvitha to Emily
Dickinson, from Elizabeth I to Georgia O'Keeffe. The colors and
designs were sometimes fierce, sometimes subtly nuanced, reflecting Chicago's response to the figures she was representing. And the
basic structure was vaginal. Too vaginal! argued some of the installation's stoniest critics. "Vaginas on plates," Chicago summed up their
attacks, encapsulating the review of Hilton Kramer, the art critic at
the *New York Times*, who concluded by calling it "an outrageous libel
on the female imagination."[76]

Yet for the one of us (Sandra) who saw the exhibit when it first
opened at the San Francisco Museum of Modern Art, there was
something ceremonial about the banquet room. King Arthur's
round table had become a female triangle, and instead of knights in
armor who would stab their food with knives, the guests would be
the very women who might have been trophies for those knights.
The installation space was hushed, as people moved around, quietly
studying each place setting, the runners, the banners: a stage-set
for a silent opera in which all the historical heroines who might

have been sacrificed by Wagner, Verdi, Puccini, et al. were instead resurrected.

But yes, there *was* something problematic about reducing each woman to her sexual parts—labia, vulva, vagina—every woman except, that is, the one Black woman represented, Sojourner Truth, whose plate featured—instead of the central vulvar core—three faces. And wait: why depict Emily Dickinson as a vagina surrounded by delicate layers of pink lace? Nothing volcanic or Vesuvian about pink lace! On the contrary, something frivolous and fragile.

Reactions to the exhibit turned out to be predictive of conversations that would evolve as later feminists built on the work of the seventies, questioning its racial awareness as well as its emphasis on a fixed essence of womanhood. Why was Sojourner Truth the only African American included in *The Dinner Party* and why was she presented without a slit? And what about that slit at the center of all the other plates?

As to the first question, maybe Judy Chicago had refrained from using the slit on the Sojourner Truth plate because she couldn't imagine a Black woman with a vagina, as Alice Walker among others speculated.[77] Or, a more sympathetic viewer might argue perhaps it was because Judy Chicago believed that Black women historically had been reduced to nothing but their reproductive/sexual parts. As to the second question, Chicago had created a work that rhymed well with what many racially diverse feminists had been brooding on throughout the seventies and indeed back into the sixties and even the fifties.

Women had for centuries been defined by that slit, which enabled them to give birth—and to be raped—and to be silenced as trophies. Whatever each one had accomplished, she had done through a flowering around and about and above the slit. Perhaps the plates had been designed to show both the immanence, the materiality, of woman (the sexual/maternal slit) *and* her transcendent/spiritual accomplishments (the flowering around the slit). If the trendy French psychoanalyst Jacques Lacan could define the penis/phallus as the "transcendental signifier," couldn't Judy Chicago counter that the vagina, too, is both immanent and transcendent?

Chicago wasn't alone in claiming that each woman is in some way rooted in the X chromosome, even if her femininity is at the same time created by societal imperatives and constraints. The opening of *The Dinner Party* at the end of the seventies confronted us all with the dilemma that feminists had long been facing: vaginas (nature) on plates (culture)! Is that what women have been—and are? This is a point that a number of trans and nonbinary thinkers would set out to refute in the twenty-first century. But the groundwork for their rebuttal was established earlier by poststructuralist feminists who decried what they called "essentialism," the idea that female anatomy determines women's destiny.

During the last two decades of the twentieth century, the category *women* started to implode within the women's movement, while the movement itself came under increasingly virulent attacks from secular as well as religious conservatives. By the end of the seventies, feminism had become fully visible to its antagonists: and, as Shulamith Firestone had warned, "Power, however it has evolved, whatever its origins, will not be given up without a struggle."[78]

REVISIONS IN THE EIGHTIES AND NINETIES

8

Identity Politics

FROM A FEMINIST PERSPECTIVE, the eighties began with grim news. The Republican Party elevated Ronald Reagan to the presidency, opposed abortion rights, and withdrew its support for the ERA, which failed to gain ratification. "It's morning again in America," proclaimed the Reagan reelection campaign in 1984, featuring images of white couples buying homes and shiny new cars in leafy landscapes. Were the eighties witnessing the dawn of a new age or, rather, a new/old age—the fifties reborn?

In what seemed to be a call for a return to the fifties, Betty Friedan argued in 1981 not only that the women's movement was over but that it should be over: "In reaction against the feminine mystique, which defined women solely in terms of their relation to men as wives, mothers and homemakers, we insidiously fell into a feminist mystique, which denied that core of women's personhood that is fulfilled through love, nurture, home."[1] And in 1982 a *New York Times Magazine* essay about "post-feminism" reported that quite a few younger women considered feminism "a dirty word."[2] This was the period when some of our undergraduates began telling us, *"We've come a long way, professor! We're shattering glass ceilings!,"* or they floated the dispiriting declaration, *"I'm not a feminist, but . . ."*

Yet gains from seventies activism kept on mounting: the armed forces, NASA, and most men's colleges had begun to welcome women. Between the years when Alice Walker and then Toni Morrison received the Pulitzer Prize in fiction, Geraldine Ferraro ran for the vice presidency and a *Newsweek* poll ascertained that 71 percent of women believed the women's movement had improved their lives.[3] TV shows such as *Murphy Brown* and *The Golden Girls* were popular, while Oprah started her media reign. Inside museums, the Guerrilla Girls protested the male monopoly on art; and inside Nora Ephron's romantic comedy *When Harry Met Sally*, Meg Ryan simulated orgasm at a deli table to the amusement of other customers and of moviegoing audiences. In the film *Nine to Five*, which generated a TV series and a Broadway musical, Jane Fonda, Lily Tomlin, and Dolly Parton waged war against their sexist boss.

Certainly, feminism had taken hold in parts of the entertainment world and in the academy. Our students could tell us that they'd "come a long way" because they had taken, or been offered, a range of courses in the women's studies programs that were proliferating on campuses. The activism of the seventies had largely disappeared from the streets, and now was cloistered in the ivory tower. The new culture of academic activism enlarged our conversations, but it was notably different from the public activism that preceded it, and that now became less a mission, more an object of study.

As social safety nets unraveled under Reagan, with his constant baiting of "welfare queens," the feminization and racialization of poverty became more evident.[4] A deadly virus afflicting the gay community led to panic that fomented prejudice against homosexuals.

When complications from AIDS became the leading cause of death among men between the ages of twenty-five and forty-four, sexual anxiety led to the scapegoating of gay men as well as feminists who supported gay liberation. Violent demonstrators tried to shut down women's health-care clinics while right-wing publications fanned the flames of what were called "the culture wars."

How should we characterize the evolution of the second wave in the mostly conservative eighties and nineties? Waves, after all, travel at different speeds and sometimes in sets. At the end of the twentieth century, two approaches reshaped feminist thinking: identity politics, which we discuss in this chapter, and poststructuralist theory, which we broach in the next. Under their influence, feminists questioned the word *women*, which became suspect for conflating people with divergent backgrounds and orientations.

Identity politics promoted coalitions of women dedicated to exploring their racial, ethnic, linguistic, or spiritual origins. Two anthologies—*This Bridge Called My Back* (1981) and *All the Women Are White, All the Blacks Are Men, But Some of Us Are Brave* (1982)[5]—inaugurated a swell of books that focused attention on Chicana, African American, Asian American, and Native American women. Suspicious of identity categories, proponents of poststructuralist theory unraveled conventional ideas of masculinity and femininity, as well as heterosexuality and homosexuality, and in the process drew attention to multiple forms of eroticism.

Within the academy, feminists began writing and lecturing for each other rather than for general audiences. To advocates of identity politics, the term *women* was too capacious and in need of adjectival qualifiers (Black women, Native American women). For poststructuralists, it was too narrowly constricted by its heterosexual antitype (men). At the peaks of their positive influence, advocates of identity politics and of poststructuralism challenged feminists to explore new areas and think in new ways. In the troughs, both groups trashed their seventies predecessors as blind to the realities of women of color ("racist") or as blind to the social construction of gender ("essentialist").[6]

Even while academic conversations became increasingly opaque, such literary women as Andrea Dworkin, Gloria Anzaldúa, Adrienne Rich, and Toni Morrison illuminated differences among women that gave rise to differences among feminists. Especially in their deployment of identity politics, they extended feminist discussions to analyze sexual and racial injustice in transnational contexts. Eventually, the concept of intersectionality arose out of identity politics as both literary critics and creative writers explored the subtle ways in which gender is inflected by economic, religious, linguistic, and geographic factors.

ANDREA DWORKIN AND THE SEX WARS

At the start of the eighties, important debates in the women's movement issued in a battle that pitted feminists against feminists. Much of the anger of seventies activists had coalesced in protests against the violence that girls and women too often experienced: rape, incest, child abuse, domestic battery, workplace harassment, and femicide (a nineteenth-century legal term that was revived). Activists questioned early sexual liberationists: how liberating is sexual freedom in a male-dominated culture?

The proliferation of pornographic magazines and movies suggested that pornography itself might be to blame for assaults on women. Snuff and slasher movies had surged in popularity. What should be done about them? This question led to the so-called porn or sex wars. Although no single crusader can represent the many voices raised against sexual violence, Andrea Dworkin often starred in that role. As activists organized the first Take Back the Night marches, Dworkin began to represent the group called Women Against Pornography. She was loud, large, and "the angriest woman in America"—a radical feminist, she explained, but "not the fun kind."[7]

At the podium, Dworkin's "dramatized martyrdom and revival-tent theatrics"[8] arose from damaging experiences: she was assaulted at the age of 9 and later fled a marriage to a physically abusive husband. Before that marriage, at freewheeling Bennington College, she prided herself on having "never slept with faculty members, only their wives." Later in life, she married the feminist activist John Stotenberg, who also identified as gay. After being arrested at an anti–Vietnam War protest and "sexually brutalized" by a gynecological examination in New York City's Women's House of Detention, Dworkin brought charges that eventually helped lead to the closing of the prison. Homeless at some points during a sojourn in Europe and resorting to prostitution, she returned to the States determined to lecture as a feminist "because I had a lot of trouble getting my work published."[9]

Claiming that she was too impoverished to buy her favorite women's movement button, "Don't Suck. Bite," Dworkin spoke out against the idea that women were to blame for the violence inflicted on them: "it was presumed that the woman was sexually provocative or was trying to destroy the man with a phony charge of rape." She called for "a generation of warriors who can't be tired out or bought off. Each woman needs to take what she endures and turn it into action. With every tear, accompanying it, one needs a knife to rip a predator apart."[10]

Dworkin opposed those feminists who aligned with civil libertarians to reject all forms of censorship and who quickly became known as "pro-sex." Wary of moral pieties that had historically inhibited women from experiencing sexual pleasure, pro-sex feminists emphasized the difficulty of distinguishing between sexually explicit art and pornography: "What turns me on is erotic; what turns you on is pornographic," Ellen Willis quipped. Dworkin dismissed this stance as a collaboration with the enemy, for she agreed with Robin Morgan that "pornography is the theory, and rape the practice."[11]

Gloria Steinem, who supported Dworkin's efforts, labeled her an "Old Testament prophet"; Susan Brownmiller dubbed her "Rolling Thunder": "Perspiring in her trademark denim coveralls, she employed the rhetorical cadences that would make her both a cult idol and an object of ridicule a few years later."[12] To others, she "seemed like a misogynist's caricature of a women's rights activist, a puritanical battle ax in overalls out to smite men for their appetites."[13] Inspired by Kate Millett's *Sexual Politics*, Dworkin's book *Pornography: Men Possessing Women* (1981) reflected many feminists' belief that the porn industry's images of female humiliation robbed women of their humanity and promoted violence. Salacious magazines and movies, Dworkin believed, indoctrinated men into what today is called toxic masculinity.

As her detractors pointed out, Dworkin often depicted sex itself as a violation, for she conflated heterosexuality with women's abjection, especially in her book *Intercourse* (1987): "Intercourse remains a means or the means of physiologically making a woman inferior: communicating to her cell by cell her own inferior status, . . . shoving it into her, over and over, . . . until she gives up and gives in— which is called *surrender* in the male lexicon."[14] She was, in other words, an early advocate of the view that men—programmed for aggression and rapacity—are from Mars, women—conditioned for reciprocity and intimacy—from Venus.[15] In a male-dominated culture, many anti-porn feminists argued, men's values were essentially distinct from women's. Separatist communities grew, along with separatist music festivals. Some of the separatist rural communities were called "Womyn's Lands," and the best known of the festivals was the Michigan Womyn's Music Festival: note that it was important to distinguish women from men linguistically, by replacing the "men" in "women" with "myn."

The separatists found confirmation in speculations that grappled once again with Freud, specifically his pre-Oedipal couple: the mother and infant. Dorothy Dinnerstein, for example, argued that misogyny is rooted in women's childbearing and child-rearing, which means that a baby's first other is generally the mother. As children grow up, she claimed, their anxieties and hostilities are projected onto a female figure who comes to embody not-quite-human otherness.[16] The psychologist Nancy Chodorow considered a different consequence of the family romance, namely that the earliest desire of female as well as male babies is for the mother. Because of girls' primary attachment to a female figure, homosexuality remains a significant component of their erotic lives. According to Chodorow, girls identify with the mother (and vice versa), whereas boys define themselves in opposition to the mother. Women who grow up invested in interdependence acquire fluid ego boundaries, whereas men with rigid ego boundaries are characterized by agonistic modes of self-definition. Carol Gilligan extended this insight into ethics.[17]

Taken together, these speculations helped generate lesbian studies in the academy and bolstered the view of separatists that women needed not equality with men but a revaluation of their differences from men: ergo the term *difference feminism* as distinct from *equality feminism*. To the extent that separatist communities espoused a unique identity for women, their founders might be considered the first advocates of identity politics. In some lesbian feminist circles, men became as suspect as the trappings of femininity: high heels, makeup, dresses. Yet such a view alienated not only women in heterosexual relationships but also those advocating for sex workers or identifying as butch or femme. Just as alarmingly, it threatened to reinstate Victorian notions of men as hypersexualized predators and women as paragons of purity, as well as longer-lasting stereotypes of men as active and rational, women as passive and emotional.

Hostility between anti-porn and pro-sex feminists escalated until it came to a head at the 1982 Barnard conference "Toward a Politics of Sexuality," where pro-sex activists sought to reclaim "pleasure and danger" for feminists.[18] Pleasure especially was at risk of being forgotten with the overemphasis on danger. Administrators at Barnard, panicked at the prospect of bad publicity, confiscated the program notes created by the planning committee, and the conference was picketed by members of Women Against Pornography whose T-shirts read "For Feminist Sexuality" on the front, "Against S/M" on the back. Their leaflets accused the pro-sex organizers of lending "support to the very sexual institutions and values that oppress all women."[19]

The foremost sex-positive thinker at the Barnard conference, the anthropologist Gayle Rubin, found herself "traumatized" by the ensuing acrimony. The anti-pornography protesters "attempted to excommunicate from the feminist movement anyone who disagreed with them, and they aggressively sabotaged events that did not adhere to the antiporn line."[20] Wanting to reclaim erotic fantasy for women, pro-sex participants delivered papers on sadomasochism, butch-femme roles, the history of sexual repression, and the sanitizing of lesbianism as sisterhood. The poets Sharon Olds and Cherríe Moraga read their verse aloud. At an off-campus speak-out, the pro-sex Lesbian Sex Mafia organized a slide presentation on dildos, nipple clamps, and bondage. Reporters from the anti-porn feminist newspaper *off our backs* decried a return to the allure of dominance, but Susie Bright soon founded a pro-sex magazine "for adventurous lesbians" and called it *On Our Backs.*[21]

In the aftermath of the Barnard conference, the spokesperson who would become Andrea Dworkin's unlikely sidekick, Catharine MacKinnon, came forward with the decorous self-presentation fostered by her Ivy League legal training. She had already pioneered the legal argument that sexual harassment functions as discrimination in the workplace: in *Sexual Harassment of Working Women* (1979), McKinnon argued that "economic power is to sexual harassment as physical force is to rape."[22] By 1983, Dworkin and MacKinnon were team-teaching a class at the University of Minnesota, where they began to argue that pornography was a civil rights violation against women.

First in Minnesota and then in Indiana, they drafted civic ordinances that would outlaw demeaning sexual representations of women.[23] "If a woman or girl was forced into making pornography or if a woman or girl was raped or assaulted because of pornography, the pornographer or retailer could be held responsible for civil damages," Dworkin explained about the legislation.[24] Why did Phyllis Schlafly back Dworkin and MacKinnon's efforts?[25] While lies and evasions proliferated about AIDS, conservatives campaigned for abstinence-only sex education and the censorship of sexually explicit representations. Both anti-pornography feminists and pro-sex feminists quickly realized, as one historian put it, "that the state's interest in restricting sexual expression had nothing to do with a commitment to enlarging women's rights."[26]

Because of the rescinding of the ordinances—they were found

to be unconstitutional—most commentators on the porn wars believe they were won by the pro-sex side.[27] On the sidelines, we found ourselves leery of any form of censorship—we had read Rabelais, Joyce, Lawrence, and Nabokov, all of whom had created works labeled obscene—and therefore enlisted on the pro-sex side.[28] But now we feel more divided. During an era in which a rape occurred every three minutes in America, both sides suffered a defeat. Both were undermined by a society that spouted puritanical pieties while commercialized forms of sexuality became perversely profitable.

What was to be done about all of this? When asked this question by a student journalist at Harvard, Andrea Dworkin had a discerning response. "That's where first-person testimony of women has been so important," she said. "Because the mainstream will say, 'Oh, that doesn't happen' and then a group of women will say, 'Well, it happened to me.'" Rebecca Traister, the author of the 2018 book *Good and Mad* (partly inspired by Andrea Dworkin), furnishes this account, and punctuates it by chiming in: "Yeah. Me too."[29] Johanna Fateman, one of the editors of a 2019 compilation of Dworkin's writings titled *Last Days at Hot Slit*, attributes to Dworkin "a prescient apocalyptic urgency."[30]

GLORIA ANZALDÚA'S *MESTIZA* CONSCIOUSNESS

While the words of Dworkin resonate with the #MeToo activists of our time, the writings of her contemporary Gloria Anzaldúa illuminate the history of immigration policies that led during the Trump administration to the separation of children from their parents at the Mexican border and their incarceration in bleak holding cells. By supplying first-person testimony about growing up as a Chicana in south Texas, Gloria Anzaldúa inspired feminist thinking about ethnic identity politics and transnational issues.

Born on a ranch settlement, at age 11 Gloria Anzaldúa moved with her family to Hargill, Texas. Throughout her childhood, she experienced pain and shame because of a hormonal imbalance that brought about very early puberty—"I was always made to feel ashamed because I was having a period and had breasts when I was six years old"— but she would soon find an "escape through reading" and eventually through writing that she associated with physical and spiritual healing. After the death of her father when she was 15, Anzaldúa labored as a migrant worker until she earned her B.A. in 1969 and then an M.A. in 1972 that enabled her to become a high school teacher. While writing *Borderlands/La Frontera* (1987), she was "much more extreme, political and angry" about the situation of Chicana women than when she had left Texas for California, but "yes, I was always angry and I am still angry," she explained after the book made her famous.[31]

Declared Anzaldúa, "gender is not the only oppression."[32] Ethnicity and geography play a major role in *Borderlands/La Frontera*, where she used history, autobiography, and myth to promote understanding within Chicano and Mexican cultures as well as communication between Chicano/Mexican cultures and Black, Native American, Anglo, and international cultures. At the heart of the book, she argues for a new awareness of the paradoxes that she calls "*mestiza* consciousness": a recognition of conflicting allegiances bequeathed to those residing in borderlands, who must learn to live with multiple identities.

For Anzaldúa, *mestiza* consciousness evolved out of rage at Anglos who appropriated the land of Mexicans when they incorporated it into the state of Texas, and at the mistreatment of legal as well as illegal immigrants. Writing about the traffic from the south to the north during the Reagan years, Anzaldúa reminds us that crises at the border have been going on for decades: "Without benefit of bridges, the '*mojados*' (wetbacks) float on inflatable rafts across *el río Grande*, or wade or swim across naked, clutching their clothes over their heads." Especially at risk, the Mexican refugee woman is often raped by "the *coyote* (smuggler)" or "he sells her into prostitution. She cannot call on country or state health or economic resources because she doesn't know English and she fears deportation": "This is her home / this thin edge of / barbwire." Even for natives, the borderland is a landscape of exploitation "where the Third World grates against the first and bleeds. And before a scab forms it hemorrhages again, the lifeblood of two worlds merging to form a third country—a border culture."[33]

Within southwestern Chicano communities, "Males make the rules and laws; women transmit them." Only "a very few" can evade subservience by "entering the world of education and career," as Anzaldúa did when she was the first in her family to go to college. Loyal to her origins, Anzaldúa nevertheless abhors how her culture "cripples its women" and "makes *macho* caricatures of its men." "Being lesbian and raised Catholic" produces "*loquería*, the crazies," since "Women are at the bottom of the ladder one rung above the deviants. The Chicano, *mexicano*, and some Indian cultures have no tolerance for deviance." She feels "sold out" by the Anglos but also by her own community: "The dark-skinned woman . . . has been a slave, a force of cheap labor, colonized by the Spaniard, the Anglo, by her own people."[34]

Because Anzaldúa's personal rebellion "was quite costly—cramped with insomnia and doubts"[35]—she knew that traumatized borderland women often needed healing. Both linguistic and spiritual practices contribute to the therapies Anzaldúa prescribes in *Border-*

lands/La Frontera. As the book's bifurcated title indicates, English and Spanish must be sutured to reflect *mestiza* consciousness. Anzaldúa writes in a potpourri of standard English, English slang, standard Spanish, Mexican Spanish, North Mexican dialect, Chicano Spanish, and Tex-Mex. Switching codes, she does not always want "to accommodate" English readers. Instead, she seeks to raise their awareness of their own linguistic limitations by leaving some passages untranslated. With creolized idioms, she mines images that function as "a bridge between evoked emotion and conscious knowledge," creating meaning out of "a state of psychic unrest, in a Borderland."[36]

Just as Lorde turned to African goddesses, Anzaldúa returned to Indian, Mexican, and Catholic myths of powerful female figures, reinventing them as supporters of her spiritual quest for self-validation. Malinali (or La Malinche), a Mexican woman who served as the adviser to the Spanish conquistador Hernán Cortés; *la Llorona*, the folkloric abandoned, wailing woman who drowns herself and her children in a river; and the *Virgen de Guadalupe* (the Virgin Mary): all needed to be reimagined. Anzaldúa also seeks to reinvent the great Aztec goddesses Coatlicue, Tlazaolteotl, and Cichuoacoatl because "Azteca-Mexica culture [gave] them monstrous attributes."[37]

Both her multilinguistic writing and her spiritual meditations foster *mestiza* consciousness by breaking down dualities (virgin/whore, supernatural/natural, human/animal, spirit/body) and enable Anzaldúa to cultivate a "tolerance for ambiguity,"[38] leading her to proclaim herself reborn as a paradoxical creature:

As a *mestiza* I have no country, my homeland cast me out; yet all countries are mine because I am every woman's sister or potential lover. (As a lesbian I have no race, my own people disclaim me; but I am all races because there is the queer of me in all races). I am cultureless because, as a feminist, I challenge the collective cultural/religious male-derived beliefs of Indo-Hispanics and Anglos; yet I am cultured because I am participating in the creation of yet another culture, a new story to explain the world and our participation it, a new value system with images and symbols that connect us to each other and to the planet.[39]

Echoing Virginia Woolf's declaration in *Three Guineas* (1938)—"as a woman, I have no country. As a woman I want no country. As a woman my country is the whole world"[40]—Anzaldúa claims her place in a trans-Atlantic feminist lineage.

The success of *Borderlands/La Frontera* reflected a growing awareness among American feminists that the women's movement had always been an international phenomenon.[41] By the mid-eighties, the allure of French feminists—Hélène Cixous, Luce Irigaray, Monique Wittig, and Julia Kristeva—prompted translations of theoretical texts that harnessed the psychoanalytic ideas of Jacques Lacan and Jacques Derrida's theory of deconstruction to address an issue comparable to the project that engaged Gloria Anzaldúa: affirming the feminine component in what has historically been subordinated, repressed, or made monstrous. Like Anzaldúa, the French feminists reinvented mythological figures (Cixous' "The Laugh of the Medusa"), envisioned alternatives to systems based on male primacy (Irigaray's "This Sex Which Is Not One"), celebrated homosexuality (Wittig's utopian *Les Guérillères*), and plumbed abject emotional states (Kristeva's *Powers of Horror* and *Black Sun*).[42]

Through their influence, American feminists began turning to international matters. Robin Morgan produced the 1984 anthology *Sisterhood Is Global*, to which even Simone de Beauvoir contributed. Determined not "to settle for monoculturalism," Morgan promoted

the Action Alerts of the Sisterhood Is Powerful Institute,[43] and at the
end of the eighties, she took over the editorship of a newly international *Ms.* magazine. Feminist multiculturalism in the eighties was
extended but also questioned by the scholarship of the postcolonial
critic Gayatri Chakravorty Spivak, who was born in Calcutta a few
years before the partition of India, attended graduate school at Cornell, and became Derrida's first English translator.

Deeply committed to comparative literature, Spivak nevertheless
wondered whether well-meaning Western intellectuals could grasp
the situation of third world women. In her 1983 paper "Can the Subaltern Speak?,"[44] she reminded Western intellectuals that the female
subaltern—a subjugated person with no public agency—cannot be
heard or read. At the same time, she established literacy programs for
children in her native India, just as Gloria Anzaldúa turned her attention to bilingual children's books so she could teach the Chicano/a
past. Anzaldúa appreciated Spivak's contribution to postcolonialism,
though like us, she found "Can the Subaltern Speak?" hard going: "it
took me a long time to decipher her sentences."[45]

ADRIENNE RICH'S JUDAISM

During the eighties, while Audre Lorde was helping to found feminist support groups in the Caribbean, South Africa, and Cuba, Adrienne Rich took a turn toward identity politics that would eventually
lead her to map her own origins as a "split at the root" Southern Jew.
"Split at the root"—a line from one of her early poems—is the title
she gave to a 1982 essay in which she struggles with the subtle anti-
Semitism she had inherited from her Jewish father.[46] Arnold Rich,
a pathologist at Johns Hopkins, never spoke of his Judaism but was
secular, "deist," and assimilated.[47]

The Rich family, she tells us in this piece, was proud and private. Helen, Adrienne's Gentile mother, had been raised in an atmosphere of Southern gentility and tried to bring Adrienne and her sister up in the same way. Were the parents—or just Arnold—deliberately repudiating Judaism? When Adrienne began to question her father about his religion, he told her "measuredly" that he had never "denied" that he was a Jew, but Judaism simply was "not important" to him. Yet (and this was to be crucial to her life) Rich quotes a note to her from one of her father's Gentile colleagues, who believed that Jews "of this [Southern] background looked down on Eastern European Jews, including Polish Jews and Russian Jews, who generally were not as well educated."[48]

Eastern European Jews, recent immigrants, were noisy and vulgar, from this assimilated perspective. Thus, when she went off to Radcliffe, Rich's mother advised her to respond to forms questioning her religion with the word "Episcopalian." And in fact, both Adrienne and her sister were baptized and sent to Sunday services as Episcopalians. Nor were the concepts of Judaism and anti-Semitism ever discussed in the household. When at 16 Rich went by herself to see one of the first films depicting the liberation of the Nazi camps, with their stacks of corpses and skeletal survivors, her parents were "not pleased"; she felt "accused of being morbidly curious, . . . sniffing around death for the thrill of it." But gradually she came to understand that though the word "Jew" and the phrase "anti-Semitism" were "taboo" in the "castle of air" where she grew up, she herself would have met the same fate as the abject victims on the screen: "According to Nazi Logic, my two Jewish grandparents would have made me a *Mischling, first degree*—nonexempt from the Final Solution."[49]

At Radcliffe, she met Jewish girls who were comfortable with their origins and taught her about Judaism. Yet even there, she was

ambivalent toward her roots. In a dress shop, she had a conversation with a refugee who knelt at her feet . . . hemming her skirt.
"You Jewish?" the woman asked in a "hurried whisper." And then
"eighteen years of training in assimilation" prompted her to mutter,
"No." "There are betrayals in my life that I have known at the very
moment were betrayals: this was one of them," she comments.[50] Yet
the betrayal was not so much a betrayal of the immigrant dressmaker,
who was just hazarding a guess, as it was of herself, the girl who was
trying to come to terms with her heritage but lied about it.

Why did Adrienne Rich's parents refuse to attend her wedding
to Alfred Conrad in Harvard's Hillel House? Conrad—né Cohen—
was the "wrong" kind of Jew, from an Orthodox Eastern European
family. "My father," she wrote, "saw this marriage as my having fallen
prey to the Jewish family, eastern European division."[51] There was a
break with her parents that lasted for several years, until they allowed
themselves to meet their three Conrad grandsons.

A companion to this essay on familial taboos, the poem "Sources"
(which Rich wrote in the same year), is a sometimes angry, sometimes
loving meditation on the confusing origins she explores in "Split at
the Root." Tellingly the poem returns, after "sixteen years," to the
Vermont farmhouse near the field where Alfred Conrad shot himself.
Brooding on the dwelling's location in a stony New England town,
she notes that she can find "No names of mine," instead descendants
of Puritans or of French Catholic trappers. Yet the house itself, perhaps a symbol of the America in which she feels increasingly uneasy,
seems to ask her questions: *From where does your strength come, you
Southern Jew? / split at the root, raised in a castle of air?*"[52] At the heart of
the text is an implicit dialogue between the two men whose warring
influences shaped her spirit: her austere deistic father and her Eastern
European Jewish husband.

"Sources" is full of evocative description—the Vermont countryside and its history, the chronicles of Judaism and the Holocaust,
family memories—but two central passages, addressed to the poet's
father and to her husband, are in prose, as if they were almost help-
lessly expressive plaints torn from her split-at-the-root self. To the
father, she writes, "For years I struggled with you: your categories,
your theories, your will, the cruelty that came inextricable from your
love. . . . All this in a castle of air, the floating world of the assimilated
who know and deny they will always be aliens."[53] But as she works
through her anger, she finds a way of reimagining this man who had
been to her "the face of patriarchy."

> I saw the power and arrogance of the male as your true water-
> mark; I did not see beneath it the suffering of the Jew, the alien
> stamp you bore, because you had arranged that it should be invis-
> ible to me. It is only now, under a powerful, womanly lens, that I
> can decipher your suffering[.][54]

A "womanly lens": Rich implies here that because of her own feminist
awakening she can finally begin to comprehend the secret suffering
that her father had made invisible to her. Her own "consciousness
raising" has raised her consciousness of her father's pain, the "split"
in *his* being.

Where the address to her dead father is both reproachful and
regretful, the plainspoken letter to her dead husband is troubled and
tender. We quote key passages from it below:

> I have resisted this for years, writing to you as if you could hear
> me. It's been different with my father: he and I always had . . . a
> battle between us, it didn't matter if one of us was alive or dead.

But, you, I've had a sense of protecting your existence, not using it merely as a theme for poetry or tragic musings. . . .

Yet I cannot finish this without speaking to you, not simply of you. You knew there was more left than food and humor. Even as you said that in 1953 I knew it was a formula you had found, to stand between you and pain. The deep crevices of black pumpernickel under the knife, the sweet butter and red onions we ate on those slices; the lox and cream cheese on fresh onion rolls; . . . these, you said, were the remnants of the culture, along with the fresh *challah* which turned stale so fast but looked so beautiful.

That's why I want to speak to you now. To say: no person, trying to take responsibility for her or his identity, should have to be so alone. There must be those among whom we can sit down and weep, and still be counted as warriors. (I make up this strange, angry packet for you, threaded with love.) I think you thought there was no such place for you, and perhaps there was none then, and perhaps there is none now; but we will have to make it, we who want an end to the suffering[.][55]

While Rich's memories of her assimilated home are passionate but abstract, she remembers Conrad warmly through imagery of food. The childhood "house on a hill," detached from reality, fades before the solidity of the Eastern European Jewish practices that Arnold Rich denied. Even after her marriage to Conrad had disintegrated, she associated him with a kind of nurturing that she didn't get from her genteel parents. What kind of food, after all, was she served in that "castle of air"?

Having mapped the ethnic geography of her childhood and of her marriage, Rich clearly felt ready to undertake a larger project: claiming and naming the landscape of her country and of others, too, in her "Atlas of the Difficult World." Here she adopted the voice and vision of a feminist Walt Whitman to explore eighties America. As Whitman did, she amassed individual stories, incantatory passages, overviews of different states, all to serve her purpose: "I am bent on fathoming what it means to love my country."[56] She followed this blunt statement with a series of questions and an argumentative conclusion:

> The history of this earth and the bones within it?
> Soils and cities, promises made and mocked, plowed contours
>   of shame and of hope?
> . . . .
> Minerals, traces, rumors I am made from, morsel, minuscule
>   fibre, one woman
> like and unlike so many, fooled as to her destiny, the scope of
>   her task?
> One citizen like and unlike so many, touched and untouched
>   in passing,
> —each of us now a driven grain, a nucleus, a city in crisis
> . . . .
> A patriot is not a weapon.   A patriot is one who wrestles
>   for the soul of her country[57]

"An Atlas of the Difficult World" is a grand manifesto, a summary of all Rich's political passions. She touches on racism (the Black activist-author George Jackson in solitary confinement within Soledad), on homophobia (the murders of lesbians), on American poverty ("here is the Sea of Indifference, glazed with salt . . . These are the suburbs of acquiescence . . . This is the capital of money and dolor"). But she roots this poem too in her own life and love. Her penultimate passage is dedicated to "M."—Michelle Cliff, the partner with whom she had lived for fifteen years. Here, concluding her tour of America, she praises her lover's "providing sensate hands, your hands of oak and silk, of blackberry juice and drums."[58]

At the center of the poem, almost unbidden, a memory of Alfred Conrad surfaces. As she catalogs objects in the Vermont house that is crucial to her imaginings, she notes:

> Some odd glasses for wine or brandy, from an ignorant,
>   passionate time—we were in our twenties—
> with the father of the children who dug for old medicine
>   bottles in the woods,
> —afternoons listening to records, reading Karl Shapiro's *Poems of*
>   *a Jew* and Auden's "In Sickness and in Health"
>   aloud, using the poems to talk to each other
> —now it's twenty years since last I heard that intake
> of living breath, as if language were too much to bear,
> that voice overcast like klezmer with echoes, uneven, edged,
>   torn, Brooklyn street crowding Harvard Yard
> —I'd have known any syllable anywhere.[59]

The warring influences of Arnold Rich and Alfred Conrad still marked this poem. Arnold may have been defeated, since he doesn't appear here. But was he? His "faithful drudging child" had grown into a prophetic woman, and the habit of "sedulous" labors in which he instructed her shaped her poetic ambitions.[60] As for Alfred Conrad, he was unforgettable, as was the trauma of his suicide. Yet for Rich, Arnold's assimilated "castle of air" had become a dystopian place, while the house in Vermont—near where Conrad shot himself—seems increasingly to have taken on a fantastic utopian quality, even after she had moved to California with Michelle.

THE INTERSECTIONALITY OF TONI MORRISON

Adrienne Rich was the poet who most vividly addressed the racism and sexism that she saw as contributing to American moral decay at the end of the twentieth century; the novelist who most resolutely tackled the intertwined forces of racism and sexism was Toni Morrison. She did so both in critical prose and in fiction. Two madwomen take central stage in *Beloved* (1987), a ghost story about the haunted house of American history. Morrison credited the women's movement for inspiring her thinking. In *Sula* (1973), she had taken up feminists' "encouragement of women to support other women," while in *Beloved* she focused on a second feminist issue, namely "freedom as ownership of the body." What if a slave mother asserted her freedom to own her body and to claim her children as her own—"to be, in other words, not a breeder, but a parent?"[61]

The opening sentence of *Beloved*—"124 was spiteful"—sets out to confuse, Morrison has explained. How can numbers be vindictive?[62] She wanted to plunge readers into the disorienting repercussions of slavery. The house in question—with its address missing the number 3—is haunted by the missing third child of the once-enslaved mother, Sethe. *Beloved* moves back in time to tell the story of Sethe's escape from slavery and her furious determination to save herself and her offspring from being recaptured. As if caught in a revision of the Medea myth, Sethe murdered her baby daughter when the white slave catchers tracked her down; she was shackled before she could kill herself. The present of the novel recounts the venom of that child who as a phantom young woman, identified as "Beloved" by the single word on her gravestone, returns to wreak vengeance on her mother.

Morrison had come across the record of this infanticide when she compiled *The Black Book* (1974), an anthology of memorabilia from the African American past. The escaped slave Margaret Garner determined to kill her children to save them from what she considered a fate worse than death: slavery. Morrison oversaw the book's publication while she was working as an editor at Random House. The novels following *The Bluest Eye* received acclaim, but it was *Beloved* that earned the Pulitzer Prize in 1988. The following year Morrison accepted a chair in the creative writing faculty at Princeton University, where she began to use nonfiction to examine the racism and sexism of her own times.

Beloved asks about slavery: what injuries accrue when human beings are treated as chattel? From the opening epigraph memorializing "Sixty Million and more"—which evokes the six million of the Holocaust—to the end of the novel, Morrison seeks to establish the scope of the suffering as well as its difference from other disasters. Unlike the Holocaust, which sought to exterminate Jews like rodents, the enormously profitable institution of slavery exploited Blacks by trying to turn them into useful animals. Her enslaved characters can breed, but they can no more marry or parent than can horses and cows.

Under the rule of her relatively benevolent owners, Sethe managed to create a sort of quasi-family, but she has no rights over her own body or those of the man she wants to be her husband or the babies she wants to be her children, a fact brought home by the most traumatic injury inflicted on her by whites: her breast milk is stolen and she is raped. Sethe has witnessed Black men reduced to studs and Black children commodified as litters and sold. *Beloved*'s cast of characters suffer these indignities while their mounting fury fuels their efforts to gain their freedom.

That most of these escapes are doomed reflects a system that enforced a white monopoly over reading, writing, and education.

Because slaves should no more learn to read or write than should horses and cows, one of the villains of *Beloved* is Schoolteacher, who enlists science, literature, and religion in the service of white supremacy. Not only the nomenclature of kinship but also all the other languages available to the slaves have been perverted by their entrapment in dehumanizing laws. *Beloved* sets against the treacherous printed word the visual, physical, and oral modes of communication devised by people who had been ripped from their homelands and deposited on foreign soil: work songs, chants, rope-tug codes, brands on the body, bits of quilting, sermons, a scrap of ribbon, the remnant of an African place-name, a phrase from a spiritual.

The formal complexity of *Beloved*—its shifting points of view and time frames and fractured soliloquies—attests to the trauma of slavery and specifically the repercussions of the traumatized maternity symbolized by stolen breast milk. When after eighteen years Beloved enters 124 as a ghost-girl, she embodies the return of the repressed horror of Sethe's loving murder. Despite Sethe's efforts to "[keep] the past at bay," Beloved's presence triggers flashbacks or "rememories" even as it inaugurates mother–daughter bonding: Beloved's urgency to get the nurturance she was denied and in the process suck dry the mother who killed her; Sethe's piteous efforts to provide limitless recompense as atonement for having put her precious daughter in a "safe" place.[63] The word "mine" echoes throughout their epic struggle as Morrison meditates on love "too thick."[64] For the dispossessed mother and daughter, love—turning possessive—cannot be disentangled from rage.

After a community exorcism of the ghost, *Beloved* concludes by repeating the phrase "It was not a story to pass on."[65] With an emphasis on the last word, the sentence suggests that the horrors of this story should not be perpetuated. With an emphasis on the next-to-the-last word, it means that we must not take a pass on this story. Its miseries cannot be ignored. As a justification of the novel's form, the repeated phrase emphasizes many incongruent stories jostling within *Beloved* that remain mysterious fragments, for most of the experiences of the slaves stolen from Africa would remain untold. As a summation of the trauma of slavery, the book underscores the muteness triggered by a calamity that inaugurated innumerable "unspeakable things unspoken," the title of a lecture Morrison gave at the University of Michigan in 1988.

But Morrison did pass it on, as did such scholars as Nellie Y. McKay, Paula Giddings, and Kimberlé Williams Crenshaw, all of whom used their scholarship to examine the psychosexual, political, and economic repercussions of the American slave trade and some of whom worked with Morrison on the anthologies in which she analyzed racial and sexual injustice. Crenshaw's concept of "intersectionality"[66]—the need to address multiple structures of oppression—became crucial to their endeavor. It fostered discussions of conflicting allegiances, just as Anzaldúa's *mestiza* consciousness did.

In the nineties, two widely covered events galvanized Morrison to deplore ongoing inequality: the Anita Hill/Clarence Thomas hearings in 1991 and then the O.J. Simpson trial in 1995. In the essays Morrison collected about the Hill/Thomas extravaganza, *Race-ing Justice, En-Gendering Power* (1992), she lambasted shortsighted racial solidarity that blinded the Black community to sexual injustice. In the book on the Simpson circus, *Birth of a Nation'hood* (1997), she concluded that deeply rooted sexuality scripts blinded the white community to racial injustice. Between these two publications, Morrison produced a study of the American literary imagination that helped found the emerging field of whiteness studies.[67]

When Anita Hill, a 35-year-old University of Oklahoma law

professor, faced a Senate Judiciary Committee consisting entirely of
white men, she testified that Clarence Thomas had sexually harassed
her while she worked for him—ironically, at the Equal Employment
Opportunity Commission. Although Hill rebuffed his overtures, she
alleged, he continued to talk about bestiality, group sex, and rape; he
asked her, "Who has put pubic hair on my Coke?" and mentioned
the porn actor Long Dong Silver, apparently to tout his own sexual
prowess.[68] Before and after Thomas stood up to decry what he called
a "high-tech lynching for uppity blacks," television audiences were
riveted.[69] Republicans on the committee weirdly invoked *The Exorcist* against Hill or referenced her "erotomania" to insinuate that she
must have fantasized the innuendos she ascribed to Thomas.[70]

Confirmed by a slim vote, Thomas (married to a right-wing
white woman) went on to become one of the most conservative jurists
on the Supreme Court, but the next year a raft of women—including
Dianne Feinstein and Carol Moseley Braun—won political races and
made 1992 the Year of Women. Because Hill wasn't connected to the
Washington elite, she believed, she was "characterized as . . . a vindictive pawn of radical feminists, a victim of erotomania, someone to
be viewed at best with pity, at worst with disdain."[71] Yet her testimony
illuminated sexual harassment in the workplace.[72] Rebecca Walker,
tapping "the rage the televised character assassination had brewed"
in her, took up the mantle of her mother, Alice Walker, to conclude:
"I am not a postfeminism feminist. I am the Third Wave."[73]

In the introduction to *Race-ing Justice, En-Gendering Power*, Toni
Morrison argued that Thomas had to be "bleached, race-free," in
order to be seated on a "stain-free" Court. He therefore raced Anita
Hill. Denying her accusations, Thomas and his supporters ascribed
them to her jealousy of lighter complexioned women—"meaning . . .
his marriage to a white woman"—because, Morrison sardonically

explains, interracial love, "as everyone knows, can drive a black woman insane." Although Professor Hill looked like the epitome of propriety, she became the repository of "madness, anarchic sexuality, and explosive verbal violence."[74]

In Morrison's view, Thomas finally emerges as a double of Robinson Crusoe's Friday, who "moves from speaking *with* to thinking *as*" his master. Having internalized "the master's tongue," Friday and Thomas are condemned to "mimic" and "adore" their rescuers, "but never to utter one sentence understood to be beneficial to their original culture." For this reason, she concludes that "the time for undiscriminating racial unity has passed."[75] The Black community supporting Thomas under the aegis of racial solidarity unintentionally abetted the aims of reactionary groups.

However, in *Birth of a Nation'hood*, a collection of essays about the Simpson trial that Morrison edited with Claudia Brodsky Lacour, she went on to accuse whites of recycling the Ku Klux Klan's most toxic myth. Their title alludes to the 1915 movie *Birth of a Nation*, a celebration of the Klan; the book interprets the media spectacle of the O.J. Simpson case as a replay. Not fundamentally concerned with the crime itself, Morrison instead takes on the national obsession that presumed Simpson's guilt. Why was an image of the light-skinned Simpson darkened on the cover of *Time* magazine?

The popular former football player had been tried on two counts of murder for brutally stabbing his ex-wife Nicole Brown Simpson and her friend Ronald Goldman. Pictures of the interracial couple and the evidence—a bloodied glove—circulated along with broadcasts from the courtroom. Acquitted on both counts in the criminal trial, Simpson was found guilty in a subsequent civil suit filed by the Brown and Goldman families. From the start, most whites presumed Simpson to be guilty, whereas most Blacks did not.

Meditating on Simpson as a crossover figure, Morrison attributes the racial gap to a belief called "reversion to type." Handsome and rich, Simpson had crossed over into the white world. Among whites, his case reflected a view that beneath the veneer of civilization lurked the irrational black beast intent on despoiling white maidenhood: precisely the rape narrative in *Birth of a Nation* that necessitates the purifying vengeance of the Klan. Presumed guilt leads Morrison to liken the "media pogrom" to a lynching: "The appetite for a live head on a stick is ravenous."[76]

One passage in this essay steers perilously close to blaming the victim, Nicole Brown Simpson, for the violence she suffered before her death. After stating that "the unpopular counterargument that concerns female responsibility" in the matters of domestic abuse "is a subversive, almost treasonable one," Morrison concludes: "As long as the wildly irresponsible claim of 'It doesn't matter what she does' is the answer to the helpless, hopeless idiocy of 'She made me do it,' the complicity in power/abuse relationships will be unaddressed." With complicity unaddressed and with "sexual brutality . . . part of the package," Simpson, according to Morrison, ended up an embodiment of "the whole race needing correction, incarceration, censoring, silencing."[77]

In making this "unpopular" argument, she surely anticipated the dismay of white feminists like Gloria Steinem who wanted to see more, not less, attention paid to Simpson's abuse of Nicole Brown Simpson.[78] Andrea Dworkin was not alone in pointing out that the jury in the criminal trial was not presented with the history of domestic violence that might have led them to link it to homicide.[79] According to the legal thinker Patricia J. Williams, "black feminists started feeling a too-familiar squeeze: Were we against domestic violence or were we against racism?"[80]

Given the gap between whites and Blacks, what does Morrison's emphasis on "female responsibility" and "complicity" tell us? It illuminates, we suspect, her conviction that Black women, aware of the systemic indignities and violence inflicted on Black men in a racist society, have a critical role to play in the women's movement, a role that not all white women will affirm. She was extending an insight of Frances Beal, whose 1970 essay "Double Jeopardy" argued that white feminists had to fight racism if they wanted to be joined by Black women, a point reiterated by bell hooks in her book *Ain't I a Woman?* (1981).[81] Morrison risks polarizing her readers to drive home her belief that Black rights cannot be subordinated to women's rights.

Morrison never shied away from depictions of indefensible male predation in her fiction; however, she filtered these representations through analyses of the injuries that racism inflicts on Black men along with portrayals of how those damages wreck the lives of Black girls and women. Patricia J. Williams brought a perspective comparable to Morrison's into a conversation with Gloria Steinem about the Simpson trial. Black women who condemn domestic violence resist speaking out "too forcefully in the public arena," because they are wary of playing into "the sort of excessive spectacle" of the "hypersexualized . . . glistening black body" that arises "any time black men are involved." Both Williams and Steinem concur with Morrison that if Nicole Brown Simpson had been "a plain black woman," as Williams put it, "nobody would have cared."[82]

In many of her novels, as in *Beloved*, Morrison balanced portraits of domestic abusers with male characters, like Paul D, whose experiences of servitude deepen their compassion for Black women. In doing so, she critiqued a large portion of the literary history she analyzed in *Playing in the Dark* (1992).[83] Under her scrutiny, American literary history reveals an urgent white need to project onto African presences the horror of all that is "not-free" and "not-me."[84] The white entitlement that she locates in imaginative works by Edgar Allan Poe, Mark Twain, Willa Cather, and Ernest Hemingway depends on an unacknowledged but powerful conviction that Black people should be enslaved or at least subordinated.

When in 1993 Toni Morrison won the Nobel Prize in Literature, supporters outraged over her not receiving the National Book Award for *Beloved* were mollified.[85] While Oprah Winfrey's book club boosted sales, as did her filming of the novel, Morrison became a muse for younger thinkers fashioning forms of feminism that could grapple with the racing of sexism and the engendering of racism. All of her work suggests that the historical circumstances of Black women have produced problems notably different from those faced by white women and that feminism must become suppler. As Audre Lorde declared in a 1986 interview, "Black feminism is not white feminism in Black face."[86]

In a 1989 lecture exhibiting her commitment to intersectionality, Morrison argued that the "self-sabotage" that "seems to be crippling the [women's] movement as a whole" will cease only when feminists address the formation of American sexism in "racism and the hierarchy of class": "When both are severed, male supremacy collapses and the sea of contention among women will dry up." She glimpses the possibility of "being viewed and respected as human beings without being male-like or male dominated" in the artists and scholars of her day, for they are traveling toward a place "where the worship of masculinity as a concept dies; where intelligent compassion for women unlike ourselves can surface."[87]

9

Inside and Outside the Ivory Closet

IN THE NAME OF "FAMILY VALUES," the Reagan administration
targeted the women's movement, shrank social welfare programs,
and disregarded the AIDS epidemic. In 1992, when African Americans rioted in Los Angeles after the acquittal of four police officers who were videotaped beating Rodney King, Vice President Dan
Quayle ascribed the violence to a "poverty of values" fostered by the
decision of the sitcom character Murphy Brown to bear and raise
a child on her own.[1] He too was invoking the "family values" that
President Reagan and the religious Right promoted. In response to
this overemphasis on the sanctity of the family, and on behalf of lesbians and gay men who could not yet marry, some feminists set out
to expand the women's movement.

While Toni Morrison sought to instruct feminists that Black
rights are women's rights, a number of her contemporaries—outraged
at public apathy about widespread suffering from AIDS in the gay
community—argued that gay men's rights are women's rights. Inside
the academy, a new breed of theorists deployed the poststructuralist

approaches of Continental thinkers to examine what Adrienne Rich had called "compulsory heterosexuality." Like Rich, they sought to undermine the idea that heterosexuality is *the* normal form of eroticism. Throughout the nineties, two gender theorists, Eve Kosofsky Sedgwick and Judith Butler, became influential on college campuses.

As we traveled to feminist meetings, we were energized by colleagues reevaluating groundbreaking poets, novelists, and dramatists whose contributions had been forgotten or dismissed. Within a decade, the imperatives of the seventies led to significant revisions in humanities curricula. Conferences that might in the past have seemed obligatory but boring events were now exciting chances to exchange innovative ideas. Poststructuralist theorists such as Sedgwick and Butler contributed to the sense of intellectual excitement, for the scope of their speculations held out the promise of reimagining gender, sex, and sexual orientation.

Helping to reclaim the word *queer* and found the field of queer studies, such thinkers inspired postmodernist artists and invigorated movements on behalf of nonbinary and trans people. Yet their publications bristled with difficult-to-understand formulations rarely found in the crossover prose of a predecessor like Adrienne Rich. A shift occurred in feminist publications: from literary writing to philosophical discourse. Thus, the emergence of queer theory signaled a growing divide between feminists within the academy and those outside it, even while the new theorists undermined the social categories that advocates of identity politics espoused.

What should we make of the fact that feminists' vying claims of radicalism emerged as the society at large—influenced by the so-called Moral Majority—turned ever more retrograde? In the same year that Anita Hill was treated dismissively by white male senators, Susan Faludi published *Backlash* (1991), which documented widespread masculinist hostility toward women's gains; the heroines of *Thelma and Louise* took a nihilistic leap into the Grand Canyon on their feminist road trip; and quite a few anti-feminist screeds were produced by women like Atwood's Serena Joy.

Amid the intensity of the growing backlash, was feminism in danger of being splintered and ghettoized within an academic niche—an ivory closet—and thus marginalized? Yet while the internet took over our lives, calls for "post-feminism" were countered by proposals for a "third-wave agenda."[2] Were the members of an emerging generation advancing into a utopian future, or retreating into a dystopian past?

THE CULTURE WARS

All the scapegoats of the increasingly powerful Christian Right—women in the workforce, homosexuality, abortion—suggested that a principal target in the culture wars was feminism. But war was also being waged against gay men, who were stigmatized as AIDS took its toll. While televangelists blamed feminists for encouraging women "to leave their husbands, kill their children, destroy capitalism, and become lesbians,"[3] President Reagan delayed effective responses to what was called "the gay plague." His foot-dragging was consonant with his aide Patrick Buchanan's pronouncement on HIV/AIDS: "The poor homosexuals. They have declared war on nature and now nature is exacting an awful retribution."[4]

The reactionary fervor is reflected in the Supreme Court decision in the 1986 case *Bowers v. Hardwick*, which upheld the constitutionality of Georgia's law criminalizing oral and anal sex between consenting adults even in the privacy of their homes. Chief Justice Warren Burger quoted the eighteenth-century jurist Sir William Blackstone as he deemed sodomy "a crime not fit to be named" and

"the infamous crime against nature."[5] The Supreme Court's ruling affected the plaintiff, Michael Hardwick, "strongly" because
"the basic human right the court denied—the right of sexual intimacy with one's chosen adult partner—seems undeniable in any but
a totalitarian vision of the legal order." No less a crime or sin than
sodomy, abortion, declared the Reverend Jerry Falwell, constituted
"murder according to the Word of God."[6]

As "right to life" volunteers in Operation Rescue blockaded
women's health clinics across the country, neoconservative artists
and intellectuals enlisted in the fight against progressive causes, adding people of color to the list of enemies. When Saul Bellow asked
an interviewer, "Who is the Tolstoy of the Zulus? The Proust of
the Papuans?," he was upholding the superiority of the Western
canon of literature created by white men.[7] With a foreword by Bellow, Alan Bloom's best-selling *The Closing of the American Mind* (1987)
associated the changes in Stanford University's Western Civilization program—the inclusion of multicultural works by Blacks and
women—with the barbarism that ensues when colleges open their
doors to African Americans, feminists, and (worst, from Bloom's
point of view) acolytes of rock 'n' roll.

For comparable reasons, George Will believed that the conservative head of the National Endowment for the Humanities, Lynne
Cheney, faced a threat to national security greater than the ones confronted by her husband, the secretary of defense.[8] On the one hand,
right-wing defenders of Western civilization mocked "PC" progressives who, they argued, were straitjacketing free speech. On the other
hand, the works of such artists as Andres Serrano, Robert Mapplethorpe, and Karen Finley should be expurgated, they argued, not
funded by the National Endowment for the Arts.[9] The conservative senator Jesse Helms instructed the nation to call "a perverted

human being a perverted human being." A few years later, he refused to vote for a lesbian nominated to become an assistant secretary at the Department of Housing: "If you want to call me a bigot, fine," he said.[10]

No wonder, then, that feminists found themselves enlisting in the fight for gay rights. During the eighties, according to the activist-author Sarah Schulman, "a number of experienced lesbian and straight women activists were moved by their own relationships with gay men, by compassion and by political understanding of the anti-gay, anti-sex rhetoric . . . around the epidemic to join the newly formed ACT UP," a group of protesters who used confrontational tactics to wake up the public and prod medical researchers.[11] These alliances would be fictionalized by Schulman in her novel *Rat Bohemia* (1995).

Schulman was part of a gay avant-garde that included Tony Kushner, whose riveting two-part play *Angels in America* (1991) mourned the AIDS catastrophe and depicted the closeted Roy Cohn—Joseph McCarthy's chief counsel and a sidekick of Donald Trump's—receiving a secret stash of a new medication, AZT, from the Reagan administration and being haunted by Ethel Rosenberg, whom he had helped sentence to death. Similar concerns about a decimated gay community and a shaming closet would motivate academic feminists to extend their analyses of sex and gender to sexual orientation and homophobia.

THE QUEER THEORIES OF EVE KOSOFSKY SEDGWICK AND JUDITH BUTLER

The backlash during the Reagan–Bush years helps explain the lengths to which feminist theorists would go to dismantle polarities that pitted one type of person against another type of person. By 1990, Eve Kosofsky Sedgwick and Judith Butler were reorienting the women's movement. What better—what more audacious—way than by blowing up normative categories of thinking? Not nature but culture was "exacting an awful retribution," they replied to Patrick Buchanan and Chief Justice Warren Burger. Our mind-sets about sex can change for the better if we recognize the destructive scripts imposed by dualistic categories of thinking. Sedgwick and Butler's target: so-called *heteronormativity*, the outlook that promotes hetero-sexuality as the only healthy and normal sexual orientation.

Paradoxically, Sedgwick and Butler were primarily influenced by male thinkers and often focused on gay men. From poststructural-ism, they inherited the idea that language, reflecting our inherited ways of knowing, imposes meanings that remain indeterminate and multiple. Deploying the insights of the Continental philosophers Jacques Derrida and Michel Foucault, Sedgwick deconstructed pre-vailing axioms of sexuality, Butler the fundamentals of sex and gen-der. Together, their work ushered in queer studies, and then—with the aid of Donna Haraway, who used the figure of the part-fleshly, part-metallic cyborg to explode the tenets of what it means to be human—transgender studies, masculinity studies, eco-feminism, cyber-feminism, post-humanism, and so on.

Trained as a literary critic, Sedgwick began her work by popular-izing the useful word *homosocial* to describe male bonding. The cover of her *Between Men* (1985) featured the painting *Le déjeuner sur l'herbe*, in which Manet portrays two (clothed) men engaging in a conversa-tion routed through the presence of a (naked) woman. For Sedgwick, Manet's nude remains necessary for the intimacy to take place but irrelevant to its substance. Through a succession of close readings, Sedgwick suggests that male cronies often defend themselves against suspicions about their intimacy through an intermediary female figure and through disavowals of homosexuality. Despite both tactics, she concludes, there can be no clear dividing line between the homosocial and homosexual desires of men.

Sedgwick's next book, *Epistemology of the Closet* (1990), analyzed how the hetero-/homosexual divide structures all aspects of Western ways of knowing. She begins with the anger in her community at the "virulent ruling" of *Bowers v. Hardwick* so as to emphasize the "anti-homophobic" imperative of the work she is undertaking.[12] Given her use of a vocabulary that most readers would find daunting—words like "pullulate," "algolagnia," "retardataire," "defalcations," "ukase," and "saltation" abound—it is not surprising that early reviews faulted her "obtuse, cumbersome" prose.[13] But passages of clarity and wit illuminate her point that the gender of a person's sexual choice, rather than many other sorts of differences, regulates the categories into which we put people.

In an attempt to demonstrate that dividing people up into hetero- or homosexuals should not be considered inevitable, Sedgwick lists alternative classifications that would work just as well: for instance, "Some people like to have a lot of sex, others little or none." To illustrate the distinctiveness of gay persecution, Sedgwick compares homosexuals to another stigmatized but not visibly identifiable group: Jews in anti-Semitic societies who, like Queen Esther, could remain closeted or come out. The "distinctive structures" that pertain to the homosexual closet explain the incongruities of the analogy. When Queen Esther comes out as a Jew, no one tells her that she is just going through a phase or asks her how she knows that she is really Jewish. This and other complications stem from "the plurality and the cumulative incoherence of modern ways of conceptualizing same-sex desire."[14]

Sedgwick tackles two contradictory approaches to defining same-sex desire. First, minoritizing versus universalizing ideas. The minoritizing view assumes that there is a distinct population of persons who "'really are' gay," whereas the universalizing view supposes that sexual orientation is unpredictable and that heterosexuals experience same-sex desires, and vice versa. Second, "inversion" versus "gender separatist" models of same-sex desire. The butch may be imagined as a male-identified woman or as a male psyche trapped in a female body; however, the lesbian separatist wants not to cross gender boundaries but instead to embrace her gender as a "woman-identified woman."[15] Sedgwick then explores how the permutations of these paradigms generated the gay literary canon.

Nor should we suppose that this tradition must be a small subset of authors, especially if we recall the ways in which universalizing views of same-sex desire have coexisted with minoritizing ones. Invoking Saul Bellows's query about a Tolstoy of the Zulus, a tongue-in-cheek Sedgwick asks, has there ever been a gay Socrates, Shakespeare, or Proust? She answers with the question "Does the Pope wear a dress?"[16] The canon, in other words, has always included gay writers, a fact that her teacher Allan Bloom surely knew.

Sedgwick herself was targeted as a danger to American culture, sometimes even before she could articulate her ideas. She explained that the conservative culture warrior Roger Kimball lambasted the title of one of her essays, "Jane Austen and the Masturbating Girl," as "an index of depravity in academe" in a book that went "to press before the offending paper was so much as written."[17] (He found the title in the program of a Modern Language Association convention.) In her subsequent essays and books, the undaunted Sedgwick would go on to explore her situation as a woman identifying with gay men, a Buddhist poet and textile artist, and a breast cancer activist. In all this work, she made it a point of political honor neither to disavow nor to claim a gay orientation, though she was married for forty years to the psychologist Hal Sedgwick, whom she met as an undergraduate at Cornell and who is today the keeper of her archive.

Like *Epistemology of the Closet*, the other founding text of queer theory, Butler's *Gender Trouble* (1990), never uses the word *queer*. Whereas the prose Sedgwick used to undercut the hetero-/homosexuality bifurcation could be needlessly esoteric, the sentences Butler crafted to undermine conventional ideas of gender and sex came draped in abstractions. Eight years after the publication of *Gender Trouble*, she won *Philosophy and Literature*'s Bad Writing Contest.[18]

In the 1999 preface to a reissued *Gender Trouble*, Butler addressed "the difficulty of its style." There might be "a value to be derived from such experiences of linguistic difficulty," she believes. "If gender itself is naturalized through grammatical norms, . . . then the alteration of gender at the most fundamental epistemic level will be conducted, in part, through contesting the grammar in which gender is given."[19] Today, when we use the pronouns "they/them" for a nonbinary or genderqueer individual—someone whose gender identity is not exclusively masculine or feminine—it is clear what she means.

Denaturalizing identity, along with sex and gender, was Butler's difficult project.[20] Trained in philosophy, she remains "permanently troubled by identity categories" because they control what they claim to describe.[21] A preconception of what *women* or *lesbians* are or should be always lurks within the category. For the people who fall under the rubric *women* do not necessarily share common characteristics, except to the extent that they experience sexism, while the people grouped under the term *lesbians* may have little in common except the sexism and homophobia they encounter. In other words, these identity categories—even when narrowed down to contain only, say, Chicana women or Black lesbians—lump together people who are quite diverse. The political solution involves *not* revaluing the category but rather "interrogating" or "queering" the framework that privileges men and heterosexuals.

Butler's second subversive intervention did just that by contesting widely accepted concepts of the sex/gender system. For more than a decade, most feminists associated sex with the fixity of biology (nature), gender with the fluidity of social conditioning (nurture). According to Butler, however, both sex and gender are socially constructed and variable. Both are constituted by words and acts that create the impression of a preexisting state. Gender seems natural only because it "produces as its *effect* the illusion of a prior and volitional subject. In this sense, gender is not a performance that a prior subject elects to do, but gender is *performative* in the sense that it constitutes as an effect the very subject it appears to express."[22]

Because the idea that gender is a compulsory performance without a prior performer is hard to handle, many readers latched on to Butler's reference to drag shows. Drag dramatizes how volatile gender can be. Yet at the end of the usual drag show, female impersonators generally disclose the secondary sex characteristics beneath the masquerade. The display of such characteristics would be irrelevant to Butler, however, given her argument that sex is also socially constructed. Whether defined through chromosomes or genital type or reproductive capacity, the sex of the physical body can be interpreted only through the cultures into which we have been inducted.[23] About sex and gender, Butler seemed to be saying, "There is no there there" (as Gertrude Stein once so infamously remarked about Oakland).[24]

Butler challenged her readers to think outside the cognitive boxes

in which we are all contained. If gender is performative, it can be performed in an unlimited number of ways. Like Sedgwick, she wanted
to rethink conventional ideas because they condemn so many men as
well as women "to a death within life."[25] To counter the conceptions
of gender, sex, and sexuality in language saturated with those concepts; to argue that gender, sex, and sexuality are surprisingly mal-
leable: these imperatives make the projects of Butler and Sedgwick
utopian.

Unlike Susan Sontag's *AIDS and Its Metaphors* (1989), which
eschewed a personal investment in the fate of homosexuals,[26] Sedgwick's and Butler's publications would convince many feminists that
gay men's rights are women's rights. Their ideas, vigorously debated
in the academy, were confusing but also revolutionary. However, as
political philosophers pointed out, it is difficult to imagine who would
enlist in feminist and antihomophobic activism if no one acknowl-
edged being a woman or a homosexual.[27]

Was the emergence of feminist theory a radical intervention in
reactionary times or simply a reflection of those times? Did intel-
lectualizing replace or impede organizing? On Gay Pride Day, in
1993, the action group Lesbian Avengers handed out cards that said
"Lesbians! Dykes! Gay Women! We want revenge and we want it
now." According to Sarah Schulman, they kept their activism going
by "stay[ing] away from abstract theoretical discussion."[28] Speaking
about the impact of Continental theory on feminist academicians
in 2005, Gloria Steinem said, "Knowledge that is not accessible is
not helpful."[29]

Maybe theoretical resistance to the category *women* recycled the
same anxiety about second-class status that Denise Levertov and
Elizabeth Bishop had earlier expressed. Was the anti-identity politics
of queer theorists a product of academic elitism, and did it neglect

the material conditions to which real people are subject?[30] One is tempted to ask, what would Audre Lorde think?

ANNE CARSON'S POETICS OF LOVE AND LOSS

Audre Lorde didn't live to see feminist academic theory take over the ivory closet, but other poets certainly did. Among the most celebrated is the classicist Anne Carson, a literary figure of whom Susan Sontag said, with uncharacteristically incoherent enthusiasm, "She is one of the few writers writing in English that I would read anything she wrote."[31] From the start, Carson has been knowledgeable about theory; and in 2013, when she was visiting at NYU, she and Judith Butler put on a performance of Carson's revisionary translation *Antigonick*.[32] Earlier, during the nineties, she had embarked on sophisticated analyses of the silencing of women.

Her first scholarly book, *Eros the Bittersweet* (1986), was both an homage to Sappho of Lesbos and an investigation of ancient erotic bonds between men and boys or men and women. Her collections of poetry, in particular the early *Glass, Irony & God* (1995), focus on the central question she asks in "The Glass Essay"—"What is love?"— while exploring the bleakness of love's ending.[33] Brooding on the pains and perverse pleasures of Eros, Carson also muses on "the gender of sound" as defined by Greek culture, in the essay of that title.[34]

"Putting a door on the female mouth has been an important project of patriarchal culture from antiquity to the present day," she observes in this theoretical piece, explaining the "ideological association of female sound with monstrosity, disorder, and death" by tracing the subliminal parallel between a woman's upper mouth (the one that has teeth and a tongue) and her lower mouth (the messy, leaky vagina). For the Greeks, "female sound" is "bad to hear" because it is irrational, bestial—a "highpitched piercing cry" uttered both on bawdy occasions outside the city limits (as in the *Bacchae*) and at funeral lamentations— whereas male sound is "urbane and orderly." Women utter "a particular kind of shriek, the *ololyga*"—a term that was to evolve into our English "ululate."[35] Women's voices, then, must be silenced or muted, lest they become howls of rage, desire, or lamentation.

"The Gender of Sound" appears almost as an annotation at the end of *Glass, Irony & God*, which begins with the long poem titled "The Glass Essay," a work that is simultaneously a meditation on Emily Brontë, a low-key howl or *ololyga* of lamentation uttered by an abandoned woman, and a dramatization of a glazed-over mental state that follows a traumatic breakup. The plot of this lyric essay is quite simple. After a lover resonantly named Law abruptly leaves her, the protagonist goes to see her mother, who "lives alone" "on a moor in the north" where "Spring opens like a blade." Here, as she "stride[s]"—Brontë-like—across a "moor, paralyzed with ice," she struggles to come to terms with the moment that broke her heart "into two pieces." "When Law left I felt so bad I thought I would die," she confesses, adding dryly, "This is not uncommon."[36]

He abandoned her "on a black night in September," as "A chill fragment of moon rose." Standing in her living room, averting his eyes, he oddly said, "Not enough spin on it," and then,

I don't want to be sexual with you, he said. Everything gets crazy.
But now he was looking at me.
Yes, I said as I began to remove my clothes.

Everything gets crazy. When nude
I turned my back because he likes the back.
He moved onto me.

Everything I know about love and its necessities
I learned in that one moment
when I found myself

thrusting my little burning red backside like a baboon
at a man who no longer cherished me.
There was no area of my mind

not appalled by this action, no part of my body
that could have done otherwise.
But to talk of mind and body begs the question.

Soul is the place,
stretched like a surface of millstone grit between body and mind,
where such necessity grinds itself out.

"That was a night that centred Heaven and Hell, / as Emily would say," the speaker comments, but soon notes, tersely, "He left in the morning."[37]

That the failed relationship between the really or allegorically named Law and the woman who laments his leaving is central to the "Glass Essay" doesn't mean it dominates the book. *Glass* as window glass, looking glass, and *glace* (French for ice) insistently recurs as an objective correlative for loss, isolation, paralysis. Emily Brontë and *Wuthering Heights* help Carson place her speaker in a tradition of gothic erotic cruelty and ferocious loss; remember how Heathcliff "clings at the lattice in the storm, sobbing / Come in! Come in! to the ghost of his heart's darling," separated from her by the glass that lets him see and hear her but keeps her out. Notes Carson, Emily put into Heathcliff "in place of a soul / the constant cold departure of Catherine from his nervous system. . . . She broke all his moments in half." And she adds, "I am not unfamiliar with this half-life."[38]

But her life also includes her therapist, rather comically named Dr. Haw (a scoff-Law?), who seeks to guide her through grief; her aging mother, who cannot understand either her feminism ("Oh I see you're one of Them") or her inability to recover from loss ("Well he's a taker and you're a giver");[39] her institutionalized father, during World War II a handsome navigator in the Royal Canadian Airforce but now suffering from Alzheimer's, who "issues a stream of vehemence at the air";[40] and finally a series of visionary "Nudes," self-images drawn from the moment of abjection when she willingly stripped herself nude to appease Law.[41]

Nudes, declares Carson's protagonist, "have a difficult sexual destiny": some of the "Nudes" are like "card[s] made of flesh. . . . The living cards are days of a woman's life."[42] And these images continue to haunt her when she returns from the moors to her own apartment. At the end of the poem, however, in a moment of reconciliation she has an almost biblical, prophetic vision of an ultimate Nude.

I saw it was a human body

trying to stand against winds so terrible that the flesh was
    blowing off the bones.
And there was no pain.
The wind

was cleansing the bones.
They stood forth silver and necessary.

It was not my body, not a woman's body, it was the body of us all.
It walked out of the light.[43]

As she crosses the icy moor of grief to this moment of ambiguous redemption, Carson is working in a long tradition of female loss
dramatized by such classical figures as Ariadne, Medea, Dido, and
Sappho herself.[44] As a postmodern poet, she was keenly aware of the
poetics of abandonment that energized the writings of one of her
foremost precursors, Sylvia Plath.

Plath, in fact, was on her mind in several short pieces published
before "The Glass Essay." In one, "On Sylvia Plath," she asks, "Did you
see her mother on television? She said plain, burned things. She said I
thought it an excellent poem but it hurt me."[45] In another, "Sylvia Town,"
she imagined Plath's "Eyes pulled up like roots."[46] She must have understood, as she was writing "The Glass Essay," that the loss she was dis-
secting was not only the same loss that Emily Brontë explored but also
the rage at abandonment that courses through so many *Ariel* poems. As
she writes in *The Beauty of the Husband*, an analysis of abandonment that
followed "The Glass Essay," "A wound gives off its own light."[47]

But Carson was also furious at the sex/gender system that shapes
the dilemma of the abandoned woman, and she discussed it in "The
Truth about God," a series following "The Glass Essay." Here is the
opening of "God's Woman," which might well serve as an epigraph
to a book titled *Still Mad*:

Are you angry at nature? said God to His woman.
Yes I am angry at nature I do not want nature stuck
up between my legs on your pink baton
or ladled out like geography whenever
your buckle needs a lick.[48]

POSTMODERNISM/TRANSSEXUALISM

Even while Anne Carson was meditating on the bittersweet classical traditions of love and loss, postmodern and transsexual thinkers were ironizing the romantic heroine. Like feminist theorists, postmodern and transsexual artists were undermining normative categories of gender, sex, and sexuality.

In popular culture, when it "wasn't cool to be associated with the gay community," Madonna was hailed as the gay-friendly idol of performativity.[49] An orgasmic shape-shifter, she was like a virgin, like Marilyn Monroe, like an androgyne, like a dominatrix, but not any one of those identities. Her ever-changing hair color, hypersexualized costumes, and elaborate sets dramatized her refusal to be fixed in any of the parts she played. Doing "everything with a wink," she troubled ideas about gender and sexuality.[50] Huge audiences relished her blaspheming of sexist and homophobic scripts. She emphasized her self-commodification in multimedia tours that empowered her to thumb her nose at the Moral Majority and become enormously rich.

Within punk rock subcultures, younger women staged more overtly political protests by proclaiming girl power in fanzines and bands that attacked a male monopoly over the music industry. In "Riot Grrrl Manifesto" (1992), Kathleen Hanna proclaimed that she and other Riot Grrrls wanted "to create revolution in our own lives every single day by envisioning and creating alternatives to the bullshit christian capitalist way of doing things."[51]

The work of Cindy Sherman prefigured Madonna's style in the art world. First in her *Untitled Film Stills* (1977–80) and then in her 1982 portrait of herself as Marilyn Monroe, Sherman displayed the "interior anxiety" that "seems to seep through the cracks" of fifties femininity.[52] In avant-garde literary circles, the postmodernist novelists Kathy Acker and Chris Kraus produced narratives that blurred fact and fiction by using pastiche and collage to emphasize the textual nature of identity.

Like Anne Carson's verse, Chris Kraus's cult feminist "autonovel" *I Love Dick* (1997) explores women's sometimes masochistic capacity for erotic thralldom. Kraus's experimental work was inspired by the performance artist Hannah Wilke, who had wondered in the seventies, *"If women have failed to make 'universal' art because we're trapped within the 'personal,' why not universalize the 'personal' and make it the subject of our art?"*[53] According to the poet Eileen Myles, Chris Kraus "turned female abjection inside out and aimed it at a man."[54]

Myles, who uses the pronoun "they," represents a group of thinkers whose investment in challenging the boxes of masculinity and femininity issued in a flurry of publications defending the rights of trans individuals. As Leslie Feinberg's realistic novel *Stone Butch Blues* (1993)—about a "he/she" character—indicates, feminists were debating trans issues before television took up the subject.[55] In 1992, Feinberg's pamphlet *Transgender Liberation* protested bigotry against "people who defy the 'man'-made boundaries of gender."[56] In the next year Sandy Stone responded to prejudice against transsexuals in "The *Empire* Strikes Back." She objected to transphobia as lesbian separatists cast Jean Burkholder out of the Michigan Womyn's Musical Festival because she was not a "womyn-born-womyn." Demanding "a deeper analytic language for transsexual theory,"[57] Stone vigorously countered the assumption that trans women were not real women but rather con men invading women's spaces.

In the 1993 performance piece "My Words to Victor Frankenstein above the Village of Chamounix," the trans theorist and filmmaker Susan Stryker adopted the persona of Mary Shelley's monster, a creature whose "unnatural body" also resembles Donna Haraway's cyborg: "It is flesh torn apart and sewn together again in a shape other than that in which it was born."[58] The stigmatization of transsexuals as unnatural or artificial led Stryker to reinvent the voice of Frankenstein's monster, just as others were reclaiming the words *dyke, queer,* and *slut*:

> Hearken unto me, fellow creatures. I who have dwelt in a form unmatched with my desire. I whose flesh has become an assemblage of incongruous anatomical parts. I who achieve the similitude of a natural body only through an unnatural process, I offer you this warning: the Nature you bedevil me with is a lie. . . . You are as constructed as me; the same anarchic womb has birthed us both. . . . Heed my words, and you may well discover the seams and sutures in yourself.[59]

Stryker's rage escalates after she witnesses a lover giving birth. She feels "abject despair over what gender had done to me": *"My body can't do that: I can't even bleed without a wound, and yet I claim to be a woman. How? Why have I always felt that way? I'm such a goddamned freak. I can never be a woman like other women, but I could never be a man. Maybe there really is no place for me in all creation."* Fury rebirths Stryker because transsexuals, who "have done the hard work of constituting ourselves on our own terms, against the natural order," must "forego the privilege of naturalness" and "ally ourselves instead with the chaos . . . from which Nature itself spills forth."[60]

In *Gender Outlaw* (1994), the performance artist Kate Bornstein described her metamorphosis from a heterosexual man to a gay woman, even as she sought to make a place for those neither male- nor female-identified. While feminists were beginning to argue that trans rights are women's rights, violence against transsexuals proliferated. The 1993 killing of Brandon Teena led to the 1999 movie *Boys Don't Cry*. The Remembering Our Dead project was founded to commemorate Rita Hester, a murdered African American trans woman.[61]

Neither male nor female, the cyborg Donna Haraway envisioned in her 1985 "A Cyborg Manifesto" represented her attempt to free feminism from contentious identity politics. A theorist with a science background, Haraway imagined a creature—part flesh, part metal—who is able to hold contradictions together. Inhabiting a post-gender world, the cyborg dissolves the distinction between nature and culture while offering hope for "potent fusions, and dangerous possibilities." Like Anzaldúa's *mestiza* consciousness, Haraway's cyborg crosses borders. Haraway, who finds "the concept of *woman* elusive," repudiates identity claims as well as Adrienne Rich's "dream of a common language." The cyborg—who was not born but made—holds out the possibility of a politics based on "affinity, not identity." After the injuries inflicted by gender and sex, "We require regeneration, not rebirth, and the possibilities for our reconstitution include the utopian dream of the hope for a monstrous world without gender."[62]

Haraway turns to feminist science fiction toward the end of her essay as a way of acknowledging the fantasy couched in her claim that "I would rather be a cyborg than a goddess."[63] With these two options, she lays bare an underlying thread of despair about humanity in the work of poststructuralist thinkers and postmodernist artists. Even more than Sedgwick and Butler, Haraway remained obscure to many feminist intellectuals and to most feminist activists.

WHO OWNS FEMINISM?

To make matters worse, a number of women produced popular attacks on feminism.[64] In 1990, Camille Paglia "skyrocketed to fame" with a book of eccentric literary criticism that celebrated the Marquis de Sade.[65] Or did *Sexual Personae* gain attention because it extolled the "spectacular glory of male civilization" by repeatedly attacking women? "If civilization had been left in female hands," Paglia declared, "we would still be living in grass huts." She also argued that urinary anatomy is destiny: "women are . . . earthbound squatters" who "merely water the ground," whereas "male urination really *is* a kind of accomplishment, an arc of transcendence."[66] Adopting the role of a perverse Serena Joy, she went on to castigate feminists for puritanical moralism and to call date rape a myth.[67]

A contrarian, Paglia was nevertheless joined by polemicists such as Christina Hoff Sommers and Katie Roiphe, some of whom called themselves feminists and all of whom wanted to save women from feminism. They often claimed, as Joan Didion had, that advocates of the women's movement turned women into victims.[68] As the name-calling escalated, bell hooks was not alone in warning feminists that they had to make a greater "effort to write and talk about feminist ideas in ways that are accessible," or else "we will be complicit in the antifeminist backlash that is at the heart of the mass media's support of antifeminist women who claim to speak on behalf of feminism."[69] Who would own feminism was clearly at issue. Unintentional misinformation and intentional disinformation would take a toll on the ways in which feminism would continue to be packaged.[70]

Of course, most Americans were less obsessed with feminist disputes than with the provocative performances of Madonna, Michael

Jackson, and Tina Turner or with video games and *Star Wars* movies—if, that is, they were not pondering Bill Cosby's advice book *Fatherhood* (1986). This queasy combination of a raunchy culture and a folksy moralism, often from suspect sources—Cosby did not author the book and was not yet known to be a sexual predator—found its way into film and politics at the end of the century. The figure who needed to be punished for the licentious behavior that Americans enjoyed watching in movie houses and in the news coverage of Washington, DC? The single, independent woman.

Fatal Attraction (1987), directed by Adrian Lyne, starred an unmarried, unhinged career woman. Its hero, a lawyer (Michael Douglas), has an extramarital fling with a book editor (Glenn Close) who becomes a madwoman: she stalks him, kills and cooks his daughter's pet rabbit, kidnaps the kid, and then attacks his wife in a bathtub until this faithful and clean lady murders the psycho and we are left with the sanctified family intact.[71] The film critic Pauline Kael nailed it when she characterized the movie as a "hostile version of feminism" in which men see "feminists as witches": "The family that kills together stays together and the audience is hyped up to cheer the killing."[72]

The year before Glenn Close dramatized the psychological damages of pursuing professional instead of personal goals, women were inundated with misinformation about the need to marry younger. In "Too Late for Prince Charming?," a *Newsweek* feature, women were told that 40-year-olds had a better chance of being killed by a terrorist than of finding a husband. The story described a "crisis" that it then ignited, though it was retracted twenty years later for misusing data.[73] The media blitz about the hazards of postponing marriage was unrelenting: settle quickly or your biological clock will run down and out. Journalism about "the mommy track"—the idea that women need different work arrangements than men—also set off a brouhaha because, as Representative Patricia Schroeder noted, it "reinforces the idea, which is so strong in our country, that you can either have a family or a career, but not both, if you're a woman."[74]

Nineties media heated up and sexy girls were its trademark. Reality TV shows, ad campaigns for Victoria's Secret and Viagra, an epidemic of STDs, the popularity of thongs and cosmetic surgeries and waif models who looked prepubescent: these were the signs of concupiscence that books by younger feminists attributed to a period that derailed the women's movement.[75] While the Dominican American novelist Julia Alvarez, the Southern regionalist Dorothy Allison, and the Bengali American short story writer Jhumpa Lahiri extended feminist inquiries into identity politics with such lauded works as *How the García Girls Lost Their Accents* (1991), *Bastard Out of Carolina* (1992), and *The Interpreter of Maladies* (1999), feminism was often co-opted to sell spandex corsets, Botox, Brazilian waxes, and President Barbie dolls.

Feminist thinkers stepped up to address the problems faced by young women as they matured in a sleazy culture, and they did so by focusing on the female body. Two examples will suffice. Susan Bordo's *Unbearable Weight* (1993) is more theoretical about the cultural construction of the body than Naomi Wolf's *The Beauty Myth* (1990), but both writers emphasized the unattainable aesthetic standards imposed on women. The more women succeed, the more the fashion, cosmetic, and media industries promulgate unrealistic ideals of the female body—ideals leading to anorexia, bulimia, and breast enhancement or reduction.[76]

Wolf and Bardo judged the overemphasis on female looks "a political weapon against women's advancement."[77] So-called chicklit, a genre widely believed to have been initiated by Helen Fielding's popular British novel *Bridget Jones's Diary* (1996), promoted stories of heterosexual romance in which heroines obsessed over their physical attractiveness and husband-hunting, issues that contrasted sharply with attacks on the overvaluation of female beauty and male protection in seventies best sellers.

National politics reflected feminist and anti-feminist quarrels over the varieties of erotic experience. When the Clinton administration legitimized the 1994 "Don't Ask, Don't Tell" policy, it produced a classic statement of sexual hypocrisy. Supposedly framed to protect gay people in the military, the policy licensed discrimination against people who refused to lie about their sexual orientation. The year after President Clinton began an adulterous affair that would force Hillary Clinton to play the role of the wronged but loyal wife, he signed the Defense of Marriage Act (1996), which denied same-sex unions government recognition.

But nothing fit the bill of salacious crudity better than Ken Starr's investigation into the Clinton presidency. At the center of his prurient report—much of which was drafted, as it turned out, by the young lawyer who would become the controversial Supreme Court justice Brett Kavanaugh—was Monica Lewinsky, a 22-year-old single woman branded a tramp, a tart, a bimbo, and (most famously) "that woman": as in "I did not have sexual relations with *that woman*."[78] Fellatio, according to President Clinton's casuistry, was apparently not sexual at all.

The remark led Monica Lewinski finally to fall out of love with her boss, she admitted during a lengthy television interview with Barbara Walters.[79] Lewinsky explained that at this point the president could have disavowed the erotic relationship but still have called her a valued friend. Instead, she was further horrified when a Clinton aide testified that she had stalked the president, demanded sex, scorned his demurrals, and threatened him. She was being turned into the relentless home wrecker of *Fatal Attraction*, and not just by the *New York Times* columnist Maureen Dowd.[80]

And what of Hillary in this devastating period? As the First Lady, she was still dogged by the seemingly immortal Whitewater scandal. After she had tried, in a clumsy sound bite, to define her own seriousness with the sentence "I don't want to stay home and bake cookies," anxious Clinton campaign officials started handing out "Hillary's cookies" at the Democratic Convention.[81] As early as 1992, when the word "impeachment" had only begun to appear in the fever dreams of hard-right Republicans, a young writer for the *Harvard Crimson* noted that "the old maxim still holds: a strong man is a leader, a strong woman is a bitch." Then she went on to conclude, in a prophetic paragraph:

> The spectacle of Hillary Clinton switching from business suits to pastels and handing out cookies isn't cute. It's degrading. And it's a depressing reminder that we're not as progressive as we think we are, that we'd rather cut the brain power of the Clinton team by half than have a strong-willed and politically active First Lady.[82]

A quarter of a century later, the 2016 election would prove that this observation was still true.

By the end of the nineteen nineties, there seemed to be no tent under which variously defined feminists—radical, liberal, straight, gay, Black, Chicana, postcolonial, poststructuralist, postmodernist, transsexual, third-wave—could take shelter from the flood of propaganda unloosed by right-wingers who scorned what the radio commentator Rush Limbaugh called "feminazis."[83] Or from the commodification of feminism, the selling of it as a fun lifestyle à la Helen Gurley Brown.

Had participants in the women's movement lost the confidence they earlier had to speak as "we" about "our" needs and demands? As if summarizing the traumas of the last decade of the twentieth century, in 1991 Adrienne Rich wrote a prescient poem titled "In Those Years." Here it is in its entirety.

In those years, people will say, we lost track
of the meaning of *we*, of *you*
we found ourselves reduced to *I*
and the whole thing became silly, ironic, terrible:
we were trying to live a personal life
and, yes, that was the only life
we could bear witness to

But the great dark birds of history screamed and plunged
into our personal weather
They were headed somewhere else but their beaks and pinions
     drove
along the shore, through the rags of fog
where we stood, saying *I*[84]

A 1998 issue of *Time* magazine featured a lineup of Susan B. Anthony, Betty Friedan, and Gloria Steinem against a black background, along with the neurotic television character Ally McBeal (played by Calista Flockhart). Red letters posed the question, "Is Feminism Dead?" If feminism was not dead yet, the cover suggested, it was surely on the brink of an abyss.[85] Although this prediction echoed the views of many, we shall see that the news of feminism's demise was greatly exaggerated.

RECESSIONS/ REVIVALS IN THE TWENTY-FIRST CENTURY

10

Older and Younger Generations

THE TWENTY-FIRST CENTURY began with confusion and anxiety.[1] As the millennium approached, computer experts began to worry about the so-called Y2K bug, a programming glitch that could cause systems to mistake the year 2000 for the year 1900, generating weird catastrophes. Planes might fall from the sky, hospitals might lose their records, the software of the government might somehow forget what it was doing. But the Y2K bug was a bust. Here and there, public clocks got mixed up, but most things were all right. Politically, however, things were not all right in the United States. The first war to include female combatants resulted in protests proving the need for an energized women's movement that would soon become more publicly active.

THE NEW MILLENNIUM

At the start of the twenty-first century, the presidential election pitting Bill Clinton's vice president, Al Gore, against George H. W.

Bush's eldest son, George W. Bush, ended with a calamitous recount in Florida and, finally, an appeal to the Supreme Court, which ruled—5–4—against Gore, who had won the popular vote. The inauguration of Bush and his Darth Vader–esque vice president, Dick Cheney, swung the country into a reactionary mode. The catastrophe of 9/11, when the Twin Towers of New York's World Trade Center were destroyed by suicidal Islamist terrorists, led to an invasion of Iraq, whose totalitarian leader, Saddam Hussein, was thought by some to have "weapons of mass destruction" and perhaps to have engineered the events of 9/11—even though the Islamist terrorist group al Qaeda, led by the Saudi Arabian Osama bin Laden, had been identified as the culprit.

Before the invasion of Iraq, however, at least one prominent woman spoke out against what she termed the "self-righteous drivel" promoted by politicians commenting on the fall of the Twin Towers. "Where is the acknowledgment that this was not a 'cowardly' attack on 'civilization' or 'liberty' or 'humanity' or the 'free world' but an attack on the world's self-proclaimed superpower undertaken as a consequence of specific American alliances and actions?" wrote Susan Sontag in a brief statement in the *New Yorker* for which she was almost universally vilified.[2]

With America's entry into that war, the country moved into a grimmer period, marked by revelations of the torture at Abu Ghraib, the waterboarding of prisoners, the secret dungeons (called "black sites") controlled by the CIA, and the use of the prison at Guantánamo Bay for the indefinite detention of prisoners. "Guantánamo Bay has become the gulag of our time," declared Amnesty International's secretary general in 2005.[3] That young women soldiers—most prominently a 21-year old private, Lynndie England—not only participated in grotesque tortures at Abu Ghraib but were photographed laughing at naked, bleeding Iraqi prisoners may have come as a special shock to supporters of women in the military. How could feminists come to moral terms with such behavior, carried out by their own government?

Soon after the Abu Ghraib photographs surfaced, Susan Sontag published "Regarding the Torture of Others" in the *New York Times Magazine*; the article was an offshoot of the book she had produced one month before the Iraq invasion, *Regarding the Pain of Others* (2003). Comparing the Abu Ghraib photos of Iraqi prisoners to those made of Jewish victims in the Holocaust and of Black men lynched in the South, Sontag argued that "the horror of what is shown in the photograph cannot be separated from the horror that the photographs were taken—with the perpetrators posing, gloating, over their helpless captives." The pictures illustrate a "culture of shamelessness" as well as a "reigning admiration for unapologetic brutality."[4] With such poems as "Wait" and "The School Among the Ruins," Adrienne Rich joined dissenters against the war, as did Grace Paley, Alice Walker, Maxine Hong Kingston, and Ursula K. Le Guin.[5]

One important feminist organization in which some participated—Code Pink: Women for Peace—was founded in 2002 to protest the war, and it has continued to flourish over the years. The group's self-definition is ambitious: they are a "women-led grassroots organization working to end U.S. wars and militarism, support peace and human rights initiatives, and redirect our tax dollars into healthcare, education, green jobs and other life-affirming programs."[6] They are also parodic and impudent. The signature color in which members dress for protests is hot pink, and their name is an allusion to the elevated terror threat codes Orange and Red that the Bush administration took to posting after 9/11—but also, of course, a send-up of the old idea that pink is a girlie color standing for sugar and spice and everything nice.

Medea Benjamin, one of the founders, wears pink all the time; her "shoulder bag, her wallet and her cellphone are all pink."[7] Appropriately, the Washington, DC, headquarters of Code Pink, a safe house where members coming to protest can stay, is decorated entirely in pink. Their strategies? Some comical: dressing in pink surgical scrubs to hand out "prescriptions for peace" on pink slips to "call for Bush's ouster"; some polemical: holding up a giant pink banner in the lobby of a Senate office building that read "VOTE PEACE / FIRE BUSH."

As the demonstrations of Code Pink suggest, the women's movement did not die at the end of the twentieth century. While feminists lost ground in politics and in popular culture, organizations like Code Pink—and its more mainstream analog EMILY's List, dedicated to the election of pro-choice Democratic women candidates— have flourished, as have the twenty-first-century successors of Sontag, Rich, Paley, Walker, Hong Kingston, and Le Guin, despite evangelical and alt-right hostility to the women's movement.

For feminism was still demonized by the Moral Majority, the evangelicals, and the Tea Party. Directly after the Twin Towers collapsed, for instance, Pat Robertson commended Jerry Falwell's analysis of the terrorist attacks: "The abortionists have got to bear some burden for this because God will not be mocked. . . . [T]he pagans, and the abortionists, and the feminists, and the gays and the lesbians who are actively trying to make that alternative lifestyle, . . . all of them who have tried to secularize America—I point the finger in their face and say, you helped this happen."[8]

Many white men, riled in part by the historic election in 2008 of the first Black president, began joining neofascist organizations based on white, male, and Christian supremacy. Although First Lady

Michelle Obama tailored her image and her advocacy with exquisite tact, she knew that she and her husband would remain vulnerable to racist caricatures. Yet the fact that America had its first African American family in the White House buoyed many feminists, as did the overturning of *Bowers v. Hardwick* in 2003, the legalization of gay marriage in 2015, and the extension of the 1964 Civil Rights Act to protect trans people in 2020.

During the first two decades of the twenty-first century, a new generation of artists engaged the issues of the day, often through innovative forms. In an altered cultural marketplace, they and their contemporaries revamped popular genres, seeking to bridge the gap between theory and practice. This phenomenon harnessed feminism to a host of causes: the queer, transnational, and trans issues that we explore in this chapter as well as the debates swirling around the Black Lives Matter protests, environmental campaigns, and the #MeToo movement, which we discuss in the next chapter. In the face of burgeoning hate crimes, school shootings, the rise of totalitarian or nativist regimes, and global warming, feminists needed to build coalitions among groups with political and ideological affinities (rather than rely on common identities)—precisely what earlier theorists had called for.

When the young activist Malala Yousafzai won the Nobel Peace Prize in 2014, her award honored her passionate advocacy of girls' education, a commitment that had led the Taliban to shoot her as she sat in a school bus. A few years later, educated women lashed back at the misogyny of the Trump administration. In 2019, 102 female representatives entered a House led by Nancy Pelosi. The newcomers made up nearly a quarter of the membership, an unprecedented demographic shift. By this time, schooling had become a central theme in the feminist imagination. Many creative thinkers depicted their own learning to emphasize the central role played by education in bringing about a more equitable future.

ALISON BECHDEL'S LITERARY GENEALOGY

What might it mean to reach maturity *after* the rise of feminism's second wave? Alison Bechdel answered this question in two graphic memoirs: *Fun Home* (2006) and *Are You My Mother?* (2012).[9] Melding the irreverence of comics with the introspection of the memoir, Bechdel examined her own coming-of-age. While the first book focuses primarily on her relationship with her father and the second on her mother, both explore the consequences of growing up before and after the emergence of the feminist and gay rights movements. "The drama between my mother and me has partly to do with her bad luck coming of age in the nineteen-fifties. We were on opposite sides of women's liberation, and I got to reap its benefits," Bechdel has explained. "With Dad and me, same story: opposite sides of Stonewall. If only my parents had been born later," she added, "they might have been happier, and I wouldn't exist."[10]

The revisionary genre in which Bechdel works is almost as new as she is. Rooted in the macho comic books of the early to midtwentieth century (*Superman*, *Batman*, and the French *Tintin* and *Asterix*), the graphic memoir grew more sophisticated in the work of the controversial R. Crumb (*Zap* comics) and the widely acclaimed Art Spiegelman (*Maus* [1980–91]); at the same time, between the seventies and the nineties comics were infiltrated by underground feminist groups (*Wimmin Comix*, *Tits and Clits*). Bechdel drew strength from this complicated inheritance. She began publishing her memoirs not long after similar works by Lynda Barry and (in Paris) Marjane Satrapi appeared. Eight years after *Fun Home* came out, *Can't*

We Talk about Something More Pleasant? appeared—Roz Chast's poignantly comic profile of her aging parents.

What distinguishes Bechdel's work is its deeply allusive literary quality. The father, Bruce Bechdel, who is the primary focus of *Fun Home*, is a high school English teacher whose library is jammed with modernist classics. Even the chapter titles here are quotes from twentieth-century masterpieces. "Old Father, Old Artificer," the title of the first chapter, is drawn from James Joyce's *Portrait of the Artist as a Young Man*. On the surface, it alludes to Bruce's mania for interior decorating; but add the rest of the sentence ("Old father, old artificer, stand me now and ever in good stead")[11] and it becomes an invocation of the father-as-muse.

Chapter 2, "A Happy Death," refers to Camus's novel with that ironic title and chapter 3, "That Old Catastrophe," is drawn from Wallace Stevens's "Sunday Morning," which we learn was one of Bruce's favorite poems. "In the Shadow of Young Girls in Flower," chapter 4, embeds Alison and her father in a Proustian text, while "The Canary-Colored Caravan of Death," chapter 5, a title drawn in part from *The Wind in the Willows*, frames Bruce's death with a childhood tale that young Alison loved and a subtextual reference to the onrushing car of Mr. Toad. Chapter 6, ironically titled "The Ideal Husband," is Wildean: Alison's mother is playing Lady Bracknell in *The Importance of Being Earnest*, but as more clues of Bruce's homosexuality come to the surface, the shadow of Reading Gaol looms over the text. Finally, chapter 7, "The Antihero's Journey," refers to the urban wanderings of Leopold Bloom in Joyce's *Ulysses* and prepares us for *Fun Home*'s moving conclusion, in which the main character, Alison, imagines herself embracing her real and spiritual father as a kind of Stephen Daedalus to Bruce's Bloom.

In this allusive context, *Fun Home* meditates on Bechdel's memories of her own life. Born in 1960 to parents who taught high school English, she and her two brothers were raised in a small Pennsylvania town, in a large Victorian house not far from the family's mortuary establishment, where her father also worked as funeral director. First at Bard College and then at Oberlin, she read widely in modernist and feminist-lesbian literature. In 1980, a year before she graduated, her 44-year old father was killed in a road accident—or committed suicide by jumping in front of a moving truck—a few months after she had come out as a lesbian to him and her mother. She was 19 years old when her mother phoned her to speak about Bruce Bechdel's closeted life and her own decision to get a divorce, and then to report his death.

The trauma of that death—its indeterminacy and the shock of her father's sexuality—would take two decades to process while Bechdel embarked on a series of jobs to fund her artwork. Her drawings changed after she encountered *Gay Comix 1*, edited by the cartoonist Howard Cruse.[12] In 1983, Bechdel's *Dykes to Watch Out For* began appearing in the feminist newspaper *WomaNews*. The strips, which Bechdel self-syndicated and continued until 2008, won numerous Lambda Awards. Bechdel's bespectacled and boyish cartoon surrogate, Mo, reacts with her close-knit community of friends to every aspect of gay life—activism, dating mores, commitment ceremonies, and coming-out parties—as they congregate in their apartments or at Madwimmin Books.

Originally, Bechdel explains in her introduction to *The Essential Dykes to Watch Out For*, she had tried more conventional writing, but a rejection letter from Adrienne Rich, which became one of her "most prized possessions," convinced her to use her drawings to "catalog" lesbians, to "depict the undepicted." Her cartoons served "as an antidote to the prevailing image of lesbians as warped, sick, humorless, and undesirable" or as "supermodels—like Olympic pentathletes, objective fodder for the male gaze." The nineties taught her that "lesbians could be reactionary provocateurs" (the cartoon box features Camille Paglia's *Sexual Personae*) and that "apparently NO ONE was essentially ANYTHING" (the drawing features Judith Butler's *Gender Trouble*).[13] An admiring response to another letter sent to Adrienne Rich spurred Bechdel to keep on going. She would have been hard-pressed to pay her bills if *Fun Home* had not landed on the *Times* best-seller list.

At the center of the book, on two unnumbered pages, "a centerfold" appears:[14] a realistically drawn sketch of a photograph of a reclining boy in Jockey shorts embodies the archival project of Bechdel the artist. The photograph of Roy, the family's yardwork assistant and babysitter, was shot by her father on a family vacation—taken without her mother—when Alison was 8 years old. The two-page spread attests to Bechdel's mix of love and anger toward her father. On the one hand, her fury at the deceptions that shaped their past leads her to expose the secret Bruce had guarded throughout his closeted life. On the other hand, she finds the picture beautiful, maybe because "I identify too well with my father's illicit awe."[15]

The recursive back-and-forth in time that characterizes *Fun Home* allows Bechdel to express her feelings in a text that functions like an elegy. "There is a gray-green ink wash throughout that Bechdel describes as 'sort of a grieving color,'" one critic points out.[16] Alison's interactions with her father over corpses in the Fun Home—the children's shortening of "funeral home"—lend graphic weight to the subject of death and mourning. A hybrid of pictures and words, *Fun Home* fuses the elegy with a portrait of the artist as a young girl and thereby juxtaposes Bruce Bechdel's secret assignations with young boys against Alison's creative coming-out story. He is the *before* (liberation movements) to her *after*.

However, *Fun Home* also resists such a simple (and potentially self-serving) narrative of progress. Although it begins with Alison's anger at her father's incessant interior decorating, which turns the family's house into a sort of museum, Bechdel returns again and again to scenes with Bruce that dramatize the connections between the father's artifice and the daughter's artistry. In the queer gene-alogy traced by Bechdel, two youthful photographs—one of him, one of her—appear with the speculation that perhaps his male lover had taken his picture, just as her female lover had taken hers. Their resemblance is "about as close as a translation can get."[17]

Throughout *Fun Home*, Bruce wants to adorn his tomboy daugh-ter with barrettes, pearls, and dresses, while she frets at her growing breasts, studies men's fashions, and tries on her father's suits. When Alison catches sight of her first "bulldyke," her "surge of joy" must be stifled since her father expects her to disavow such a masculinized look.[18] Yet in their generational struggle, the adversaries function as doubles. As a boy, he had dressed up as a girl; as a girl, she dressed up as a boy. She shares his admiration for male nudes; they are both connoisseurs of masculinity. His obsessive decorating surfaces in her obsessive-compulsive disorder, which results at one point in her ornamenting every statement in her childhood diary first with the words "I think" and then with a typographical caret that eventually expands in size to cover entire pages.[19] After Alison comes out to her parents, her mother outs Bruce.

Despite his irascible temper, in a family of isolates who rarely display physical affection, Bruce and Alison share their most intimate contact through books that further clarify why Bechdel refuses to dismiss the unliberated past. Drawings of libraries, scenes of reading and instruction, typescripts of manuscripts, book covers, and bookstores abound, emphasizing the intertextuality of *Fun Home*. Alison imagines her mother as a Henry James character, her father as an F. Scott Fitzgerald character. "The line that Dad drew between reality and fiction was indeed a blurry one," Bechdel writes,[20] but the same could be said of his daughter.

Many of the coming-out panels in *Fun Home* portray Alison during her college years in bed with a lover and books—including Adrienne Rich's *Dream of a Common Language* and Olga Broumas's *Beginning with O*—"in what was for me a novel fusion of word and deed." Laughing, naked and entwined with her lover, Alison relearns the significance of *James and the Giant Peach*, for "in the harsh light of my dawning feminism, everything looked different."[21] (The lovers' glee nicely contrasts with the assumption that the dawning light of feminism needs to be "harsh.") Fascinated by the lesbian past, Alison wonders if she would have had the courage of Eisenhower dykes and prides herself on knowing "the three-articles-of-women's-clothing rule." She relishes Proust's use of the word "invert," even though she realizes that "it's imprecise and insufficient, defining the homosexual as a person whose gender expression is at odds with his or her sex": "Not only were we inverts," she thinks about herself and her father, "We were inversions of one another."[22]

Bruce, who had given the child Alison a calendar so she could keep a diary, also gives the college student Alison his copies of Colette's *Earthly Paradise* and Joyce's *Ulysses*. Colette's account of women sharing "their predilections" in Montmartre becomes a welcome addition to the stacks of texts entrancing Alison, which could have qualified as an independent reading course in "contemporary and historical perspectives on homosexuality." After Alison comes out "officially" in a newspaper piece titled with a line by Colette—"of this pure but irregular passion"—Bechdel draws Alison holding Colette's book with her left hand and masturbating with her right: "she was even good for a wank."[23] Hers is a textual and sexual awakening.

Although a seminar on *Ulysses* bores Alison, Bechdel draws on it throughout the close of *Fun Home*. And the confluence of her father's two gifts of Joyce and Colette leads to a page toward the end of *Fun Home* in which Bechdel provides portraits of Margaret Anderson and Jane Heap, who ran episodes of *Ulysses* in their *Little Review*, and of Sylvia Beach, who published "a manuscript no one else would touch." Bechdel concedes that it may have been "just a coincidence that these women—along with Sylvia's lover Adrienne Monnier, who published the French edition of *Ulysses*—were all lesbians," but over a frame of Alison reading Colette, Bechdel writes, "I like to think they went to the mat for this book *because* they were lesbians, because they knew a thing or two about erotic truth."[24] What helps redeem Bruce Bechdel is the literary genealogy he bequeaths to his daughter, a lineage that crosses the divide of the before and after of the second wave of feminism and of pre- and post-Stonewall.[25]

Fun Home ends with a double image of Bruce's death (the front of the oncoming truck) and his resurrection: Bruce standing in a swimming pool, looking up with arms outstretched as young Alison prepares to launch herself from a diving board into his arms and into the water where he stands. She is symbolically diving into the wreck of her family's life, just as Adrienne Rich recorded herself imaginatively diving into the wreck of her marriage.

ARE YOU MY MOTHER?

When *Fun Home* opened as a Broadway musical in 2013, it won five Tony Awards. By that time, Bechdel had moved to rural Vermont with the painter Holly Rae Taylor and published *Are You My Mother?* The smart but distant mother in *Fun Home* evolved into a central character in its sequel, which met with fewer accolades—possibly because of its investment in psychoanalysis, in particular the theories of the pediatric psychiatrist D. W. Winnicott. Yet here Bechdel concentrates on the effect a mother born before the women's movement has on a daughter coming into maturity after it. In doing so, she illuminates the psychology of many girls mothered by women who assumed that they and their daughters were born to be defined as the second sex.

Within numerous frames in *Are You My Mother?* Helen Bechdel is remembered trying to breast-feed her baby daughter, protecting little Alison from Bruce's wrath, and later assisting the young woman financially. Yet in pictures of Alison's face-to-face conversations with her therapists and of her phone chats with Helen, Bechdel portrays a self-absorbed mother. Had she been, in Winnicott's terms, a good-enough mother? The aging Helen responds to Alison's phone calls by going "on and on about" people and events Alison doesn't know. "She doesn't want to hear about my life," Alison thinks. Maybe "it's partly the lesbian thing, like she's afraid if I get a word in edgewise, it'll be 'cunnilingus'": "It's like I'm the mother," she concludes.[26]

Alison suffers when her mother belittles her autobiographical work ("Isn't that a rather narrow scope?"), finds it embarrassing ("You're not going to use your real name, are you?"), and ends up sounding as homophobic as Kate Millett's mother: "I would love to see your name on a book but not on a book of lesbian cartoons." When Alison reveals that she has a contract for a book of lesbian cartoons, Helen says, "I'm not comfortable with it. You know I'm not."[27] Alison hunches over the hung-up phone in tears.

Throughout many of these hurtful exchanges, Helen is reading a newspaper. We begin to judge her a narcissistic mother, one not-good-enough to give her daughter the affirmation she needs. But Bechdel knows that the thousands of pictures she has drawn of herself prove that she is just as or even more narcissistic than Helen. Since these illustrations also manifest her artistry, they suggest that Bechdel's mother must have done something right.

The mystery of what it means to be born before the women's movement is solved after a therapist convinces Alison to ask her mother, "What's the main thing you learned from your mother?" Without skipping a beat, Helen says, "That boys are more important than girls."[28] Helen's mother worshipped her sons, just as Helen adored hers. Here the period before feminism clearly implies the devaluing of daughters even by loving mothers. This mother–daughter exchange immediately leads to a flurry of thought boxes about penis envy, Virginia Woolf's novel *To the Lighthouse* (1927), and the brutality of Woolf's own father, maybe because Woolf articulated the anger of daughters at the privileges accorded their brothers by mothers who accepted their husbands' values.[29]

"Before" and "after" were terms that haunted Woolf too, especially in a diagram of *To the Lighthouse* that Bechdel reproduces.[30] The lingering Victorian order with its traditional women in part I of *To the Lighthouse* is set before the chaotic "long night" of the Great War in part II; in part III, the modern world with its liberated women emerges in the aftermath of devastating destruction. Like Lily Briscoe, Woolf's surrogate in the novel, Alison struggles to come to terms with the traditional wife and mother who serves the needs of autocratic men. Just as Woolf eased her grief for her own mother by writing about the emergence of the New Woman, Bechdel comes to terms with her mother by analyzing what her own liberation from traditional womanhood means about her mother's mothering.

Toward the close of *Are You My Mother?* Bechdel associates Helen's reserve less with rejection and more with "aesthetic distance." Changing with the times, has she begun to accept her daughter's talents? Helen is depicted putting up with the publication of *Fun Home* and even defending her daughter's commitment to serving the needs of the story, instead of the needs of the family. After Helen reads part of the sequel, her generous judgment—"it coheres," "It's a metabook"—serves as a welcome confirmation that triggers an important memory of the "crippled child" game that Bechdel associates with "the moment my mother taught me to write."[31]

As a preschooler pretending, oddly, to be a disabled child, Alison had playacted the sense of lack she acquired from Helen's assumption that "boys are more important than girls": to be born the daughter of such a mother is to be born disabled or, as Freud would have put it, castrated. But Helen's willingness to share her "disabled child's" playacting enables Bechdel to weigh that injury against a gift she also received. The something Helen did right: she encouraged her hobbled daughter's imagination. Helen is pictured offering the make-believe "crippled" toddler make-believe braces and make-believe special shoes. Bechdel thinks, "She could see my invisible wounds because they were hers too."[32]

On the last page, little Alison decides, "I think I can get up now," and Bechdel concludes about Helen, "She has given me the way out."[33] Like Woolf's Lily Briscoe, who resists the instructions of the mother-woman but nevertheless finds her a source of inspiration, Bechdel has made her injurious but beloved mother a muse. With a generosity born of good-enough nurturing, the liberated woman honors the traditional woman whose mold she has broken.

Freed from the family romance by her two autobiographies, Bechdel understandably wanted to leave the subject of childhood behind.

Her next project, *The Secret of Superhuman Strength*, will apparently focus on fitness and mortality, but the political climate has slowed its progress. The inhabitants of *Dykes to Watch Out For* were resurrected because they served as much needed "therapy" during the Trump presidency, a period she associates with rising attacks on transgender and Black people, with "unleashed forces" that make her feel "completely impotent and powerless and terrified."[34]

EVE ENSLER'S V-DAYS

While Bechdel explored the psychological injuries of girlhood, many of her peers addressed the physical traumas of womanhood. Seven years older than Bechdel, the performance artist Eve Ensler has dedicated her career to fighting "unleashed forces" that terrify women around the world. Back on Valentine's Day, 1998, Ensler established annual V-Days to call for an end to violence against human beings born with vaginas—a word that, she believed, many still found difficult to utter.

Having grown up with a remote mother and a physically as well as sexually abusive father, Ensler became dependent on drugs and alcohol after graduating from Middlebury College. Her then husband got her into rehab, and after the ten-year-old marriage ended, she remained close to his son, whom she adopted. Dedicated to using the theater to make the world a safer place, she enlisted a range of organizations to produce her celebrated 1996 play *The Vagina Monologues* in order to raise funds for antiviolence activism.

Distilled from hundreds of interviews, the first-person narratives in *The Vagina Monologues* describe women's ignorance and shame about their bodies as well as their conflicted reactions to menstruation, masturbation, childbirth, domestic abuse, rape, and female genital mutilation. Translated into forty-eight languages and staged in more than 140 countries, *The Vagina Monologues* was originally performed by Ensler herself but has since starred such celebrity actresses as Jane Fonda, Whoopi Goldberg, and Susan Sarandon, as well as countless undergraduates in college productions.

When Ensler was diagnosed with endometrial cancer in 2009, while working with war and torture victims in the Democratic Republic of the Congo, she realized that "the cancer had done exactly what rape had done to so many thousands of women in the Congo." "Fistulas"—holes between the vagina, bladder, and rectum—"have been caused by rape, in particular gang rape, and rape with foreign objects like bottles or sticks. So many thousands of women in eastern Congo have suffered fistulas from rape that the injury is considered a crime of combat."[35] Wanting to relate her own suffering to the pain she witnessed "in the body of the world," she produced a memoir with that title as well as a one-woman performance piece.[36]

Ensler's subsequent global campaign, One Billion Rising, arose in 2012 out of the V-Day movement. The election of "our predator-in-chief" only strengthened her commitment to it.[37] Since now one in three women worldwide experiences sexual assault in the course of a lifetime, Ensler organizes internationally to raise consciousness about threats produced by terrorism, fundamentalism, and warfare. In addition, she has helped create safe houses for young girls seeking refuge from female genital mutilation.[38]

In the States, Rebecca Solnit has explained, "The more than 11,766 corpses from domestic-violence homicides between 9/11 and 2012 exceed the number of deaths of victims on that day *and* all American soldiers killed in the 'war on terror.' "[39] The online harassment of women in social media (as in the "Gamergate" controversy arising from misogynist video game culture) and on dating websites (with men sending unsolicited "dick pics") also proves the ongoing relevance of Ensler's work. So do Patricia Lockwood's 2013 poem "Rape Joke," which went viral and earned a Pushcart Prize, and Emma Sulkowicz's 2014 "Mattress Performance (Carry That Weight)," which made headlines when she carried a 50-pound dorm mattress around Columbia's campus to publicize her allegation that she had been raped by a fellow student.[40]

In 2019, possibly influenced by the #MeToo movement, Ensler published *The Apology*, a text written as if it issued from her (dead) father, who here provides the words of regret she longed to hear from him. The book was dedicated to "every woman still waiting for an apology."[41] And after its publication, Ensler—feeling that she had rid herself of her father's ghost—shed the patronymic, renaming herself as simply V.

Ensler's V-Day and One Billion Rising campaigns epitomize many earlier feminist efforts to extend global activism. Just as Kate Millett traveled to Iran weeks after the revolution there, to assist women protesting the mandatory veil, so in the mid-eighties Robin Morgan established the Sisterhood Is Global Institute, while the ailing Audre Lorde resettled in Germany, where she joined with Afro-German women to campaign against the racism and xenophobia they confronted.[42] Between 1993 and 1996, Susan Sontag—in her sixties—made eleven visits to besieged Sarajevo, where she protested the Bosnian genocide and, amid the shelling, directed a production of *Waiting for Godot*.[43]

Also on the international scene, two feminist humanists—the theorist Gayatri Chakravorty Spivak and the philosopher Martha Nussbaum—were awarded the Kyoto Prize, the Japanese version of the Nobel, for their work in philosophy and ethics. Like Spivak's, Nussbaum's activism on behalf of the marginalized can be understood as part of the enterprise that postcolonial academics called "feminism without borders" or "transnational feminism."[44] Spivak donated the prize money to schools in impoverished regions in her native West Bengal,[45] and Nussbaum gave it to philosophy and law programs at her home institution, the University of Chicago. Both believe, as Nussbaum put it, that education is "a key for women in making progress on many other problems in their lives." In one-quarter of the nations of the world, she has noted, male literacy rates are higher than the female rate by 15 percentage points or more.[46] The night after Trump's election, when she was in Japan to receive the Kyoto Prize, Nussbaum began writing her next book, *The Monarchy of Fear: A Philosopher Looks at Our Political Crisis* (2018).

Similarly turning to education, the feminist psychologist Carol Gilligan translated the "shock" of the 2016 election into a question needing analysis in the classroom and in a book titled *Why Does Patriarchy Persist?* She collaborated with Naomi Snider, who had enrolled in her 2014 law seminar "Resisting Injustice," and together both teacher and student became "sounding boards for one another," holding out hope for the demise of patriarchy and the victory of democracy, which "like love, is contingent on relationship: on everyone having a voice that is grounded in their experience."[47]

TRANSGENDER VISIBILITY: FROM SUSAN STRYKER TO MAGGIE NELSON

Ensler must have realized that *The Vagina Monologues* would make her vulnerable to charges of essentialism,[48] but she was unprepared for another sort of attack from younger feminists. Because Ensler had composed a new monologue for trans actors who consulted her in 2004 about performing the play, she was quite surprised when, several years later, a number of groups on college campuses labeled *The*

Vagina Monologues transphobic and canceled its staging. In response, she argued that new forms of activism should not erase or tarnish older forms of activism.[49] Trans rights, important as they are, should not invalidate earlier efforts to highlight women's rights, especially in the resurgent backlash: "Trump is teaching us how deeply racist and sexist and homophobic our country is," Ensler pointed out.[50] But that transgender people and trans studies have begun to find a home in the academy is apparent from the controversy. Growing efforts to advance trans visibility have engaged a number of twenty-first-century writers.

In 2008, Susan Stryker brought out her *Transgender History*. Yet trans issues remained widely unacknowledged until Laverne Cox, herself a trans woman, was cast as a trans woman on the television show *Orange Is the New Black* in 2013. Jill Soloway's *Transparent* debuted in 2014, Caitlyn Jenner came out as a trans woman in 2015, and *Pose*, a television series about trans ballroom culture during the AIDS epidemic, as well as *Gentleman Jack*, based on the coded diaries of the swashbuckling Victorian Anne Lister, began appearing on television in 2018 and 2019, respectively. As Stryker has explained, numerous terms surfaced as the word *transgender* started to replace the older word *transsexual*.[51] The population that resists both female and male classifications is growing, a fact reflected in the discussions in a growing number of state legislatures about adding to the "F" for female and the "M" for male on drivers' licenses an "X" for nonbinary people.

Like nonbinary identities, transgender identifications may involve sexual orientation but they also and more fundamentally engage gender. "Simply put," the trans woman of color Janet Mock explains in her memoir *Redefining Realness* (2014), "our sexual orientation has to do with whom we get into bed *with*, while our gender identity has to do with whom we get into bed *as*." She was recycling the words of the trans *New York Times* columnist Jennifer Finney Boylan, whose memoir, *She's Not There: A Life in Two Genders* (2003), argued that "being gay or lesbian is about sexual orientation. Being trans is about identity."[52] Explaining that "a trans person can be straight, gay, bisexual, etc.," Janet Mock goes on to state "that the world can be a brutal place for a girl with a penis."[53]

Before and after transitioning surgically, Mock was repeatedly told "that I am not 'real,' meaning that I am not, nor will I ever be, a cis woman; therefore, I am fake." But "if a trans woman who knows herself and operates in the world as a woman is seen, perceived, treated, and viewed as a woman, isn't she just being herself? She isn't *passing*; she is merely *being*."[54] Seeking to clarify their sexual politics, trans advocates like Mock—who helped direct, write, and produce the TV show *Pose*—frequently employ ideas about gender, sex, and sexual orientation that feminist theorists had developed in the nineties.

One youthful writer, who calls herself "a gay trans girl," has turned to an unlikely figure in feminism's lineage to fortify her sense of self. Andrea Long Chu learned about trans women as "some kind of feminist vanguard" when she read Valerie Solanas's *SCUM Manifesto* in her junior year of college.[55] Chu enjoyed the fact that Solanas rejected men on aesthetic grounds. One passage in *SCUM* especially fascinates Chu: "If men were wise they would seek to become really female, would do intensive biological research that would lead to men, by means of operations on the brain and nervous system, being able to be transformed in psyche, as well as body, into women."[56] Chu believes that Solanas here provides a vision of "how male-to-female gender transition might express not just disidentification with maleness but disaffiliation with men." From this perspective, "transsexual women decided to transition not to 'confirm' some kind of innate gender identity, but because being a man is stupid and boring."

Needless to say, Chu is fully aware that Solanas's emphasis on eliminating babies with Y chromosomes has led to her being labeled essentialist and transphobic. Chu understands both the strangeness of excavating the *SCUM Manifesto* to legitimize the trans community and the conflicts certain to continue between that community and some cis feminists, or so her references to Germaine Greer indicate. In 2015, when the editors of *Glamour* decided to give their Woman of the Year award to Caitlyn Jenner, Germaine Greer released what Chu rightly calls a "gem of a statement": "Just because you lop off your dick and then wear a dress doesn't make you a fucking woman," Greer declared. "I've asked my doctor to give me long ears and liver spots and I'm going to wear a brown coat but that won't turn me into a fucking cocker spaniel."[57] Yet it remains a "supreme irony of feminist history," Chu concludes, "that there is no woman more woman-identified than a gay trans girl like me." And because of other trans women, "there are literally *fewer men on the planet*. Valerie, at least, would be proud. The Society for Cutting Up Men is a rather fabulous name for a transsexual book club."

Maggie Nelson's *The Argonauts*, the winner of the 2015 National Book Critics Circle Award in Criticism, extended the feminist/trans conversation with none of Greer's or Solanas's vitriol. Instead, Nelson redirected the lyricism she had brought to poetry into poetic prose about her feminist education. The title of her genre-bending memoir alludes to a passage by the French thinker Roland Barthes that associates reiterated declarations of love with "the Argonaut renewing his ship during its voyage without changing its name."[58] In a form Nelson calls autotheory—a mix of autobiography and theory—she provides a succession of quotations to round up the tribe of fellow travelers who patch the vessel that keeps her and her beloved safely sailing, buoyed by their commitment to gender fluidity.

Nelson's argonauts are the "sappy crones" who constitute "'the many gendered-mothers of my heart,'" her teachers and sages.[59] They consist of the queer theorists Wayne Koestenbaum, Judith Butler, and especially Eve Kosofsky Sedgwick; the artists Gertrude Stein, Djuna Barnes, Alison Bechdel, Maya Angelou, Alice Munro, Catherine Opie, Annie Sprinkle, and especially Eileen Myles; and the feminist thinkers Susan Fraiman, Denise Riley, Sara Ahmed, Susan Sontag, and Mary Ann Caws. Nelson assembles these "good witches" to bless the queer family she seeks to preserve in a book that implicitly questions the attack on the nuclear family launched by many radical feminists back in the early seventies.

The first paragraph of *The Argonauts*—a collection of sometimes fragmentary and nonchronological paragraphs—sets out to shock. Beginning with an I-love-you spoken "in an incantation the first time you fuck me in the ass," it upends readers with its reference to anal eroticism and with its ambiguous use of "you," a pronoun benignly ungendered. Both celebrate the nonnormative partnership of Maggie Nelson with the neither male nor female artist Harry Dodge. By various onlookers at various moments, they are greeted as a butch with a femme, a heterosexual couple, and two female friends.

The Argonauts goes on to narrate the love affair of Maggie and Harry and then the metamorphoses of Maggie's pregnancy (through a sperm donor) and Harry's transitioning (through testosterone and top surgery), two profoundly physical conversions. "On the surface, it may have seemed as though your body was becoming more and more 'male,' mine, more and more 'female.' But that's not how it felt on the inside. On the inside, we were two human animals undergoing transformations beside each other, bearing each other loose witness. In other words, we were aging."[60]

Suspicious not only of gender-specific pronouns but of any identities that are inflicted rather than adopted, Nelson returns repeatedly to conventional stereotypes that confine women in uncongenial boxes. Her pregnant body at a lecture podium elicits "the spectacle of that wild oxymoron, *the pregnant woman who thinks*. Which is really just a pumped-up version of that more general oxymoron, *a woman who thinks*": "But I was enough of a feminist to refuse any kneejerk quarantining of the feminine or the maternal from the realm of intellectual profundity."[61]

Exploring the paranoia that accompanies parenting, Nelson describes the terror ensuing from the realization that our children make us hostages to fortune. And in a moving sequence toward the end of *The Argonauts*, Nelson counterpoints the labor of childbearing—the counting up toward the effacement of her cervix—with the labor of dying, the counting down toward the last breath of Harry's mother. Recalling that Rita Mae Brown purportedly "once tried to convince fellow lesbians to abandon their children in order to join the movement," she observes that "generally speaking, even in the most radical feminist and/or lesbian separatist circles, there have always been children around (Cherríe Moraga, Audre Lorde, Adrienne Rich, Karen Finley, Pussy Riot . . . the list could go on and on)" (ellipsis hers). And in any case, she has had it with "the tired binary that places *femininity, reproduction, and normativity on one side and masculinity, sexuality, and queer resistance on the other.*" Instead, she broods on "the rise of homonormativity and its threat to queerness."[62]

Like Alison Bechdel, Nelson writes comically about her feminist education: in Nelson's case, the eccentric pedagogy of Eve Kosofsky Sedgwick, who got to know her graduate students by asking about their totem animals. "I burped out *otter*," Nelson admits. She was thinking about the need to be quick and dexterous, and then more generally about wanting to flee or refuse "the menacing pressure to take sides." But she knows "that a studied evasiveness has its own limitations," so she ends up embracing what we have been calling lifelong learning: "the pleasure of recognizing that one may have to undergo the same realizations, write the same notes in the margin, return to the same themes in one's work, relearn the same emotional truths, write the same book over and over again—not because one is stupid or obstinate or incapable of change, but because such revisitations constitute a life."[63]

11

Resurgence

B Y THE TURN OF THE CENTURY, quite a few of those who
ushered in the second wave were encountering the losses that
accompany aging. Before Audre Lorde died of liver cancer in 1992,
she adopted the name Gamba Adisa, which means "Warrior: She
Who Makes Her Meaning Known."[1] Both Gloria Anzaldúa and
Susan Sontag received public accolades after their deaths in 2004.
Andrea Dworkin died in 2005, Betty Friedan in 2006, Grace Paley in
2007, Marilyn French and Eve Kosofsky Sedgwick in 2009, Joanna
Russ in 2011. Adrienne Rich died of complications related to rheumatoid arthritis in 2012. Kate Millett died in 2017 in her beloved
Paris. After Ursula K. Le Guin's death in 2018, a documentary film
appeared that recorded her fear that she had failed to subvert the
masculinist assumptions of science fiction.[2]

The literary critic Nancy K. Miller gravitated toward elegy. In
My Brilliant Friends (2019), she paid tribute to the Italian novelist
Elena Ferrante (the author of *My Brilliant Friend*) as she mourned the
deaths of her and our mentor Carolyn Heilbrun, the feminist theorist

Naomi Schor, and the feminist biographer Diane Middlebrook. To our great sorrow, Toni Morrison died while we were finishing a draft of this book in the summer of 2019. Like Carolyn Heilbrun, she had been a friend and a source of inspiration to us both.

The rest of us kept on working, for feminist studies continued to proliferate. Yet deteriorating conditions in the humanities demoralized those within the academy. As enrollments shifted out of the liberal arts, traditional departments shrank. When women integrate a profession, we began to worry, does it inevitably become devalued?

Inside and outside the academy, feminists had cause for alarm. There were few advances in affordable childcare or flexible work/family arrangements, even though working women were spending more time with housework, children, and elder care than men did.[3] While female students took their rightful share of places in law, medical, and business schools, Arlie Hochschild's 1989 *The Second Shift* was reissued in 2012 and remained all too relevant in its analysis of the doubled burdens of employed mothers. Despite a number of protests, African American, Chicana, and Native American women continued to receive substandard medical attention. "In the wealthiest nation in the world," the sociologist Tressie McMillan Cottom noted in 2019, "black women are dying in childbirth at rates comparable to those in poorer, colonized nations."[4]

Abortion rights were seriously weakened—especially for rural and economically disadvantaged women—with many states passing restrictive laws and others trying to outlaw abortion altogether.[5] The conservative pundit Ann Coulter went on talk shows to argue that single mothers should give their babies up for adoption and that the feminists who supported them were "angry, man-hating lesbians."[6] The fervor of the right-to-life movement mounted, even as biotechnologies gave parents more control over their families with such developments as the morning-after pill, in vitro fertilization, and sperm and egg freezing. As white supremacists rallied, hate crimes, drug overdose deaths, and cyberattacks escalated, as did the "fake news" circulated on social media by those who followed the lead of President Trump in libeling mainstream journalists. And, of course, many began to realize that melting glaciers, wildfires, and floods signaled serious climate change.

In the face of such threats, twenty-first-century literary women cultivated multiple alliances with, for instance, the Black Lives Matter movement and environmental activists. As the poet Claudia Rankine, the science fiction writer N. K. Jemisin, and the memoirist Patricia Lockwood brooded on racial injustice, ecological disaster, and patriarchal religious institutions, various celebrities saluted the continuing vitality of the women's movement. When it became clear that many paths would be needed to find ways through the swamp of the Trump reign, new routes were mapped by younger activists and by veteran politicians.

CLAUDIA RANKINE MAKES
BLACK LIVES MATTER

What would it mean to relearn the insights of Black feminism in order to make antiracist interventions in an America that needs them now more than ever, given the severe wealth and health gaps between white and Black families? Contemporary African American activists and artists answer this question in a range of ways.

Patrisse Cullors, Alicia Garza, and Opal Tometi—defining themselves as "three black women, two of whom are queer women and one who is a Nigerian-American"—founded #BlackLivesMatter in 2013 because they wanted to go beyond "the narrow nationalism" that has kept "straight cis Black men in the front of the movement while our sisters, queer and trans and disabled folk take up roles in the background or not at all."[7] Established a year after Trayvon Martin was killed because a hoodie somehow made him look "suspicious" and seven years before George Floyd's murder was captured on a cellphone video, #BlackLivesMatter generated #SayHerName in 2015 to foreground the violence regularly encountered by girls and women of color in a racist society, even (or perhaps especially) from the police and justice systems meant to protect them.[8]

Deepening despair about race relations marks the contributions of Black literary women in this decade. And, as is often the case, pain inspires innovative art. While the videos of the deaths of Trayvon Martin, Michael Brown, and Sandra Bland went viral, Claudia Rankine—who featured an empty hoodie on the cover of her book *Citizen: An American Lyric* (2014)—titled many poems and sketches "In the Memory of . . ." so as to mourn those subjected to racist epithets, unprovoked beatings, neglect in the midst of natural disasters like Hurricane Katrina, and police misconduct.

A year before *The Argonauts* appeared, Rankine's mixed genre book won the National Book Critics Circle Award in poetry. Whereas Maggie Nelson is invested in the gender neutrality of the pronoun "you," Rankine uses it to examine the self-alienation experienced by Blacks confronting systemic racism. *Citizen*'s hybrid form—the book contains accounts of micro-aggressions, prose poems, an essay, surrealistic visions, elegies, and reproductions of artworks—contrasts Rankine's psychological condition with that of her foremost predecessor, Zora Neale Hurston, whose words appear in the text and in reprinted etchings by Glenn Ligon.

Both the quote and the etchings derive from Hurston's 1928 autobiographical essay "How It Feels to Be Colored Me," in which the

Harlem Renaissance author reports that she sometimes feels "cosmic," belonging to "no race," although she becomes magnificently colored while listening to jazz and becomes "most colored when I am thrown against a sharp white background."[9] Implying that race, like gender, is a social construct, she also remembers "the very day that I became colored." In various settings, Hurston insists, "I am not tragically colored."[10] The same assertion can hardly be made by or about Rankine's speaker.

Many of *Citizen*'s anecdotes record "you" encountering, against a "sharp white background,"[11] a series of seemingly slight but hurtful speech acts. A girl cheats by copying your schoolwork and then thanks you with the explanation that "you smell good and have features more like a white person"; a colleague tells you that "his dean is making him hire a person of color when there are so many great writers out there"; a friend calls you by the name of her housecleaner; a mother and daughter have to negotiate which one will sit next to you on a plane. "I didn't know black women could get cancer," a woman with multiple degrees tells you.[12] These micro-aggressions take a toll as they contribute to the speaker's mounting fatigue, headaches, and numbness.

What is the purpose of this "you"? The speaker, who is female and privileged with an education as well as a profession, has been robbed of personhood, rendered invisible or hypervisible, dissociated from the agency of "I." Each white speech act chips away at the assumption that she is fully human. Seeing herself through alien eyes, Rankine's speaker does not embody the schizophrenic "double consciousness" or "two-ness" that W. E. B. Du Bois diagnosed in the hyphenated Afro-American psyche.[13] Rather, she suffers a sense of perpetual estrangement and diminishment. "You" is not a self but an alienated Other. As a rhetorical strategy, the pronoun forces

Rankine's white readers to enter her text by identifying with a "you" repeatedly sickened by the racist assumptions of white Americans.

Besides rage, what possible response could such white interlocutors elicit from you? But rage itself has been problematized for Rankine's speaker. *Citizen*'s essay on the tennis star Serena Williams, situated against the "sharp white background" of tennis etiquette, meditates on the personal danger of Black anger, a topic that President Obama took up at the 2015 White House Correspondents' Dinner when "Luther" (played by the comedian Keegan-Michael Key) reprised his role as Obama's "anger translator."[14] On the campaign trail, Michelle Obama found that her being "female, black, and strong . . . translated only to 'angry'" for some audiences, and their reaction started to make her feel "a bit angry": "It's remarkable how a stereotype functions as an actual trap."[15] Rankine, who associates stereotypically angry figures with "commodified anger," considers honest anger "really a type of knowledge: the type that both clarifies and disappoints."[16]

No force could shield Serena Williams "from people who felt her black body didn't belong on their court." Questionable calls by umpires, punishments for alleged violations of tennis rules, and biased press coverage fuel the rage that bursts out in strings of profanity. All "the boos, the criticisms that she has made ugly the game of tennis—through her looks as well as her behavior"—contribute to frustrations and more angry outbursts, earning Williams further opprobrium. When a "newly contained Serena" emerges, Rankine wonders if the athlete has decided "that the less that is communicated the better" and whether "this ambiguity could also be diagnosed as dissociation": Serena Williams "has had to split herself off from herself and create different personae."[17] She has entered the domain signified by "you." Hurston's view at the start of the twentieth century that she could be a color-changing chameleon contrasts with Rankine's belief in the twenty-first century that "what happens to you doesn't belong to you": "You nothing. // You nobody. // You."[18]

A number of Rankine's predecessors in the eighties and nineties were less pessimistic as they weighed racial injustice against Hurston's vision of a world in which all people could experience themselves as cosmically raceless or brilliantly colorful. When the performance artist Adrian Piper participated in white social events where she was presumed to be white, she handed a printed card to anyone who made a prejudiced comment:

> I am black.
>
> I am sure you did not realize this when you made/laughed at/ agreed with that racist remark. . . .
>
> I regret any discomfort my presence is causing you, just as I am sure you regret the discomfort your racism is causing me.[19]

Piper began this performance, which she called *My Calling (Card)*, in 1986, three years after Toni Morrison produced "Recitatif," a story with ambiguous markers that made readers conscious of the arbitrariness of racial labels.[20] In 1997, Morrison's novel *Paradise* also kept matters of race indeterminate. She "wanted the readers to wonder about the race of those girls until those readers understood that their race didn't matter."[21] Like the legal thinker Patricia J. Williams, Morrison attributed sexism's and racism's persistence to a persistent "habit" of thinking that could be countered "if only we could imagine" breaking it,[22] as did the extraordinarily talented actress and playwright Anna Deavere Smith.

During the nineties, Anna Deavere Smith conducted interviews with participants in racially charged conflicts and then replicated their words, mannerisms, and appearances in two dramatic one-woman shows: *Fires in the Mirror* (1992), about the 1991 Crown Heights riots, and *Twilight: L.A.* (1994), about the 1992 Los Angeles riots. "If only a man can speak for a man, a woman for a woman, a Black person for all Black people," Smith believes, "then we, once again, inhibit the *spirit* of theater."[23]

The actress is a chameleon; for instance, in *Fires in the Mirror* she plays Al Sharpton and Angela Davis as well as Letty Cottin Pogrebin and Rabbi Joseph Spielman. She has said about the antiracists and the racists she performs, "I come to love" them, which may be why she has refrained from impersonating the politician she calls our "Narcissist-in-Chief."[24] Smith's incarnations emphasize the links between people who do not feel connected. This connectedness—so evident to the drama's spectators, so invisible to the dramatized participants—promoted xenophilia, an antidote to the xenophobia expressed by many of her characters. Whether Smith played white or Black, Asian or Latino, female or male characters, her imaginative identification was fully evident.

Less optimistic, the visual artist Kara Walker—especially in her hit installation of murals, *Gone, An Historical Romance of a Civil War as It Occurred b'tween the Dusky Thighs of One Young Negress and Her Heart* (1994)—captured the interracial violence that Rankine deplores. Walker's scenes of perversity in the antebellum South were displayed in the most genteel of art forms, the silhouette. Unlike the multicultural Harlem Renaissance rendered by Faith Ringgold in the story quilts of her *French Collection* (1990–97), the past depicted by Kara Walker featured Black figures against a stark white wall engaged in the pornographic rituals of the sexual politics first critiqued by Kate Millett and Andrea Dworkin: cartoon pickaninnies and Jezebels and bucks voluptuously assaulting and assaulted by cartoon plantation masters and mistresses (who, of course, are also black silhouettes).[25]

In 2019, Kara Walker's huge sculpture *Fons Americanus*—riffing on the Victoria Memorial outside Buckingham Palace—arose in the Tate Modern. As the artist has explained, the work is a meditation on the intersection of America, Britain, and Africa in "the Black Atlantic"—the sea crisscrossed by slave ships for several centuries. Some three million visitors poured into the museum to admire the parodic details of this installation, which featured "Queen Vicky" at the top, along with drowning Black children, rebellious Black captains, a tree trunk adorned with a noose, and waters gushing over all. But though Walker had hoped to find another home for the piece when its term at the Tate was up, it was dismantled in early April 2020, as the COVID-19 pandemic shut down galleries around the world. Still, it has been amply documented and can be seen on the internet, along with Walker's shrewd commentary on it.[26]

THE BROKEN EARTH OF N. K. JEMISIN

Walker's and Rankine's bleak view of sexual and racial relations is shared by a major science fiction writer of the early twenty-first century. But while Walker looked back in anger at the Civil War, N. K. Jemisin looks forward in horror at a resurgence of slavery during the end times. Each volume in her Broken Earth trilogy won the prestigious Hugo Award for Best Novel, in 2016, 2017, and 2018— a feat never before accomplished by any writer. Jemisin describes the destruction of the environment on a planet suffering climate changes far worse than global warming. In her postapocalyptic dystopia, earthquakes and volcanic eruptions have long ago buried an advanced civilization—perhaps ours—and the survivors live on one broken continent, called the Stillness. Amid remnants of a wrecked culture, they subsist on a devastated planet intermittently wracked by convulsions.

The psychology degree Jemisin earned at Tulane University and the masters of education she received from the University of Maryland, as well as her work in counseling, undoubtedly shaped her insights into the traumas triggered by a shattered Earth and a grotesque slave system. She was watching the police abusing protesters in Ferguson when she began the trilogy, which depicts the Stills of the Stillness ruling over enslaved "orogenes," a race endowed with the ability to mitigate the geological disasters to which the earth is subject.[27] They are instruments or tools for human beings, not considered human themselves.

The powers of the orogenes—often called "roggas," a derogatory label—are needed to protect against seismic upheavals, but those very powers make them feared, since they can obliterate anyone or anything in their path. They are therefore either killed as soon as their powers are recognized or used as tools (sometimes weapons) by Guardians of the state, after rigorous training and testing. Like the pioneering African American science fiction writer Octavia Butler, to whom she has paid tribute, Jemisin grapples with the racial, sexual, and ecological nightmares confronting humanity.[28]

Three intertwined narratives enable Jemisin to analyze slavery in *The Fifth Season*. Essun's story is told in the second-person present: an orogene mother discovers that her husband has killed their son (who inadvertently displayed his orogenic nature) and goes in quest of the daughter her husband has abducted. Damaya's story is told in the third-person past: a child newly discovered to be an orogene is removed from her home to the Fulcrum, a training station, where she is indoctrinated to become a mere instrument in the service of the state. Syenite's story is told in the third-person present: embarked on a daunting mission, a highly trained orogene realizes that she is expected to become a breeder of future orogenes whose lives will be wrecked by the uses to which they will be put.

In vivid and often violent scenes, Jemisin explores the griefs that accrue as all three negotiate between a dehumanizing system and stubborn efforts to maintain life, limb, and a shred of autonomy on a ruined planet. Only at the end of this first novel of the Broken Earth trilogy, when we discover that the three female characters—the mother, the schoolgirl, the weaponized slave—are the same woman at different stages of development, does the novel reconfigure itself as a powerful tale of survival at great cost. And through this revelation, Jemisin illuminates the book's dedication: "For all those who have to fight for the respect that everyone else is given without question."[29]

The Broken Earth trilogy issues a warning about slavery and about an environment so chaotic that human life is constantly under assault from natural disasters. While ecofeminists analyzed the destruction of the ecosystem portrayed in Jemisin's fiction,[30] such literary women as Annie Dillard, Mary Oliver, Barbara Kingsolver, Leslie Marmon Silko, Louise Erdrich, and Margaret Atwood sought to cultivate reverence for the natural world or to raise awareness of the possibility of global pandemics. The current U.S. poet laureate, Joy Harjo, a Creek Indian and student of First Nation history, frequently calls on a spirit world to heal the wounds of women, tribal cultures, and the earth.[31]

Quite a few feminist activists have also begun to tackle the threat of global warming in multiple media.[32] Mining a tradition pioneered by Rachel Carson in *Silent Spring* (1962), Elizabeth Kolbert's *The Sixth Extinction*, which won the Pulitzer Prize in 2015, predicted the disappearance of 20–50 percent of living species by the end of the twenty-first century. Kolbert hopes that humans can be forward-thinking and altruistic: "Time and time again, people have demonstrated that they care about what Rachel Carson called 'the problem of sharing our earth with other creatures,' and that they're willing to make sacrifices on those creatures' behalf."[33] Similarly, Rebecca Solnit, arguing that we must keep moving toward "a vision of a world in which everything is connected," draws on the words of Ursula K. Le Guin: "Any human power can be resisted and changed by human beings."[34]

PATRICIA LOCKWOOD SENDS UP THE CHURCH AND THE FAMILY ROMANCE

But can any power be resisted and changed? In a secular, postmodern world, how does the patriarchy of the church continue to operate— and how does it shape the patriarchy of the family? This question, which inspired many feminists to critique the masculinism not only of Catholicism but of all institutionalized religions,[35] shapes Patricia Lockwood's memoir *Priestdaddy* (2017), a coming-of-age story that records the evolution of a young poet whose real-life father was an honest-to-God Catholic Father. Her book, as one enthusiastic reviewer commented, gives "'confessional memoir' a new layer of meaning"; and as another critic noted, it is often "brilliantly silly."[36] A surrealist poet who gained fame on the internet with tweets she called "Sexts" (e.g., "A ghost teasingly takes off his sheet. Underneath he is so sexy that everyone screams out loud") and with a ferocious "Rape Joke" ("The rape joke it wore a goatee"), Lockwood couldn't have invented the family that she traces in *Priestdaddy*.[37]

How could someone *have* a "priestdaddy"? Not because a local confessor seduced one of his confessees, who then gave illicit birth to his child, but because this particular Father was once stationed in a submarine where he converted to Lutheranism and became a minister after watching *The Exorcist* more than seventy times; then, "tired of [Protestant] grape juice" and wanting wine, he converted all over again to Catholicism and became a priest.[38] But because throughout all these conversions Greg Lockwood already had a wife and children, only a special dispensation from the Vatican could enable his ordination—at which, the author tells us, she wore an itchy dress.

In its ambivalent focus on a peculiarly problematic father, *Priestdaddy* has much in common with Alison Bechdel's *Fun Home*. But while Bechdel's father is enigmatic because of the dissonance between his role as paterfamilias and his closeted sexuality, Lockwood's father is odd because of the dissonance between his churlish behavior as a private paterfamilias and his public role as a theological Pater. Around the house, he is almost always dressed in nothing but boxer shorts while listening simultaneously to Rush Limbaugh and Bill O'Reilly, shouting "Hoo-eee" at televised games, cooking himself lavish servings of bacon or hamburger, and strumming on his expensive collection of guitars—a collection so pricey (one once belonged to Paul McCartney) that he can't find the money to send his daughters to college. In public, sporting his white clerical collar, he sponsors anti-abortion protests, hosts seminarians, and tends to the rites of baptism, marriage, and death.

How can one man be both a thuggish daddy and a pastoral Daddy? This is a question that lurks behind the hilarious façade that Lockwood erects in her book, which often seems to be a giddy analysis of every aspect of patriarchy: male privilege, male self-indulgence, male authority, male childishness, male selfishness, and, yes, male misogyny. Though Greg Lockwood adores his energetic wife, his children seem to exist mostly as props in an ongoing fleshly/spiritual game of "Father knows best." And his daughter knows that the church he serves is colluding in multiple cover-ups of dank sexual secrets.

Is Lockwood's memoir an extended iteration of Sylvia Plath's "Daddy, daddy, you bastard, I'm through"?[39] In the center of the book, this seems to be the case. At 16, she tells us, she thought "the house seemed made of screaming, and I roamed it looking for a cell of silence . . . in that thunderous and warlike score." Such feelings, she adds, drove her to take "a hundred Tylenol" and end up in a mental ward not unlike the one where Plath's Esther Greenwood lands. There, when her father first visits (and not in the role of Father), he sardonically says, "I just want to thank you for ruining our anniversary."[40] But then, just as there is a difference between Greg Lockwood and Bechdel's poignant father, so too there is a difference between him and Plath's mythic "man in black with a Meinkampf look."[41]

For one thing, at the age of 19 Patricia Lockwood has the luck to meet and marry a kinder, gentler man than any of these fathers. For another, she acknowledges that for his parishioners Father Lockwood's living room (where his children weren't allowed) was a space where they went to discuss loss and fear: "Sunday after Sunday in our living room sat the unthinkable and spoke to my father." And, too, though her father "lounged horizontal at home, and sent us up and down the stairs to fetch for him," when "the call came at three in the morning, he was up and out the door without the smallest sigh or protest, to serve the unthinkable, to read the ritual words to it, to plump the pillow under its head. His Last Rites kit sat on the stairs just by the front door."[42]

So is Greg Lockwood redeemable, despite his awful politics, bad behavior, and misogyny? A "lapsed" Catholic,[43] his daughter nonetheless respects his commitment to what is, on the one hand, a patriarchal ceremonial role, and, on the other hand, at least for some a comforting ceremonial role. Half-naked, he is a bully or a solipsist. Attired in Catholic black with white collar, he struggles to do what is best for those who have put their trust—their *faith*—in him. Nonetheless, his daughter concludes her memoir by taking her mother on a sentimental journey to Key West, where they ignore the Hemingway lookalikes who patrol the streets of the tropical town and picnic on the beach. "Oh, it was *so fun*," the mother whispers when Lockwood and her husband leave her back in Kansas with the father about whom she has said, "He is who he is and that's all he's ever gonna be."[44] Should we say the same thing, we wonder as we close the book, about the patriarchy outlined by church and state?

HEADLINING FEMINISM: FROM REBECCA SOLNIT TO BEYONCÉ

"What is patriarchy," N. K. Jemisin asked in a *New York Times* book review, "but a con being run on all genders, whispering to both victims and beneficiaries that any suffering they experience is for their own good?"[45] Jemisin's Otherworldly column for the *New York Times*—in which she reviewed fantasy and science fiction between 2016 and early 2019—points to the ways in which feminists have established themselves in journalism. Although the *Times* did not accept the usage "Ms." until 1986, in the past few years it has hired a growing number of female columnists and promoted all sorts of feminist ventures, most notably the In Her Words biweekly newsletter and Overlooked No More, a series of obituaries whose subjects had been disregarded at the time of their death because of editorial racist or sexist biases. In other words, the evolution of the *Times* reflects the growing impact and visibility of feminism in American culture today.

After earning a master's degree in journalism, Rebecca Solnit, who grew up "in a house full of male violence," has made such violence "a public issue" in writings about a world "full of strangers who seemed to hate me and wished to harm me for no reason other than my gender."[46] After her essay "Men Explain Things to Me" was posted online in 2008, "hundreds of university women shared their stories of being patronized, belittled, talked over, and more" on the website "Academic Men Explain Things to Me."

"The term 'mansplaining' was coined soon after the piece appeared, and . . . my essay, along with all the men who embodied the idea, apparently inspired it."[47] The origins of the coinage *bropriate*—to steal or appropriate the words or ideas of women—remain murkier. *Manspreading* appeared in the context of online complaints about men taking up excessive public space on New York City subways by spreading their legs.[48]

By 2020, when we were disheartened by too much mansplaining, we could watch Rachel Maddow or peruse innumerable feminist blogs, all of which exhibit the multiple and discordant points of view that commentators like Roxane Gay were calling for.[49] Quirky protests were abounding. The online Crunk Feminist Collective used the neologism *crunk*—crazy drunk—to define its mission: "we are drunk off the heady theory of feminism that proclaims that another world is possible." In her *Tiny Pricks Project*, Diana Weymar and her collaborators protested Trump's imbecilic statements—"I am a very stable genius"—by embroidering them onto heirloom textiles. The delicacy of the stitches highlights the crudity of the words. The trans feminist Natalie Wynn, hailed as the "Oscar Wilde of YouTube," created the channel ContraPoints to dispute the agenda of the alt-right.[50]

In the meantime, major feminist novelists continue to produce new works in this country and elsewhere. When Margaret Atwood released *The Testaments* in 2019, it was a newsworthy event—she was featured in haute couture on the front page of the Saturday *New York Times* "Style" section on September 7, a week before the Sunday review—perhaps especially because the novel held out hope in a bleak time. The madwoman who emerges to right the wrongs against women in the puritanical Gilead of the earlier *Handmaid's Tale* turns out to be its prime female architect, Aunt Lydia.

The Testaments explains why Aunt Lydia signed up to become patriarchy's enforcer; it includes a secret memoir in which she describes how, when the Commanders were taking over the country, she was rounded up with other female judges and lawyers and herded into a concentration camp. There she was penned up in filthy barracks, forced to witness mass executions, and then isolated in a Thank Tank, where she was tortured until a resolution formed within her: "*I will get you back for this. I don't care how long it takes or how much shit I have to eat in the meantime, but I will do it.*"[51]

Atwood makes the case that some female enforcers of patriarchy collaborate with the enemy in order to survive and that they may ultimately undermine the misogynist powers they were forced to serve. *The Testaments* is thus an optimistic book, one that envisions the collapse of patriarchal Gilead and the restoration of the United States of America. To revenge herself against the patriarchs, Aunt Lydia unites Offred's two daughters to act as messengers relaying information about the nefarious dealings of the Gilead Commanders to the Underground Femaleroad in Canada. Sisterhood, it turns out, is powerful. That her testimonies speak truth to power and that the truth sets America free led the *New York Times* columnist Michelle Goldberg to conclude that *The Testaments* is "utopian," for in the reign of Trump "truth has lost its political salience."[52]

Popular culture also featured a figure holding out hope in hard times. In a succession of videos especially loved by youthful audiences,

Beyoncé and her co-writers delved into the feminist past to revitalize its present and future. Her 2019 film *Homecoming*, documenting her performance at the Coachella festival in 2018, opens with an epigraph from Toni Morrison: "If you surrendered to the air, you could ride it."[53] The movie is punctuated throughout by quotations from Nina Simone, Maya Angelou, the children's advocate Marian Wright Edelman, and Alice Walker, some of whom are identified by the colleges they attended because *Homecoming* highlights the importance of historically Black colleges and universities. The movie's title, evoking college homecoming parades and the halftime shows at football games, is emphasized by brass marching bands, drum majorettes, and high-rise bleachers on a stage crowded with singers, dancers, and musicians.

"Without community, there's no liberation":[54] these words from Audre Lorde flash on the screen toward the climactic conclusion of the film, a sort of bacchanalia with singers, dancers, and Beyoncé dedicating themselves to all women who "opened up the doors." In the midst of the song "Run the World (Girls)," the voice of the Nigerian American novelist Chimamanda Ngozi Adichie can be heard: "We teach girls to shrink themselves, to make themselves smaller. We say to girls, 'You can have ambition, but not too much. You should aim to be successful but not too successful, otherwise you will threaten the man.'"[55] After the song "Say My Name," Maya Angelou's voiceover tells us "to make this country more than it is today," and Beyoncé concludes by launching into her last song, "Love on Top," singing "Honey, I see the stars."

KEEPING THINGS STIRRING

Moving forward, contemporary artists look backward by summoning voices from feminism's past. Sometimes they explicitly call on foundational texts. Sometimes they refine tactics to help vulnerable populations deal with patriarchy. With a laugh or a sigh or a shout, American women continue to protest conditions of being that they experience as an affliction or infirmity. All seem motivated by the prophetic intuition expressed in one of the Irish poet Eavan Boland's last verses: "Our Future Will Become the Past of Other Women."[56]

To safeguard that future, and as a result of feminist consciousness-raising, more and more women were eager to testify to assaults by powerful men. In 2017, thousands of people tweeted #MeToo after the actress Alyssa Milano, complaining of sexual assault from the predatory Hollywood producer Harvey Weinstein, picked up the phrase from Tarana Burke, who had used it in 2006 to promote empathy for women of color who had experienced sexual abuse. From Rose McGowan and Gwyneth Paltrow to Rosanna Arquette and Cate Blanchett, a range of well-known women raised their voices against Weinstein and joined the #MeToo movement that spread around the world. Harvey Weinstein was convicted of assault and imprisoned in New York. The equally predatory investor Jeffrey Epstein was arrested, was jailed, and (evidently) committed suicide in his cell. At the same time, women accused more "ordinary" figures of sexual harassment or assault. All resoundingly cried out *Me Too! It has happened to Me Too, my body has been manhandled, I have been wounded, I am a survivor and I am sore, angry, weary of seeking help to no avail: Me Too!*

"There's #MeToo in 2017 and 2018. In 2014, there was #YesAllWomen. And in 1991, there was 'I Believe Anita.' It can feel like we've been defeated . . . but I think that every time we get a little louder, and we get a little closer to making changes that actually need to be made." So said Moira Donegan, who created a spreadsheet on which women anonymously listed men in the media industry accused of sexual misconduct.[57] The success of Susan Choi's metafictional novel

Trust Exercise—which won the 2019 National Book Award—indicates that such issues will continue to shape women's fiction.

When Anita Hill appeared at protests against sexual harassment, she recalled that back in 1991, two-thirds of Americans believed she was lying under oath: "I think in today's atmosphere more people would believe my story, would understand my story."[58] At the close of 2017, Merriam-Webster chose *feminism* as the word of the year and *Newsweek* featured "The Silence Breakers" who came forward in numbers to report sexual misconduct as its composite Person of the Year.[59]

Chillingly, however, the Anita Hill story was recycled in September 2018, when 51-year-old Christine Blasey Ford testified before the House Judicial Committee that Brett Kavanaugh was not fit for a seat on the Supreme Court. Explaining that she felt it was her "civic duty" to disclose a traumatic experience from her girlhood, Ford told the committee that Kavanaugh had sexually assaulted her when she was 15 and he was 17. At both the Hill/Thomas and the Ford/Kavanaugh hearings, wounded women spoke quietly, struggling to contain their emotions and especially their anger. "There is not a woman alive," the media analyst Soraya Chemaly noted, "who does not understand that women's anger is openly reviled."[60] In response, injurious men reveled in righteous rage.

From a historical perspective, women have made progress toward equality, but uneven progress that is perpetually threatened. By whom? One answer to this question became evident when the shocking public slaughters witnessed by Americans in the twenty-first century—mass shootings at malls, in bars, at schools, in houses of worship—were perpetrated by white men seeking to salvage what they experienced as an endangered masculinity. Noted the *New York Times* in a stunning headline, "A Common Trait among Mass Killers: Hatred toward Women."[61] Another source of backlash may be the insufficient democratization of higher education. So suggested analyses revealing that most Trump supporters were white people who had not gone to college: "I love the poorly educated," Trump declared at riotous rallies.[62]

When Nora Ephron gave the 1996 commencement speech at Wellesley, she emphasized that progress is perpetually threatened by an "undertow" at work in American culture, cautioning her audience that "American society has a remarkable ability to resist change."[63] Similarly, Michelle Obama's 2016 commencement address at the City College of New York warned against those who view "diversity as a threat to be contained rather than as a resource to be tapped."[64] Implicit in her words: the danger of racism sanctioned by the Trump administration. When in July 2019 President Trump told four congresswomen of color, "the Squad," to "go back" to the countries they came from—three were born in America and the fourth was a naturalized citizen—that threat came into plain view.[65]

One member of the Squad, Alexandria Ocasio-Cortez, would go on to face the cameras while funneling her anger into a cool, lucidly argued speech on the House floor. When AOC stood up to Representative Ted Yoho for calling her "a fucking bitch" on the steps of the Capitol, she noted that this "kind of language is not new," but it reflects "a culture of lack of impunity, of accepting of violence and violent language against women, and an entire structure of power that supports" it. Defying this "pattern" of "dehumanization," AOC rightly labeled Representative Yoho's alleged apology—"I cannot apologize for my passion or for loving my God, my family and my country"—a non-apology before she went on to assert her own values.

Mr. Yoho mentioned that he has a wife and two daughters. I am two years younger than Mr. Yoho's youngest daughter. I am someone's daughter too. My father, thankfully, is not alive to see how Mr. Yoho treated his daughter. My mother got to see Mr. Yoho's disrespect on the floor of this House towards me on television and I am here because I have to show my parents that I am their daughter and that they did not raise me to accept abuse from men.

Acknowledging that the verbal abuse she refused to accept "happens every day in this country," Alexandria Ocasio-Cortez declared: "It happens when individuals who hold the highest office in this land admit to hurting women and using their language against us all."[66]

Even before the Squad began to question dehumanizing patterns in the structures of power in Washington, DC, Stacey Abrams became the first African American woman to run for governor as the candidate of a major party. The leader of the minority Democrats in Georgia's House of Representatives, she took on Georgia's secretary of state, whose office had systematically disenfranchised hundreds of thousands of mostly minority voters. When she lost by a narrow margin in 2018, rather than legally contest the election Abrams created Fair Fight Action, an organization that would successfully raise public awareness of voter suppression and combat it both in Georgia and nationally.

Before, during, and after mounting these political challenges, Stacey Abrams was writing and publishing eight romantic spy and crime novels under the pseudonym Selena Montgomery. All of them feature adventurous and attractive black heroines. "Whether I'm writing about an ethno-botanist or a woman who's raising orphans in South Georgia, the challenge of telling their stories is the same challenge I face as a legislator who has to talk to someone about passing a bill on kinship care, helping grandparents raising grandchildren, or blocking a tax bill because I'm using expertise they don't realize I have," Abrams told an interviewer in 2018. "I revel in having been able to be a part of a genre that is read by millions and millions of women, in part because it respects who they are. It respects the diversity of our experiences, and it creates space for broader conversations."[67] To this same end—to respect diversity and create broader conversations—Stacey Abrams was chosen by the Democratic Party to respond to President Trump's 2019 State of the Union address.

Trump's years in the White House intensified many women's shock at the 2016 election. Toward the end of her autobiography, Michelle Obama recalled her reaction to the *Access Hollywood* tapes that captured Trump bragging about sexually assaulting women. She heard him to be saying "something painfully familiar" and menacing: "*I can hurt you and get away with it.*" This "expression of hatred" was one that "Every woman I know recognized. . . . Every person who's ever been made to feel 'other' recognized it." Before the election she protested publicly: "This is not politics as usual. This is disgraceful. It is intolerable." Afterward she could only "wonder what led so many women, in particular, to reject an exceptionally qualified female candidate and instead choose a misogynist as their president."[68]

That same question has troubled us and accounts for our attention to the succession of Serena Joys who have made it their business to urge women to forgo their equal rights. This sort of public (generally white) spokeswoman appears only during those times when there *is* a vocal feminist movement, for she commits herself to sabotaging it. Think, for instance, of such hard-right figures as Sarah Huckabee Sanders and Kellyanne Conway, and more recently Congresswoman Marjorie Taylor Greene. As useful as such figures have been to the Trump administration, we're all too well aware that it featured a set of high-level masculinist bullies—from Trump himself to Mike Pompeo, Bill Barr, and Mitch McConnell—who made it *their* business to dismantle the social and environmental safety nets put in place by their predecessors. One indomitable senior woman stood in their way: Nancy Pelosi, who at 80 has scripted for herself a profile in courage.

Like Hillary Clinton, Nancy Pelosi has played a pivotal role in American feminism. As the first female Speaker of the House of Representatives, she became the most powerful woman in American politics, second in line of succession to the presidency, and widely considered the most adept at this crucial job since (half a century ago) the legendary Sam Rayburn. Yet she started out in life from the sort of conventional background that Hollywood movies celebrated in the fifties.

Born in 1940, Nancy Patricia D'Alesandro was the pretty youngest child and only daughter in a well-off Baltimore family. Her father, Thomas D'Alesandro, was a prominent politician who served both in Congress and as the mayor of Baltimore; one of her five brothers was also mayor of Baltimore; and her mother was a political activist in the community. An Italian American, Nancy D'Alesandro seems always to have been comfortable in her ethnicity. After graduating from Trinity College in Baltimore, she married another Italian American, Paul Pelosi, a businessman whom she followed first to New York City and then to San Francisco, where she bore five children in six years and devoted herself to bringing them up as what we've come to call a stay-at-home mom.

Unlike such near contemporaries as Rich and Plath, Pelosi does not seem to have expressed ambivalence toward marriage, maternity, or domesticity. On the contrary, as she parented a gang of lively kids, she developed strategies that would serve her in good stead throughout her political career. Testified her daughter Alexandra on CNN, "She'll cut your head off and you won't even know you're bleeding." Her daughter Christine added that her skill at "coalition politics" was honed in the family, where "with five kids it could be three-on-two, four-on-one," until she achieved the kind of consensus that works just as well in the House of Representatives.[69] And as she herself has noted, a busy mother learns a lot about human nature. When Donald Trump walked out of a meeting in a rage because she wasn't going to help him get funds for his beloved border wall, she remarked, "I'm the mother of five, grandmother of nine. I know a temper tantrum when I see one."[70]

Even while mothering a houseful of kids, Pelosi began fundraising for the Democratic Party; she was so skillful that eventually she became the chair of the California Democratic Party and "the most successful nonpresidential fundraiser in U.S. history."[71] From her father, the consummate politician in Baltimore's Little Italy, she had learned to count votes, learned how to run for office. And run she did, once her youngest daughter had graduated from high school. The rest is, in fact, history, as Pelosi rose through the ranks of the House to become, as one observer put it, "the strongest and most effective speaker of modern times."[72]

Recurrently called "a shrew," "the Wicked Witch of the West," and "a yenta" by right-wing commentators,[73] Pelosi has always understood her place in feminist history. When she was sworn in as Speaker for the first time, in 2007, she exulted, "For our daughters and granddaughters, the sky is the limit, anything is possible for them," and she later declared, "Think of me as a lioness—you threaten my cubs, you have a problem."[74] Reelected to the Speakership when Democrats reclaimed the House in 2018, she took the oath of office surrounded by a horde of her own grandchildren and a mass of other kids. And once installed, she preached optimism while staunchly opposing Trump and his enablers, but she prepared, too—when it became necessary—for the articles of impeachment that her colleague Adam Schiff would eloquently defend in the Senate.

Pelosi has her quirks. She has confided to reporters that she has "been eating dark chocolate ice cream for breakfast for as long as I can remember"—two scoops![75] And despite all that sweetness and her sartorial elegance, she is notoriously but coolly vengeful, which is how she keeps her congressional troops in line.

Consider Tuesday, February 4, 2020. This is the day before a zombified Republican Senate majority will vote to acquit President Trump of the charges sent them by Pelosi and her colleagues in the House. Both senators and representatives are seated before the podium at which Trump is to deliver his State of the Union address, along with Supreme Court justices and distinguished guests. When the president arrives, Pelosi courteously holds out her hand, but he turns away. She is dressed in a tailored suffragist white pantsuit, as are most of the women who are her Democratic colleagues.

The president finishes his address—defending gun rights, bestowing a Presidential Medal of Freedom on (of all people) Rush Limbaugh, loudly celebrating his great big strong border wall, and intoning lie after lie about his record.[76] As he spoke, Pelosi, presiding behind him along with Vice President Mike Pence, was shaking her head from time to time, with a small ironic half-smile. But now there is clapping and booing in the hall.

Pelosi stands, looking severe, and then in a gesture as symbolic and theatrical as it is scandalous, she calmly rips each of the different sections of the president's speech in half. She is tearing up the text of lies, the text of narcissism and bullying that has sought to divide our country and dismantle its safety nets. Some people might think she is just the "Crazy Nancy" of Trump's tirades. But she isn't.

She is still mad, for good reason. And so are we.

EPILOGUE

White Suits, Shattered Glass

O N Saturday, November 7, 2020, at exactly 11:24 a.m. East
Coast time, Wolf Blitzer declared to the nation that CNN had
projected victory for presidential candidate Joe Biden and his running
mate Kamala Harris, ending four years of Trump's misrule. People in
cities and towns around the country danced in the streets. Car horns
honked exuberantly. In Rochester, New York, citizens thrilled by the
election of the first woman vice president—and the first woman of
color to rise so high on the national scene—swarmed to Susan B.
Anthony's grave to leave tokens of gratitude. In some of the Donald's
rural strongholds, rifle-toting emulators of the far-right Proud Boys
gathered in savage clusters. And within two days Senate Majority
Leader Mitch McConnell sulkily observed that the president, who
was refusing to concede the election, was "100 percent within his
right" to resist the truth.[1] The country, sickened by COVID and dis-
eased by political divisiveness, was both relieved and enraged.

The night of the 7th, in Wilmington, Delaware—Biden's home
state—the winning candidates mounted a huge open-air stage to

speak to a socially distanced crowd of cheering voters. Biden appeared wise and distinguished by contrast with the childishly recalcitrant Trump: President Grandpa was ousting President Toddler. Wearing an elegant white silk pantsuit designed by the Venezuelan-born designer Carolina Herrera, Harris circled the platform as if to display the historical costume she was wearing; she then introduced the president-elect with a beautifully articulated speech, in which she expressed her gratitude to her Indian American mother and to "all the women who worked to secure and protect the right to vote for over a century: 100 years ago with the 19th Amendment, 55 years ago with the Voting Rights Act and now, in 2020, with a new generation of women in our country who cast their ballots and continued the fight for their fundamental right to vote and be heard." Most memorably, she added, "While I may be the first woman in this office [of vice president–elect], I won't be the last."[2]

Nor was she, as we have seen, the first woman to wear the emblematic white suit. Nancy Pelosi had worn it when she tore up the text of Trump's mendacious State of the Union address. Most of the congresswomen who listened to that speech wore it too, as did Alexandria Ocasio-Cortez when she was sworn into office, and Hillary Clinton when she accepted the Democratic nomination in 2016, and Geraldine Ferraro when she ran for vice president in 1984, and Shirley Chisholm when she entered Congress in 1969.

Inspired by the white dresses in which women on both sides of the Atlantic marched and fought for suffrage, the white suit was not a fashion statement: it was a political assertion, a point repeatedly made by doyennes of style from Vanessa Friedman of the *New York Times* to the new website whatkamalawore.com.[3] On the day of her installation, Ocasio-Cortez had tweeted forcefully on the subject: "I wore all-white today to honor the women who paved the path before me, and for all the women yet to come. From suffragettes to Shirley Chisholm, I wouldn't be here if it wasn't for the mothers of the movement."[4]

"White, the emblem of purity, symbolizes the quality of our purpose," proclaimed a 1913 newsletter published by the American National Woman's Party,[5] but the color was also, as many commentators have pointed out, media-savvy. White-clad suffragists parading down Pennsylvania Avenue stood out in photographs against the grim ranks of dark-suited male spectators. At the same time, because white is the traditional hue of bridal gowns, the suffragists' dramatic deployment of the color was also, in a sense, parodic: what the yearning for suffrage meant was a yearning for selfhood instead of subjugation, reason instead of romance, sacramental sisterhood rather than sacramental marriage. But white is also the color of spirits, indeed of ghosts. Highlighted by tricolor sashes, were the white-dressed suffragists marching in America and England a kind of ghost army, demanding to be incarnated as material citizens of their countries?

It is now a century since the Nineteenth Amendment was ratified in the United States, and more than half a century since the pantsuit became not only a comfortable but a stylish outfit for women. But Harris was a new kind of candidate in this attire. As journalists tirelessly noted, she is not only the first woman to rise to such victorious prominence but also the first woman of color, daughter of immigrants, and graduate of a historically Black institution: Howard University. Harris's mother, a Hindu Brahman from Tamil Nadu, came to the United States at the age of 19 to study at the University of California, Berkeley, where she became (tellingly, from a feminist perspective) a major researcher of breast cancer. Harris's Black Jamaican father, Donald Harris, met Shyamala on campus, where he was studying economics; he is now a professor emeritus at Stanford.

Kamala was born in Oakland and bused from an apartment in

the Berkeley flats to the hills as part of the first wave of integration in California. Yet though Harris spent her elementary school years in a predominantly white neighborhood, and though she herself was biracial, her parents had deliberately chosen Blackness for themselves and their family. They had first come to know each other through their mutual engagement with the university's Afro-American Association, where, as the flamboyant spirit of the sixties took hold in Berkeley, they met with African Americans from their school and nearby community colleges (think Huey Newton) in a group that birthed both the Black studies movement and the Black Panthers.[6]

As Harris herself has commented, growing up in that environment meant being wheeled through protests in her stroller, amid masses of marching legs.[7] And once she was older, after her parents divorced and her mother brought her and her younger sister Maya to Canada, where she was teaching at McGill, Harris herself deliberately chose Blackness, opting for Howard University, the star of historically Black institutions, rather than Harvard University, the apex of the white academy.

After graduation, Harris became both an activist and an ambitious insider. Her relationship in the mid-nineties with the African American Assembly Leader and later San Francisco Mayor Willie Brown may or may not have aided her ascent to the top of California politics, but it did give her a clear view of the establishment she was entering and seeking to seriously reform, if not to disrupt. And as she joined that world, she doubled down on her Blackness, celebrating her "line sisters" from an elite sorority at Howard, as well as the fiercely feminist family she formed with her lawyer sister Maya, her niece Meena, and her grandnieces. Yes, she had visited her elegant Indian family often, as well as her equally elegant Jamaican family, but as a politician she chose to be an advocate of an African American race that was not exactly her own.[8] No wonder Michelle Obama, knowing that Kamala Harris was on the presidential slate, told her millions of followers, "We have to vote for Joe Biden like our lives depend on it."[9]

But in the meantime, Joe Biden had another supporter who also identified as a twenty-first-century New Woman: namely, his wife. Like Harris the offspring of immigrants—one half Sicilian, one half Anglo-Scottish—Jill Biden grew up in a working-class family; and while raising children with Joe Biden, she studied for higher degrees in English and worked as a teacher at local community colleges. She kept on keeping on at that job throughout her husband's years as vice president; on campaign planes, as her friend Michelle Obama noted, "Jill is always grading papers."[10] The couple were regularly introduced not as Vice President and Mrs. Biden but as Vice President and Dr. Biden.

Dr. Biden wasn't a stay-at-home Second Lady and she won't be a stay-at-home First Lady. She plans to continue teaching at Northern Virginia Community College during her husband's presidency. As one observer has noted, it will "be a real modernizing of the first ladyship . . . to have the president's spouse live the kind of life that the majority of women live, which is working outside the home professionally."[11]

Inevitably there was backlash against both Vice President–elect Harris and Dr. Biden. Sneering at Harris, xenophobic opponents were fond of mispronouncing her first name: *Kamalala—Kamalalalala?*[12] In Biden's case, they went after her title. An op-ed writer took her to task for daring to preface her name with the sacred word "Dr." Titled "Is There a Doctor in the White House? Not If You Need an M.D.," his screed was so vicious in its assault on Jill Biden that it quickly went viral.[13]

Here's how this curmudgeonly misogynist addressed her: "Madame First Lady—Mrs. Biden—Jill—kiddo: a bit of advice on

what may seem like a small but I think is a not unimportant matter. Any chance you might drop the 'Dr.' before your name? 'Dr. Jill
Biden' sounds and feels fraudulent, not to say a touch comic." Then
he went on to snobbishly point out that her doctorate is merely "an
Ed.D, a doctor of education, earned at the University of Delaware
through a dissertation" with an "unpromising title." Worse, he adds,
she didn't receive the degree until she was 55—a fact sympathetic
observers might have admired (she had, after all, brought up three
children and taught in high school while married to a senator and
doing advanced study). But no, as an accomplished woman she must
be reduced to a person offensively derided as "kiddo"!

Misogyny won't fade and go away like an old soldier. It raises its
ugly head both in the worst of times and in the best of times. Nevertheless, Jill Biden persists.

In Wilmington on the night of November 7, Jill Biden and
Kamala Harris enacted an extraordinary transformation of what
used to be the world of *Good Housekeeping* and the *Ladies' Home Journal*. Each in her own way had broken the same glass ceiling that
Hillary Clinton and Nancy Pelosi, among others, had begun to
crack. They had carved out spaces through which many more could
ascend. And though obdurate slivers lay all around them, these two
women of a future that has become our present weren't mad. They
were deeply sane and delighted to take their proper places.

Every shard of glass that had fallen around them glittered with
possibility. Yet within two months such fragments would evoke not
ceilings broken by women, but windows of the Capitol shattered by
marauders.

*January 6, 2021. A day that will live in infamy, as Franklin Roosevelt
said about Pearl Harbor.*

"Be there, will be wild!"[14]

For weeks after the election of Joe Biden, Donald Trump had been complaining that his "sacred landslide victory" in the 2020 presidential contest had been stolen by the so-called fraudulent Democrats.[15] In December, he sent a message to his MAGA followers all over the country. They were instructed to come to a rally near the White House. This last chance to "STOP THE STEAL" would be on January 6, when Congress met so that Vice President Mike Pence could certify electoral votes.[16]

Will be wild. Wild, they came en masse, some in army camouflage, some in crazier costumes—Proud Boys and Oath Keepers in full body armor, some loaded with zip cuffs, many bearing guns or bear spray, one raider bare chested with phallic horns on his head.

The President told them to "walk down [Pennsylvania Avenue] to the Capitol," that he'd be with them.[17] Then he retreated to the White House and watched the television with evident delight.

Outside the Senate and the House arose great bangings, boomings, and shouts. The MAGA mob was breaching the seat of the legislature, smashing windows, crashing through doorways, overwhelming the undermanned and underprepared Capitol Police. Later, when Trump was impeached for inciting this unprecedented violence, the House prosecutors wrote that he had "exhorted them into a frenzy" and "aimed them like a cannon down Pennsylvania Avenue."[18]

Inside the halls of the Capitol, even in the suites of Speaker Pelosi, they hunted down the enemies of "their" president. During the second impeachment trial, a traumatized nation was to watch a Capitol policeman screaming as he was being crushed between two doors, a rioter shot as she tried to climb through a broken window into the House chamber, Mitt Romney and Chuck Schumer narrowly escaping massacre when the Capitol Police turned them away from the mob.

The nation was to hear AOC confide, in an hour-long Instagram live, that "I thought I was going to die" as she hid in her office's bathroom.[19] The nation was to hear the raw craziness of a lynch mob splintering the gravity of the Capitol as they chanted "Hang Mike Pence! Hang Mike Pence!" Viewers were to gaze, horrified, at a gibbet the mob had already set up in their lust to lynch.[20] The nation was to watch as a single, sinister miscreant strolled down the hall outside the Speaker's offices, calling out a taunting elongation of her name: "Oh, Naaaaaaancy!"

Commented a *Washington Post* columnist, "*Oh, Naaaaaaancy. A woman who hears it thinks of a specific kind of danger, and a man who says it thinks of that danger, too. That's why he says it. To make clear that he is the hunter, and guess what you are?*"[21]

Donald Trump kept on watching the events on TV, refusing—despite repeated pleas from his aides and family—to call off the crazed mob.

The battle costumes, the stolen legislative artifacts, the breakage and the filth the rioters left behind (they smeared shit on the marble floors), and the five people who died in the attack on the seat of government—did all this portend an unbinding of the social contract? This furious crowd seemed at first to have come from the underbelly of America—from shacks and mudflats, backwoods and lonely prairies. But it turned out that many were "respectable" middle-class citizens, policemen, retired army officers, even though yes, they were also Proud Boys and Three Percenters and Oath Keepers.

Was theirs a backlash not only against democracy but against the equal rights that feminists in white suits have for so long sponsored? Throughout these pages, after all, we have traced the historical link between white male violence and the dominance/submission structure of patriarchal culture. The white supremacist insurgents at the Capitol—with their Confederate flags and Camp Auschwitz T-shirts—dramatized the toxic masculinism and proto-fascism of Trumpism. Had the lunatic crowd been maddened by the maddening accomplishments of feminism itself? Must madwomen necessarily create madmen?

Within two weeks, however, at the January 20 inauguration of Joe Biden and Kamala Harris, it began to look as though the feminist imagination might prevail. The peaceful order of those seated on the inaugural platform—ex-presidents, ex-candidates— strikingly contrasted with the chaos of January 6. Among former leaders, only Trump was absent. In the accomplished poem that twenty-two-year-old African American Amanda Gorman recited on the inaugural stage, she contended that such a catastrophe could not and would not go unanswered, that she and those she repre- sented could not march backward but would move forward, for "We will not be turned around / or interrupted by intimidation."[22]

All the women of the feminist movement who met, marched, struggled, fought, and brought a new order into being helped teach her those words—and now would echo them.

ACKNOWLEDGMENTS

I N THE PAINFUL AFTERMATH of the 2016 election, it was bracing to resume a collaboration that had paused at the start of the twenty-first century. Over the years, the two of us have developed in somewhat different directions. Yet in the process of putting this book together, we found that our separate interests inspired and enlivened each of us and then melded.

We tried throughout to capture not only the pioneering achievements of second-wave feminism but also the sometimes edgy dialogues, disagreements, and divisions within feminism, most of which ended up enriching the collectivity that feminists seek to foster and promote. For those who want a more capacious social history of the second wave, we recommend Ruth Rosen's excellent 2000 account *The World Split Open: How the Modern Women's Movement Changed America*, a book whose broad sociocultural vision enabled us to focus on the unique contributions of poets, novelists, dramatists, memoirists, and literary theorists.

We have been encouraged to persevere by many guides in our

lives. Sandra is grateful for the help of her research assistants, Rebecca Gaydos and Laura Ritland, and also indebted to advice and counsel from Gayle Greene, Susan Griffin, and especially Ruth Rosen. She is also thankful for support over the years from many friends, including Marlene Griffith Bagdikian, Wendy Barker, Elyse Blankley, Dorothy Gilbert, Marilyn Hacker, Diane Johnson, Marilee Lindemann, Wendy Martin, Eugenia Nomikos, Joan Schenkar, Elaine Showalter, Martha Nell Smith, and Anne Winters.

Susan would like to thank her three research assistants—Patrick Kindig, Brooke Opel, and Rory Boothe—as well as friends and colleagues: Matt Brim, Judith Brown, Shehira Davezac, Ellen Dwyer, Dyan Elliott, Mary Favret, Georgette Kagan, Jon Lawrence, George Levine, Stephanie Li, Julia Livingston, Nancy K. Miller, Alexandra Morphet, Jean Robinson, Rebekah Sheldon, Jan Sorby, and Alberto Varon. The knowledge and intelligence of Jonathan Elmer informed Susan's approach to this project from start to finish.

Our collaborative process was of course also facilitated by our families. As always, Sandra is grateful for intellectual and emotional support from her son, Roger Gilbert; his wife, Gina Campbell; and her oldest grandson, Val Gilbert, along with his partner, Noreen Giga. Her daughter Kathy Gilbert-O'Neill and daughter-in-law Robin Gilbert-O'Neill, together with their two lively sons, Aaron and Stefan, grounded her life with feasts, fun, and technical help. Her daughter Susanna Gilbert was always available for analytic discussions as well as much personal aid, while her granddaughter Sophia Gilbert continually lightened and brightened her days. But her deepest debt for sustenance while she was working on this book is to her partner, Dick Frieden, who—as she coped with a hard year—kept her going while things were stirring, reading chapter drafts, cooking meals, and traveling everywhere with her, both mentally and physically.

More than ever, Susan is indebted to the editorial and connubial genius of Don Gray. She has also been buoyed by the wit of her step-daughters and daughters, Julie Gray, Susannah Gray, Marah Gubar, and Simone Silverbush; the kindness of her sons-in-law, John Lyons, Kieran Setiya, and Jeff Silverbush; and the hilarity and insights of her grandchildren, Jack, Eli, Samuel, Jonah, and Gabriel. Her extended family overseas—Bernard and Colin David as well as her honorary son-in-law Suneil Setiya—could not have been more supportive.

Our sage agent, Ellen Levine, emboldened us to take on this project and inspired us to stay on track. An astute intervention by our savvy editor, Jill Bialosky, and her perceptive assistant, Drew Elizabeth Weitman, helped us transform a ponderous draft into the readable book we hope it has become. And we give thanks for the meticulous brilliance of our copyeditor, Alice Falk, and the enthusiasm of our publicist, Erin Sinesky Lovett. As we got this book ready for production, we were especially grateful for the generosity of Erica Jong and Robin Morgan, who kindly waived permission fees for their verse. In addition, we thank the administrators of Indiana University for helping us with research costs along the way.

All of our benefactors support the networks upon which feminists depend, but we remember moments that seem like yesterday when each of us knew what it meant to inhabit pre-feminist environments. Toward the end of her doctoral training at Columbia University, Sandra was counseled to forgo a job search since, one professor informed her, she would have to follow in the footsteps of her husband, who was also an academic. Upon Susan's arrival at the English department in Indiana

University, she was handed a syllabus to type by a senior colleague who assumed she was a secretary. Such events, which now seem faintly comical, were not long ago and far away. They were quite common everywhere and all the time before the remarkable transformations wrought by the feminist imagination.

NOTES

INTRODUCTION: THE POSSIBLE AND THE IMPOSSIBLE

1 Molly Haskell, *Love and Other Infectious Diseases* (William Morrow, 1990), p. 248.

2 Sojourner Truth, "Keeping the Thing Going While Things Are Stirring," in *The Norton Anthology of Literature by Women: The Traditions in English*, ed. Sandra M. Gilbert and Susan Gubar, 3rd ed., 2 vols. (W. W. Norton, 2007), 1:512–13.

3 Sandra M. Gilbert and Susan Gubar, *The Madwoman in the Attic* (Yale University Press, 1979), p. 3.

4 After Elizabeth Warren dropped out of the Democratic primaries, Jimmy Kimmel said, "In spite of her experience, her track record and her skills in the debates, American voters ultimately decided she just didn't have what they were looking for in a president, which is a penis": quoted in "Best of Late Night: Late Night Says Elizabeth Warren 'Realized She Was Overqualified,'" *New York Times*, 6 Mar. 2020, www.nytimes.com/2020/03/06/arts/television/late-night-elizabeth -warren.html.

5 Jay Inslee, quoted in Joseph O'Sullivan, "Inslee Rebukes the President, as Trump Encourages Rebellion to States' Coronavirus Stay-Home Orders," *Seattle Times*, 17 Apr. 2020, www.seattletimes.com/seattle-news/politics/inslee-rebukes-the -president-as-trump-encourages-rebellion-to-states-coronavirus-stay-home -orders/; @realDonaldTrump, *Twitter*, 17 Apr. 2020, 11:21 a.m., twitter.com/real DonaldTrump/status/1251168994066944003; 11:22 a.m., twitter.com/realDonald Trump/status/1251169217531056130; 11:25 a.m., twitter.com/realDonaldTrump /status/1251169987110330372.

6 @realDonaldTrump, *Twitter*, 29 Nov. 2020, 10:05 p.m., twitter.com/realDonald Trump/status/1333245684011642881; @realDonaldTrump, *Twitter*, 1 Dec. 2020,

8:59 a.m., twitter.com/realDonaldTrump/status/1333772740483026944; Nicholas Fandos and Maggie Haberman, "Impeachment Case Argues Trump Was 'Singularly Responsible' for Capitol Riot," *New York Times*, 2 Feb. 2021; Peter Baker, "The Last Act of the Trump Drama: Rage, Denial and Retribution," *New York Times*, 6 Dec. 2020.

7 Hillary Rodham Clinton, interview, *60 Minutes*, aired 26 Jan. 1992, on CBS; Clinton, "Remarks to the United Nations Fourth World Conference on Women Plenary Session," United Nations Fourth World Conference, 5 Sept. 1995, Beijing.

8 See Elaine Showalter, "Pilloried Clinton," *Times Literary Supplement*, 26 Oct. 2016, www.the-tls.co.uk/articles/public/hillary-clinton-vs-misogyny/.

9 James Robenalt, *January 1973: Watergate, Roe v. Wade, Vietnam and the Month That Changed America Forever* (Chicago Review Press, 2015).

10 E-mail correspondence between Ruth Rosen and Sandra M. Gilbert, 4 May 2020.

11 For more about women's utopian efforts to seek the presidency, see Ellen Fitzpatrick, *The Highest Glass Ceiling: Women's Quest for the American Presidency* (Harvard University Press, 2016).

12 See Gail Collins, "The Senate Bathroom Angle," *New York Times*, 22 Dec. 2016; Judith Plaskow, "Embodiment, Elimination, and the Role of Toilets in Struggles for Social Justice," *Cross Currents* 58, no. 1 (Spring 2008): 51–64, at 52–53.

13 Consider such feminist publications as *Signs: Journal of Women in Culture and Society, Feminist Studies, Women's Studies, Chrysalis, Frontiers*, and *Aphra*, as well as the Feminist Press.

14 See two striking exceptions to this rule: Jeannette Howard Foster, *Sex Variant Women in Literature: A Historical and Quantitative Survey* (Vantage Press, 1956), and Gwen Needham, *Pamela's Daughters* (Russell and Russell, 1972).

15 W. B. Yeats, "Easter, 1916," in *The Collected Poems of W. B. Yeats*, ed. Richard J. Finneran (Scribner, 1996), pp. 180–81, at 180.

16 D. H. Lawrence, *Studies in Classic American Literature* (1923; repr., Cambridge University Press, 2003), p. 14.

17 Gilbert and Gubar, *Norton Anthology of Literature by Women*, 2:618.

18 Gloria Steinem, "In Defense of the 'Chick-Flick,'" *Alternet*, 6 July 2007, www.alternet.org/2007/07/gloria_steinem_in_defense_of_the_chick_flick/.

19 Hillary D. Rodham, "Hillary D. Rodham's 1969 Student Commencement Speech," *Wellesley College*, www.wellesley.edu/events/commencement/archives/1969commencement/studentspeech. Edward Brooke, the first African American popularly elected to the Senate, was a liberal Republican in the Nelson Rockefeller mode. For his address, see "Progress in the Uptight Society: Real Problems and Wrong Procedures," *Wellesley College*, www.wellesley.edu/events/commencement/archives/1969commencement/commencementaddress.

20 See Charles Bethea, "Race, Activism, and Hillary Clinton at Wellesley," *New Yorker*, 11 June 2016, www.newyorker.com/news/news-desk/race-activism-and-hillary-clinton-at-wellesley.

21 Hillary Rodham Clinton, *What Happened* (Simon and Schuster, 2017), p. 117.

22 "Hillary Rodham Clinton Interview, 1979," *YouTube*, uploaded by AlphaX News, 13 May 2015, www.youtube.com/watch?v=bg_sEZg7-rk.

23 Nancy Sinatra, "These Boots Are Made for Walkin'," on *Boots* (Reprise Records, 1966).

24 Clinton, *What Happened*, p. 118.

25 Ibid., pp. 113–14.

26 Bethea, "Race, Activism, and Hillary Clinton at Wellesley."

27 Clinton, *What Happened*, p. 115. Misogynist attacks, which have been amply studied by scholars, included outré pictures of her as the snake-headed Medusa as well as images of her face imprinted on toilet paper, both of which can be found on the internet.

28 Sheryl Sandberg, *Lean In: Women, Work, and the Will to Lead* (Knopf, 2013).

29 Claire Cain Miller, "Sexes Differ on Persistence of Sexism," *New York Times*, 19 Jan. 2017 (published online as "The Upshot: Republican Men Say It's a Better Time to Be a Woman Than a Man," 17 Jan. 2017, www.nytimes.com/2017/01/17/upshot /republican-men-say-its-a-better-time-to-be-a-woman-than-a-man.html).

30 Rebecca Solnit, *The Mother of All Questions* (Haymarket Books, 2017), p. 69. For Emma Watson and Miss Piggy, see Andi Zeisler, *We Were Feminists Once: From Riot Grrrl to CoverGirl®, the Buying and Selling of a Political Movement* (PublicAffairs, 2016), p. xii.

31 Zeba Blay, "How Feminist TV Became the New Normal," *HuffPost*, 18 June 2015, www.huffpost.com/entry/how-feminist-tv-became-the-new-normal_n_7567898.

32 Kirsten Gillibrand, speech at Women's March on Washington, 21 Jan. 2017, Washington, DC, www.c-span.org/video/?c4650727/user-clip-senator-gillibrand -speaks-womens-march-washington.

33 Margaret Atwood, "Margaret Atwood on What 'The Handmaid's Tale' Means in the Age of Trump," *New York Times Book Review*, 19 Mar. 2017.

34 The television adaptation deviates from the novel in casting black women as Handmaids.

35 Margaret Atwood, *The Handmaid's Tale* (1985; repr., Anchor, 1998), p. 45.

36 Alison Bechdel, "The Rule," in *Dykes to Watch Out For* (Firebrand Books, 1986), p. 22.

37 Virginia Woolf, *A Room of One's Own* [1929], annotated and with an introduction by Susan Gubar (Harcourt, 2005), p. 75.

38 Ruth Rosen argues that Cold War panics led the United States to educate girls: *The World Split Open: How the Modern Women's Movement Changed America* (2000; repr., Penguin Books, 2006), p. 42.

39 Atwood, *The Handmaid's Tale*, pp. 90, 186.

CHAPTER 1: MIDCENTURY SEPARATE SPHERES

1 For Robert Lowell's characterization, see "Memories of West Street and Lepke," in *Selected Poems*, expanded ed. (Farrar, Straus and Giroux, 2006), pp. 129–30, at 129.

2 Adrienne Rich, unpublished letters to Hayden Carruth, quoted in Michelle Dean, "Adrienne Rich's Feminist Awakening," *New Republic*, 4 Apr. 2016; she

recalls her merciful discovery in Adrienne Rich, "The Distance between Language and Violence," in *What Is Found There: Notebooks on Poetry and Politics,* expanded ed. (W. W. Norton, 2003), pp. 181–89, at 187.

3 Jacqueline Rose, *The Haunting of Sylvia Plath* (Virago, 1991), p. 26.

4 In a September 1952 interview for *Pageant,* Monroe said, "I'm personally opposed to a deep tan because I like to feel blond all over" (p. 125).

5 *The Journals of Sylvia Plath,* ed. Ted Hughes (Knopf, 1982), p. 319.

6 Ibid., p. 212.

7 See Ginia Bellafante's "Suburban Rapture," *New York Times,* 24 Dec. 2008, www .nytimes.com/2008/12/28/books/review/Bellafante-t.html. For "blessed Rombauer," see *The Unabridged Journals of Sylvia Plath,* ed. Karen V. Kukil (Anchor, 2000), p. 249.

8 The exhibition *Paper Doll,* curated by Anne Koval at Owens Art Gallery (2011) and Mendel Art Gallery (2012), displayed Plath's dolls. See Koval's catalog entry, "Paper Doll," for a description of the "romantic titles" that Plath gave the doll's outfits (*Paper Doll* [Owens Art Gallery/Mendel Art Gallery, 2011], p. 14). The dolls can also be seen in Plath's archives at the Lilly Library at Indiana University, Bloomington. Darlene J. Sadlier describes and reprints some of them in *The Lilly Library from A to Z* (Indiana University Press, 2019), pp. 39–40.

9 *Varsity,* 26 May 1956.

10 Sylvia Plath, *Letters Home,* ed. Aurelia Schober Plath (Faber and Faber, 1975), pp. 236–37.

11 *The Letters of Sylvia Plath,* vol. 1, *1940–1956,* ed. Peter K. Steinberg and Karen V. Kukil (Harper, 2017), pp. 1203, 1063.

12 Plath, *Unabridged Journals,* p. 211.

13 *Letters of Sylvia Plath,* 1:1247.

14 Ibid., 1:1228.

15 Ted Hughes, "You Hated Spain," in *Birthday Letters* (Farrar, Straus and Giroux, 1998), pp. 39–40, at 39.

16 Plath, *Unabridged Journals,* pp. 22, 20, 160.

17 Ibid., pp. 54, 77 (the final ellipsis is hers).

18 Sylvia Plath, *The Bell Jar* (1963; repr., Harper, 2013), p. 85.

19 For a personal memoir of a *Mademoiselle* guest editorship and an extended reading of Plath in that context, see Sandra M. Gilbert, "'A Fine, White Flying Myth': The Life/Work of Sylvia Plath" [1978], in her *Rereading Women: Thirty Years of Exploring Our Literary Traditions* (W. W. Norton, 2011), pp. 114–33.

20 See Cailey Rizzo, "A Sylvia Plath Retrospective Finally Puts Her Visual Art on Display," *Vice,* 28 July 2017, www.vice.com/en/article/zmva5x/sylvia-plath -retrospective-visual-art-smithsonian. The collage is held in the Mortimer Rare Book Collection at Smith College. See also *Eye Rhymes: Sylvia Plath's Art of the Visual,* ed. Kathleen Connors and Sally Bayley (Oxford University Press, 2007).

21 The catchphrase "the man in the gray flannel suit" comes from the title of Sloan Wilson's best-selling 1955 novel.

22 Phyllis McGinley, "The 5:32," *New Yorker,* 25 Oct. 1941, p. 19.

23 For the comment of McGinley's daughter, see Bellafante, "Suburban Rapture."

24 Elaine Tyler May, *Homeward Bound: American Families in the Cold War Era* (Basic Books, 1999), p. 14.

25 Ibid., p. 121.

26 Sylvia Plath, "Barren Woman," in *The Collected Poems*, ed. Ted Hughes (1981; repr., HarperCollins, 2018), p. 157; "Munich Mannequins," in ibid., pp. 262–63, at 262.

27 Adrienne Rich, *Of Woman Born: Motherhood as Experience and Institution* (W. W. Norton, 1995), p. 224.

28 More savagely, in "Inauguration Day: January 1953"—a prefiguring of Plath's collage—Lowell added that "the Republic summons Ike, / the mausoleum in her heart" (*Selected Poems*, p. 57).

29 W. H. Auden, *The Age of Anxiety: A Baroque Eclogue*, ed. Alan Jacobs (Princeton University Press, 2011).

30 See David K. Johnson, *The Lavender Scare: The Cold War Persecution of Gays and Lesbians in the Federal Government* (University of Chicago Press, 2004).

31 See Shaun Usher, "Utopian Turtletop," *Lists of Note*, 8 Feb. 2012, www.listsofnote .com/2012/02/utopian-turtletop.html. Was Moore serious, or was she slyly subverting that great American institution, the Ford Motor Company? Duplicitous or not, she dominated the *New Yorker*, along with the "housewife poet" Phyllis McGinley.

32 Moore's letter is quoted in Vivian R. Pollak, "Moore, Plath, Hughes, and 'The Literary Life,'" *American Literary History* 17, no. 1 (Spring 2005): 95–117, at 103.

33 Ibid., p. 107.

34 Marianne Moore, letter of November 1961 to Henry Allen Moe, in ibid.

35 Ibid., p. 108.

36 *The Letters of Sylvia Plath*, vol. 2, *1956–1963*, ed. Peter K. Steinberg and Karen V. Kukil (Harper, 2018), p. 110.

37 Plath, *Unabridged Journals*, p. 354.

38 David Holbrook, *Sylvia Plath: Poetry and Existence* (1976; repr., Bloomsbury, 2013), p. 89.

39 Posted in 2010 at www.youtube.com/watch?v=UOH-PyZecVM.

40 Ferdinand Lundberg and Marynia F. Farnham, *Modern Woman: The Lost Sex* (Harper and Brothers, 1947), p. 143. The quote appears in a chapter titled "The Feminist Complex." Joanne Meyerwitz has cautioned that the book was considered extreme at the time and "did not represent the mainstream in the mass culture": see "Beyond the Feminine Mystique: A Reassessment of Post-War Mass Culture, 1946–1958," *Journal of American History* 79, no. 4 (March 1993): 1455–82, at 1476.

41 Lundberg and Farnham, *Modern Woman*, pp. 166, 265, 271.

42 Ibid., pp. 266, 271, 270, 280, 304–5.

43 Jane Gerhard, *Desiring Revolution: Second-Wave Feminism and the Rewriting of American Sexual Thought, 1920–1982* (Columbia University Press, 2001), p. 47.

44 Helene Deutsch, *The Psychology of Women: A Psychoanalytic Interpretation*, 2 vols. (Grune and Stratton, 1944–45), 1:xiii.

45 Ibid., 1:228, 229, 230.

46 Ibid., 1:227, 228 (quoting Horney).

47 Ibid., 2:79; 1:291, 292, 319.

48 As a girl, Deutsch later admitted, she "hated" her mother, who beat her because she was not a son and who kept a "tyrannical vigil over [her daughter's] chastity" because she valued only "status, conformity, and a good reputation." Helene Deutsch, *Confrontations with Myself: An Epilogue* (W. W. Norton, 1973), pp. 62–63.

49 Alfred C. Kinsey et al., *Sexual Behavior in the Human Female* (W. B. Saunders, 1953), p. 582.

50 See, e.g., Karl E. Bauman, "Volunteer Bias in a Study of Sexual Knowledge, Attitudes, and Behavior," *Journal of Marriage and Family* 35, no. 1 (Feb. 1973): 27–31.

51 Kinsey et al., *Sexual Behavior in the Human Female*, pp. 574, 657.

52 See James H. Jones, "To Deal Directly with the Rockefeller Foundation," chap. 27 of *Alfred C. Kinsey: A Public/Private Life* (W. W. Norton, 1997), pp. 442–47.

53 Jonathan Gathorne-Hardy, *Alfred C. Kinsey: Sex the Measure of All Things: A Biography* (Pimlico Press, 1999), p. 439.

54 Sharon R. Cohany and Emy Sok, "Trends in Labor Force Participation of Married Mothers of Infants," *Monthly Labor Review*, Feb. 2007, pp. 9–16, at 10.

55 On popular forms of contraception in the fifties, see Vern L. Bullough and Bonnie Bullough, *Contraception: A Guide to Birth Control Methods* (Prometheus Books, 1990); on unsafe abortion practices in the United States before *Roe v. Wade* in 1973, see David A. Grimes with Linda G. Brandon, *Every Third Woman in America: How Legal Abortion Transformed Our Nation* (Daymark, 2014).

CHAPTER 2: RACE, REBELLION, AND REACTION

1 Allan Ginsberg, "Howl," in *Howl and Other Poems* (City Lights, 1956), pp. 9–20, at 17, 18.

2 Diane di Prima, *Recollections of My Life as a Woman: The New York Years* (Penguin, 2001), pp. 92, 93, 101.

3 Diane di Prima, *Memoirs of a Beatnik* (1969; repr., Last Gasp of San Francisco, 1988), p. 131. The veracity of this book needs to be gauged against di Prima's need to make money and her editor's response to the manuscript: di Prima noted in her afterword that Maurice Girodias always wrote "MORE SEX" across the top of her pages (p. 137).

4 Di Prima, *Recollections*, pp. 108, 107, 108.

5 Ibid., p. 157.

6 Ibid., p. 233.

7 Ibid., p. 227.

8 Ibid., p. 225.

9 Gwendolyn Brooks, "The Bean-Eaters," in *Selected Poems* (Harper and Row, 1963), p. 72.

10 Gwendolyn Brooks, *Maud Martha* (AMS Press, 1953).

11 Gwendolyn Brooks, "Bronzeville Woman in a Red Hat," in *Selected Poems*, pp. 103–6, at 103.

12 Ibid., p. 104.

13 Ibid., p. 106.

14 Harry Belafonte, vocalist, "Man Smart (Woman Smarter)," probably composed by Norman Span, on *Calypso* (RCA Victor, 1956).

15 In the recent *Looking for Lorraine: The Radiant and Radical Life of Lorraine Hansberry* (Beacon, 2018), Imani Perry fills in many details. Perry discusses the indebtedness of "Flag from a Kitchenette Window" to Brooks's work on p. 44.

16 Lorraine Hansberry, *To Be Young, Gifted, and Black: An Informal Autobiography of Lorraine Hansberry*, adapted by Robert Nemiroff (Signet, 1969), p. 36.

17 Anne Cheney, *Lorraine Hansberry* (Twayne, 1984), p. 10.

18 Hansberry, *Young, Gifted, and Black*, pp. 73, 85.

19 Lorraine Hansberry, "The Negro Writer and His Roots: Toward a New Romanticism," *Black Scholar* 12, no. 2 (Mar./Apr. 1981): 2–12, at 12.

20 Lorraine Hansberry, "In Defense of the Equality of Men," in *The Norton Anthology of Literature by Women: The Tradition in English*, ed. Sandra M. Gilbert and Susan Gubar (W. W. Norton, 1985), pp. 2058–67, at 2066.

21 Hansberry, *Young, Gifted, and Black*, pp. 98, 103.

22 Perry, *Looking for Lorraine*, p. 59.

23 The photograph is available on a webpage of the Lorraine Hansberry Literary Trust, www.lhlt.org/gallery?page=2.

24 Perry, *Looking for Lorraine*, p. 74.

25 Lorraine Hansberry, "Simone de Beauvoir and *The Second Sex*: An American Commentary," in *Words of Fire: An Anthology of African-American Feminist Thought*, ed. Beverly Guy-Sheftall (New Press, 1995), pp. 128–42, at 129, 128, 129, 130. Hansberry's essay went unprinted until it appeared in this anthology.

26 Ibid., pp. 139, 140, 141.

27 Lorraine Hansberry, *A Raisin in the Sun* (1959; repr., Benediction Classics, 2017), p. 61.

28 In the resulting blitz of invitations and TV appearances, Hansberry defended the play against those attributing its success to the fact that "everybody associated with it was a Negro." Its outstanding director and actors, she argued, made it a smash hit, along with her own awareness of Anouilh, Beckett, Dürrenmatt, Brecht, and O'Casey. [Lillian Ross], "How Lorraine Hansberry Wrote 'A Raisin in the Sun,'" *New Yorker*, 9 May 1959, p. 34.

29 Hansberry, *Young, Gifted, and Black*, pp. 51, 63.

30 Hansberry, *Raisin in the Sun*, pp. 92, 87.

31 Langston Hughes, "Harlem" (1951), in *Selected Poems of Langston Hughes* (Vintage Classics, 1990), p. 268.

32 Hansberry, *Raisin in the Sun*, p. 42.

33 bell hooks, *Killing Rage: Ending Racism* (Henry Holt, 1995), p. 67.

34 Hansberry, "The Negro Writer and His Roots," pp. 4, 5.

35 Ibid., pp. 8, 10.

36 Hansberry, "In Defense of the Equality of Men," pp. 2060, 2064.

37 Perry, Looking for Lorraine, p. 135.

38 Adrienne Rich, "The Problem with Lorraine Hansberry," Freedomways 19, no. 4 (4th Quarter 1979): 247–55, at 252.

39 Hansberry, Young, Gifted, and Black, p. 137.

40 See Del Martin and Phyllis Lyon, Lesbian/Woman (Bantam Books, 1972), pp. 121–22, as well as Kevin J. Mumford, Not Straight, Not White: Black Gay Men from the March on Washington to the AIDS Crisis (University of North Carolina Press, 2016), p. 18.

41 Hansberry, Young, Gifted, and Black, p. 137. Too much of what we know about Hansberry has remained filtered through her well-intentioned husband, who after her death produced her so-called autobiography, To Be Young, Gifted and Black. According to Kevin Mumford, the restricted papers in the Schomberg Center for Research in Black Culture contain diary entries and letters about Hansberry's responsiveness to female lovers, FBI files on her Communist affiliations, an essay on white backlash, accounts of recurrent bouts of despondency, and full runs of homophile journals that indicate "how deeply she felt about her lesbian desire." E-mail from Professor Mumford to Susan Gubar, 21 Sept. 2017.

42 Audre Lorde, Zami: A New Spelling of My Name (Crossing Press, 1982), p. 242.

43 Di Prima, Recollections, p. 73.

44 Interview with Marion Kraft in 1986 in Conversations with Audre Lorde, ed. Joan Wylie Hall (University Press of Mississippi, 2004), pp. 146–53, at 149.

45 Lorde, Zami, p. 24.

46 Audre Lorde, "An Interview: Audre Lorde and Adrienne Rich," in Sister Outsider: Essays and Speeches (Crossing Press, 1984), pp. 81–109, at 82.

47 Lorde, Zami, pp. 59, 58.

48 Ibid., pp. 86, 91, 100–103.

49 "Memorial II," in The Collected Poems of Audre Lorde (W. W. Norton, 1997), p. 3; Lorde, Zami, p. 82.

50 Alexis De Veaux, Warrior Poet: A Biography of Audre Lorde (W. W. Norton, 2004), p. 26.

51 Lorde, Zami, pp. 136, 133, 139, 142.

52 Ibid., p. 126.

53 Ibid., p. 232.

54 Ibid., pp. 224, 178, 224, 187.

55 Ibid., p. 204.

56 Audre Lorde, "Learning from the 60s," in Sister Outsider, pp. 134–44, 134.

57 Tracy Daugherty, The Last Love Song: A Biography of Joan Didion (Macmillan, 2015), p. 80.

58 Ibid.

59 Joan Didion, "People Are Talking About" column, Vogue, January 1963, 34; quoted in ibid., p. 104.

60 Daugherty's biography draws from Noel Parmentel's recollections of Didion; see The Last Love Song, p. 95.

61 Joan Didion, "People Are Talking About" column, *Vogue*, July 1963, 31; quoted in ibid., p. 142.

62 Betty Friedan, *Life So Far* (Simon and Schuster, 2000), p. 99.

63 Ibid., p. 98.

64 Betty Friedan, *The Feminine Mystique* [50th anniversary ed.] (W. W. Norton, 2013), p. 83. She describes the education required for women in her book's final chapter, "A New Life Plan for Women" (chap. 14, pp. 407–56).

65 Friedan's unpublished notes on Bruno Bettelheim's *The Informed Heart* (1960), quoted in Kirsten Fermaglich, *American Dreams and Nazi Nightmares: Early Holocaust Consciousness and Liberal America, 1957–1965* (Brandeis University Press, published by University Press of New England, 2000), p. 68. Fermaglich and Lisa M. Fine further contextualize this quotation in their introduction to the Norton Critical Edition of *The Feminine Mystique* (W. W. Norton, 2013), pp. xi–xx, at xv–xvi.

66 Phyllis Lee Levin, "Road from Sophocles to Spock Is Often a Bumpy One; Former Co-eds Find Family Routine Is Stifling Them," *New York Times*, 28 June 1960; quoted in Friedan, *The Feminine Mystique*, p. 10; for "the trapped American housewife," see p. 14.

67 Friedan, *The Feminine Mystique*, p. 10.

CHAPTER 3: THREE ANGRY VOICES

1 See Sandra M. Gilbert, *The Culinary Imagination: From Myth to Modernity* (W. W. Norton, 2014), p. 205, for a description of the Eisenhowers' menu. For descriptions and visuals of the Kennedys' luncheon menu, see *The Gilded Age Era* blogspot, "Grace Kelly Visits the Kennedys," 10 May 2014, thegildedageera.blogspot .com/2014/05/grace-kelly-visits-kennedys.html.

2 "Jacqueline Kennedy in the White House," *John F. Kennedy Presidential Library and Museum*, www.jfklibrary.org/learn/about-jfk/jfk-in-history/jacqueline-kennedy -in-the-white-house.

3 See Mary Ann Watson, "A Tour of the White House: Mystique and Tradition," *Presidential Studies Quarterly* 18, no. 1 (Winter 1998): 91–99, at 92, 95, and "A Tour of the White House with Mrs. John F. Kennedy," dir. Franklin J. Schaffner (CBS, 14 Feb. 1962).

4 "When Marilyn Monroe happened to die that month," Warhol explained, "I got the idea to make screens of her beautiful face, the first Marilyns." Andy Warhol and Pat Hackett, *POPism: The Warhol Sixties* (Houghton Mifflin Harcourt, 1980), p. 28.

5 Sylvia Plath, *Letters Home*, ed. Aurelia Schober Plath (Faber and Faber, 1975), p. 473.

6 Marilyn Hacker, "The Young Insurgent's Commonplace Book," *Field*, no. 77 (2007): 16–20 (Hacker's contribution—a discussion of "Snapshots of a Daughter-in-Law"—to a section titled "Adrienne Rich: A *Field* Symposium"). Within the next decade feminist critics were to criticize Friedan for omitting any discussion of working-class white women and women of color.

7 Imani Perry, *Looking for Lorraine: The Radiant and Radical Life of Lorraine Hansberry* (Beacon, 2018), p. 164.

8 "It didn't bother me that much that [Kennedy] was dead," Warhol recalled. "What bothered me was the way the television and radio were programming everybody to feel sad" (Warhol and Hackett, *POPism*, p. 77).

9 *The Unabridged Journals of Sylvia Plath*, ed. Karen V. Kukil (Anchor, 2000), pp. 648, 647.

10 Sylvia Plath, "Morning Song," in *Ariel* (Harper, 1965), p. 1.

11 Sylvia Plath, "Nick and the Candlestick," in ibid., pp. 33–34, at 34.

12 Plath, *Letters Home*, p. 446.

13 For a granular account of this episode, see Heather Clark's *Red Comet: The Short and Blazing Life of Sylvia Plath* (Knopf, 2020), pp. 700–35.

14 Sylvia Plath, "Letter in November," in *The Collected Poems*, ed. Ted Hughes (1981; repr., Harper, 2018), pp. 253–54, at 253.

15 Plath, *Letters Home*, p. 446.

16 Ibid., p. 468.

17 Plath, "Stings," in *Ariel*, pp. 61–63, at 61.

18 Ibid., pp. 62, 63.

19 Anne Stevenson, *Bitter Fame: A Life of Sylvia Plath* (Mariner, 1998), p. 277: "Sylvia . . . read 'Daddy' aloud [to her friend Clarissa Roche] in a mocking, comical voice that made both women fall about with laughter."

20 Plath, "Daddy," in *Ariel*, pp. 49–51, at 50.

21 "Script for the BBC Broadcast 'New Poems by Sylvia Plath,'" appendix II in Sylvia Plath, *Ariel: The Restored Edition* (HarperCollins, 2004), pp. 195–97, at 195.

22 Plath, "Daddy," pp. 50, 49. It is of course deeply significant here that Otto Plath had to have his leg amputated after gangrene set in due to an advanced case of untreated diabetes. Sylvia blamed her father for never seeking medical attention.

23 Ibid., pp. 51, 49.

24 Ibid., p. 51.

25 Plath, "Ariel," in *Ariel*, pp. 26–27.

26 Ibid., p. 27.

27 The facsimile of Plath's manuscript is reproduced in *Ariel: The Restored Edition*; see pp. 91–174.

28 Plath, *Letters Home*, p. 491.

29 Ted Hughes, "The Inscription," in *Collected Poems*, ed. Paul Keegan (Farrar, Straus and Giroux, 2003), p. 1154.

30 *The Letters of Sylvia Plath*, vol. 2, *1956–1963*, ed. Peter K. Steinberg and Karen V. Kukil (Harper, 2018), p. 968.

31 See Sandra M. Gilbert, "Introduction: The Treasures That Prevail," in Adrienne Rich, *Essential Essays: Culture, Politics, and the Art of Poetry*, ed. Gilbert (W. W. Norton, 2018), pp. xi–xx, at xvi.

32 W. H. Auden, foreword to Adrienne Cecile Rich, *A Change of World* (Yale University Press, 1951), pp. 7–11, at 11.

33 Randall Jarrell, "New Books in Review," *Yale Review* 46 (1956): 100.

34 Adrienne Rich, "Juvenilia," in *Collected Poems: 1951–2012* (W. W. Norton, 2016), pp. 126–27, at 127.

35 See Gilbert, "Introduction: The Treasures That Prevail," p. xvi.

36 Ibid.

37 Plath, *Unabridged Journals*, p. 368.

38 Ibid., p. 354.

39 Adrienne Rich, "Split at the Root: An Essay on Jewish Identity" (1982), in *Essential Essays*, pp. 198–217, at 212.

40 Adrienne Rich, "When We Dead Awaken: Writing as Re-Vision" (1971), in ibid., pp. 3–19, at 14.

41 Adrienne Rich, "Snapshots of a Daughter-in-Law," in *Collected Poems*, pp. 117–21, at 117. Literarily, moldering wedding cake evokes Miss Havisham, the perpetually unmarried bride in Dickens's *Great Expectations*, whose unconsumed cake has sat for decades in a cobwebby room while the marriage it was supposed to celebrate never took place.

42 Ibid.

43 Significantly, Rich always insisted that her children—and later, her grandchildren—call her "Adrienne," as if "mother" and "grandmother," those placeholders of family identity, might prove as ruinous as the cake "heavy with useless experience." Yet by all accounts she was a loving parent and grandparent. Even more than Plath, however, she regularly transmuted the personal into the political and the poetical. The lovely essay "For Adrienne," written by her granddaughter Julia Conrad, gives in a short space a vivid sense of the way in which Rich related to her family. See *Massachusetts Review* 57, no. 4 (Winter 2016): 799–804.

44 Rich, "Snapshots of a Daughter-in-Law," p. 118. This last phrase is drawn from Baudelaire's poem "Au lecteur" ("To the Reader"), in which he addresses both the reader and himself with some contempt: "Hypocrite lecteur,—mon semblable,—mon frère!" Charles Baudelaire, "Au lecteur," in *Flowers of Evil and Other Works/Les Fleurs du Mal et Oeuvres Choisies*, ed. and trans. Wallace Fowlie (1964; repr., Dover, 1992), p. 18.

45 Rich, "Snapshots of a Daughter-in-Law," p. 118.

46 Ibid., p. 119.

47 Ibid.

48 Ibid., pp. 120, 121.

49 Ibid., p. 121. The passage from *The Second Sex* that yielded this vision was like yet unlike Rich's literally fabulous conclusion to "Snapshots." For Beauvoir, she is an archetypal and problematic figure, the very paradigm of the *other* who is the "second sex." For Rich, however, in her otherness she becomes a utopian redeemer. Simone de Beauvoir, *The Second Sex*, trans. and ed. H. M. Parshley (1952; repr., Vintage, 1989), p. 729.

50 Rich, "When We Dead Awaken," p. 14.

51 See John Ashbery's review of Rich's *Necessities of Life*, quoted in Albert Gelpi's *American Poetry After Modernism: The Power of the Word* (Cambridge University

Press, 2015), p. 141. Ashbery dismissed her with faint praise as "an Emily Dickinson of the suburbs."

52 See Michelle Dean, "The Wreck," *New Republic*, 3 Apr. 2016, newrepublic.com /article/132117/adrienne-richs-feminist-awakening.

53 Adrienne Rich, "Blue Ghazals: 9/29/86," in *Collected Poems*, p. 310.

54 Angela Davis, quoted in Alan Light, *What Happened, Miss Simone? A Biography* (Crown Archetype, 2016), p. 103; Toni Morrison, quoted in David Brun-Lambert, *Nina Simone: The Biography* (Aurum, 2009), pp. 156–57; Amiri Baraka, quoted in Michael Gonzales, "Natural Fact: The Nina Simone Story," *WaxPoetics*, 25 June 2015, backend.waxpoetics.com/blog/features/natural-fact -the-nina-simone-story.

55 Both movies made about Nina Simone include these three incidents: see *Nina*, dir. Cynthia Mort (RLJ Entertainment, 2016), and *What Happened, Miss Simone?*, dir. Liz Garbus (Netflix, 2015).

56 Nina Simone with Stephen Cleary, *I Put a Spell on You: The Autobiography of Nina Simone* (Da Capo Press, 1991), p. 26.

57 Ibid., p. 42.

58 Simone Signoret would go on to translate and produce Hansberry's *A Raisin in the Sun* in Paris.

59 Light, *What Happened, Miss Simone?*, p. 59; Nina Simone, quoted in ibid., p. 136.

60 Simone with Cleary, *I Put a Spell on You*, p. 77.

61 Ibid., p. 78.

62 Simone, quoted in Light, *What Happened, Miss Simone?*, p. 120.

63 Simone with Cleary, *I Put a Spell on You*, p. 83.

64 Perry, *Looking for Lorraine*, p. 129.

65 Simone with Cleary, *I Put a Spell on You*, pp. 87, 89.

66 Ibid., p. 90.

67 Nina Simone, "Mississippi Goddam" (1964), *Genius*, genius.com/Nina-simone -mississippi-goddam-lyrics.

68 Lisa Simone, quoted in Light, *What Happened, Miss Simone?*, p. 100.

69 Nina Simone, quoted in Joe Hagan, "I Wish I Knew How It Would Feel to Be Free: The Secret Diary of Nina Simone," *The Believer*, no. 73 (1 July 2010), www .believermag.com/i-wish-i-knew-how-it-would-feel-to-be-free/.

70 Nina Simone, "Pirate Jenny" (1964), *Genius*, www.genius.com/Nina-simone -pirate-jenny-lyrics.

71 Angela Davis, quoted in Light, *What Happened, Miss Simone?*, p. 103; Ruth Feldstein, *How It Feels to Be Free: Black Women Entertainers and the Civil Rights Movement* (Oxford University Press, 2013), p. 96.

72 For "the United Snakes of America," see Claudia Roth Pierpoint, "A Raised Voice: How Nina Simone Turned the Movement into Music," *New Yorker*, 11 and 18 Aug. 2014, pp. 44–51, at 49.

73 Nina Simone, "Go Limp" (1964), *Genius*, www.genius.com/Nina-simone-go -limp-lyrics.

74 Angela Davis, *Angela Davis—An Autobiography* (Random House, 1974), p. 161.

75 Stokely Carmichael, quoted in Mary King, *Freedom Song: A Personal Story of the 1960s Civil Rights Movement* (William Morrow, 1985), pp. 451–52.

76 Nina Simone, "Four Women" (1965), *Genius*, www.genius.com/Nina-simone -four-women-lyrics.

77 Nina Simone, "Images" (1966), *Genius*, www.genius.com/Nina-simone-images -lyrics.

78 Mary Anne Evans's lengthy interview with Nina Simone about "Four Women" is reprinted in Light, *What Happened, Miss Simone?*, pp. 132–34. All of Simone's comments about the characters that follow derive from this interview. In the biography, the interview appears in italics.

79 Al Schackman, quoted in ibid., 134–35.

80 Simone with Cleary, *I Put a Spell on You*, p. 117.

81 Nina Simone, "I Wish I Knew How It Would Feel to Be Free" (1967), *Genius*, www.genius.com/Nina-simone-i-wish-i-knew-how-it-would-feel-to-be-free -lyrics.

82 Simone with Cleary, *I Put a Spell on You*, p. 118.

83 Nina Simone, quoted in Light, *What Happened, Miss Simone?*, p. 91. The description of her being worked "like a carthorse" is from Simone with Cleary, *I Put a Spell on You*, p. 114.

84 Nina Simone, quoted in Nadine Cohadas, *Princess Noire: The Tumultuous Reign of Nina Simone* (University of North Carolina Press, 2010), p. 224.

85 Simone, quoted in ibid., 162.

86 Bryant Rollins and Les Matthews, "Candidates Warned: Must Deal with Black Nationalists and Integrationists or Get No Support," *New York Amsterdam News*, 16 Oct. 1971.

87 Hansberry's lecture "The Nation Needs Your Gifts" is discussed by Perry, *Looking for Lorraine*, p. 197.

CHAPTER 4: THE SEXUAL REVOLUTION AND THE VIETNAM WAR

1 Philip Larkin, "Annus Mirabilis," in *The Complete Poems*, ed. Archie Burnett (Farrar, Straus and Giroux, 2012), p. 90.

2 See Loren Glass, "Redeeming Value: Obscenity and Anglo-American Modernism," *Critical Inquiry* 32, no. 2 (Winter 2006): 341–61.

3 See Elaine Tyler May, *America and the Pill: A History of Promise, Peril, and Liberation* (Basic Books, 2010).

4 On the "little marriages," see Carolyn Heilbrun, *The Education of a Woman: The Life of Gloria Steinem* (Ballantine Books, 1996), pp. 112, 115.

5 Gloria Steinem, "Introduction: Life between the Lines," in *Outrageous Acts and Everyday Rebellions* (Holt, Rinehart and Winston, 1983), pp. 1–26, at 16.

6 Gloria Steinem, "I Was a Playboy Bunny," in ibid., pp. 29–69, at 30, 35. The piece was originally published in *Show* magazine in two parts, under the title "A Bunny's Tale."

7 Hugh Hefner's 1967 interview is quoted in Carina Chocano, *You Play the Girl: On*

Playboy Bunnies, Stepford Wives, Train Wrecks, and Other Mixed Messages (Houghton Mifflin Harcourt, 2017), p. 6.

8 Ibid., p. 5.

9 Steinem, "Introduction: Life between the Lines," p. 16.

10 Steinem, "I Was a Playboy Bunny," p. 69.

11 Steinem, "Introduction: Life between the Lines," p. 16.

12 Gloria Steinem, "The Moral Disarmament of Betty Coed," *Esquire*, Sept. 1962, pp. 97–157, at 97, 153, 154. Mary McCarthy's novel *The Group* (1963) discusses many of these same issues raised by contraception.

13 Steinem, "The Moral Disarmament of Betty Coed," pp. 155, 156.

14 Ibid., pp. 156, 157.

15 Ibid., p. 157.

16 Helen Gurley Brown, *Sex and the Single Girl* (Bernard Geis, 1962), p. 4.

17 This was famously her "favorite motto," according to Judith Thurman, "Owning Your Desire: Remembering Helen Gurley Brown," *New Yorker*, 15 Aug. 2012, www.newyorker.com/books/page-turner/owning-your-desire-remembering-helen-gurley-brown.

18 Brown, *Sex and the Single Girl*, pp. 24, 65, 76, 78.

19 Ibid., pp. 111, 120, 222, 252, 267.

20 Jennifer Scanlon, *Bad Girls Go Everywhere: The Life of Helen Gurley Brown* (Oxford University Press, 2009), p. 101.

21 William H. Masters and Virginia E. Johnson, *Human Sexual Response* (Little, Brown, 1988), pp. 21, 67, 45.

22 Mary Ann Sherfey's was the first major response to Masters and Johnson: "The Evolution and Nature of Female Sexuality in Relation to Psychoanalytic Theory," *Journal of the American Psychoanalytic Association* 14, no. 1 (1966): 28–128 (quotation at 123).

23 Masters and Johnson, *Human Sexual Response*, pp. 65, 131, 285, 314.

24 Susan Sontag, *Reborn: Journals and Notebooks, 1947–1963*, ed. David Rieff (Picador, 2009), pp. 213, 220.

25 Benjamin Moser, *Sontag: Her Life and Work* (HarperCollins, 2019), p. 90.

26 Sontag, *Reborn*, p. 73.

27 Moser, *Sontag*, p. 116.

28 Sontag, *Reborn*, p. 196.

29 Terry Castle, "Desperately Seeking Susan," *London Review of Books*, 17 Mar. 2005, pp. 17–20, at 17.

30 Daniel Stern, "Life Becomes a Dream," *New York Times Book Review*, 8 Sept. 1963.

31 Carolyn G. Heilbrun, "Speaking of Susan Sontag," *New York Times Book Review*, 27 Aug. 1967.

32 Susan Sontag, "Notes on Camp," in *Susan Sontag: Essays of the 1960s & 70s*, ed. David Rieff (Library of America, 2013), pp. 259–74, at 263.

33 Simone de Beauvoir, *The Second Sex*, trans. and ed. H. M. Parshley (1952; repr., Vintage, 1989), p. 267.

34 In Sontag's vision of "camp" culture, pronounced Simon with distaste, the "outre and the inverted become the quotidian"; for his part, Howe bizarrely (and misogynistically) dismissed Sontag as a "brilliant publicist who makes brilliant quilts from Grandmother's patches." Both are quoted in James Penner, "Gendering Susan Sontag's Criticism in the 1960s: The New York Intellectuals, the Counter Culture, and the *Kulturkampf* over 'the New Sensibility,'" *Women's Studies* 37, no. 8 (2008): 921–41, at 935, 926.

35 See Theodore Roszak, *The Making of a Counter Culture: Reflections on the Technocratic Society and Its Youthful Opposition* (University of California Press, 1969). For a similar argument, see also Charles A. Reich, *The Greening of America* (Random House, 1970).

36 Susan Sontag, "What's Happening in America?" in *Susan Sontag: Essays of the 1960s & 70s*, pp. 452–61, at 452, 453, 460.

37 Ibid., pp. 457–58, 459.

38 Joan Didion, "John Wayne: A Love Song," *Saturday Evening Post*, 14 Aug. 1965, pp. 76–79.

39 Joan Didion, "A Preface," in *Slouching Towards Bethlehem* (Farrar, Straus and Giroux, 1968), pp. xi–xiv, at xi.

40 Joan Didion, "Slouching Towards Bethlehem," in ibid., pp. 84–128, at 84–85.

41 Ibid., p. 85.

42 Ibid., p. 93.

43 Ibid., pp. 88, 92, 97.

44 Ibid., p. 101.

45 Ibid., pp. 95, 127.

46 *The Centre Will Not Hold*, dir. Griffin Dunne (Netflix, 2017).

47 All quoted material in this paragraph is drawn from Michael J. Kramer, "Summer of Love, Summer of War," *New York Times*, 15 Aug. 2017.

48 Susan Sontag, quoted in Ellen Hopkins, "Susan Sontag Lightens Up," *Los Angeles Times*, 16 Aug. 1992.

49 Alice Herz, quoted in Jon Coburn, "'I Have Chosen the Flaming Death': The Forgotten Self-Immolation of Alice Herz," *Peace & Change* 43, no. 1 (2018): 32–60 (quotation at 32).

50 Todd Gitlin, *The Sixties: Years of Hope, Days of Rage* (1989; repr., Bantam, 1993), p. 265.

51 Ruth Rosen, *The World Split Open: How the Modern Women's Movement Changed America* (Penguin Books, 2000), p. 59.

52 See also such figures as Barbara Deming, "Southern Peace Walk: Two Issues or One?" (1962), and Angela Davis, "The Liberation of Our People" (1969), in *War No More: Three Centuries of American Antiwar and Peace Writing*, ed. Lawrence Rosenwald (Library of America, 2016), pp. 348–61, 507–13.

53 Denise Levertov, interview with William Packard, "Craft Interview with Denise Levertov" (1971), in *Conversations with Denise Levertov*, ed. Jewel Spears Brooker (University Press of Mississippi, 1998), p. 50. Denise Levertov is talking about the post-1966 movement.

54 Denise Levertov, "Life at War," in *Poems 1968–1972* (New Directions, 1987), pp. 121–22, at 121, 122.

55 Denise Levertov, "Advent 1966," in ibid., p. 124.

56 Muriel Rukeyser, "Poem" (1968), in *The Collected Poems of Muriel Rukeyser*, ed. Janet E. Kaufman and Anne F. Herzog with Jan Heller Levi (University of Pittsburgh Press, 2005), p. 430.

57 Mary McCarthy, *Vietnam* (Harcourt, Brace and World, 1967), p. 33.

58 Mary McCarthy, *Hanoi* (Harcourt, Brace and World, 1968), p. 123.

59 Mary McCarthy, letter quoted in Michelle Dean, *Sharp: The Women Who Made an Art of Having an Opinion* (Grove Press, 2018), p. 165.

60 McCarthy, *Hanoi*, p. 127.

61 Susan Sontag, "Trip to Hanoi," in *Styles of Radical Will* (Picador, 1969), pp. 205–74, at 223, 263.

62 Grace Paley, "Report from North Vietnam" (1969), in *A Grace Paley Reader: Stories, Essays, and Poetry*, ed. Kevin Bowen and Nora Paley (Farrar, Straus and Giroux, 2017), pp. 263–69, at 265, 267.

63 Robert Duncan, quoted in Donna Krolik Hollenberg, *A Poet's Revolution: The Life of Denise Levertov* (University of California Press, 2013), p. 240; Denise Levertov, "Part IV: Daily Life," in *Poems 1968–1972*, p. 188.

64 Robert Duncan and Denise Levertov, letters quoted in Hollenberg, *A Poet's Revolution*, p. 284.

65 Sara Evans, *Personal Politics: The Roots of Women's Liberation in the Civil Rights Movement and the New Left* (Alfred A. Knopf, 1979), p. 188.

66 Quoted in ibid., p. 188. In 1967, a "Women's Manifesto" by the Women's Liberation Workshop at a national conference of the Students for a Democratic Society compared women's status with the colonized and demanded that their "brothers" deal with their "male chauvinism." See Gayle Graham Yates, *What Women Want: The Ideas of the Movement* (Harvard University Press, 1975), pp. 7–8.

67 Shulamith Firestone, "The Jeannette Rankin Brigade: Woman Power?" in *Notes from the First Year*, by New York Radical Women (New York Radical Women, 1968), pp. 18–19. The pamphlet is available online at library.duke.edu/digital collections/wlmpc_wlmms01037/.

68 Ibid., pp. 19, 18 (quoting Kathie Amatniek).

69 Kathie Sarachild, "Consciousness-Raising: A Radical Weapon," talk at the First National Conference of Stewardesses for Women's Rights, 12 Mar. 1973, New York City; see www.organizingforwomensliberation.wordpress.com/2012/09/25/consciousness-raising-a-radical-weapon/. Also see Rosen, *The World Split Open*, p. 197.

70 *Ramparts*, quoted in Rosen, *The World Split Open*, p. 131.

71 See Breanne Fahs, *Valerie Solanas: The Defiant Life of the Woman Who Wrote SCUM (and Shot Andy Warhol)* (Feminist Press, 2014). There is an excellent account of the Warhol shooting in Olivia Laing, *The Lonely City: Adventures in the Art of Being Alone* (Picador, 2016), pp. 77–93.

72 Valerie Solanas, *SCUM Manifesto* (1967; repr., AK Press, 1997), pp. 1, 4, 26, 39, 37.

73 Ti-Grace Atkinson believed that "Solanas has brought feminism up-to-date for the first time in history" (quoted in Fahs, *Valerie Solanas*, p. 174).

74 Robin Morgan, *Saturday's Child: A Memoir* (W. W. Norton, 2001), p. 315.

75 Kate Millett, quoted in Fahs, *Valerie Solanas*, p. 164.

76 Morgan, *Saturday's Child*, p. 315.

77 Gail Collins, *America's Women: Four Hundred Years of Dolls, Drudges, Helpmates, and Heroines* (HarperCollins, 2003), p. 440; Kathie Sarachild, quoted in Sara Evans, *Personal Politics: The Roots of Women's Liberation in the Civil Rights Movement and the New Left* (Knopf, 1979), p. 203.

78 See Susan Brownmiller, *In Our Times: Memoir of a Revolution* (Dial Press, 199), pp. 36–40.

79 See Rosen, *The World Split Open*, p. 205; Gloria Steinem, quoted in Joy Press, "The Life and Death of a Radical Sisterhood," *New York: The Cut*, [Nov. 2017], www.thecut.com/2017/11/an-oral-history-of-feminist-group-new-york-radical -women.html.

80 Erica Jong, "Don't Forget the F-Word," *The Guardian*, 11 Apr. 2008, www .theguardian.com/books/2008/apr/12/featuresreviews.guardianreview11; Laura Kaplan, *The Story of Jane: The Legendary Underground Feminist Abortion Service* (1995; repr., University of Chicago Press, 2019), pp. 27, 47; Shirley Chisholm, recorded in Walter Ray Watson, "A Look Back on Shirley Chisholm's Historic 1968 House Victory," *Morning Edition*, NPR, 6 Nov. 2018, www.npr .org/2018/11/06/664617076/a-look-back-on-shirley-chisholm-s-historic-1968 -house-victory; Alexis De Veaux, *Warrior Poet: A Biography of Audre Lorde* (W. W. Norton, 2004), p. 105.

81 Jerry Rubin, quoted in Todd Gitlin, *The Sixties: Years of Hope, Days of Rage*, rev. ed. (Bantam Books, 1993), pp. 219, 404.

82 Mary King and Casey Hayden, quoted in Susan Brownmiller, *In Our Times: Memoir of a Revolution* (Dial Press, 1999), p. 14. See also Winifred Breines, *The Trouble between Us: An Uneasy History of White and Black Women in the Feminist Movement* (Oxford University Press, 2006), p. 26. On the parallels between the nineteenth- and the twentieth-century feminist movements' outgrowth from protests against racial injustice, see Elaine Showalter, "A Criticism of Our Own: Autonomy and Assimilation in Afro-American and Feminist Literary Theory," in *The Future of Literary Theory*, ed. Ralph Cohen (Routledge, 1989), pp. 347–69.

83 Eldridge Cleaver, *Soul on Ice* (1968; repr., Delta, 1999), p. 33.

84 Amiri Baraka, "Babylon Revisited," in *Selected Poetry of Amiri Baraka/LeRoi Jones* (William Morrow, 1979), p. 119.

85 Quoted in Evans, *Personal Politics*, p. 80.

86 Kathleen Cleaver and Frances Beale, quoted in Alice Echols, *Daring to Be Bad: Radical Feminism in America, 1967–1975* (1989; repr., University of Minnesota Press, 2003), p. 107.

87 Robin Morgan, "Introduction: The Women's Revolution," in *Sisterhood Is Pow-*

erful: An Anthology of Writing from the Women's Liberation Movement, ed. Morgan (Vintage Books, 1970), pp. xiii–xl, at xx.

88 Evans, *Personal Politics*, p. 201.

89 Anne Koedt, quoted in Fahs, *Valerie Solanas*, p. 84.

90 Anne Koedt, "The Myth of the Vaginal Orgasm," in *Notes from the Second Year: Women's Liberation: Major Writings of the Radical Feminists*, ed. Shulamith Firestone and Anne Koedt (Radical Feminism, 1970), pp. 37–41, at 41. A shorter version of this essay originally appeared in 1968 in *Notes from the First Year*.

91 Jane O'Reilly's 1971 *Ms.* essay "The Housewife's Moment of Truth" popularized the click of recognition of sexism. For a more recent treatment of the idea, see Courtney E. Martin and J. Courtney Sullivan, eds., *Click: When We Knew We Were Feminists* (Seal Press, 2010).

92 Steinem, "Introduction: Life between the Lines," pp. 17–18.

93 Marge Piercy, "The Grand Coolie Dam," in Morgan, *Sisterhood Is Powerful*, pp. 421–38, at 430, 438. The Chicana students formed Las Hijas de Cuauhtémoc in Long Beach 1969: see Benita Roth, *Separate Roads to Feminism: Black, Chicana, and White Feminist Movements in America's Second Wave* (Cambridge University Press, 2004), p. 138.

94 Robin Morgan, "Goodbye to All That," in *Dear Sisters: Dispatches from the Women's Liberation Movement*, ed. Rosalyn Baxandall and Linda Gordon (Basic Books, 2000), pp. 53–57, at 53, 54, 57; for the dolls, see Morgan, *Saturday's Child*, p. 30. Ellen Willis, one of the founders of the Redstockings, had already announced the emergence of "women's liberation as an independent revolutionary movement, potentially representing half the population. We intend to make our own analysis of the system and put our interests first, whether or not it is convenient for the (male-dominated) Left" (Willis, "Women and the Left" [1969], in *Radical Feminism: A Documentary Reader*, ed. Barbara A. Crow [New York University Press, 2000], pp. 513–15, at 513).

CHAPTER 5: PROTESTING PATRIARCHY

1 *Time* used the Alice Neel portrait for the cover of its 31 Aug. 1970 issue because Millett refused to sit for a photo shoot.

2 Proposed Amendment to the Constitution of the United States, H. J. Res. 208, 92nd Cong. (1972), www.govinfo.gov/content/pkg/STATUTE-86/pdf/STATUTE-86 -Pg1523.pdf.

3 "Who's Come a Long Way, Baby?," *Time*, 31 Aug. 1970, p. 16.

4 In 1969 Carol Hanisch wrote an essay titled "The Personal Is Political" when it was published in *Notes from the Second Year: Women's Liberation: Major Writings of the Radical Feminists*, ed. Shulamith Firestone and Anne Koedt (Radical Feminism, 1970), pp. 76–78, but no feminist claims authorship of the phrase since it quickly became ubiquitous.

5 Adrienne Rich, "When We Dead Awaken" (1971), in *Essential Essays: Culture, Politics, and the Art of Poetry*, ed. Sandra M. Gilbert (W. W. Norton, 2018), pp. 3–19, at 13, 3.

6 Adrienne Rich, "Arts of the Possible" (1997), in ibid., pp. 326–44, at 332.

7 Rachel Blau DuPlessis, *Blue Studios: Poetry and Its Cultural Work* (University of Alabama Press, 2006), p. 22. Elaine Showalter used the phrase "a Great Awakening" in "Women's Time, Women's Space: Writing the History of Feminist Criticism," *Tulsa Studies in Women's Literature* 3, no. 1/2 (Spring–Autumn 1984): 29–43, at 34.

8 Ann Snitow, *The Feminism of Uncertainty: A Gender Diary* (Duke University Press, 2015), p. 71.

9 On the emergence of all these groups, see Winifred D. Wandersee, *On the Move: American Women in the 1970s* (Twayne, 1988).

10 Kate Millett, "Introduction to the Touchstone Paperback," in *Sexual Politics* (1969; repr., Columbia University Press, 2016), pp. xxv–xxviii, at xxv.

11 Millett, *Sexual Politics*, p. 5.

12 Cherryblossomlife, "Sexual Politics Part III: Jean Genet," *Radfem Hub: A Radical Feminist Collective Blog*, 30 Jan. 2012, radicalhubarchives.wordpress.com/2012/01/30/sexual-politics-part-iii-jean-genet/.

13 Millett, *Sexual Politics*, p. 22.

14 Ibid., p. 54.

15 Ibid., p. 363.

16 Kate Millett, *Flying* (1974; repr., University of Illinois Press, 2000), pp. 23, 403, 502, 505.

17 Ibid., p. 15.

18 Radicalesbians, "The Woman-Identified Woman" (1970), in *Women's Rights in the United States: A Comprehensive Encyclopedia of Issues, Events, and People*, ed. Tiffany K. Wayne and Louis Banner, 4 vols. (ABC-CLIO, 2015), 3:358–61, at 358. Also see Karla Jay, *Tales of the Lavender Menace: A Story of Liberation* (Basic Books, 1999).

19 Jill Johnston, *Lesbian Nation: The Feminist Solution* (Simon and Schuster, 1973), p. 179.

20 Ti-Grace Atkinson, quoted in Alice Echols, *Daring to Be Bad: Radical Feminism in America, 1967–1975* (1989; repr., University of Minnesota Press, 2003), p. 238; Johnston, *Lesbian Nation*, p. 166.

21 Millett, *Flying*, pp. 328, 433.

22 Ibid., p. 357.

23 Ibid., pp. 357, 358, 359.

24 *Town Bloody Hall*, dir. Chris Hegedus and D. A. Pennebaker (Pennebaker Hegadus Films, 1979).

25 Ibid.

26 Irving Howe, "The Middle-Class Mind of Kate Millett," *Harper's*, Dec. 1970, pp. 110–29, at 118, 110, 124.

27 Gore Vidal, "In Another Country," *New York Review of Books*, 22 July 1971, pp. 8–10.

28 *Town Bloody Hall.*

29 Kate Millett, *The Basement: Meditations on a Human Sacrifice* (Simon and Schuster, 1979).

30 Joyce Carol Oates, "To Be Female Is to Die," *New York Times*, 9 Sept. 1979.

31 Susan Sontag, "The Pornographic Imagination," in *Susan Sontag: Essays of the 1960s & 70s*, ed. David Rieff (Library of America, 2013), pp. 320–52, at 337.

32 Ibid.

33 Susan Griffin, *Pornography and Silence: Culture's Revenge against Nature* (Harper and Row, 1981), pp. 227–28.

34 Susan Sontag, "The Double Standard of Aging" (1972), in *Susan Sontag: Essays of the 1960s & 70s*, pp. 745–68, at 766, 754, 755.

35 Susan Sontag, "A Woman's Beauty: Put-Down or Power Source?" (1975), in ibid., pp. 803–5, at 804, 805.

36 Susan Sontag, "The Third World of Women" (1973), in ibid., pp. 769–99, at 782.

37 Ibid., pp. 792, 772, 776.

38 Ibid., pp. 793, 779.

39 Ibid., p. 783.

40 Ibid., p. 788.

41 Ibid., p. 797.

42 But on Sontag's implicit feminism in the sixties, and her forthright feminism in the early seventies, as well as the hostility she evoked from Old Left members of the *Partisan Review* "family," see James Penner, "Gendering Susan Sontag's Criticism in the 1960s: The New York Intellectuals, the Counter Culture, and the *Kulturkampf* over 'the New Sensibility,'" *Women's Studies* 37, no. 8 (2008): 921–41.

43 Adrienne Rich and Susan Sontag, "Feminism and Fascism: An Exchange," *New York Review of Books*, 20 Mar. 1975, pp. 31–32.

44 Hilary Holladay, *The Power of Adrienne Rich* (Doubleday, 2020), p. 269.

45 Benjamin Moser, *Sontag: Her Life and Work* (HarperCollins, 2019), pp. 397, 399.

46 Terry Castle, "Desperately Seeking Susan," *London Review of Books*, 17 Mar. 2005, pp. 17–20, at 20.

47 Sigrid Nunez, *Sempre Susan: A Memoir of Susan Sontag* (Riverhead Books, 2014).

48 Needless to say, other novels also captured feminist experience in the seventies, in particular Sue Kaufman's *Diary of a Mad Housewife* (1970) and Marge Piercy's *Small Changes* (1973), as well as Lisa Alther's *Kinflicks* (1976).

49 Toni Morrison, *The Bluest Eye* (1970; repr. Alfred A. Knopf, 1993), pp. 45–46.

50 Ibid., p. 122. Objecting to the slogan "Black is beautiful," Toni Morrison wrote in 1974, "The concept of physical beauty as a *virtue* is one of the dumbest, most pernicious and destructive ideas of the Western world, and we should have nothing to do with it" ("Behind the Making of *The Black Book*," *Black World* 23, no. 4 [Feb. 1974]: 86–90, at 89).

51 Morrison, *The Bluest Eye*, pp. 123, 126.

52 Toni Morrison, "A Slow Walk of Trees (as Grandmother Would Say), Hope-

less (as Grandfather Would Say)" (1976), in *What Moves at the Margin: Selected Nonfiction*, ed. Carolyn C. Denard (University Press of Mississippi, 2008), pp. 6, 7.

53 Fanny Hurst's novel, published in 1933, was adapted in two successful films (1934, 1959).

54 Morrison, *The Bluest Eye*, p. 20.

55 Ibid., pp. 42, 151, 162–63, 206.

56 Toni Morrison, "What the Black Woman Thinks about Women's Lib," *New York Times Magazine*, 22 Aug. 1971, reprinted in *What Moves at the Margin*, pp. 18–30, at 19.

57 Alix Kates Shulman, *Memoirs of an Ex-Prom Queen*, rev. ed. (Penguin, 1997), pp. 18, 22, 42, 46, 63, 58.

58 Ibid., pp. 33, 149, 159.

59 Shulman does not sound penitent when she recalls one reader who chastised her, "complaining that his wife left him, taking the baby with her, after reading *Memoirs of an Ex-Prom Queen*" (preface to *Memoirs of an Ex-Prom Queen*, p. ix).

60 Paul Theroux, for instance, excoriated "Erica Jong's witless heroine" for "loom[ing] like a mammoth pudenda, as roomy as the Carlsbad caverns, luring amorous spelunkers to confusion in her plunging grottoes" (introduction to *Sunrise with Seamonsters: Travels & Discoveries, 1964–1984* [Houghton Mifflin, 1985], p. 5, quoting his own review of *Fear of Flying*).

61 Erica Jong, *Fear of Fifty: A Midlife Memoir* (HarperCollins, 1994), p. 295.

62 Olive Schreiner, *Woman and Labor* (Bernard Tauchnitz, 1911), p. 74.

63 Erica Jong, *Fear of Flying* (Holt, Rinehart and Winston, 1973), pp. 9–10, 96.

64 Ibid., pp. 11, 205, 295.

65 Jong, *Fear of Fifty*, pp. 153–54.

66 Joan Didion, "The Women's Movement" (1972), in *The White Album* (Simon and Schuster, 1979), pp. 109–18, at 112, 115.

67 Rita Mae Brown, *Rita Will: Memoir of a Literary Rabble-Rouser* (Bantam Books, 1997), pp. 280–81.

68 "All you got is a wad of pink wrinkles hangin' around it. It's ugly": Rita Mae Brown, *Rubyfruit Jungle* (1973; repr., Bantam Books, 1977), p. 4.

69 Ibid., p. 107.

70 Ibid., p. 142. One straight-defined female lover asks Molly to pretend they are at a urinal "and you say, 'That's a nice cock, big and juicy'" (p. 202). A straight-defined man wants her to imagine "We're in the ladies room at the Four Seasons and you're admiring my voluptuous breasts" (p. 206).

71 For the quotation, see ibid., p. 147. The novel does sustain her optimism at the end. As if operating under the aegis of Huck Finn, Molly prepares to bolt her way into the forbidden territory of moviemaking until she's "the hottest fifty-year-old this side of the Mississippi" (p. 246).

72 Margaret Atwood, *Lady Oracle* (Simon and Schuster, 1976), pp. 46, 50, 50–51, 74.

73 Ibid., pp. 82, 310, 313.

74 Ibid., p. 319.

75 Margaret Atwood, "You Fit into Me," in *Power Politics* (1971; repr., House of Anansi Press, 2005), p. 1.

76 Margaret Atwood, *Surfacing* (Simon and Schuster, 1972), pp. 162, 163, 176. The "Americans" are associated with murder —"To prove they could do it, they had the power to kill" (p. 134)—and are often actually Canadians from whom the troubled narrator wants to distance herself and her countrymen.

77 Ibid., pp. 187, 222.

78 French protests the horror of pregnancy "because it wipes you out, it erases you"; the misery of lecherous husbands; drunken dinner parties; the "poverty, stigma, and loneliness" associated with divorce; the "boring and painful and full of despair" routines of housekeeping; the wife beatings; the marital rapes ("It was over fast and he never looked at her"); the snarling at kids; the electric shock treatments. Marilyn French, *The Woman's Room* (Summit Books, 1977), pp. 49, 133, 141, 162.

79 Ibid., pp. 189, 199.

80 Ibid., pp. 245, 433.

81 Kim A. Loudermilk, *Fictional Feminism: How American Bestsellers Affect the Movement for Women's Equality* (Routledge, 2004), pp. 45–51, 62–63.

82 For more on Judy Chicago and Miriam Shapiro's installation, see the 1974 documentary *Womanhouse*, directed by Johanna Demetrakas and available at judy chicago.arted.psu.edu/womanhouse-video/; further information is supplied by Penn State's Jude Chicago Art Education Collection at judychicago.arted.psu .edu/about/onsite-archive/teaching-projects/womanhouse/.

83 Betsey Stevenson and Justin Wolfers, "Marriage and Divorce: Changes in Their Driving Forces," *Journal of Economic Perspectives* 21, no. 2 (Spring 2007): 27–52.

84 *The Unabridged Journals of Sylvia Plath*, ed. Karen V. Kukil (Anchor, 2000), p. 275.

85 Sylvia Plath, *The Bell Jar* (Faber and Faber, 1963), p. 1.

86 Ibid., pp. 6, 7.

87 Ibid., pp. 74, 71.

88 Ibid., p. 80. For figs as vulvas see, for example, D. H. Lawrence's poem "Fig," which Plath would have known well.

89 Sylvia Plath, "Hanging Man," in *Collected Poems*, ed. Ted Hughes (1981; repr., HarperCollins, 2018), p. 141.

90 Betty Friedan, *The Feminine Mystique* [50th anniversary ed.] (W. W. Norton, 2013), p. 14.

91 Robin Morgan, "Arraignment," in *Monster* (Random House, 1972), pp. 76–78, at 76.

92 The friend is Elizabeth Compton Sigmund, whose account of this conversation is quoted in Elaine Feinstein, *Ted Hughes: The Life of a Poet* (Weidenfeld and Nicolson, 2001), p. 149.

93 Ted Hughes, "The Dogs Are Eating Your Mother," in *Birthday Letters: Poems* (Farrar, Straus and Giroux, 1998), pp. 195–96, at 195.

94 Diane Seuss, "Self-Portrait with Sylvia Plath's Braid," in *Still Life with Two Dead Peacocks and a Girl* (Graywolf, 2018), p. 84.

95 Erica Jong, "Alcestis on the Poetry Circuit," in *Half-Lives* (Holt, Rinehart and Winston, 1973), pp. 25–26.

96 Anne Sexton, "Sylvia's Death." *Poetry* 103, no. 4 (Jan. 1964): 224–26, at 224.

97 Catherin Bowman, *The Plath Cabinet* (Four Way Books, 2009). See also *The Plath Poetry Project*, plathpoetryproject.com/.

98 Joanna Biggs, "I'm an Intelligence," *London Review of Books*, 20 Dec. 2018, pp. 9–15, at 15.

CHAPTER 6: SPECULATIVE POETRY, SPECULATIVE FICTION

1 Jane Austen, *Northanger Abbey* [1818], ed. Marilyn Butler (Penguin Classics, 1995), p. 104.

2 See *Bradley v. State*, 1 Miss. (1 Walker) 156, 157 (1824).

3 Adrienne Rich, interview in David Montenegro, *Points of Departure: International Writers on Writing and Politics* (University of Michigan Press, 1991), pp. 5–21, at 11.

4 W. B. Yeats, "Easter, 1916," in *The Collected Poems of W. B. Yeats*, ed. Richard J. Finneran, rev. 2nd ed. (Scribner Paperback Poetry, 1996), pp. 180–81, at 180.

5 The quotation, from Alfred Conrad, appears in his obituary in the *New York Times*, 20 Oct. 1970.

6 Adrienne Rich to Hayden Carruth, letter quoted in Michelle Dean, "The Wreck," *New Republic*, 3 Apr. 2016, newrepublic.com/article/132117/adrienne -richs-feminist-awakening.

7 Rich, interview in Montenegro, *Points of Departure*, p. 17.

8 Hilary Holladay, *The Power of Adrienne Rich* (Doubleday, 2020), p. 222. Rich wrote the book for Joseph Goldberg, a film professor at the New School.

9 Dean, "The Wreck."

10 Ibid.

11 Adrienne Rich, quoted in John O'Mahoney, "Poet and Pioneer," *The Guardian*, 14 June 2002, www.theguardian.com/books/2002/jun/15/featuresreviews .guardianreview6.

12 Hayden Carruth, quoted in ibid.

13 See ibid.

14 Elizabeth Hardwick, quoted in Dean, "The Wreck."

15 See Emily Dickinson, "Tell all the truth but tell it slant," in *The Poems of Emily Dickinson*, ed. R. W. Franklin, reading ed. (Belknap Press of Harvard University Press, 1999), p. 494.

16 Sandra M. Gilbert, "A Life Written in Invisible Ink," *American Scholar*, 6 Sept. 2016, theamericanscholar.org/a-life-written-in-invisible-ink/#.XWdLF -hKhPY.

17 Adrienne Rich, "Diving into the Wreck," in *Diving into the Wreck: Poems, 1971– 1972* (W. W. Norton, 1973), pp. 22–24, at 24.

18 Margaret Atwood, "Diving into the Wreck," *New York Times Book Review*, 30 Dec. 1973.

19 Leslie H. Farber, "He Said, She Said," *Commentary*, Mar. 1972, pp. 53–59, at 53.

20 Adrienne Rich, "Waking in the Dark," in *Diving into the Wreck*, pp. 7–10, at 8.

21 Adrienne Rich, "From an Old House in America," in *Collected Poems, 1950–2012* (W. W. Norton, 2016), pp. 425–37, at 435.

22 Adrienne Rich, "Trying to Talk with a Man," in *Diving into the Wreck*, pp. 3–4, at 4.

23 William Blake, *The Marriage of Heaven and Hell* (ca. 1790–93), in *The Poetry and Prose of William Blake*, ed. David V. Erdman (Doubleday, 1965), pp. 33–44, at 39 (plate 14).

24 Adrienne Rich, "From the Prison House," in *Diving into the Wreck*, pp. 17–18, at 17; "The Stranger," in ibid., p. 19.

25 Rich, "Diving into the Wreck," pp. 22, 23.

26 Ibid., pp. 23, 24.

27 Ibid., p. 24.

28 Adrienne Rich, "A Marriage in the 'Sixties," in *Collected Poems*, pp. 137–39, at 139 (originally published in *Snapshots of a Daughter-in-Law*, 1963); "Like This Together," in ibid., pp. 174–76 (originally published in *Necessities of Life*, 1966).

29 Rich, "Diving into the Wreck," p. 24.

30 Adrienne Rich, "From a Survivor," in *Diving into the Wreck*, p. 50.

31 Adrienne Rich, "When We Dead Awaken" (1971), in *Essential Essays: Culture, Politics, and the Art of Poetry*, ed. Sandra M. Gilbert (W. W. Norton, 2018), pp. 3–19, at 3–4.

32 Adrienne Rich, "Compulsory Heterosexuality and Lesbian Existence" (1980), in ibid., pp. 157–97, at 159, 160.

33 Holladay, *The Power of Adrienne Rich*, p. 264.

34 Adrienne Rich, "Twenty-One Love Poems," in *Collected Poems*, pp. 465–77, at 465.

35 Ibid., pp. 468, 470, 471.

36 Ibid., pp. 472–73.

37 Adrienne Rich, "Split at the Root: An Essay on Jewish Identity" (1982), in *Essential Essays*, pp. 198–217, at 216.

38 Rich, "Twenty-One Love Poems," pp. 476–77.

39 Other notable works in this tradition include Christine de Pizan's *City of Ladies* (1405) and Margaret Cavendish's *The Blazing World* (1666), as well as, closer to Gilman's era, Mary Elizabeth Bradley Lane's *Mizora* (1880–81) and Elizabeth Corbett's *New Amazonia* (1889).

40 Julie Phillips, *James Tiptree Jr.: The Double Life of Alice B. Sheldon* (St. Martin's, 2007), p. 245.

41 Ibid., p. 337.

42 James Tiptree, Jr., "The Women Men Don't See" (1973), in *Her Smoke Rose Up Forever* (Tachyon, 2004), pp. 115–43, at 115.

43 Ibid., p. 134.

44 Ibid., pp. 141, 138, 142.

45 James Tiptree, Jr., "The Girl Who Was Plugged In" (1973), in *Her Smoke Rose Up Forever*, pp. 43–79.

46 Ibid., p. 77.

47 Ibid., p. 47.

48 James Tiptree, Jr., "The Screwfly Solution" (1977), in *Her Smoke Rose Up Forever*, pp. 9–31, at 9.

49 Ibid., pp. 24, 25–26.

50 Whether or not there was any direct influence, the two tales are strikingly similar, for in each three male travelers confront an all-female utopia whose customs fascinate, baffle, and befuddle them. Both stories are narrated from the perspective of one of the bemused (and often confused) explorers. Both portray peaceful all-female worlds characterized by almost stereotypically—and sometimes comically—"feminine" traits: both feminist utopias stress the significance of maternity and education. In both, the women reproduce without male assistance: in *Herland* through parthenogenesis and in "Houston" through a sophisticated form of cloning. And in each, one of the three men temporarily disrupts the serene fabric of the community by inappropriately (hetero)sexualizing the women and ultimately attempting to rape one of them. Julie Phillips, Tiptree's biographer, has said there is no evidence that Alice Sheldon knew *Herland*—and indeed Gilman's utopia wasn't published in book form until 1979, several years after Tiptree's tale appeared in print. But *The Forerunner*, the feminist journal where *Herland* was first published, had in fact been reprinted in 1968, so it's possible that Sheldon—who had just recently earned a Ph.D. in psychology and was a serious academic—might have seen it.

51 James Tiptree, Jr., "Houston, Houston Do You Read?" (1976), in *Her Smoke Rose Up Forever*, pp. 163–216, at 186, 189, 173, 175.

52 Ibid., pp. 191, 163.

53 Ibid., pp. 212, 215.

54 James Tiptree, Jr., to Joanna Russ, letter quoted as the epigraph to Pat Wheeler, "'That Is Not Me. I Am Not That': Anger and the Will to Action in Joanna Russ's Fiction," in *On Joanna Russ*, ed. Farah Mendlesohn (Wesleyan University Press, 2009), pp. 99–113, at 99.

55 Joanna Russ, "The New Misandry," *Village Voice*, 12 Oct. 1972, villagevoice .com/2011/03/21/the-new-misandry-man-hating-in-1972/.

56 Joanna Russ, *The Female Man* (Bantam Books, 1975), p. 7.

57 Wheeler, "'That Is Not Me. I Am Not That,'" 99. Yet as Judith Gardiner noted in the nineties, *The Female Man* began to feel dated within two decades. The book, wrote Gardiner, was "a heavy-handed treatment of a situation that I now find embarrassing even to recall. It's hard for me to recapture the fresh moral indignation of that time, its conviction of rightness, the enthusiasm and group solidarity of its feminist anger, yet also its despair at patriarchal odds" (quoted in ibid.). But for a recent, highly positive review of the novel, see B. D. McClay, "Joanna Russ, the Science-Fiction Writer Who Said No,"

New Yorker, 30 Jan. 2020, www.newyorker.com/books/under-review/joanna -russ-the-science-fiction-writer-who-said-no.

58 Russ, *The Female Man*, pp. 213–14.

59 Letter from Ursula K. Le Guin to James Tiptree, Jr., quoted in Phillips, *James Tiptree Jr.*, 371. See also "Ursula K. Le Guin: An Interview," conducted by Paul Walker, *Luna Monthly*, no. 63 (Mar. 1976): 1–7, at 1.

60 Ursula K. Le Guin, *The Left Hand of Darkness* (1969; repr., Ace Books, 2010), p. 100.

61 See Ursula K. Le Guin, "Is Gender Necessary? Redux," in *Dancing at the Edge of the World: Thoughts on Words, Women, Places* (Grove, 1989), pp. 7–16.

62 Ursula K. Le Guin, introduction to "Winter's King," in *The Wind's Twelve Quarters* (Bantam Books, 1975), p. 85.

63 See "Coming of Age in Karhide" (1995), reprinted in *The Birthday of the World: And Other Stories* (HarperCollins, 2002), pp. 1–22.

64 Ursula K. Le Guin, "Sur" (1982), in *The Compass Rose* (Harper and Row, 1982), pp. 230–46, at 234, 236.

65 Ibid., pp. 239, 240.

66 Ibid., pp. 242, 243–44.

67 Ibid., p. 246.

68 Adrienne Rich, "Phantasia for Elvira Shatayev," in *Collected Poems*, pp. 443–46, at 446.

CHAPTER 7: BONDED AND BRUISED SISTERS

1 Vivian Gornick, "Who Says We Haven't Made a Revolution? A Feminist Takes Stock," *New York Times Magazine*, 15 Apr. 1990; she is quoting Wordsworth's "French Revolution" (1809).

2 Gloria Steinem, quoted in Rebecca Traister, *Good and Mad: The Revolutionary Power of Women's Anger* (Simon and Schuster, 2018), pp. 109–10; Steinem, "Alice Walker: Do You Know This Woman? She Knows You" (1982), in *Outrageous Acts and Everyday Rebellions* (Holt, Rinehart, and Winston, 1983), pp. 259–75, at 275.

3 Carolyn G. Heilbrun, *The Education of a Woman: The Life of Gloria Steinem* (Dial Press, 1995), p. 255.

4 Ibid., p. 268.

5 Betty Friedan, *It Changed My Life: Writings on the Women's Movement* (Random House, 1976), p. 244; the passage appears in a section titled "Betty Friedan's Notebook: Struggling for Personal Truth (1971–1973)." Friedan disagreed with *Ms.* essays advising women not to do anything that "would make them attractive to men. It was so annoying to me that Gloria would preach this kind of doctrine in *Ms.*, and at the same time be dating some very glamorous men and having her hair streaked at Kenneth, a very fancy New York salon" (Betty Friedan, *Life So Far* [Simon and Schuster, 2000], pp. 249–50).

6 Nora Ephron, "Women," *Esquire*, Nov. 1972, pp. 10–18, 28, at 10, 18.

7 Heilbrun, *The Education of a Woman*, p. 255.

8 "The fact that [Alice] didn't want to work full-time and refused to come to meetings was fine," Steinem thought. Evelyn C. White, *Alice Walker: A Life* (W. W. Norton, 2004), pp. 265, 266.

9 Adrienne Rich, quoted in Alexis De Veaux, *Warrior Poet: A Biography of Audre Lorde* (W. W. Norton, 2004), p. 133. The money was earmarked for the New York advocacy group Sisterhood of Black Single Mothers. In fact, the actual award was divided between Rich and Allen Ginsberg, but, as Walker explained, "I think she felt unable to accept anything for herself in the context of our exclusion" (White, *Alice Walker*, p. 271).

10 Hilary Holladay, *The Power of Adrienne Rich* (Doubleday, 2020), pp. 256, 257.

11 The essay was reprinted in Alice Walker, *In Search of Our Mothers' Gardens: Womanist Prose* (1974; repr., Harcourt Brace Jovanovich, 1983), pp. 231–43, at 232, 235.

12 Ibid., pp. 237, 243.

13 When collected in *In Search of Our Mothers' Gardens*, the essay appeared as "Looking for Zora," pp. 93–116 (quotation at 102).

14 Ibid., pp. 107, 110.

15 White, *Alice Walker*, pp. 258, 259. Sara Blackburn wrote the review of *Sula*; *New York Times Book Review*, 30 Dec. 1973.

16 White, *Alice Walker*, p. 272. Walker's biographer, Evelyn C. White, suggests that envy was the motive for the estrangement: "Rukeyser had never imagined that her own literary light might be outshone by the impoverished black woman from Georgia whom she had taken 'under her wing'" (p. 271).

17 Alice Walker to Muriel Rukeyser, letter quoted in ibid., p. 273.

18 Rukeyser never mailed the letter she composed in response, where she mentions the money she gave Walker at a difficult period in her life (ibid., pp. 125–26, 275).

19 Susan Brownmiller, *In Our Time: Memoir of a Revolution* (Dial Press, 1999), p. 234.

20 Statement quoted in ibid., p. 235.

21 Ibid., p. 238; Ellen Willis is quoted on p. 236.

22 Gloria Steinem, quote in Heilbrun, *The Education of a Woman*, pp. 290, 291.

23 The story of the demise of the Sagaris Collective, whose members could not decide whether to accept funding from *Ms.*, is told by both Heilbrun (*The Education of a Woman*, pp. 297–99) and Brownmiller (*In Our Time*, pp. 239–42).

24 Jo Freeman, "Trashing," *Ms.*, Apr. 1976, pp. 49–51, 92–98, at 49.

25 Friedan, *It Changed My Life*, pp. 373, 382.

26 Heilbrun, *The Education of a Woman*, pp. 280–81. See Ruth Rosen's chapter on the FBI, "The Politics of Paranoia," in *The World Split Open: How the Modern Women's Movement Changed America* (Penguin Books, 2000), pp. 227–60.

27 Letty Cottin Pogrebin, "Have You Ever Supported Equal Pay, Child Care, or Women's Groups? The FBI Was Watching You," *Ms.*, June 1977, pp. 37–44, at 37, 44.

28 Heilbrun, *The Education of a Woman*, p. 309. In the same year as the radical feminists' allegation against Steinem, Elizabeth Forsling Harris—the first publisher of *Ms.*, who left after the first issue—sued Steinem, alleging stock fraud.

29 Erica Jong, *Fear of Fifty: A Midlife Memoir* (HarperCollins, 1994), pp. 286, 290.

30 Phyllis Chesler, *Letters to a Young Feminist* (Four Walls Eight Windows, 1997), pp. 56, 59.
31 Jill Lepore, *These Truths: A History of the United States* (W. W. Norton, 2018), p. 660.
32 Winifred Breines, *The Trouble between Us: An Uneasy History of White and Black Women in the Feminist Movement* (Oxford University Press, 2006), p. 152.
33 Sheila Tobias, *Faces of Feminism: An Activist's Reflections on the Women's Movement* (Westview Press, 1997), pp. 155, 156.
34 Lepore, *These Truths*, p. 662.
35 One cynical view of Schlafly's successful "pro-family" and anti-ERA campaign is offered by Sheila Tobias: it provided "a vehicle for a politically ambitious woman. Unable to 'make it' in other arenas and having a tremendous drive to wield power and hold office, Schlafly was clever enough to realize that of the range of issues available to a conservative in 1972, the ERA could be her own" (*Faces of Feminism*, p. 140). See the Hulu television series *Mrs. America* for a dramatization of Schlafly's rise to power.
36 Marjorie J. Spruill, *Divided We Stand: The Battle over Women's Rights and Family Values That Polarized American Politics* (Bloomsbury, 2017), p. 91.
37 Lillian Faderman, "Enter, Anita," chap. 18 of *The Gay Revolution: The Story of the Struggle* (Simon and Schuster, 2015), pp. 321–35, at 332.
38 "Feminine Fulfillment," season 5, episode 19, of *Maude* (originally aired 28 Feb. 1977 on CBS). The episode "Trouble in Chapter 17" of *The Rockford Files* (season 4, episode 2; originally aired 23 Sept. 1977 on NBC) depicts a character named Anne Louise Clement (Claudette Nevins), who is closely based on Marabel Morgan.
39 Audre Lorde, "An Interview: Audre Lorde and Adrienne Rich," in *Sister Outsider: Essays and Speeches* (Crossing Press, 1984), pp. 81–109, at 90, 92.
40 Audre Lorde, "The Master's Tools Will Never Dismantle the Master's House," in *Sister Outsider*, pp. 110–13, at 112.
41 Audre Lorde, "Love Poem," in *The Collected Poems of Audre Lorde* (W. W. Norton, 1997), p. 127.
42 De Veaux, *Warrior Poet*, pp. 130–31.
43 Lorde, "An Interview," p. 98. To Adrienne Rich, who recalled hearing Lorde read the poem at a coffeehouse the year before—"It was incredible. Like defiance. It was glorious" (quoted in ibid.)—Lorde explained, "Being an open lesbian in the Black community is not easy, although being closeted is even harder" (p. 99).
44 The quoted phrase is from Audre Lorde, "Scratching the Surface: Some Notes on Barriers to Women and Loving," in *Sister Outsider*, pp. 45–52, at 49. Possibly she was also trying to protect her comrade in the emerging Combahee River Collective, Barbara Smith, when she said, "The Black lesbian has come under increasing attack from both Black men and heterosexual Black women" (ibid.). On the evolution and significance of the Combahee River Collective, see Winifred Breines, "Alone: Black Socialist Feminism and the Combahee River Collective," chap. 4 of *The Trouble between Us*, pp. 117–49.

45 Audre Lorde, "Sexism: An American Disease in Blackface," in *Sister Outsider*, pp. 60–65, at 64. See, for example, Lorde's discussion of the murder of the young actress Patricia Cowan in the poem "Need: A Choral of Black Women's Voices" (*Collected Poems*, p. 353) and in this essay.

46 Audre Lorde, "An Open Letter to Mary Daly," in *Sister Outsider*, pp. 66–71, at 66, 67.

47 De Veaux, *Warrior Poet*, pp. 151–52.

48 Lorde, "An Open Letter to Mary Daly," pp. 67, 68.

49 Ibid., p. 71.

50 De Veaux, *Warrior Poet*, 252–53, 252.

51 Lorde, "An Interview," p. 103.

52 Lorde, "Power," in *Collected Poems*, pp. 251–16, at 215. She later explained what she meant: "if we are really ready to put ourselves behind what we believe, then we can bring about change. Other than that, it is only empty rhetoric, and it is our children who will have to live out our destinies." Interview with Marion Kraft in 1986 in *Conversations with Audre Lorde*, ed. Joan Wylie Hall (University of Mississippi Press, 2004), pp. 146–53, at 148.

53 Lorde, "The Master's Tools Will Never Dismantle the Master's House," pp. 110–11, 112, 113.

54 Audre Lorde, "The Transformation of Silence into Language and Action," in *Sister Outsider*, pp. 40–44, at 41, 42, 44.

55 Audre Lorde, "Poetry Is Not a Luxury," in *Sister Outsider*, pp. 36–39, at 37, 38; "Uses of the Erotic: The Erotic as Power," in ibid., 53–59, at 55.

56 Blanche Cook, quoted in De Veaux, *Warrior Poet*, p. 257.

57 Jonathan Rollins, quoted in ibid., p. 225.

58 Audre Lorde, "Breast Cancer: A Black Lesbian Feminist Experience," *Sinister Wisdom*, no. 10 (Summer 1979): 44–61, at 60, 61

59 Audre Lorde, "The Uses of Anger: Women Responding to Racism," in *Sister Outsider*, pp. 124–33, 127; this essay was given as a keynote at the National Women's Studies Association Convention in 1981.

60 Casey Cep, "Fighting Mad: Reconsidering the Political Power of Women's Anger," *New Yorker*, 15 Oct. 2018, pp. 83–86, at 84; the essay is a review of Soraya Chemaly's *Rage Becomes Her: The Power of Women's Anger*, Brittney Cooper's *Eloquent Rage: A Black Feminist Discovers Her Superpower*, and Rebecca Traister's *Good and Mad: The Revolutionary Power of Women's Anger*.

61 Alice Walker, quoted in "Dorothy Bryant," in *Feminist Writers*, ed. Pamela Kester-Shelton (St. James Press, 1996), p. 77.

62 Though the work was controversial in the Chinese American community, with some of Kingston's male contemporaries claiming that its author hadn't represented the "real" China, by the nineties *The Woman Warrior* and its companion volume, *China Men*, were "the most frequently taught texts on college campuses by any living American writer" (Amy Ling, "Maxine Hong Kingston," in *Contemporary Authors* [Gale Research, 1991]). In the view of the prominent Chinese American playwright Frank Chin, for instance, *The Woman Warrior* represents a

"fake" China described in a pseudo-Christian autobiographical mode. See Chin, "Come All Ye Asian-American Writers of the Real and the Fake," in *The Big Aiiieeeee!: An Anthology of Chinese American and Japanese American Literature*, ed. Jeffrey Paul Chan et al. (Meridian, 1991), pp. 1–92, at 8.

63 See Kimberlé Crenshaw, "Demarginalizing the Intersection of Race and Sex: A Black Feminist Critique of Antidiscrimination Doctrine, Feminist Theory and Antiracist Politics," *University of Chicago Legal Forum* 1989 (1989): 139–67.

64 The "American" children, all born in the States, are compared to two older children who died in China: the "Chinese" children. But of course all the American children grapple with the ghosts of China.

65 Alex Zwerdling, "Imagining the Facts in Kingston's Memoirs," chap. 7 of *The Rise of the Memoir* (Oxford University Press, 2017), pp. 185–218.

66 Maxine Hong Kingston, *The Woman Warrior: Memoirs of a Girlhood among Ghosts* (1976; repr., Vintage, 1989), pp. 96–97.

67 Ibid., pp. 3, 16.

68 Ibid., pp. 6, 7.

69 Ibid., p. 9.

70 Ibid., p. 22.

71 Ibid., pp. 47, 52, 53. There was of course a Disney movie titled *Mulan* that appeared in 1998, but accounts of its production suggest that the creative team hadn't read *The Woman Warrior*.

72 Ibid., pp. 90–92.

73 Ibid., p. 152.

74 Virginia Woolf, *A Room of One's Own* [1929], annotated and with an introduction by Susan Gubar (Harcourt, 2005), p. 66 (on Austen); Robert Southey to Charlotte Brontë, letter of 12 Mar. 1837, and Brontë to Southey, letter of 16 Mar. 1837, in *The Letters of Charlotte Brontë: With a Selection of Letters by Family and Friends*, vol. 1, *1829–1847*, ed. Margaret Smith (Clarendon Press, 1995), pp. 166–67, at 166–67, and pp. 168–69, at 169. On the Dickinson anecdote, see Adrienne Rich, "Vesuvius at Home: The Power of Emily Dickinson" (1976), in *Shakespeare's Sisters: Feminist Essays on Women Poets*, ed. Sandra M. Gilbert and Susan Gubar (Indiana University Press, 1979), pp. 99–121, at 99.

75 "The Dinner Party: Entry Banners," *Brooklyn Museum*, www.brooklynmuseum .org/eascfa/dinner_party/entry_banners.

76 Judy Chicago, quoted in Nadja Sayej, "Judy Chicago: 'In the 1960s, I Was the Only Visible Woman Artist,'" *The Guardian*, 20 Oct. 2017, www.theguardian .com/artanddesign/2017/oct/20/judy-chicago-the-dinner-party-history-in-the -making; Hilton Kramer, "Art: Judy Chicago's 'Dinner Party' Comes to Brooklyn Museum," *New York Times*, 17 Oct. 1980.

77 Alice Walker, "*One* Child of One's Own: A Meaningful Digression within the Work(s)," in *In Search of Our Mothers' Gardens*, pp. 361–83, at 373. See also Hortense Spillers, "Interstices: A Small Drama of Words," chap. 6 of *Black, White, and in Color: Essays on American Literature and Culture* (University of Chicago Press, 2003), pp. 152–75, at 156–57.

78 Shulamith Firestone, "On American Feminism," in *Woman in Sexist Society*, ed. Vivian Gornick and Barbara K. Moran (Basic Books, 1971), pp. 485–501, at 495.

CHAPTER 8: IDENTITY POLITICS

1 Betty Friedan, "Feminism's Next Step," *New York Times Magazine*, 5 July 1981.
2 Susan Bolotin, "Voices from the Post-Feminist Generation," *New York Times Magazine*, 17 Oct. 1982.
3 Walker received the prize in 1983 for *The Color Purple* and Morrison in 1988 for *Beloved*. The *Newsweek* poll came out in 1986; see Eloise Salholz, "Feminism's Identity Crisis," *Newsweek*, 31 Mar. 1986, pp. 58–59, at 58.
4 Marilyn Power, "Falling through the 'Safety Net': Women, Economics Crisis, and Reaganomics," *Feminist Studies* 10, no. 1 (Sept. 1984): 31–58. Tax cuts for the rich were matched by cuts in "funding for education, public housing, and most other social welfare programs," according to Corey Dolgon; see Dolgon, *Kill It to Save It: An Autopsy of Capitalism's Triumph over Democracy* (Policy Press, 2017), p. 182.
5 *This Bridge Called My Back* was edited by Cherríe Moraga and Gloria Anzaldúa; *All the Women Were White, All the Men Were Black, But Some of Us Were Brave* was edited by Gloria T. Hull, Patricia Bell Scott, and Barbara Smith.
6 Needless to say, the two of us came in for our share of invective. One of Susan's former graduate students informed us (much later) that she failed to get tenure because feminist members of her department believed that her scholarship was based on our "problematic" work, which had been "disproven." See Kathleen Davies, *Sacred Groves: Or, How a Cemetery Saved My Soul* (Bedazzled Ink Publishing, 2019), pp. 86, 119.
7 Dworkin was called "the angriest woman" by Ariel Levy, quoted in Rebecca Traister, *Good and Mad: The Revolutionary Power of Women's Anger* (Simon and Schuster, 2018), p. 154; "not the fun kind" describes a fictional character who is clearly a surrogate of Dworkin in Andrea Dworkin, *Ice and Fire* (Weidenfield and Nicolson, 1987), p. 110.
8 Susan Brownmiller, *In Our Time: Memoir of a Revolution* (Dial Press, 1999), p. 302.
9 Andrea Dworkin, *Heartbreak: The Political Memoir of a Feminist Militant* (Basic Books, 2002), pp. 4, 77, 139.
10 Ibid., pp. 142, 149, 180.
11 Ellen Willis, "Feminism, Moralism, and Pornography" (1979), in *Powers of Desire: The Politics of Sexuality*, ed. Anne Snitow, Christine Stansell, and Sharon Thompson (Monthly Review, 1983), pp. 460–67, at 464; Robin Morgan, *Going Too Far: The Personal Chronicle of a Feminist* (Random House, 1977), p. 169.
12 Gloria Steinem, quoted in Traister, *Good and Mad*, p. 155, Brownmiller, *In Our Time*, p. 302.
13 Michelle Goldberg, "Not the Fun Kind of Feminist," op-ed, *New York Times*, 22 Feb. 2019.

14 Andrea Dworkin, *Intercourse* (Free Press, 1987), p. 137.

15 John Gray's book *Men Are from Mars, Women Are from Venus* (HarperCollins) did not appear until 1992.

16 Dorothy Dinnerstein, *The Mermaid and the Minotaur: Sexual Arrangement and Human Malaise* (Harper and Row, 1976).

17 Nancy Chodorow, *The Reproduction of Mothering: Psychoanalysis and the Sociology of Gender* (University of California Press, 1978). Carol Gilligan argued that girls are not inferior to boys in moral reasoning, as Gilligan's mentor Lawrence Kohlberg had asserted; instead, they commit themselves to an ethic of care, whereas boys tend to espouse more abstract notions of justice. See Gilligan, *In a Different Voice: Psychological Theory and Women's Development* (Harvard University Press, 1982).

18 Carole Vance associated "the positive possibilities of sexuality" with "exploration of the body, curiosity, intimacy, sensuality, adventure, excitement, human connection, basking in the infantile and non-rational—are not only worthwhile but provide sustaining energy." Carole S. Vance, "Pleasure and Danger: Toward a Politics of Sexuality," in *Pleasure and Danger: Exploring Female Sexuality*, ed. Vance (Routledge and Kegan, 1984), pp. 1–27, at 1.

19 Carole S. Vance, epilogue to ibid., pp. 431–39, at 433.

20 Gayle Rubin, "Blood under the Bridge: Reflections on 'Thinking Sex,'" *GLQ: A Journal of Lesbian and Gay Studies* 17, no. 1 (2011): 15–48, at 16. In "Thinking Sex," her contribution to *Pleasure and Danger*, Rubin objected to both right-wing and anti-porn efforts to regulate sexuality through the state and called for a new "sexuality studies" that heralded the emergence of queer studies. See Gayle Rubin, "Thinking Sex: Notes for a Radical Theory of the Politics of Sexuality," in Vance, *Pleasure and Danger*, pp. 267–319.

21 Brownmiller, *In Our Time*, p. 316.

22 Catharine A. McKinnon, *Sexual Harassment of Working Women* (Yale University Press, 1979), pp. 217–18.

23 Actually, in Indianapolis a city councilwoman who fought against the ERA enlisted the help of MacKinnon but not Dworkin, "whose passionate radical feminist rhetoric and unruly appearance would not have been well received." Carolyn Bronstein, *Battling Pornography: The American Feminist Anti-Pornography Movement, 1976–1986* (Cambridge University Press, 2011), p. 325.

24 Dworkin, *Heartbreak*, p. 170. In Minneapolis, the ordinance was vetoed as a violation of the First Amendment. In Indianapolis, it gained the endorsement of Phyllis Schlafly and Christian conservatives and was signed into law in 1984—the year that Mississippi ratified the Nineteenth Amendment giving women the vote!—but its constitutionality was soon under attack in federal court (Bronstein, *Battling Pornography*, 328). The Supreme Court found the Indianapolis anti-pornography ordinance unconstitutional in 1986.

25 Schlafly was a woman whom Betty Friedan wanted "to burn at the stake" for stalling the progress of the ERA. See Donald T. Critchlow, *Phyllis Schlafly and Grassroots Conservatism* (Princeton University Press, 2005), p. 12.

26 Bronstein, *Battling Pornography*, p. 329.

27 According to Sarah Schulman, "the 'sex radicals' won control of the lesbian community." Schulman, *My American History: Lesbian and Gay Life during the Reagan/ Bush Years* (Routledge, 1994), p. 8. Traister declares: "The prosex feminists won, conclusively" (*Good and Mad*, 154).

28 Susan Gubar, "Representing Pornography: Feminism, Criticism, and Depictions of Female Violation" (1987), in *For Adult Users: The Dilemma of Violent Pornography*, ed. Gubar and Joan Hoff (Indiana University Press, 1989), pp. 47–67.

29 Traister, *Good and Mad*, p. 189.

30 Johanna Fateman, "The Power of Andrea Dworkin's Rage," *New York Review of Books*, 15 Feb. 2019, www.nybooks.com/daily/2019/02/15/the-power-of-andrea -dworkins-rage/.

31 Gloria Anzaldúa, interview with Karin Ikas, in *Borderlands/La Frontera*, by Anzaldúa, 2nd ed. (Aunt Lute Books, 1999), pp. 227–46, at 238, 229.

32 Ibid., pp. 230–31.

33 Anzaldúa, *Borderlands/La Frontera*, pp. 33, 34, 35, 25.

34 Ibid., pp. 38, 59, 43, 41, 40, 44–45.

35 This is the translation in Sonia Saldivar-Hull's introduction (in ibid., p. 4) of a passage that appears on p. 37, where it is written in Spanish.

36 Anzaldúa, *Borderlands/La Frontera*, pp. 78, 81, 95.

37 Ibid., p. 49.

38 Ibid., p. 52.

39 Ibid., pp. 102–3.

40 Virginia Woolf, *Three Guineas* [1938], annotated and with an introduction by Jane Marcus (Harcourt, 2006), p. 129.

41 Anzaldúa's book had not yet been published when we decided to document female literary lineages with a Norton anthology of works by women around the world who wrote in English. When our *Norton Anthology of Literature by Women* was published in 1985, the volume did represent quite a few African American, Native American, and Asian American authors along with Anglophone writers from India, Africa, Australia, Canada, and the Caribbean. In the expanded 1996 edition, they were joined by Gloria Anzaldúa and also by Bessie Head, Bharati Mukherjee, Buchi Emecheta, Lorna Dee Cervantes, and others. Between 1985 and 1996, in other words, we saw the female literary tradition in English expand to include more literary women around the globe because of the increasingly international reach of feminism itself.

42 For an overview of some of the major French feminists, see Kelly Ives, *Cixous, Irigaray, Kristeva: The Jouissance of French Feminism* (Crescent Moon, 1998). See also part II of Toril Moi's *Sexual/Textual Politics: Feminist Literary Theory* (Methuen, 1985), "French Feminist Theory" (pp. 89–173).

43 Robin Morgan, *Saturday's Child: A Memoir* (W. W. Norton, 2001), p. 424.

44 Spivak's essay was first presented at a 1983 conference; it has been printed in several versions, first Gayatri Chakravorty Spivak, "Can the Subaltern Speak? Speculations on Widow-Sacrifice," *Wedge*, no. 7/8 (Winter/Spring 1985): 120–30, and

more accessibly as "Can the Subaltern Speak?," in *Marxism and the Interpretation of Culture*, ed. Cary Nelson and Lawrence Grossberg (University of Illinois Press, 1988), pp. 271–313.

45 Gloria Anzaldúa, "Toward a Mestiza Rhetoric: Gloria Anzaldúa on Composition, Postcoloniality, and the Spiritual," in *Gloria E. Anzaldúa: Interviews/Entrevistas*, ed. AnaLouise Keating (Routledge, 2000), pp. 251–80, at 255, 259 (quotation). For Spivak's efforts in establishing literacy programs, see Gayatri Chakravorty Spivak, "Critical Intimacy: An Interview with Gayatri Chakravorty Spivak," by Steve Paulson, *Los Angeles Review of Books*, 29 July 2016, lareviewofbooks.org/article/critical-intimacy-interview-gayatri-chakravorty-spivak/#!.

46 Adrienne Rich, "Split at the Root: An Essay on Jewish Identity" (1982), in *Essential Essays: Culture, Politics, and the Art of Poetry*, ed. Sandra M. Gilbert (W. W. Norton, 2018), pp. 198–217. The poem is "Readings of History"; see Rich's *Collected Poems, 1950–2012* (W. W. Norton, 2016), pp. 130–34, at 133.

47 Adrienne Rich, "Not How to Write Poetry, but Wherefore" (1993), in *Essential Essays*, pp. 264–69, at 267.

48 Rich, "Split at the Root," pp. 206, 208.

49 Ibid., pp. 203, 204, 202, 201.

50 Ibid., pp. 205, 206.

51 Ibid., p. 210.

52 Adrienne Rich, "Sources," in *Collected Poems*, pp. 571–89, at 573, 574.

53 Ibid., pp. 576–77.

54 Ibid., p. 577.

55 Ibid., pp. 587–88.

56 Adrienne Rich, "An Atlas of the Difficult World," in *Collected Poems*, pp. 707–28, at 725.

57 Ibid., pp. 725–26.

58 Ibid., pp. 711, 727. These lines echo André Breton's "My Wife" and comparable poems by Pablo Neruda and Federico García Lorca.

59 Ibid., p. 714.

60 Rich, "Sources," p. 586; Adrienne Rich, "Juvenilia," in *Collected Poems*, pp. 126–27, at 127.

61 Toni Morrison, "On *Beloved*," in *The Source of Self-Regard: Selected Essays, Speeches, and Meditations* (Alfred A. Knopf, 2019), pp. 280–84, at 282.

62 Toni Morrison, *Beloved* (1987; repr., Plume, 1988), p. 3; Morrison, "Unspeakable Things Unspoken: The Afro-American Presence in American Literature," in *The Source of Self-Regard*, pp. 161–97.

63 Morrison, *Beloved*, pp. 42, 95, 163.

64 Ibid., pp. 145, 164.

65 Ibid., pp. 274–75.

66 Kimberlé Crenshaw first used this term in 1989 in "Demarginalizing the Intersection of Race and Sex: A Black Feminist Critique of Antidiscrimination Doctrine, Feminist Theory and Antiracist Politics," *University of Chicago Legal Forum* 1989 (1989): 139–67, at 140.

67 See Toni Morrison, ed., *Race-ing Justice, En-gendering Power: Essays on Anita Hill, Clarence Thomas, and the Construction of Social Reality* (Pantheon Books, 1992); Toni Morrison and Claudia Brodsky Lacour, eds., *Birth of a Nation'hood: Gaze, Script, and Spectacle in the O.J. Simpson Case* (Pantheon Books, 1997); and Toni Morrison, *Playing in the Dark: Whiteness and the Literary Imagination* (Harvard University Press, 1992).

68 Anita Hill, in *Complete Transcripts of the Clarence Thomas–Anita Hill Hearings: October 11, 12, 13, 1991*, ed. Anita Miller (Academy Chicago, 2005), p. 24.

69 Clarence Thomas, in ibid., p. 118.

70 Orrin Hatch alluded to *The Exorcist* during the hearing (ibid., pp. 160–61), and during a press conference John C. Danforth suggested Hill might have "eroto-mania." See "Excerpts from Anita Hill's Interview with the Times," *New York Times*, 29 Apr. 2019. Also see Andrew Rosenthal, "Psychiatry's Use in Thomas Battle Raises Ethics Issue," *New York Times*, 20 Oct. 1991.

71 Anita Faye Hill, "Marriage and Patronage in the Empowerment and Disempowerment of African American Women," in *Race, Gender, and Power in America: The Legacy of the Hill-Thomas Hearings*, ed. Hill and Emma Coleman Jordan (Oxford University Press, 1995), pp. 271–91, at 273.

72 Anna Deavere Smith makes this point best in "The Most Riveting Television: The Hill-Thomas Hearings and Popular Culture," in ibid., pp. 248–70.

73 Andi Zeisler, *We Were Feminists Once: From Riot Grrrl to CoverGirl®, the Buying and Selling of a Political Movement* (PublicAffairs, 2016), p. 153; and Rebecca Walker, "Becoming the Third Wave," *Ms.*, Jan./Feb. 1992, pp. 39–41, at 41.

74 Toni Morrison, "Introduction: Friday on the Potomac," in Morrison, *Race-ing Justice, En-gendering Power*, pp. vii–xxx, at xiii, xviii, xvi, xxii, xv–xvi.

75 Ibid., pp. xxv, xxix, xxx.

76 Toni Morrison, "Introduction: The Official Story: Dead Men Golfing," in Morrison and Brodsky Lacour, *Birth of a Nation'hood*, pp. vii–xxviii, at xxvii.

77 Ibid., pp. xxiii, xxiv, xxviii.

78 See "Race and Gender: Charlie Rose Interviews: Gloria Steinem and Patricia Williams" (transcript of program of 9 Oct. 1995), in *Postmortem: The O.J. Simpson Case: Justice Confronts Race, Domestic Violence, Lawyers, Money, and the Media*, ed. Jeffrey Abramson (Basic Books, 1996), pp. 91–101.

79 See Andrea Dworkin, "In Memory of Nicole Brown Simpson, 1994–1995," in *Last Days at Hot Slit: The Radical Feminism of Andrea Dworkin*, ed. Johanna Fateman and Amy Scholder (Semiotext(e), 2010), pp. 342–53, esp. 350. Also see Elizabeth M. Schneider, "What Happened to Public Education about Domestic Violence?" in Abramson, *Postmortem*, pp. 75–82, esp. 78–79. A number of feminist attorneys and social workers dealing with domestic abuse victims believed that the criminal trial did not focus sufficiently on the issue: see Lin S. Lilley, "The Trial of the Century in Retrospect," in *The O.J. Simpson Trials: Rhetoric, Media, and the Law*, ed. Janice Schuetz and Lilley (Southern Illinois University Press, 1999), pp. 161–73. Lilley writes, "Both Denise Brown, sister of victim Nicole Brown Simpson, and Kim Goldman, sister of victim Ronald Godman,

have become spokespersons for domestic abuse organizations" (p. 166). The head of NOW's Los Angeles branch, Tammy Bruce, denounced "the largely black and female jury" as "'an embarrassment'" to her city, although NOW censured her for the comment. Bruce is quoted in Darnell M. Hunt, *O.J. Simpson Facts and Fictions: News Rituals in the Construction of Reality* (Cambridge University Press, 1999), p. 83.

80 Patricia J. Williams, "American Kabuki," in Morrison and Brodsky Lacour, *Birth of a Nation'hood*, pp. 273–92, at 274.

81 bell hooks, *Ain't I a Woman? Black Women and Feminism* (South End Press, 1981), p. 122; see Frances Beal, "Double Jeopardy: To Be Black and Female," in *The Black Woman: An Anthology*, ed. Toni Cade Bambara (Washington Square Press, 1970), pp. 109–22.

82 "Race and Gender: Charlie Rose Interviews," pp. 92, 101.

83 In a gesture toward that history, Morrison framed her criticism of the media's role in both the Hill/Thomas and the Simpson investigations with references to Herman Melville's "Benito Cereno" (1855), a story told by a white spectator whose unreliable observations spring from his racist assumptions. See Morrison, "The Official Story," p. viii, and "Friday on the Potomac," p. xv.

84 Morrison, *Playing in the Dark*, p. 38.

85 See Edwin McDowell, "48 Black Writer Protest by Praising Morrison," *New York Times*, 19 Jan. 1988; William Grimes, "Toni Morrison Is '93 Winner of Novel Prize in Literature," *New York Times*, 8 Oct. 1993; and Yogita Goyal, "No Strangers Here," *Los Angeles Review of Books*, 7 Feb. 2018, www.lareviewofbooks.org/article/no-strangers-here/.

86 Audre Lorde, interview with Marion Kraft in 1986, in *Conversations with Audre Lorde*, ed. Joan Wylie Hall (University Press of Mississippi, 2004), pp. 146–53, at 150.

87 Morrison, "Women, Race, and Memory" (1989), in *The Source of Self-Regard*, pp. 86–95, at 91, 93, 94–95.

CHAPTER 9: INSIDE AND OUTSIDE THE IVORY CLOSET

1 Dan Quayle, quoted in Douglas Jehl, "Quayle Deplores Eroding Values; Cites TV Show," *Los Angeles Times*, 20 May 1992.

2 Leslie Haywood and Jennifer Drake, *Third-Wave Agenda: Being Feminist, Doing Feminism* (University of Minnesota Press, 1997). See also Jennifer Baumgardner and Amy Richards, *Manifesta: Young Women, Feminism, and the Future* (Farrar, Straus and Giroux, 2000).

3 Pat Robertson, quoted in Michael Schaller, *Right Turn: American Life in the Reagan-Bush Era, 1980–1992* (Oxford University Press, 2006), p. 41.

4 Patrick Buchanan, quoted in ibid., pp. 163–64.

5 *Bowers v. Hardwick*, 478 U.S. 186, 197 (1986), quoted in Lillian Faderman, *The Gay Revolution: The Story of the Struggle* (Simon and Schuster, 2015), p. 429. On the ruling, see Nan D. Hunter, "Banned in the U.S.A.: What the Hardwick Rul-

ing Will Mean" (1986) and "Life After Hardwick" (1992), both in *Sex Wars: Sexual Dissent and Political Culture*, ed. Lisa Duggan and Hunter (Routledge, 1995), pp. 77–81, 85–98.

6 Michael Hardwick, quoted in Joyce Murdoch and Deb Price, *Courting Justice: Gay Men and Lesbians v. the Supreme Court* (Basic Books, 2001), p. 331; Jerry Falwell, quoted in Andrew Hartman, *A War for the Soul of America: A History of the Culture Wars* (University of Chicago Press, 2015), p. 95.

7 Saul Bellow, quoted in James Atlas, "Chicago's Grumpy Guru," *New York Times Magazine*, 3 Jan. 1988. Bellow defended himself against the outrage his comment elicited in an op-ed, "Papuans and Zulus," *New York Times*, 10 Mar. 1994: "We can't open our mouths without being denounced as racists, misogynists, supremacists, imperialists or fascists." When asked by another interviewer about a female character who was "sexually enslaved without a mind of her own," Bellow retorted, "Well, I'm sorry girls—but many of you are like that, very much so. It's going to take a lot more than a few books by Germaine Greer or whatshername Betty Friedan to root out completely the Sleeping Beauty syndrome." Quoted in Nathaniel Rich, "Swiveling Man," *New York Review of Books*, 21 Mar. 2019, www.nybooks.com/articles/2019/03/21/saul -bellow-swiveling-man/.

8 "The foreign adversaries her husband, Dick, must keep at bay are less dangerous, in the long run, than the domestic forces with which she must deal." George F. Will, "Literary Politics," *Newsweek*, 21 Apr. 1991, p. 72. Lynne Cheney, who headed the NEH from 1986 to 1993, believed that Foucault's "ideas were nothing less than an assault on Western civilization." See Lynne V. Cheney, *Telling the Truth: Why Our Culture and Our Country Have Stopped Making Sense—and What We Can Do about It* (Simon and Schuster, 1995), p. 91.

9 Serrano's photograph of a crucifix in a jar of urine, Mapplethorpe's homoerotic themes, and Finley's performance of smearing chocolate pudding over her body to symbolize the crap that women take are discussed in terms of the culture wars by Robert M. Collins, *Transforming America: Politics and Culture in the Reagan Years* (Columbia University Press, 2007), p. 188.

10 Jesse Helms, quoted in Edward I. Koch, "Senator Helms's Callousness toward AIDS Victims," op-ed, *New York Times*, 7 Nov. 1987; Jesse Helms, quoted in "Jesse, You're a Bigot," editorial, *Baltimore Sun*, 26 May 1993.

11 Sarah Schulman, *My American History: Lesbian and Gay Life during the Reagan/ Bush Years* (Routledge, 1994), p. 11.

12 Eve Kosofsky Sedgwick, *Epistemology of the Closet*, updated ed. (University of California Press, 2008), p. 6.

13 Ibid., pp. 6, 8, 16, 24, 41, 69. The *Publishers Weekly* review of the book concludes: "Obtuse, cumbersome, academic prose limits the appeal of this treatise" (publishersweekly.com/978-0-520-07042-4).

14 Sedgwick, *Epistemology of the Closet*, pp. 25, 78, 82.

15 Ibid., pp. 85, 87.

16 Ibid., p. 52.

17 See Eve Kosofsky Sedgwick, "Jane Austen and the Masturbating Girl," *Critical Inquiry* 17, no. 4 (Summer 1991): 818–37, at 818. For Roger Kimball's deployment of the title, in a book first published in 1990, see *Tenured Radicals: How Politics Has Corrupted Our Higher Education*, 3rd ed. (Rowman and Littlefield, 2008), pp. 7, 219, 282, 300.

18 Responding in a nicely titled op-ed in the *New York Times*, "A 'Bad Writer' Bites Back" (20 Mar. 1999), Judith Butler pointed out that the prize generally goes to "scholars on the left" and also that "common sense sometimes preserves the social status quo." Ergo, the supposition goes, uncommon writing can topple it.

19 Judith Butler, "Preface (1999)," in *Gender Trouble: Feminism and the Subversion of Identity*, 2nd ed. (Routledge, 1999), pp. vii–xxvi, at xix, xx.

20 In our teaching and anthologizing of feminist theory, we found it easier to introduce Butler's ideas through the essay "Imitation and Gender Insubordination," maybe because she begins it with the poignant confession that "the prospect of *being* anything . . . has always produced in me a certain anxiety": Judith Butler, "Imitation and Gender Insubordination" (1990), in *Feminist Literary Theory and Criticism: A Norton Reader*, ed. Sandra M. Gilbert and Susan Gubar (W. W. Norton, 2007), pp. 708–22, at 709.

21 Ibid. Butler was extending Monique Wittig's argument that lesbians are not women, because they do not operate within the heterosexual system. See Wittig, *"The Straight Mind" and Other Essays* (Beacon, 1992).

22 Butler, "Imitation and Gender Insubordination," p. 718.

23 Judith Butler explores the issue of sex in *Bodies That Matter: On the Discursive Limits of "Sex"* (1993; repr., Routledge Classics, 2011). In addition, variations in chromosomes or genitals or other biomarkers render sex unstable in the work of Anne Fausto-Sterling, especially *Myths of Gender: Biological Theories about Women and Men* (Basic Books, 1992) and *Sexing the Body: How Biologists Construct Human Sexuality* (Basic Books, 2000).

24 Gertrude Stein, *Everybody's Autobiography* (Random House, 1937), p. 289.

25 Butler, "Preface (1999)," in *Gender Trouble*, p. xxi.

26 Benjamin Moser, *Sontag: Her Life and Work* (HarperCollins, 2019), pp. 517–21.

27 See Nancy Frazer, *Unruly Practices: Power Discourse and Gender in Contemporary Social Theory* (University of Minnesota Press, 1989), and Gayatri Chakravorty Spivak's discussion of "strategic essentialism" in "Subaltern Studies: Deconstructing Historiography" (1985), in *The Spivak Reader*, ed. Donna Landry (Routledge, 1996), pp. 203–36.

28 Schulman, *My American History*, p. 290.

29 Gloria Steinem, quoted in Melissa Denes, "Feminism? It's Hardly Begun," *The Guardian*, 16 Jan. 2005, www.theguardian.com/world/2005/jan/17/gender .melissadenes.

30 In "The Professor of Parody: The Hip Defeatism of Judith Butler" (*New Republic*, 22 Feb. 1999, pp. 37–45), Martha Nussbaum associates Butler's approach with a loss of commitment to material change. Also see Heather Love, "Feminist Criti-

cism and Queer Theory," in *A History of Feminist Literary Criticism*, ed. Gill Plain and Susan Sellers (Cambridge University Press, 2007), pp. 301–21, at 302, 309.

31 Susan Sontag is quoted on the back cover of Anne Carson's *Glass, Irony & God* (New Directions, 1995).

32 See Sam Anderson, "The Inscrutable Brilliance of Anne Carson," *New York Times Magazine*, 14 Mar. 2013.

33 Anne Carson, "The Glass Essay," in *Glass, Irony & God*, pp. 1–38, at 17. In *Eros the Bittersweet* (Princeton University Press, 1998), p. 124, she quotes Roland Barthes on the "pure portion of anxiety" that is the (present) absence of the beloved.

34 Anne Carson, "The Gender of Sound," in *Glass, Irony & God*, pp. 119–42. Carson did in fact dramatize homoerotic love in her widely admired *Autobiography of Red: A Novel in Verse* (Alfred A. Knopf, 1998).

35 Carson, "The Gender of Sound," pp. 121, 124, 125.

36 Carson, "The Glass Essay," pp. 7, 2, 11, 8.

37 Ibid., pp. 11–12.

38 Ibid., pp. 4, 14.

39 Ibid., pp. 22, 3.

40 Ibid., pp. 24, 25.

41 Ibid., pp. 35–38, 22, 3, 25.

42 Ibid., p. 35.

43 Ibid., p. 38.

44 On the tradition of loss, see Lawrence Lipking, *Abandoned Women and Poetic Tradition* (University of Chicago Press, 1988), which studies the aggrieved lamentations of lovelorn heroines over the centuries.

45 Anne Carson, "On Sylvia Plath," in *Plainwater: Essays and Poetry* (Alfred A. Knopf, 1995), p. 38.

46 Anne Carson, "Sylvia Town," in ibid., p. 97.

47 Anne Carson, *The Beauty of the Husband: A Fictional Essay in 29 Tangos* (Alfred A. Knopf, 2001), p. 1.

48 Anne Carson, "God's Woman," in *Glass, Irony & God*, p. 46.

49 Ali Katz, "Transcript of Madonna's Controversial 2016 'Woman of the Year Award' Thank You Speech at Billboard Music Awards," 11 Dec. 2016, *Medium.com*, medium.com/makeherstory/transcript-of-madonnas-controversial-2016-woman -of-the-year-award-thank-you-speech-at-billboard-5f34cfbf8644 (the webpage also contains a link to a video of the speech). Also see Sarah Churchwell, "Sarah Churchwell on Madonna: 'She remains the hero of her own story,'" *The Guardian*, 15 July 2018, www.theguardian.com/music/2018/jul/15/sarah-churchwell-on -madonna-power-success-feminist-legacy; Laura Barcella, ed., *Madonna & Me: Women Writers on the Queen of Pop* (Soft Skull Press, 2012); and Georges-Claude Guilbert, *Madonna as Postmodern Myth: How One Star's Self-Construction Rewrites Sex, Gender, Hollywood, and the American Dream* (McFarland, 2002).

50 Madonna, quoted in Jock McGregor, "Madonna: Icon of Postmodernity," *AFA Journal*, Feb. 2001, afajournal.org/past-issues/2001/february/madonna-icon-of

-postmodernity/. Guilbert describes conflicting feminist views of Madonna in *Madonna as Postmodern Myth*, pp. 175–84.

51 Kathleen Hanna/Bikini Kill, "Riot Grrrl Manifesto" (1992), in *The Essential Feminist Reader*, ed. Estelle B. Freedman (Modern Library, 2007), pp. 394–96, at 395. Girls need to riot "BECAUSE we are unwilling to let our real and valid anger be diffused and/or turned against us via the internalization of sexism" (p. 396). Girl power was also on display in TV shows like *Buffy the Vampire Slayer* (1997–2003) and in the performances of rappers like Queen Latifah.

52 Laura Mulvey, "A Phantasmagoria of the Female Body," in *Cindy Sherman: [A Cindy Book]*, exhib. catalogue (Flammarion, 2007), pp. 284–303, at 299.

53 Chris Kraus, *I Love Dick* (Semiotext(e), 1998), p. 211.

54 Eileen Myles, foreword to ibid., pp. 13–15, at 15.

55 In 1990, for example, Jennie Livingston's prize-winning film *Paris Is Burning* documented the culture of Latino and African American drag balls in New York City.

56 Leslie Feinberg, *Transgender Liberation: A Movement Whose Time Has Come* (World View Forum, 1992), p. 5.

57 Sandy Stone, "The *Empire* Strikes Back: A Posttranssexual Manifesto," *Camera Obscura* 10, no. 2 (29) (May 1992): 151–76, at 166. Among other works critical of transsexualism from a radical feminist perspective, Stone was responding to Janice Raymond's *The Transsexual Empire: The Making of the She-Male* (Beacon, 1979).

58 Susan Stryker, "My Words to Victor Frankenstein above the Village of Chamounix: Performing Transgender Rage," *GLQ* 1, no. 3 (1994): 237–54, at 238.

59 Ibid., p. 241.

60 Ibid., pp. 248, 251.

61 See Jaqueline Rose, "Who Do You Think You Are?" *London Review of Books*, 5 May 2016, pp. 3–13.

62 Donna Haraway, "A Cyborg Manifesto: Science, Technology, and Socialist-Feminism in the Late Twentieth Century" (1985), in *Manifestly Haraway* (University of Minnesota Press, 2016), pp. 3–90, at 10, 14, 17, 67.

63 Ibid., p. 68.

64 Ann Snitow identifies 1986 as the "peak year for backlash at least partially internalized by feminism." Snitow, *The Feminism of Uncertainty: A Gender Diary* (Duke University Press, 2015), p. 106.

65 The description of Paglia's rise comes from Hartman, *A War for the Soul of America*, p. 146.

66 Camille Paglia, *Sexual Personae: Art and Decadence from Nefertiti to Emily Dickinson* (1990; repr., Yale University Press, 2001), pp. 9, 38, 21. See Terry Teachout, "Siding with the Men," *New York Times Book Review*, 22 July 1990. Paglia, who liked to think of herself as Susan Sontag's successor, baited Sontag to gain media attention, but Sontag refused to play the game, claiming never to have heard of her (Moser, *Sontag: Her Life and Work*, pp. 546–47).

67 Reflecting on the Clarence Thomas/Anita Hill case, Paglia declared that Hill's inability to communicate her "discomfort with mild off-color banter strained credulity. That Thomas could be publicly grilled about trivial lunchtime conver-

sations that occurred 10 years earlier was an outrage worthy of Stalinist Russia." Camille Paglia, "A Call for Lustiness: Just Say No to the Sex Police," *Time*, 23 Mar. 1998, p. 54.

68 Also see *Sex and Destiny: The Politics of Human Fertility* (Harper and Row, 1984), in which Germaine Greer touted chastity and the chador, as well as Daphne Patai and Noretta Koertge, *Professing Feminism: Cautionary Tales from the Strange World of Women's Studies* (Basic Books, 1995), and Daphne Patai, *Heterophobia: Sexual Harassment and the Future of Feminism* (Rowman and Littlefield, 1998).

69 bell hooks, "Camille Paglia: 'Black' Pagan or White Colonizer?," chap. 7 of *Outlaw Culture: Resisting Representations* (Routledge, 1994), pp. 83–90, at 90. Tania Modleski cautioned against a "feminism without women," and Susan Lurie against self-critiques indifferent to "feminist politics"; see Modleski, *Feminism without Women: Culture and Criticism in a "Postfeminist" Age* (Routledge, 1991), and Lurie, *Unsettled Subjects: Restoring Feminist Politics to Poststructuralist Critique* (Duke University Press, 1997), pp. 2–3.

70 At a 2016 Billboard Woman of the Year event, an angry Madonna defended herself against "the feminist" Camille Paglia's accusation that she had set women back by objectifying herself; see Katz, "Transcript of Madonna's Thank You Speech." But in the 1990s, Paglia had defended Madonna and the MTV-banned video "Justify My Love," which she called "pornographic" and "truly avantgarde," while hailing Madonna as "the future of feminism." Camille Paglia, "Madonna—Finally a Real Feminist," op-ed, *New York Times*, 14 Dec. 1990.

71 To Clarence Thomas's wife, *Fatal Attraction* explained Anita Hill: "I always believed she was probably someone in love with my husband and never got what she wanted." Virginia Lamp Thomas, "Breaking Silence," interview with Jane Sims Podesta, *People*, 11 Nov. 1991, www.people.com/archive/cover-story -breaking-silence-vol-36-no-18/.

72 Pauline Kael, "The Current Cinema: The Feminine Mystique," *New Yorker*, 19 Oct. 1987, pp. 106–12, at 109.

73 Eloise Salholz, "Too Late for Prince Charming?," *Newsweek*, 2 June 1986, pp. 54–58; Megan Garber, "When *Newsweek* 'Struck Terror in the Hearts of Single Women,'" *The Atlantic*, 2 June 2016, www.theatlantic.com/entertainment/archive /2016/06/more-likely-to-be-killed-by-a-terrorist-than-to-get-married/485171/.

74 Patricia Schroeder, quoted in Tamar Lewin, "'Mommy Career Track' Sets Off a Furor," *New York Times*, 8 Mar. 1989.

75 See Ariel Levy's *Female Chauvinist Pigs: Women and the Rise of Raunch Culture* (Free Press, 2005), Andi Zeisler's *We Were Feminists Once: From Riot Grrrl to CoverGirl®, the Buying and Selling of a Political Movement* (PublicAffairs, 2016), and Allison Yarrow's *90s Bitch: Media, Culture, and the Failed Promise of Gender Equality* (Harper Perennial, 2018).

76 See Jennifer Armstrong, "Revisiting 'The Beauty Myth,'" *HuffPost*, 12 June 2013, www.huffpost.com/entry/revisiting-the-beauty-myth_b_3063414. Wolf's book was found to exaggerate statistics on anorexia; Wolf answered this criticism by pointing out that later printings of her book corrected the inaccuracy (Naomi

Wolf, letter to *Washington Post*, 28 Aug. 1994: responding to Deirdre English's "Their Own Worst Enemies," *Washington Post*, 17 July 1994, a review of Christine Hoff Sommer's *Who Stole Feminism? How Women Have Betrayed Women* [1994]).

77 Naomi Wolf, *The Beauty Myth: How Images of Beauty Are Used against Women* (William Morrow, 1991), p. 10. Both her book and Susan Bordo's *Unbearable Weight: Feminism, Western Culture, and the Body* (University of California Press, 1993) build on Laura Mulvey's argument that the male gaze shapes representations of women in the movies. See Mulvey, "Visual Pleasure and Narrative Cinema," *Screen* 16, no. 3 (Autumn 1975): 6–18.

78 Clinton issued his denial during a televised press conference, 26 Jan. 1998. See, e.g., www.youtube.com/watch?v=VBe_guezGGc.

79 "Monica Lewinski Interview," with Barbara Walters, *20/20*, aired 3 Mar. 1999, on ABC, www.youtube.com/watch?v=fpCv-UT2yCU.

80 Maureen Dowd, "Liberties: Monica Gets Her Man," op-ed, *New York Times*, 23 Aug. 1998.

81 Jendi B. Reiter, "A Tale of Two Stereotypes," *Harvard Crimson*, 21 July 1992, www.thecrimson.com/article/1992/7/21/a-tale-of-two-stereotypes-pbtbhis/. Hilary Clinton told the journalist Gail Sheehy that to many "wounded men," she represented "the boss they never wanted to have" or "the wife who went back to school and got an extra degree and a job as good as theirs. . . . It's not me, personally, they hate—it's the changes I represent": quoted in Marjorie J. Spruill, *Divided We Stand: The Battle over Women's Rights and Family Values That Polarized American Politics* (Bloomsbury, 2017), p. 324.

82 Reiter, "A Tale of Two Stereotypes."

83 Zeisler, *We Were Feminists Once*, pp. 25, 156. As Sheila Tobias has observed of the nineties, the women's movement was "no longer united, which meant politically that feminism was no longer a force to be reckoned with" (*Faces of Feminism: An Activist's Reflections on the Women's Movement* [Westview Press, 1997], p. 225). Others emphasize the stalling or commandeering of feminism. Besides the writings of Ariel Levy, Andi Zeisler, and Allison Yarrow, see Jessa Crispin, *Why I Am Not a Feminist* (Melville House, 2017), and Lynn S. Chancer, *After the Rise and Stall of American Feminism: Taking Back a Revolution* (Stanford University Press, 2019).

84 Adrienne Rich, "In Those Years," in *Collected Poems, 1950–2012* (W. W. Norton, 2016), pp. 755–56.

85 See the cover of *Time*, 29 June 1998. *Harper's* magazine had featured the identical question as the title of an essay by Genevieve Parkhurst published back in May 1935; see Laura Ruttum, "Is Feminism Dead?," *New York Public Library Blogs*, 25 Mar. 2009, www.nypl.org/blog/2009/03/25/feminism-dead.

CHAPTER 10: OLDER AND YOUNGER GENERATIONS

1 Although the twentieth century did not end until 2001, the emotional force of a new century's beginning was attached to the year 2000.

2 See Sontag's entry in *New Yorker* writers' response to 9/11, "Comment: Tuesday, and After," *New Yorker*, 24 Sept. 2001, p. 32. On right-wing criticism of Sontag's analysis, see Daniel Lazare, "The New Yorker Goes to War," *The Nation*, 2 June 2003, pp. 25–30.

3 Irene Khan, foreword to *Amnesty International Report 2005: The State of the World's Human Rights* (Amnesty International Publications, 2005), pp. i–ii, at i.

4 Susan Sontag, "Regarding the Torture of Others," *New York Times Magazine*, 23 May 2004.

5 Rich's poem "The School Among the Ruins" and Le Guin's poem "American Wars" are published in the antiwar anthology *Poets against the War*, ed. Sam Hamill (Nation Books, 2003), pp. 190–93, 119. See also Adrienne Rich, *The School Among the Ruins: Poems 2000–2004* (W. W. Norton, 2006). Both Walker and Kingston were arrested at antiwar protests.

6 "What is CODEPINK?" *Codepink.org*, www.codepink.org/about.

7 Benjamin told a reporter, "We wanted Code 'Hot Pink,' . . . but it was already a porn site." And like the organization she leads, she is sardonically self-named. She was born Susan Benjamin, a "nice little Jewish girl" on Long Island, but redefined herself in college as Medea Benjamin, in a curious act of homage to the tragic Greek heroine. The quotations in this paragraph are from Libby Copeland, "Protesting for Peace with a Vivid Hue and Cry," *Washington Post*, 10 June 2007.

8 Jerry Falwell, quoted in Jeffrey D. Howison, *The 1980 Presidential Election: Ronald Reagan and the Shaping of the American Conservative Movement* (Routledge, 2014), p. 78. See also Laurie Goodstein, "After the Attacks: Finding Fault: Falwell's Finger-Pointing Inappropriate, Bush Says," *New York Times*, 15 Sept. 2001.

9 Alison Bechdel, *Fun Home: A Family Tragicomic* (2006; repr., Mariner Books, 2007) and *Are You My Mother? A Comic Drama* (Houghton Mifflin Harcourt, 2012).

10 Alison Bechdel, quoted in Judith Thurman, "Profiles: Drawn from Life: The World of Alison Bechdel," *New Yorker*, 23 Apr. 2012, pp. 48–55, at 50.

11 James Joyce, *A Portrait of the Artist as a Young Man* (B. W. Huebsch, 1916), p. 299; this is the final line of the book.

12 Edward Austin Hall, "Alison Bechdel," in *Dictionary of Literary Biography: American Radical and Reform Writers, Second Series*, ed. Hester Lee Furey (Gale, 2008), pp. 40–45, at 41.

13 Alison Bechdel, "Cartoonist's Introduction," in *The Essential Dykes to Watch Out For* (Houghton Mifflin, 2008), pp. vii–xviii, at xiii, xiv, xv, xvi.

14 "An Interview with Alison Bechdel," by Hillary Chute, *Modern Fiction Studies* 52, no. 4 (Winter 2006): 1004–13, at 1006.

15 Bechdel, *Fun Home*, p. 101.

16 Hillary L. Chute, *Graphic Women: Life Narrative & Contemporary Comics* (Columbia University Press, 2010), p. 179.

17 Bechdel, *Fun Home*, p. 120.

18 Ibid., pp. 119, 118.

19 Ibid., pp. 141–43.

20 Ibid., p. 59.

21 Ibid., pp. 80, 81.

22 Ibid., pp. 107, 97, 98.

23 Ibid., pp. 205, 207.

24 Ibid., p. 229.

25 One feminist critic who postulates a similar posture toward the past is Heather Love, whose *Feeling Backward: Loss and the Politics of Queer History* (Harvard University Press, 2007) argues: "Paying attention to what was difficult in the past may tell us how far we have come, but that is not all it will tell us; it also makes visible the damage that we live with in the present" (p. 29).

26 Bechdel, *Are You My Mother?*, p. 60.

27 Ibid., pp. 181, 182, 228.

28 Ibid., pp. 262, 263, 264.

29 Ibid., p. 265. Especially in *Three Guineas*, Woolf expresses anger at the educational and economic impoverishment of daughters.

30 Bechdel, *Are You My Mother?*, p. 255.

31 Ibid., pp. 283, 285, 287.

32 Ibid., pp. 264, 287.

33 Ibid., p. 289.

34 Rachel Cooke, "*Fun Home* Creator Alison Bechdel on Turning a Tragic Childhood into a Hit Musical," *The Guardian*, 5 Nov. 2017, www.theguardian.com/books/2017/nov/05/alison-bechdel-interview-cartoonist-fun-home.

35 Eve Ensler, *In the Body of the World* (Henry Holt, 2013), p. 41.

36 The one-woman show, also called *In the Body of the World*, premiered in 2016 and was directed by Diane Paulus.

37 Eve Ensler, "Even with a Misogynist Predator-in-Chief, We Will Not Be Silenced," *The Guardian*, 24 Aug. 2017, www.theguardian.com/commentisfree/2017/aug/24/20-years-after-the-vagina-monologues-breaking-silence-is-still-a-radical-act.

38 More than 200 million girls and women alive today have endured female genital mutation, according to the World Health Organization; see "Prevalence of Female Genital Mutilation," *World Health Organization*, 2020, www.who.int/reproductive health/topics/fgm/prevalence/en/.

39 Rebecca Solnit, *Men Explain Things to Me* (Haymarket Books, 2014), p. 23. One in five American women will be raped in their lifetime, according to "Statistics about Sexual Violence," *National Sexual Violence Resource Center*, 2015, www.nsvrc.org/sites/default/files/publications_nsvrc_factsheet_media-packet_statistics-about-sexual-violence_0.pdf.

40 See Vanessa Grigoriadis, *Blurred Lines: Rethinking Sex, Power, and Consent* (Houghton Mifflin Harcourt, 2017), pp. xiii–xvi; the student in question was exonerated, and Columbia University settled with him for an undisclosed sum. Patricia Lockwood's poem was published online: "Rape Joke," *The Awl*, 25 July 2013, www.theawl.com/2013/07/patricia-lockwood-rape-joke/.

41 Eve Ensler, *The Apology* (Bloomsbury, 2019), dedication page.

42 For more on Kate Millett in Iran, see her 1982 book *Going to Iran*. For more on Audre Lorde in Germany, see the 2012 documentary *Audre Lorde—The Berlin Years: 1984–1992*, directed by Dagmar Schultz. In the early nineties, Ann Snitow helped to found the Network of East-West Women, to organize with "often isolated and beleaguered Central and East European feminist colleagues" (Snitow, *The Feminism of Uncertainty: A Gender Diary* [Duke University Press, 2015], p. 204).

43 Similarly, numerous indigenous feminist organizations such as Ni Una Menos (Not One Less) in South and Central America and Aware Girls in Pakistan have galvanized women to fight gender-based violence. The campaign by the Yazidi activist Nadia Murad to end mass rape in war earned her a Nobel Peace Prize in 2018.

44 See Chandra Talpade Mohanty, *Feminism without Borders: Decolonizing Theory, Practicing Solidarity* (Duke University Press, 2003), as well as Inderpal Grewal and Caren Kaplan, eds., *Scattered Hegemonies: Postmodernity and Transnational Feminist Practices* (University of Minnesota Press, 1994).

45 Spivak speaks about her pedagogic work in her interview with Steve Paulson, "Critical Intimacy: An Interview with Gayatri Chakravorty Spivak," *Los Angeles Review of Books*, 29 July 2016, lareviewofbooks.org/article/critical-intimacy -interview-gayatri-chakravorty-spivak/. Also see Gayatri Chakravorty Spivak, "Righting Wrongs," *South Atlantic Quarterly* 1, no. 2/3 (Spring/Summer 2004): 523–81, at 557.

46 Martha C. Nussbaum, "Women's Education: A Global Challenge," *Signs* 29, no. 2 (Winter 2004): 325–55, at 327–28, 331.

47 Carol Gilligan and Naomi Snider, *Why Does Patriarchy Persist?* (Polity Press, 2018), pp. 5, 16, 25, 145.

48 *The Vagina Monologues* was accused of essentialism in Christine M. Cooper, "Worrying about Vaginas: Feminism and Eve Ensler's *The Vagina Monologues*," *Signs* 32, no. 3 (Spring 2007): 727–58.

49 Watch interviews with Eve Ensler: "Eve Ensler: Transforming Abuse with Apology," Commonwealth Club, 12 June 2019, www.youtube.com/watch ?v=TNss3qVhpog, and "The War and Peace Report," interview by Amy Goodman, *Democracy Now!*, 14 Feb. 2017, www.democracynow.org/2017/2/14/the _predatory_mindset_of_donald_trump.

50 Eve Ensler, quoted in Katherine Gillespie, "Do We Still Need 'The Vagina Monologues'?" *Vice*, 2 Oct. 2017, www.vice.com/en_nz/article/j5gk8p/is-the -vagina-monologues-still-woke.

51 *Trans* is now used to include people engaged in MTF (male to female) or FTM (female to male) crossings; *cisgender* is associated with normativity and characterizes those who are not trans; *genderqueer* or *nonbinary* stands for people who resist conforming to either masculine or feminine roles; and the acronym *TERF* arose to label the transphobia of trans-exclusionary radical feminists. See Susan Stryker, *Transgender History: The Roots of Today's Revolution*, 2nd ed. (Seal, 2017), pp. 10–40.

52 Janet Mock, *Redefining Realness: My Path to Womanhood, Identity, Love & So Much More* (Atria, 2014), p. 50; Jennifer Finney Boylan, *She's Not There: A Life in Two Genders* (Broadway, 2013), p. 21. Boylan is quoted with attribution in Jacqueline Rose, "Who Do You Think You Are?" *London Review of Books*, 5 May 2016, www.lrb.co.uk/the-paper/v38/n09/jacqueline-rose/who-do-you -think-you-are.

53 Mock, *Redefining Realness*, pp. 50, 161.

54 Ibid., p. 155.

55 Andrea Long Chu, "On Liking Women," *n+1*, no. 30 (Winter 2018), nplus onemag.com/issue-30/essays/on-liking-women/. She ultimately does not defend this idea, because "nothing good comes of forcing desire to conform to political principle."

56 Valerie Solanas's *SCUM Manifesto* (1967; repr., AK Press, 1997), p. 34, quoted in ibid.

57 Germaine Greer, quoted in Chu, "On Liking Women." For the rest of Greer's statement, and fuller context, see Cleis Abeni, "Feminist Germaine Greer Goes on Anti-Trans Rant over Caitlyn Jenner," *The Advocate*, 26 Oct. 2015, www .advocate.com/caitlyn-jenner/2015/10/26/feminist-germaine-greer-goes-anti -trans-rant-over-caitlyn-jenner.

58 Maggie Nelson, *The Argonauts* (Graywolf Press, 2015), p. 5.

59 Ibid., p. 57. The last phrase is attributed to the poet Dana Ward.

60 Ibid., p. 83.

61 Ibid., pp. 91, 42.

62 Ibid., pp. 75, 74.

63 Ibid., p. 112.

CHAPTER 11: RESURGENCE

1 "Audre Lorde," *The Ubuntu Biography Project*, 18 Feb. 2017, ubuntubiography project.com/2017/02/18/audre-lorde/.

2 *Worlds of Ursula K. Le Guin* (2018), directed by Arwen Curry, is discussed by Alison Flood in "Ursula K Le Guin Film Reveals Her Struggle to Write Women into Fantasy," *The Guardian*, 30 May 2018, www.theguardian.com/books/2018/ may/30/ursula-k-le-guin-documentary-reveals-author.

3 See Bobbie Mixon, "Chore Wars: Men, Women and Housework," *National Science Foundation*, 28 Apr. 2018, www.nsf.gov/discoveries/disc_summ.jsp?org=NSF &cntn_id=111458&preview=false.

4 Tressie McMillan Cottom, "Dying to Be Competent," in *Thick and Other Essays* (New Press, 2019), pp. 73–98, at 86–87.

5 The Guttmacher Institute maintains fact sheets on the incidence of and restrictions on abortion in each state; for example, Georgia and Ohio both severely limit abortions after 20 weeks, even in the case of rape or incest (www.guttmacher.org /fact-sheet/state-facts-about-abortion-georgia and /state-facts-about-abortion

-ohio), while Alabama, which has similar restrictions, has aimed to ban abortion altogether, in a law blocked by a federal court; see Kate Smith, "Alabama Governor Signs Near-Total Abortion Ban into Law," *CBS News*, 16 May 2019, www .cbsnews.com/news/alabama-abortion-law-governor-kay-ivey-signs-near-total -ban-today-live-updates-2019-05-15/.

6 See, as one of many examples of Ann Coulter's virulent anti-feminism, her interview on SVT/TV 2, 5 Oct. 2018, posted to YouTube by Skavlan as "Feminists Are Angry Man-Hating Lesbians," 8 Oct. 2018, www.youtube.com/watch ?v=hxTtjGamJtI.

7 Opal Tometi, Alicia Garza, and Patrisse Cullors-Brignac, "Celebrating MLK Day: Reclaiming Our Movement Legacy," 18 Jan. 2015, updated 20 Mar. 2015, *Huffpost*, www.huffpost.com/entry/reclaiming-our-movement-l_b_6498400; Alicia Garza, "A Herstory of the #BlackLivesMatter Movement," *The Feminist Wire*, 7 Oct. 2014, www.thefeministwire.com/2014/10/blacklivesmatter-2. Both quotes appear in Leigh Gilmore, *Tainted Witness: Why We Doubt What Women Say about Their Lives* (Columbia University Press, 2017), pp. 161, 163.

8 According to the released 911 call, George Zimmerman reported Trayvon Martin to the police because Martin looked "real suspicious"; quoted in Charles M. Blow, "The Curious Case of Trayvon Martin," op-ed, *New York Times*, 17 Mar. 2012.

9 Zora Neale Hurston, "How It Feels to Be Colored Me," in *The Norton Anthology of Literature by Women: The Traditions in English*, ed. Sandra M. Gilbert and Susan Gubar, 2 vols., 3rd ed. (W. W. Norton, 2007), 2:357–59, at 360, 359; this essay was first published in *The World Tomorrow* (May 1928). Glenn Ligon's *Untitled: Four Etchings*— which incorporate Hurston's sentence—are reproduced in Claudia Rankine, *Citizen: An American Lyric* (Graywolf Press, 2014), pp. 52, 53; Hurston is quoted on p. 25.

10 Hurston, "How It Feels to Be Colored Me," 2:357, 358. On her remembering "the very day that I became colored," see Barbara Johnson, "Thresholds of Difference: Structures of Address in Zora Neale Hurston," *Critical Inquiry* 12, no. 1 (Autumn 1985): 278–89.

11 Rankine, *Citizen*, p. 5.

12 Ibid., pp. 5, 10, 7, 12, 45.

13 W. E. B. Du Bois, *The Souls of Black Folk* (1903), ed. Brent Hayes Edwards (Oxford University Press, 2007), p. 8.

14 Barack Obama with Keegan-Michael Key, "President Obama at White House Correspondents' Dinner," 25 Apr. 2015, Washington, DC,www.youtube.com /watch?time_continue=873&v=oi86E5GgawY.

15 Michelle Obama, *Becoming* (Crown, 2018), p. 265.

16 Rankine, *Citizen*, pp. 23–24.

17 Ibid., pp. 26, 31, 35, 36.

18 Ibid., pp. 141, 142.

19 See Judith Wilson's summary of Piper's career changes in "In Memory of the News and of Our Selves: The Art of Adrian Piper," *Third Text* 5, nos. 16/17 (1991): 39–64; she quotes Piper at p. 42. Piper, Toni Morrison, Anna Deavere Smith, and

Faith Ringgold are discussed in Susan Gubar, *Critical Condition: Feminism at the Turn of the Century* (Columbia University Press, 2000), pp. 21–44.

20 Toni Morrison, "Recitatif" (1983), in Gilbert and Gubar, *The Norton Anthology of Literature by Women*, 2:996–1008.

21 Toni Morrison, quoted in Paul Gray, "Paradise Found: The Nobel Prize Changed Toni Morrison's Life But Not Her Art, as Her New Novel Proves," *Time*, 19 Jan. 1998, pp. 62–68, at 67.

22 Patricia J. Williams, *Seeing a Color-Blind Future: The Paradox of Race* (Farrar, Straus and Giroux, 1998), p. 16.

23 Anna Deavere Smith, introduction to *Fires in the Mirror* (Anchor Books, 1993), pp. xxiii–xlii, at xxix.

24 Anna Deavere Smith, in Richard Schechner, "There's a Lot of Work to Do to Turn This Thing Around: An Interview with Anna Deavere Smith," *Drama Review* 62, no. 3 (Fall 2018): 35–50, at 47, 49.

25 Kara Walker, *Gone: An Historical Romance of a Civil War as It Occurred b'tween the Dusky Thighs of One Young Negress and Her Heart* (1994), Museum of Modern Art, New York, www.moma.org/collection/works/110565. Some of the material in this section, as well as Faith Ringgold's more hopeful work *Dancing at the Louvre*, is discussed in Gubar's *Critical Condition*, pp. 26–37.

26 See "Look Closer: Kara Walker's Fons Americanus," *The Tate*, www.tate.org.uk /art/artists/kara-walker-2674/kara-walkers-fons-americanus.

27 Ari Shapiro, "At the End of the Year, N. K. Jemisin Ponders the End of the World," *All Things Considered*, National Public Radio, 26 Dec. 2018, www.npr .org/2018/12/26/680201486/at-the-end-of-the-year-n-k-jemisin-ponders-the -end-of-the-world.

28 See N. K. Jemisin's foreword to the new edition of Octavia Butler's 1993 *Parable of the Sower* (Grand Central Publishing, 2019).

29 N. K. Jemisin, *The Fifth Season* (Orbit, 2015).

30 Annette Kolodny's many books and Carol J. Adams, *The Sexual Politics of Meat: A Feminist-Vegetarian Critical Theory* (Continuum, 1990), were followed by a number of touchstone texts on ecofeminism: Maria Mies and Vandana Shiva, *Ecofeminism* (Zed Books, 1993); Greta Gaard, *Ecological Politics: Ecofeminists and the Green* (Temple University Press, 1998); and Karen J. Warren, *Ecofeminist Philosophy: A Western Perspective on What It Is and Why It Matters* (Rowman and Littlefield, 2000).

31 For an overview of Joy Harjo, see her entry at the Academy of American Poets website, "Joy Harjo," *Poets.org*, poets.org/poet/joy-harjo.

32 In 2016, for instance, the trans musician Anohni produced the album *Hopelessness* (Secretly Canadian, 2016) to protest imminent climate catastrophe. For excerpts from the album, see Anohni's Bandcamp page, anohni.bandcamp.com/album /hopelessness. And in 2019, Linda Cheung founded the nonprofit initiative Before It's Too Late to create an augmented reality mural in south Florida. Passersby can aim their smartphones at paintings of the animals to see videos about the extinction they will soon face because of heedless human activities. See Meg

O'Connor, "New Wynwood Mural Uses Augmented Reality to Spark Conversation on Climate Change," *Miami New Times*, 15 Jan. 2019.

33 Elizabeth Kolbert, *The Sixth Extinction: An Unnatural History* (Henry Holt, 2014), p. 261. For the quotation from Rachel Carson, see *Silent Spring*, 40th anniversary ed. (Houghton Mifflin, 2002), p. 296.

34 Rebecca Solnit, "Everything's Coming Together While Everything Falls Apart" (2014), in *Hope in the Dark: Untold Histories, Wild Possibilities* (Haymarket Books, 2016), pp. 126–36, at 136. She quotes Le Guin's "Speech in Acceptance of the National Book Foundation Medal for Distinguished Contribution to American Letters," 19 Nov. 2014, www.ursulakleguin.com/nbf-medal.

35 From Rosemary Radford Ruether and Mary Daly (Catholicism) to E. N. Broner and Judith Plaskow (Judaism), Lila Abu-Lughod and Leila Ahmed (Islam), and Phyllis Trible (Protestantism), feminists in religious studies have questioned the masculinism of virtually every major religion.

36 The first critic is Solane Crosley, "What to Read Right Now: Elizabeth Strout's *Anything Is Possible*, Patricia Lockwood's *Priestdaddy*, and Secret Recipes from the Chiltern Firehouse," *Vanity Fair*, 16 May 2017, www.vanityfair.com/style/2017/05/what-to-read-right-now-elizabeth-strout-patricia-lockwoods; the second is Paul Laity, "*Priestdaddy* by Patricia Lockwood Review—A Dazzling Comic Memoir," *The Guardian*, 27 Apr. 2017, www.theguardian.com/books/2017/apr/27/priestdaddy-by-patricia-lockwood-review.

37 @TriciaLockwood, "A ghost teasingly takes off his sheet. Underneath he is so sexy that everyone screams out loud," *Twitter*, 7 June 2011, 1:59 p.m., twitter.com/TriciaLockwood/status/78159153884958720; Patricia Lockwood, "Rape Joke," *The Awl*, 25 July 2013, www.theawl.com/2013/07/patricia-lockwood-rape-joke/.

38 Patricia Lockwood, *Priestdaddy* (Riverhead, 2017), p. 11.

39 Sylvia Plath, "Daddy," in *Ariel* (Harper, 1965), pp. 49–51, at 51.

40 Lockwood, *Priestdaddy*, pp. 214, 216.

41 Plath, "Daddy," p. 51.

42 Lockwood, *Priestdaddy*, pp. 287, 288.

43 Ibid., p. 8.

44 Ibid., pp. 332, 331.

45 N. K. Jemisin, "Three Sisters, an Island and an Apocalyptic Tale of Survival," *New York Times Book Review*, 8 Jan. 2019.

46 Rebecca Solnit, *The Mother of All Questions* (Haymarket Books, 2017), p. 171.

47 Rebecca Solnit, "Men Explain Things to Me," in *Men Explain Things to Me* (Haymarket Books, 2014), pp. 1–18, at 13–14.

48 See "Manspreading," *Know Your Meme*, [2019], knowyourmeme.com/memes/manspreading.

49 Roxane Gay criticizes what she calls "essential feminism" in "Bad Feminist: Take One," in *Bad Feminist: Essays* (Harper Perennial, 1914), pp. 303–14, at 304–6.

50 "Mission Statement," *Crunk Feminist Collective*, www.crunkfeministcollective.com/about/; Diana Weymar, *Tiny Pricks Project*, www.tinypricksproject.com/; and see Katherine Cross, "The Oscar Wilde of YouTube Fights the Alt-Right

with Decadence and Seduction," *The Verge*, 24 Aug. 2018, www.theverge.com/tech /2018/8/24/17689090/contrapoints-youtube-natalie-wynn, as well as Andrew Marantz, "The Stylish Socialist Who Is Trying to Save YouTube from Alt-Right Domination," *New Yorker*, 19 Nov. 2018, www.newyorker.com/culture/persons -of-interest/the-stylish-socialist-who-is-trying-to-save-youtube-from-alt-right -domination.

51 Margaret Atwood, *The Testaments* (Doubleday, 2019), p. 149.

52 Michelle Goldberg, "Margaret Atwood's Dystopia, and Ours," op-ed, *New York Times*, 15 Sept. 2019.

53 *Homecoming*'s epigraph quotes the final words of Toni Morrison, *Song of Solomon* (1977; repr., Vintage International, 2004), p. 337.

54 The quotation, slightly altered, comes from Audre Lorde's "The Master's Tools Will Never Dismantle the Master's House" (1979), in *Sister Outsider: Essays and Speeches* (Crossing Press, 1984), pp. 110–13, at 112.

55 Chimamanda Ngozi Adichie, *We Should All Be Feminists* (Anchor Books, 2012), pp. 27–28.

56 Eavan Boland, "Our Future Will Become the Past of Other Women" (2018), in *The Historians: Poems* (W. W. Norton, 2020), pp. 63–67.

57 Moira Donegan, "What Comes After the Media Men List? 'A Lot of Hard Work,'" video interview by Ainara Tiefenthäler, *New York Times*, 18 Jan. 2018, www.nytimes.com/2018/01/18/business/media/men-media-spreadsheet.html; ellipsis hers.

58 Anita Hill, quoted in Dana Goodyear, "Exposure: In the Wake of Scandal, Can Hollywood Change Its Ways?," *New Yorker*, 8 Jan. 2018, pp. 20–26, at 26. (Published online as "Can Hollywood Change Its Ways? In the Wake of Scandal, the Movie Industry Reckons with Its Past and Its Future," 1 Jan. 2018.)

59 "Word of the Year 2017: 'Feminism' Is Our Word of the Year," *Merriam-Webster*, www.merriam-webster.com/words-at-play/woty2017-top-looked-up-words -feminism# (announced 12 Dec.); *Time*, cover of 18 Dec. 2017 issue (announced 6 Dec.).

60 Soraya Chemaly, *Rage Becomes Her: The Power of Women's Anger* (Atria, 2018), p. xvi.

61 The story, written by Julie Bosman, Kate Taylor, and Tim Arango, was published 10 Aug. 2019, www.nytimes.com/2019/08/10/us/mass-shootings-misogyny -dayton.html.

62 Thomas B. Edsall, "We Aren't Seeing White Support for Trump for What It Is," op-ed, *New York Times*, 28 Aug. 2019, www.nytimes.com/2019/08/28/opinion /trump-white-voters.html; Josh Hafner, "Donald Trump Loves the 'Poorly Educated'—and They Love Him," 24 Feb. 2016, usatoday.com/story/news/politics /onpoliics/2016/02/24/Donald-trump-nevada-poorly-educated/80860078.

63 Recalling that one of her friends in the class of 1962 believed that "our education was a dress rehearsal for a life we never led," Nora Ephron told the class of 1996: "Your education is a dress rehearsal for a life that is yours to lead." "Nora Eph-

ron '62 Addressed the Graduates in 1996," *Wellesley College*, www.wellesley.edu /events/commencement/archives/1996commencement.

64 Michelle Obama, "Commencement Address by First Lady Michelle Obama," *City College of New York*, 2016, www.ccny.cuny.edu/commencement/commencement -address-first-lady-michelle-obama.

65 Katie Rogers and Nicholas Fandos, "Fanning Flames, Trump Unleashes a Taunt: 'Go Back,'" *New York Times*, 15 July 2019.

66 Nicholas Wu, "'I Am Someone's Daughter Too': Read Rep. Ocasio-Cortez's Full Speech Responding to Rep. Ted Yoho," *USA Today*, 24 July 2020, www.usatoday .com/story/news/politics/2020/07/24/aoc-response-ted-yoho-read-text-rep-ocasio -cortezs-speech/5500633002/. For Yoho's "apology," see Luke Broadwater, "Ocasio-Cortez Upbraids Republican After He Denies Vulgarly Insulting Her," *New York Times*, 22 July 2020, www.nytimes.com/2020/07/22/us/politics/aoc-yoho.html.

67 Stacey Abrams, "Stacey Abrams Talks the Shared Values of Her Political Campaign and Writing Romance," interview by Maureen Lee Lenker, *EW.com*, 5 Sept. 2018, ew.com/books/2018/09/05/stacey-abrams-interview/.

68 Michelle Obama, *Becoming* (Crown, 2018), pp. 408, 409, 411.

69 Alexandra Pelosi, interview by John Berman, *New Day*, CNN, 2 Jan. 2019, transcripts.cnn.com/TRANSCRIPTS/1901/02/nday.05.html; Ellen McCarthy, "'Makes going to work look easy': Decades Before She Was House Speaker, Nancy Pelosi Had an Even Harder Job," *Washington Post*, 23 Feb. 2019, www .washingtonpost.com/lifestyle/style/makes-going-to-work-look-easy-how -being-a-full-time-mom-prepared-nancy-pelosi-for-this-moment/2019/02/12 /416cd85e-28bc-11e9-984d-9b8fba003e81_story.html.

70 Nancy Pelosi, video at @ABCPolitics, *Twitter*, 11 Jan. 2019, 5:27 p.m., twitter. com/ABCPolitics/status/1083852879922847744.

71 John Bresnahan, Heather Caygle, and Kyle Cheney, "Pelosi Faces Growing Doubts among Dems after Georgia Loss," *Politico*, 21 June 2017, www.politico .com/story/2017/06/21/nancy-pelosi-fallout-georgia-special-election-239804. By the date of this article, Pelosi had "rais[ed] more than $560 million for the House Democrats since she became leader in 2003."

72 The Brookings Institution scholar Thomas Mann, quoted in Andy Kroll and National Journal, "The Staying Power of Nancy Pelosi," *The Atlantic*, 11 Sept. 2015, www.theatlantic.com/politics/archive/2015/09/the-staying-power-of-nancy -pelosi/440022/.

73 Epithets quoted in Ronald M. Peters, Jr., and Cindy Simon Rosenthal, *Speaker Nancy Pelosi and the New American Politics* (Oxford University Press, 2010), pp. 215–16.

74 Nancy Pelosi, quoted in ibid., pp. 233, 193.

75 M. Elizabeth Sheldon, "Nancy Pelosi Traces Her Food Heritage to Risotto, Eats Dark Chocolate Ice Cream for Breakfast Every Day," *Food & Wine*, 23 May 2017, www.foodandwine.com/news/nancy-pelosi-traces-her-food-heritage-risotto -eats-dark-chocolate-ice-cream-breakfast-every-day.

76 Glenn Kessler, Salvador Rizzo, and Sarah Cahlan list thirty-one stretched and dubious claims in "Fact-Checking President Trump's 2020 State of the Union Address," *Washington Post*, 4 Feb. 2020, washingtonpost.com/politics/2020/02/04/fact-checking-president-trumps-2020-state-union-address.

EPILOGUE: THE WHITE SUIT

1 Mitch McConnell, quoted in Amy Gardner, Ashley Parker, Josh Dawsey, and Emma Brown, "Top Republicans Back Trump's Efforts to Challenge Election Results," *Washington Post*, 9 Nov. 2020, www.washingtonpost.com/politics/trump-republicans-election-challenges/2020/11/09/49e2c238-22c4-11eb-952e-0c475972cfc0_story.html.

2 Matt Stevens, "Read Kamala Harris's Vice President–Elect Acceptance Speech," *New York Times*, 8 Nov. 2020, www.nytimes.com/article/watch-kamala-harris-speech-video-transcript.html.

3 See Vanessa Friedman, "Message about the Past and the Future of Politics in a Fashion Statement," *New York Times*, 9 Nov. 2020.

4 @AOC, *Twitter*, 3 Jan. 2019, 10:39 p.m., twitter.com/aoc/status/108103230726234 5216?lang=en.

5 *The Suffragist*, 6 Dec. 1913.

6 See Ellen Barry, "How Kamala Harris's Immigrant Parents Found a Home, and Each Other, in a Black Study Group," *New York Times*, 13 Sept. 2020, updated 6 Oct. 2020, www.nytimes.com/2020/09/13/us/kamala-harris-parents.html.

7 For more about Kamala Harris's experience growing up in Berkeley's Black community, see her memoir *The Truths We Hold: An American Journey* (2019; repr., Penguin Books, 2020); for her early memories of demonstrations, see pp. 7–8.

8 On her Jamaican background, see Donald J. Harris, "Reflections of a Jamaican Father," *Jamaica Global*, updated 18 Aug. 2020, www.jamaicaglobalonline.com/kamala-harris-jamaican-heritage/.

9 "Transcript: Michelle Obama's DNC Speech," *CNN Politics*, 18 Aug. 2020, www.cnn.com/2020/08/17/politics/michelle-obama-speech-transcript/index.html.

10 Michelle Obama, quoted in Yada Yuan and Annie Linskey, "Jill Biden Is Finally Ready to Be First Lady: Can She Help Her Husband Beat Trump?," *Washington Post*, 18 Aug. 2020. They are drawing on an "exit interview" of Obama and Biden conducted by Jess Cagle, the editor in chief of *People* magazine; see www.youtube.com/watch?v=eZDfztfau9A.

11 Ohio University professor Katherine Jellison, "who studies first ladies," quoted in Nicole Guadiano, "First Professor: Jill Biden to Make History as a First Lady with a Day Job," *Politico*, 12 Nov. 2020 (ellipsis hers), www.politico.com/states/california/story/2020/11/12/first-professor-jill-biden-to-make-history-as-a-first-lady-with-a-day-job-1336242.

12 Most notoriously, Senator David Purdue (R-GA), campaigning for reelection at

a rally on October 16, 2020, badly mangled the name of his Senate colleague; see www.nbcnews.com/video/perdue-mispronounces-sen-kamala-harris-name-at -rally-94021701947.

13 Joseph Epstein, "Is There a Doctor in the White House? Not If You Need an M.D.," op-ed, *Wall Street Journal*, 11 Dec. 2020, www.wsj.com/articles/is-there -a-doctor-in-the-white-house-not-if-you-need-an-m-d-11607727380. All quotations in the following paragraph are taken from this piece.

14 Quoted in Dan Barry and Sheera Frenkel, " 'Be There. Will be Wild!': Trump All But Circled the Date," *New York Times*, 6 Jan. 2021, updated 8 Jan. 2021, www.nytimes.com/2021/01/06/us/politics/capitol-mob-trump-supporters .html; @realDonaldTrump, "Peter Navarro releases 36-page report alleging election fraud 'more than sufficient' to swing victory to Trump https://t.co/ D8KrMHnFdK. A great report by Peter. Statistically impossible to have lost the 2020 Election. Big protest in D.C. on January 6th. Be there, will be wild!" *Twitter*, 19 Dec. 2020, 1:42 a.m., thetrumparchive.com.

15 Quoted in Maggie Haberman and Jonathan Martin, "After the Speech: What Trump Did as the Capitol Was Attacked," *New York Times*, 13 Feb. 2021, www .nytimes.com/2021/02/13/us/politics/trump-capitol-riot.html; @realDonaldTrump, "These are the things and events that happen when a sacred landslide election victory is so unceremoniously & viciously stripped away from great patriots who have been badly & unfairly treated for so long. Go home with love & in peace. Remember this day forever!" *Twitter*, 6 Jan. 2021, 6:01 p.m., the trumparchive.com.

16 "Stop the Steal" was an alt-right campaign that protested alleged voter fraud in the 2020 election. See Sheera Frenkel, "Beware of This Misinformation from 'Stop the Steal' Rallies This Weekend," *New York Times*, 13 Nov. 2020, www.nytimes .com/2020/11/13/technology/beware-of-this-misinformation-from-stop-the -steal-rallies-this-weekend.html.

17 "Transcript of Trump's Speech at Rally Before US Capitol Riot," *U.S. News*, 13 Jan. 2021, www.usnews.com/news/politics/articles/2021-01-13/transcript-of -trumps-speech-at-rally-before-us-capitol-riot.

18 Quoted in Mike Dorning and Steven T. Dennis, "What to Know About Trump's Second Impeachment Trial," *Washington Post*, 4 Feb. 2021, www.washington post.com/business/what-to-know-about-trumps-second-impeachment -trial/2021/02/03/d88f5a08-6669-11eb-bab8-707f8769d785_story.html.

19 @aoc, "What happens after the Capitol attacks?" *Instagram*, 13 Jan. 2021, www .instagram.com/p/CJ-OkgNAO1N/.

20 Quoted in Peter Baker, Maggie Haberman, and Annie Karni, "Pence Reached His Limit With Trump. It Wasn't Pretty," *New York Times*, 12 Jan. 2021, updated 13 Jan. 2021, www.nytimes.com/2021/01/12/us/politics/mike-pence-trump.html.

21 Monica Hesse, "Capitol Rioters Searched for Nancy Pelosi in a Way That Should Make Every Woman's Skin Crawl," *Washington Post*, 10 Feb. 2021, www .washingtonpost.com/lifestyle/style/nancy-pelosi-capitol-insurrection-foot

age-impeachment-trial/2021/02/10/34bb843c-6bec-11eb-9f80-3d7646ce1bc0
_story.html.

22 " 'The Hill We Climb,' A Transcript. Amanda Gorman's Poem Recited at Biden's
Inauguration Captures the Times," *Baltimore Sun*, 20 Jan. 2021, www.baltimore
sun.com/opinion/editorial/bs-ed-0121-gorman-transcript-20210120-5ojxffrfb
5cybjabhgiffgiyhi-story.html.

CREDITS

Sylvia Plath. Copyright © 2004 by the Estate of Sylvia Plath. Previously unpublished Plath material copyright © 2004 by the Estate of Sylvia Plath. Foreword copyright © 2004 by Frieda Hughes. Notes and editorial material © 2004 by HarperCollins Publishers. Used by permission of HarperCollins Publishers and Faber and Faber Ltd.

CLAUDIA RANKINE. Excerpts from *Citizen: An American Lyric*, pp. 5, 10, 23, 24, 26, 31, 35, 36, 45, 141, and 145. Copyright © 2014 by Claudia Rankine. Reprinted with the permission of the Permissions Company, LLC, on behalf of Graywolf Press, graywolfpress.org. From *Citizen: An American Lyric* by Claudia Rankine, published by Penguin Press. Copyright © Claudia Rankine, 2014. Reprinted by permission of Penguin Books Limited.

ADRIENNE RICH. Excerpts from "Diving into the Wreck," "Waking in the Dark," "From an Old House in America," "From the Prison House," "The Stranger," and "From a Survivor." Copyright © 2016 by the Adrienne Rich Literary Trust. Copyright © 1973 by W. W. Norton & Company, Inc. Excerpts from "Twenty-One Love Poems" and "Phantasia for Elvira Shatayev." Copyright © 2016 by the Adrienne Rich Literary Trust. Copyright © 1978 by W. W. Norton & Company, Inc. Excerpt from "Snapshots of a Daughter-in-Law." Copyright © 2016 by the Adrienne Rich Literary Trust. Copyright © 1967, 1963 by Adrienne Rich. Excerpt from "Sources." Copyright © 2016 by the Adrienne Rich Literary Trust. Copyright © 1986 by Adrienne Rich. Excerpts from "An Atlas of the Difficult World." Copyright © 2016 by the Adrienne Rich Literary Trust. Copyright © 1991 by Adrienne Rich. Excerpt from "In Those Years." Copyright © 2016 by the Adrienne Rich Lit-

INDEX